FIRESIDE

PARKSIDE

D1204887

FIRESIDE ✦ PARKSIDE BOOKS

Anatomy of a Food Addiction: The Brain Chemistry of Overeating, by Anne Katherine, M.A.

Behind the 8-Ball: A Guide for Families of Gamblers, by Linda Berman, M.S.W., and Mary-Ellen Siegel, M.S.W.

Believing in Myself: Daily Meditations for Healing and Building Self-Esteem, by Earnie Larsen and Carol Hegarty

Blues Ain't Nothing But a Good Soul Feeling Bad: Daily Steps to Spiritual Growth, by Sheldon Kopp with Bonnie B. Hesse

Codependents' Guide to the Twelve Steps, by Melody Beattie

Family Intervention, by Frank L. Picard, M.S.

Freedom from Food: The Secret Lives of Dieters and Compulsive Eaters, by Elizabeth Hampshire

From Love That Hurts to Love That's Real: A Recovery Workbook, by Sylvia Ogden Peterson

Growing Through the Pain: The Incest Survivor's Companion, by Catherine Bronson

Growing Up Gay in a Dysfunctional Family: A Guide for Gay Men Reclaiming Their Lives, by Rik Isensee

Help for Helpers: Daily Meditations for Those Who Care

Hooked on Exercise: How to Understand and Manage Exercise Addiction, by Rebecca Prussin, M.D., Philip Harvey, Ph.D., and Theresa Foy DiGeronimo

Meditations for Men Who Do Too Much, by Jonathon Lazear

Repressed Memories: A Journey to Recovery from Sexual Abuse, by Renee Fredrickson, Ph.D.

Soul Survivors: A New Beginning for Adults Abused as Children, by J. Patrick Gannon, Ph.D.

Understanding the Twelve Steps: An Interpretation and Guide for Recovering People, by Terence T. Gorski

ADDICTIONARY

A PRIMER OF RECOVERY TERMS AND CONCEPTS

FROM ABSTINENCE TO WITHDRAWAL

JAN R. WILSON
AND
JUDITH A. WILSON

A Fireside/Parkside Recovery Book
Published by Simon & Schuster

NEW YORK   LONDON   TORONTO   SYDNEY   TOKYO   SINGAPORE

FIRESIDE/PARKSIDE
Simon & Schuster Building
Rockefeller Center
1230 Avenue of the Americas
New York, New York 10020

Designed by Irving Perkins Associates
Manufactured in the United States of America

1   3   5   7   9   10   8   6   4   2

Library of Congress Cataloging-in-Publication Data

Wilson, Jan. R.
Addictionary : a primer of recovery terms and concepts, from
abstinence to withdrawal / Jan R. Wilson and Judith A. Wilson.
p.   cm.—(A Fireside/Parkside recovery book)
Includes bibliographical references and index.
1. Compulsive behavior—Encyclopedias.   2. Twelve-step programs—
Encyclopedias.   I. Wilson, Judith A.   II. Title.   III. Series.
RC533.W48   1992
616.86'003—dc20   92-19070
                                                                  CIP

ISBN: 0-671-76696-1

Parkside Medical Services Corporation is a full-service
provider of treatment for alcoholism, other drug addiction,
eating disorders, and psychiatric illness.

Parkside Medical Services Corporation
205 West Touhy Avenue
Park Ridge, IL 60058
1-800-PARKSIDE

Introduction

How to Use This Book

This is a recovery manual for anyone interested in recovery from addiction to alcohol, drugs, food, overeating, purging, starving, gambling, sex, tobacco, exercise, work, relationships, codependency, or any other addiction or its effects. It is for addicts, for family and others concerned about addicts, or for therapists who work with all of these people.

Topics, or modules, are arranged alphabetically to make them easy to use for ongoing recovery. Whether in crisis or just working a recovery program, turn directly to a relevant module. At the end of each module are names of other modules that may help. If you are looking for a topic that does not have its own module, look at the index and you will find a place to start.

Individuals, therapists, and programs can also use this book as a textbook. We have supplied some "Addictionary Paths" for those wishing to set up a logical sequence for a thorough study of addiction recovery.

Sharing Recovery

We wrote this book as a way to share what we have learned through many years of treating all kinds of addiction, researching information for the *Eating Disorders Digest,* and in gratitude for our own recovery as both food addicts and alcoholics. You may also want to use this book to help share recovery with those you sponsor or others who need help with their recovery. We want to acknowledge a few of those who have contributed, whether they knew it or not, to make this book possible. They include (alphabetically): Leigh Cohn, Kathy Evans, Lindsey Hall, Ernest Kurtz, Julie Leavitt, John Lovern, Carol Price, Jean Fox Pritchett, Fr. Bob Skeris, Rozanne

Skoller, John Small, Robert H. Smith, Terry Spohn, Michael Trachtenberg, Lois Wilson, William G. Wilson, all the participants in the Food Addiction Workshops, and every addict we have known.

—Jan R. Wilson, B.S., C.E.D.C., C.A.P.
—Judith A. Wilson, M.A., C.A.P.

Addictionary Paths

A. STYLES OF ADDICTION:
   PATTERNS OF THE DISEASE

   Alcoholism
   Drugs
   Food addiction
   Anorexia nervosa
   Bulimia nervosa
   Obesity
   Exercise & activity
   Excitement
   Gambling
   Sex
   Spending
   Religiosity
   Chronic pain
   Adolescents

B. PHYSICAL ASPECTS OF
   ADDICTION

   Physical aspects
   Allergies
   Tolerance
   Withdrawal
   Biochemistry
   Metabolism
   Bingeing
   Purging
   Constipation

   Edema
   Blackouts
   Fetal alcohol syndrome
   Flashbacks
   Panic attacks
   Weight
   Progression

C. EMOTIONAL ASPECTS OF
   ADDICTION

   Emotional aspects
   Feelings
   Fear
   Anger
   Craving
   Body image
   Stress & strain

D. MENTAL ASPECTS OF
   ADDICTION

   Mental aspects
   Disease concept
   Obsession
   Dichotomous thinking
   Diet mentality
   Magical thinking
   Judgment

Habit & structure
Paradoxes in addiction
Psychological problems

Acceptance
Willingness
Surrender

E. SPIRITUAL ASPECTS OF
ADDICTION

Spiritual aspects
Beliefs
Integrity & values
Spirituality
Steps of AA

I. AA's STEPS FOUR AND FIVE:
INVENTORY

Step Four
Step Five
Assertiveness
Energy levels
Defenses
Perfectionism
Inventory

F. AA's STEP ONE: AWARENESS

Step One
Crisis
Delusion
Half-measures
Hitting bottom
Honesty
Powerlessness
Unmanageability

J. AA's STEPS SIX AND SEVEN:
SURRENDER

Step Six
Step Seven
Character defects
Self-centeredness
Behavior
Grief
Guilt & shame
Resentments
Responsibility
Money
Affirmations
Slogans

G. AA's STEP TWO: SANITY

Step Two
Sanity
Power
Higher Power
Openmindedness

K. AA's STEPS EIGHT AND
NINE: ATONEMENT

Step Eight
Step Nine
Amends
Forgiveness

H. AA's STEP THREE:
LETTING GO

Step Three
Attitudes
Trust

L. AA's STEP TEN: HUMILITY

Step Ten
Humor & fun
Humility

M. AA's STEP ELEVEN:
MEDITATION

Step Eleven
Prayer & meditation
Grace
Gratitude
Serenity

N. AA's STEP TWELVE:
SERVICE

Step Twelve
Intervention
Service & giving

O. RELAPSE PREVENTION:
WHEN THE ROAD GETS
ROUGH

Relapse prevention
Sabotage of recovery
Stinking thinking
Celebrations
Relaxation
Sleep
Pregnancy
Premenstrual syndrome
  (PMS)
Prevention of addiction
Priorities

A

Abstinence

What is abstinence from addiction? In addictions other than alcoholism, there is no greater source of confusion and conflict, for those who have the disease as well as for the professionals who treat them.

Abstinence from addictive behavior is where recovery begins. It gives you the freedom to begin a good recovery program. For compulsive eaters or compulsive gamblers or even relationship addicts, it is just as important as sobriety for the alcoholic.

Abstinence means to refrain from addictive behavior. Many people would say, "I know what abstinence means for alcoholism, but what about the other addictions?" Our understanding of addiction has been shaped by our familiarity with alcoholism, and alcohol is one of the few addictive substances that is not necessary for life under almost any circumstances and therefore can be totally avoided. But most recovering alcoholics would be quick to agree that recovery requires more than just not drinking—someone who exhibits all kinds of addictive behavior except alcohol consumption is called a "dry drunk," implying that they are dry but not well.

We believe that a look at abstinence for all addictions can help even pure "alcohol only" addicts (if you can find one) to understand the role of abstinence in the overall concept of recovery.

Individual addicts' definitions of abstinence vary considerably, especially with those other than alcohol and other drug addiction. As long as individualized abstinence *works*, with no fooling, there is no need for someone to dictate a "one size fits all" definition.

If you can identify your problem as addiction to a particular substance, or to biochemical imbalances caused by a particular

11

behavior, you will find the tool of abstinence to be a powerful ally in recovery.

THE FOUR FREEDOMS OF ABSTINENCE

Since we view addiction as having four aspects—physical, emotional, mental, and spiritual (PEMS model)—you can also see direct benefits in each area.

Freedom from intoxication (physical)   By abstaining from whatever amount of the drug, food, or activity that profoundly changes your bodily functions, your mood, your thinking process, and your spirit, you become sober or clearheaded enough to begin to understand and work the rest of the program.

Freedom from craving (emotional)   Abstinence also stabilizes your mood swings and reduces the emotional effects of craving. Then you can learn what it means to share your feelings appropriately. Your life becomes less crisis-oriented, mood swings and guilt decrease, and you can begin to see glimpses of serenity.

Freedom from obsession (mental)   By removing the constant access to and preoccupation with addictive substances and behavior, you reduce the obsession and mental mismanagement that has disrupted your life. Obsession with alcohol, other drugs, activities, weight, and physical appearance decreases. Delusion fades away, and judgment improves.

Freedom from isolation (spiritual)   Finally, to the extent that addiction has isolated you from your Higher Power and other people, you begin to gain or regain these vital relationships. Through your abstinence and working the program you become open to the love others have for you, and you can experience peace and surrender.

ABSTINENCE FROM MOODIFIERS

We have coined the word *moodifier* to mean any externally or internally induced chemical imbalance that has the potential to cause the profound mood swings associated with addiction. This includes the body's reaction to alcohol, cocaine, marijuana, heroin, and other drugs, as well as excessive sugar or other foods, exercise, sex, or excitement.

It seems much simpler to think about abstinence when talking about a drug like alcohol that is not needed for life, than from something like food, which you cannot avoid entirely. Many addicts do not have the "luxury" of being able totally to cease using the drug, other substance, or activity that seems so central to their addiction.

For example, most food addicts are sensitive to sugar, fat, or sugar-fat combinations, to some degree. This means that the bio-chemical imbalances caused by *excessive* amounts of these foods affect them significantly. The greater these foods modify their judgment and mood, the more careful they should be to avoid large amounts of them. Excesses of other foods, like protein, also can produce abnormal mood swings or distortions of judgment.

Binge abstinence   Bingeing (overdoing it with drugs like alcohol or heroin, substances like food or certain foods, or activities like sex or gambling) should be included in a definition of abstinence, even if the excess is not directly associated with extreme mood and judgment distortions.

Purging/starving abstinence   For food addiction, purging (vomiting, using laxatives or other attempts to get rid of food) or starving (fasting, near fasting, or very low calorie diets) also can be moodifiers. Bingeing, purging, and starving have no place in abstinence.

Between-meals abstinence   By avoiding food between meals, food addicts experience the *ability* to be free of the obsession about whether to eat now, and if so what and how much. Most people do allow reasonable amounts of low-calorie beverages (like diet sodas and artificially sweetened coffee or tea) between meals. Some OA members talk about "3-0-1," which means three moderate meals, nothing between, and one day at a time.

Rigid diet abstinence   When asked about their abstinence, some food addicts describe a rigid diet (which they may proudly call a "food plan"). This diet mentality is a setup to break their abstinence and "fail." A food plan, formal or informal, is your guide to selecting a moderate meal, but abstinence will be hard to maintain if you think that any tiny deviation from that food plan is a break of abstinence.

Activity abstinence   Addicts can exclude certain definite activities if they consider them to be part of their addiction. Some examples are gambling, having sex with a prostitute, using credit cards, writing bad checks, shoplifting, hitting people, or exceeding the speed limit. These activities are similar to drinking alcohol in that you could decide to abstain from them and be able to count the days since your last such activity.

Addictive behavior   Some behaviors are not so clear. You may need to abstain from a particular pattern, rather than a clear activity. If you want to avoid unhealthy sex, then you need to know what an unhealthy or addictive sexual pattern is, so you can recognize and abstain from it. You may exclude prostitution and adultery, but what about masturbation and sex between unmarried people? If you can establish the pattern in your mind, then you can abstain from it. If you did a lot of your drinking in bars or lounges, then excluding that type of "bar behavior" might become part of your abstinence. That may not preclude meeting a prospective client in a hotel lounge, if you believe you have a good reason for being there. If you can identify with the feeling of a "feeding frenzy," then you can recognize and take steps to avoid that sharklike approach to food in your abstinence. If you binged on excitement by taking unreasonable risks while driving or playing, you might want to avoid these patterns as part of your abstinence.

Alcohol abstinence   All addicts must abstain from the use of alcohol and other mind-altering drugs (unless prescribed for a good medical reason), especially during early recovery. If you are not an acknowledged alcoholic, this may seem extreme. But here are some good reasons:

- Even if you have no history of alcohol or other drug abuse, there is such a strong tendency for addiction to mutate into another form that the chance of developing alcoholism/ chemical dependency does not seem worth the risk.
- Alcohol is a powerful mind-altering drug, so it will be much more difficult to maintain good judgment about your specific abstinence or other choices while drinking.
- Alcohol usually metabolizes into fat, not carbohydrates, and it interferes with carbohydrate metabolism, so it makes no sense for anyone with weight concerns to use it.
- Alcohol has a very poor nutritional value, increases appetite in many people, and may stimulate various kinds of cravings.
- We have seen virtually no addicts of any sort who could drink alcohol, even occasionally, and still maintain long-term recovery from other addictions.

For most addicts, getting honest will help you find the best compromise between abstinence that is too lax and abstinence that is too rigid. It may include your own interpretation of many of the above suggestions.

Abstinence, see also: Addiction, Allergies, Dichotomous thinking, Diet mentality, Drugs, Excitement, Freedoms, Hitting bottom, Moderation, Moodifiers, Physical aspects, Powerlessness, Purging, Recovery, Sex, Step One.

Abuse

The use of the word *abuse,* particularly child abuse, started in the legal field. Courts used parameters to declare a child abused, such as physical bruises or injuries. Neglect was also a legal term that applied to situations where a child's physical needs were ignored, such as not feeding a child or not attending to illness or injuries.

When you use the word *abuse* it is important to remember that you can be talking about anything from the most horrendous of physical acts to poor parenting behaviors that we know are unhealthy, like verbally discounting children or discouraging their independence. What you call abuse is a matter of opinion.

Pia Mellody (1989) defines abuse broadly, identifying it as any experience that was less than nurturing. She says abuse is the major factor in codependency.

John Bradshaw (1989) perceives abuse as an underpinning of toxic shame that results in the inability to have a good relationship with oneself. According to his model, this is the basis for most maladaptive and unhealthy behavior.

DYNAMICS OF ABUSE

Studies of abuse suggest that abuse, especially in its extreme forms, is usually handed down through generations. Among the many factors that perpetuate it are low self-esteem, self-pity, feeling trapped, and addiction to the neurochemistry of excitement.

Overt or covert   Mellody discusses abuse as overt (out in the open) or covert (hidden, devious, and indirect). Overt abuse is easy to see, even for the child, because it is so obvious. Overt abuse can include yelling and screaming, or cause bruises or other physical damage. This does not mean that overt abuse is identified, acknowledged, or understood by anyone involved. It is just more visible.

Covert abuse is more subtle, devious, and manipulating. Mellody includes certain kinds of parental neglect as covert abuse, like not addressing the child's emotional and intellectual needs.

Recognizing abuse   When we use the term *abuse*, we mean that level of behavior beyond partial neglect or insensitivity (like not having ideal parents), when the relationship becomes adverse or destructive to the people involved.

You have been abused if someone physically harms you, if you feel in any way threatened, or if you have a sense that "something is very wrong here."

EMOTIONAL ABUSE

Emotional abuse includes neglecting a child's needs, verbal abuse (such as name-calling), and extreme over- or underprotectiveness. Emotional abuse is probably the most common form of abuse.

PHYSICAL ABUSE

Anything that causes bodily damage, especially if accompanied with violence, is physical abuse. Incest and rape are physical abuse. We also consider any serious *threat* of physical damage to be physical abuse.

Violence   Any act that injures or damages a person's body is abuse. We excuse it by calling it discipline when it comes to children, but an untold number of children continue to suffer serious physical and psychological damage at the hands of their "disciplinarians."

How damaging violence is depends on several factors. Is the act habitual or an isolated incident? How old are the children? Do they fear for their lives? Is there anyplace they feel safe?

Incest   Incest and other types of sexual abuse of children wreak psychological havoc. Incest is possible in all dysfunctional families, especially where one or both caregivers are violent, authoritarian, or chemically addicted. Among women with eating disorders, estimates of sexual abuse range from about 25 percent to about 75 percent. These figures are shocking. Unfortunately, you would find about the same rate of incest in any other addicted family as well as in many psychiatric disorders.

Incest is a special kind of abuse because it involves not only the powerful feelings around sexuality and childhood fears but it also disrupts the very fabric of the family. Once incest meant sexual activity between people who were closely related biologically. Recent studies, however, indicate that an emotional bond as well as a blood bond can determine what is incest. There is a violation of an ongoing bond of trust between a child and a caretaker (Blume, 1990). See the module on Incest for more information.

Rape   Rape can result in both psychological damage and devastating physical injury. Our society is beginning to understand that rape is an act of violence more than an act of sex.

If rape involves physical force or obvious violence, it is more likely to result in criminal prosecution of the rapist. But even the threat of violence can be extremely traumatic, and besides the need for justice, the victim(s) probably will need assistance with the healing process, such as a counselor and a support group.

Date rape   Rape that happens while on a date, or with someone you know, is still rape. The courts are beginning to make it clear that regardless of the relationship, sexual activity must be voluntary or it is rape.

There is also sexual activity that is common in addiction and dysfunctional relationships. If you consent to sex with someone because of poor self-esteem, romantic addiction, or to obtain drugs, alcohol, food, or other addictive substances or activities, it may not be called rape, but you are still being abused, and the resulting emotions can perpetuate your sense of powerlessness and shame.

RECOVERY FROM ABUSE

Any degree or type of abuse warrants attention for recovery and healing. Bringing repressed or forgotten experiences into conscious awareness can help you understand your present feelings and fears. You may be using a lot of energy to keep these memories down.

Recovery from abuse is a process. You must identify abuse and experience feelings associated with it. You need a safe, supportive place to express the fear, hurt, anger, hatred, and other emotions that come with your awareness. You can then move through the negative feelings and attitudes to acceptance, letting go, and eventual forgiveness and healing.

Freedom   In abuse recovery you do not need to forget what happened, place yourself in peril, or maintain a relationship with the person who abused you. Yet hanging onto resentments (literally, continuing to refeel) will block you from the emotional, mental, and spiritual freedom that recovery has to offer.

Therapy   Professional help may include individual and group therapy with siblings or family, family reconstruction, or other techniques to work through the issues. Brief therapy, say, four to six weeks of inpatient or outpatient treatment, is not usually enough to resolve the trauma of abuse or incest—you should be referred to a competent therapist for continuing work. Abuse and incest especially require the attention of an experienced, trained, professional therapist. Personality disorders can result from these traumas, and they tax the expertise of any counselor to the limit. These are not issues to try to resolve with an amateur.

Abuse, see also: Acceptance, Adolescents, Affirmations, Amends, Anorexia nervosa, Attitudes, Behavior, Children of addicts, Codependency, Control, Crisis, Defenses, Detachment, Emotional aspects, Enabling, Family of origin, Fetal alcohol syndrome, Forgiveness, Guilt & shame, Incest, Intimacy, Love & caring, Power, Psychological problems, Relationships, Resentments, Sabotage of recovery, Self-image, Step Four, Survival roles, Therapy & treatment.

Acceptance

Lasting recovery from addiction requires acceptance of the addiction itself, and surrender to the recovery process. Acceptance is the door to the spiritual awakening that leads to the joy and freedom promised by the Twelve-Step programs.

Acceptance means to take with a consenting mind. It begins a process that leads to surrender. Acceptance is an awareness of the reality that further struggle or conflict is useless.

Acceptance is a natural process, simple unless whatever needs to be accepted somehow threatens you. Accepting that you have been selected for a raise is one thing; accepting a hurt or a loss is not so easy.

Suppose you were expecting a raise, because you thought you were doing a great job, but you are told you will be laid off. It may be very hard to accept. You may try to deny reality, blame others, rationalize, talk yourself into self-pity, or employ any number of defenses to avoid or postpone acceptance.

RESISTANCE TO ACCEPTANCE

Why is accepting an addiction so difficult? There are some fears and resistance that may inhibit admitting that you are an addict, such as:

- I don't want to be different from a normal person.
- It means I'll never be able to drink/eat/use/do the things I like.

- I hate having to talk to others about my problems.
- My family might think I'm joining another weird group.
- I can't get to meetings, especially several each week.
- It's embarrassing to think I can't do this myself.
- This is too hard—all I want to do is cut back, lose weight, stop getting into trouble with it.

These are only some of the common barriers to accepting addiction and all that recovery entails. You may be able to think of many others. If you come from a dysfunctional family, you may have additional resistance to accepting powerlessness and unmanageability. The survival techniques, like bucking authority or always being "in control," that worked well to get you through childhood may now be inhibiting your recovery.

DYSFUNCTIONAL FAMILY

If you come from a dysfunctional family or had any reason to be suspicious of authority or outside guidance, you may have trouble with your recovery. Cathleen Brooks (1987), a popular lecturer on adult children of addicts, says that many ACOAs have trouble working the first three Steps of the program when they find themselves in an active addiction. After taking care of your life to survive, it's very hard to turn your will and your life over to an outside power. By continuing to go to meetings you can learn how and whom to trust. Acceptance will become easier.

FEAR

Fear is a major barrier to acceptance. You may fear what will happen to you if you honestly admit and accept your condition. This fear may be residual fear from the past that does not fit your current situation. It may lead to paranoid (untrusting) attitudes and delusions. But you can begin with just a little willingness. By going to meetings you have begun the process that leads to acceptance. With time, you will have less difficulty trusting people, the program, and things outside yourself to help you get started on the Steps.

STEPS

With a clear understanding of your need for recovery, you can turn to the Steps for help. The first three, for example, can be applied directly to acceptance.

Defiance becomes need (Step One) The First Step suggests admitting that your life has become unmanageable because you are powerless over your addiction. Without Step One, you might never see the need to accept your addiction. While you deny its existence your addiction is likely to flourish.

Escape becomes hope (Step Two)   The Second Step says that a power greater than yourself can restore you to sanity. Opening yourself to the love of a Higher Power and the care of others in the program can give you the hope you need to accept your addiction. It also supercharges your recovery program.

Control becomes acceptance (Step Three)   The Third Step advises you to decide to let that Higher Power work in your life. Thus you can ask the God *of your understanding* to help you accept your disease and other realities of life and recovery. After seeing the need in Step One, and the means in Step Two, the Third Step asks you to dispel the illusion and make the conscious choice to let your Higher Power guide you in your recovery from addiction. Step Twelve recommends expanding this success to the rest of your life as well.

Acceptance, see also: Abuse, Amends, Attitudes, Fear, Grace, Gratitude, Love & caring, Openmindedness, Perfectionism, Powerlessness, Prayer & meditation, Recovery, Sanity, Self-image, Serenity, Step Three, Step Seven, Surrender, Trust, Willingness. Next on path H: Willingness.

Addiction

Addiction is a primary, progressive, chronic, and potentially fatal disease characterized by:

- a physical sensitivity to excessive externally or internally induced biochemical imbalances, causing
- unusually strong mood changes and other emotional volatility, and
- mental obsession, poor judgment, and other mental mismanagement that support the continuance of the disease, and
- a spiritual isolation that effectively blocks outside help and guidance, resulting in a self-centered lifestyle.

ALCOHOL

Alcoholism is probably the best known, although not the most common, addiction. It is not just addiction to alcohol, but to the biochemistry that results when alcohol is ingested.

PRESCRIPTION DRUGS

Depressants, analgesics (painkillers), tranquilizers, stimulants, and many other prescription drugs can produce an addicted biochemistry.

STREET DRUGS

Illegal drugs such as heroin, cocaine, marijuana, LSD, and "designer drugs" are powerful biochemical agents that can dramatically change the body's neurochemistry, often producing addiction.

NICOTINE

Nicotine and other chemicals in tobacco share with crack cocaine the dubious distinction of being the most physically addicting substances currently known. Tobacco is also society's most costly addiction, each year killing three times as many people as alcoholism.

CAFFEINE

Caffeine is a stimulant drug that can easily produce addiction. It stimulates various cravings and exaggerates certain processes' mood-altering capabilities (see the sugar-insulin-serotonin reaction under the module Sugar).

GAMBLING

Gambling can be understood as an addiction to excitement. It is probably an addiction to an excess of catecholamines, like dopamine, norepinephrine, epinephrine (adrenaline), and other neurotransmitters, which are biochemicals that are produced when we become excited or afraid.

SPENDING

Spending also may be an excitement addiction. Compulsive spenders tend to flirt with danger, whether from shoplifting, passing bad checks, or facing the wrath of their spouse.

RELATIONSHIPS

The most powerful relationship addictions seem grounded in excitement, as "women [or men] who love too much" (Norwood,

1985) continually get themselves into physically or emotionally dangerous situations.

SEX

The powerful biochemistry associated with sex alters mood and motivates us as few other substances can. Although this is necessary for preservation of the species, excessive sexual behavior can become a full-fledged addiction.

WORK

What is called "workaholism" is probably several things, some of which include addiction. Those who must work long hours in minimum-wage jobs to support a large family may see no alternative. Someone who works long hours because there is conflict at home may be addicted to work, or may simply be avoiding a painful situation. People with low self-esteem who get most of their self-worth from work are not *necessarily* work-addicted. Genuine work addiction seems to involve addiction to the power associated with certain high-intensity jobs, or with the excitement and danger the work provides.

EXCITEMENT

As we have already seen, many addictions include the biochemistry of excitement as a part of or often most of the addiction process. You may know people who get into trouble for driving too fast, or literally risking their lives for adventure. Excitement may also play an addictive role in crime, including theft, murder, family violence, and incest.

IDENTIFYING ADDICTION

It is easy to recognize alcoholism in a skid row drunk, or food addiction in someone who weighs more than 500 pounds. But these are extremes; we would like to recognize addiction before it becomes a threat to survival itself.

The most common way to identify addiction is by looking at consequences that seem way out of scale with what we accept as normal. People who have lost jobs, been convicted of DUIs, or wrecked cars because of drinking are hardly paying a reasonable price for their "recreational" use of the drug alcohol.

Many people are well into addiction before they experience clearly unreasonable consequences. It may be easier to identify addiction by the struggle required to maintain an illusion of control. For example, elaborate and excessive measures to control your weight can suggest food addiction, though you are not overweight, and seldom binge or purge.

PROGRESSION

One characteristic of addiction is that over time things tend to get worse. This means not only the physical aspects of tolerance and the breakdown of the body's immune system but a progressive emotional, mental, and spiritual deterioration.

DELUSION

When you begin to believe the lies and half-truths you have been telling others to cover your addiction, you fall prey to delusion. You start making decisions based on the way you would like things to be, rather than how they are. You are operating in fantasy rather than reality, with predictable results.

Addiction, see also: Abstinence, Addiction model (PEMS), Alcoholism, Allergies, Arousal, Binge history, Biochemistry, Chronic pain, Codependency, Counseling, Disease concept, Drugs, Excitement, Impaired professionals, Intervention, Moderation, Moodifiers, PEMS model, Powerlessness, Progression, Recovery, Step One, Therapy & treatment.

Addiction model (PEMS)

This manual is structured by the PEMS addiction model. Using the physical, emotional, mental, and spiritual aspects of the disease we will explore everything we have learned to help your recovery.

The PEMS model of addiction can be described by the following diagram:

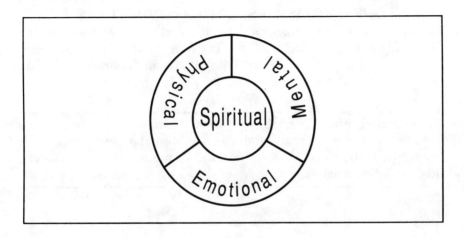

Notice that each aspect—physical, emotional, mental, and spiritual—touches every other aspect. In fact, if you can imagine each area overlapping and gradually blending into each other area it would be a more accurate picture.

PHYSICAL ASPECTS

Physical aspects of addiction include the physical effects of drugs and other substances (whether they originate from outside or inside the body), the reality of the environment that surrounds the addict, and the addict's actual behavior (including what is done for recovery).

EMOTIONAL ASPECTS

Cravings, mood swings, and other emotional factors play a part in the development of addiction and its recovery. Emotions are bio-chemical, and they affect and are affected by what we drink, eat, use, how we act, and how we think.

MENTAL ASPECTS

Obsession, dichotomous thinking, deprivation or diet mentality, delusion, and other forms of mental mismanagement degrade judgment and insure continuation of the addiction. Thoughts are also neurochemical processes, so whatever affects our biochemistry is likely to affect our thoughts, and vice versa.

SPIRITUAL ASPECTS

Isolation from family and friends and from a Higher Power insures that this distorted judgment will proceed down the road of addictive behavior without productive guidance.

ALCOHOLISM VS. OTHER ADDICTIONS

There is almost nothing we have learned about alcoholism that does not have its counterpart in every other addiction. Below each addiction's thin but important layer of specific characteristics, all addictions are the same.

Addiction model (PEMS), see also: Abstinence, Addiction, Alcoholism, Allergies, Emotional aspects, Mental aspects, Models & concepts, Moderation, Moodifiers, PEMS model, Physical aspects, Recovery, Spiritual aspects.

Adolescents

Addictive families encounter abuse, incest, addictive or inconsistent behavior, kids (or even parents) who act out, double messages, and other dynamics that make it hard to learn what the adolescent should learn. Children adapt for survival, learning to fight, to hide, to conceal their feelings, to lie, to entertain, or whatever it takes to survive. With this background, they face the universal crises of puberty, dating, school, love, and career choices.

Over half of all children that grow up with addicts develop some kind of addiction or addictive behaviors. Several questions face anyone concerned about children of addicts. How do you recognize their addiction? What do you do about it? Whether or not they develop their own addictions, what can you do to help them overcome the effect of their childhood and youth?

DIAGNOSING ADOLESCENTS

Mental health professionals are rightly hesitant to diagnose and label adolescents as having an addiction or a mental illness. Many of the diagnostic categories used by psychiatrists, psychologists, and others cannot be applied to adolescents. There is a whole set of similar diagnostic categories that pertain to children and adolescents, and they essentially leave open the possibility that the condition will disappear with adulthood.

There are plenty of adults who drank heavily in high school or college but seemed to grow out of it when they got a job and started a family. At least half the young women who binge and purge in college dorms report that they stopped doing that when they left the college environment. Almost everyone can think of something they did for excitement in their youth that they would not consider doing today.

It is just as possible for parents and others to deny that anything is wrong, to ignore the "rhinoceros in the living room." Adolescents do die of accidents related to addictions. Suicide is a leading cause of adolescent death, and addiction is often involved. It is common to hear adult addicts lament their own lack of academic or other skills due to addiction that was established during their teens.

Parents who suspect addiction in their children will need some professional help to assess and refer the problem to the right resource for recovery. The parents and the rest of the family may also need counseling or other treatment.

Adolescents, see also: Addiction, Alcohol, Alcoholism, Anorexia nervosa, Bingeing, Biochemistry, Bulimia nervosa, Craving, Drugs, Excitement, Exercise & activity, Families Anonymous, Family, Food addiction, Nutrition, Prevention of addiction, Purging, Self-image, Sex, Stress & strain, Unmanageability. End of path A.

Affirmations

A TOOL FOR CHANGE

Recovery involves change, and that is what Steps Six and Seven are all about. Change may require healing and transforming old negative ideas and beliefs about yourself, others, or the world. Affirmations are a tool for this change.

SELF-TALK INJUNCTIONS

Listen to some of the things you say to yourself, or about yourself, that might sabotage your recovery at the onset. Any significantly negative attitudes form barriers to your recovery and personal growth. Imagine bad, old audio tapes that keep repeating, "It is hopeless," and, "I don't deserve recovery."

Committee in the head   You can recognize the negative messages from these old tapes, or the disease itself, that would deter you from getting better or from taking risks for recovery. Some people have fun calling them "the committee in the head." If you plan to be assertive, these voices in your head might snicker, "Nobody will like you if you are pushy."

BELIEFS

You may have many old beliefs that can sabotage recovery, including those about yourself, your relationships, your family, your career, the world, or your idea of a Higher Power.

Many of your beliefs are deeply embedded, but remember that you learned them, and you can now learn something different. A good way to start is by using affirmations. These can help change negatives into positives.

CREATING AFFIRMATIONS

Douglas Bloch (*Words That Heal,* 1988) suggests that you take an area of your life that needs change and write positive statements about how you want things to be. It is important to write them in the first person, present tense, and avoid negative words. For example, instead of saying, "I don't want to keep drinking/using/gambling/ eating compulsively," say, "I deserve health and recovery."

Initially you may find self-defeating thoughts and ideas coming up, such as, "I've been too bad a person to deserve anything good." Continue to replace each negative with a positive affirmation. Change thoughts like the above to "I am wonderful and I am now recovering."

Repetition is the key   Write the affirmation on a card, say it several times a day, and you will start to believe there is truth in what you are saying. It also will help you practice behavior that will reinforce the new belief.

Many meditation books have an affirmation after each daily reading. Using appropriate ones can be very helpful.

Exchange affirmations   You can exchange affirmations with a friend, using the second person. "You are in recovery now. I support your recovery." This will help each of you validate your feelings and self-worth.

Affirmations, see also: Acceptance, Assertiveness, Attitudes, Behavior, Body image, Character defects, Dichotomous thinking, Family, Fear, Feelings, Forgiveness, Guilt & shame, Habit & structure, Obsession, Perfectionism, Prayer & meditation, Resentments, Self-image, Slogans, Step Six, Step Seven, Stinking thinking, Surrender, Willingness. Next on path J: Slogans.

Aftercare

Aftercare is the term used to describe a program of activities to support recovery following inpatient or residential treatment. It usually includes group therapy to address ongoing issues and to help prevent or deal with relapse. Aftercare groups are generally sponsored by a treatment program for their own graduates. Patients return once or twice a week to help each other deal with problems encountered in living addiction free. These therapy groups are usually facilitated by members of the treatment staff.

Many people go to treatment in places far from their home towns, and attending an aftercare group at the treatment center is impossible. They will then need to learn how to reinforce recovery in an aftercare plan. This plan could include recommendations for individual or group therapy and will most certainly include involvement in local Twelve-Step groups.

Treatment centers and programs for addiction should be able to assess the addict's needs and should make appropriate recommendations. These may involve improvements in career, education, family and other relationships, or other activities. The more support available in early recovery, the better the chance for avoiding relapse.

SUPPORT GROUPS

Those who will become involved in AA or NA will have no difficulty finding good groups anywhere in the United States. Other fellowships such as Overeaters Anonymous, Gamblers Anonymous, or Sex and Love Addicts Anonymous, may still be struggling to become strong. In such cases it is especially important that the person be provided with a good understanding of the tools necessary for recovery, perhaps including how to start their own Twelve-Step meetings.

Aftercare, see also: Codependency, Counseling, Dual diagnosis, Employee assistance programs, Half-measures, Halfway house, Impaired professionals, Psychological problems, Therapy & treatment.

AIDS

Acquired immunodeficiency syndrome (AIDS) is a disease that breaks down the immune system, leaving a person defenseless against a variety of life-threatening illnesses. AIDS is caused by a virus called human immunodeficiency virus, or HIV. Because HIV is usually transmitted by sharing needles or having sex with an infected person, most addicts have been or are at increased risk of being exposed to AIDS.

RISK FACTORS IN ADDICTION

When we first started hearing about AIDS, we heard that those at risk included intravenous drug users, transfusion recipients, gay men, and people from Haiti. This idea was dangerous because many people assumed that they were safe if they were not in one of those groups. Today, AIDS organizations are saying that these generalizations do not hold anymore. In 1985 only 1 percent of AIDS cases resulted from heterosexual sex; by 1991 the figure had risen to 6 percent, and it is increasing rapidly.

Addicts who share needles or syringes are at high risk. Needles and syringes could be sterilized by thoroughly cleaning them, soaking them in 10 percent chlorine bleach, and rinsing them well, and then repeating that cycle. The problem is that drug addicts are not known for being very careful about taking precautions.

In 1991, the U.S. city with the highest incidence of HIV positives was Belle Glade, Florida. Researchers flocked to this southern Florida town to find out why. It was not from I.V. drug use, as they expected. Instead, they found heavy use of crack cocaine, and a major part of that addictive behavior was the exchange of sex for crack. They found women who had dozens of partners a night. With this exposure, it is no mystery how the HIV virus could spread so rapidly.

Alcoholics and drug addicts may not remember whether or with whom they had sex because of blackouts. Sex addicts are likely to be exposed to HIV infection, partly because of the impulsiveness of addiction. In fact, any kind of addict will experience loss of judgment that could result in exposure to the virus.

The poor self-esteem and body image problems that often accompany eating disorders and other addictions and codependency can increase the vulnerability to sexual advances, and we expect to see more HIV positives among addicts of all kinds.

TESTING FOR AIDS

What can you do if you are worried that you might have been exposed to AIDS? Even if you know you had unprotected sex with a person who is HIV positive, you may not have it. There have been cases where the spouse of an AIDS patient never got the virus, even after years of exposure.

You can get an HIV-antibody blood test to find out. This simple test is available through your doctor, a special clinic, or a public health unit. You should discuss the test and what it may mean before and after the test is done. The test would not show anything for several weeks after exposure, and it may take a week or more to get the results back.

AVOIDING AIDS

The virus is spread by anal, vaginal, or oral intercourse with an infected person, by sharing drug needles or syringes with an infected person, or by transmission by mother to baby during pregnancy or birth or breast-feeding. Also, since 1985, careful screening and laboratory testing of blood donations have greatly reduced the risk of getting AIDS from transfusions (there is no risk in donating blood).

Assuming you are not using intravenous drugs, you have little danger of exposure to AIDS if you abstain from sexual intercourse or if you and your partner are negative and you both abstain from sex with anyone else. Many people have been exposed by mates they thought were having sex exclusively with them, however.

If you are not absolutely sure about your partner, the greatest safety comes from proper use of a condom. Some experts believe that a spermacide (like nonoxynol-9) may kill the virus during intercourse, too. So the combination of condom and spermacide is best. Select a latex condom with a disease prevention claim on the package label, never reuse condoms, make sure they are not gummy or stuck to themselves, and are within any expiration dates. If you use external spermacide or lubricant, make sure they are water-based and not oil-based, as these may weaken the latex in the condom.

LIVING WITH AIDS

About half of those with HIV develop AIDS within ten years, but this length of time can vary greatly. If you find out you are HIV positive, you should remember that it is not necessarily fatal. While a cure or vaccine may be many years away, there are promising treatments being tested all the time.

Addicts in recovery have a great advantage: they already have a strong support group to help them cope with HIV or AIDS. You can turn to your Twelve-Step or other existing support groups, and you can locate AIDS support groups in your area. As in any serious crisis in life, your spirituality will be tested and quite likely strengthened as you search for meaning and restructure your life to deal with AIDS. Many recovering addicts find themselves doing another kind of Twelve Stepping, as they reach out to share their experience, strength, and hope with others with HIV.

If you are HIV positive, you have a moral responsibility to share that information with recent, present, and future sex partners. Recovery from addiction hinges on honesty and love for self and others, and we find it hard to believe that spirituality includes knowingly endangering another's life. You have a chance to demonstrate love by caring about others, even in your time of crisis.

OTHER SEXUALLY TRANSMITTED DISEASES

There are many other sexually transmitted diseases (STDs) that are not as dramatic as AIDS but still are serious and some potentially fatal. A lot of what we have said about risk factors and prevention of AIDS applies to the more common STDs: chlamydial infections, trichomoniasis, genital herpes, pubic lice, genital warts, and others, including classic gonorrhea and syphilis.

For more information, call the National AIDS Hotline, 1-800-342-AIDS or 1-800-AIDS-TTY (for deaf access), or the National STD Hotline, 1-800-227-8922. They provide information twenty-four hours a day. Ask for their pamphlet, "Condoms and Sexually Transmitted Diseases . . . Especially AIDS."

AIDS, see also: Acceptance, Abuse, Behavior, Blackouts, Body image, Crisis, Guilt & shame, Honesty, Incest, Intimacy, Love & caring, Responsibility, Self-image, Sex, Sex addiction groups, Spirituality, Surrender, Therapy & treatment.

Al-Anon and Alateen

Al-Anon is a Twelve-Step self-help fellowship for family and friends of alcoholics. It began in the 1940s when Lois W., the wife of AA's cofounder Bill W., decided she needed a support group of her own. Families were involved in meetings with alcoholics from the start, but as AA grew the fellowship tended to include only alcoholics. This is where the idea of closed (alcoholics only) and open (for anyone interested) developed.

FAMILY GROUPS

Lois realized she was still suffering from problems caused by alcoholism even though Bill had been sober for several years. Family support groups began to meet around the country, and in 1951 Lois and a friend set up an office in New York to help them. They called their new organization Al-Anon.

Al-Anon adopted AA's Twelve Steps and Twelve Traditions with only minor changes in the wording as needed to make sense for family members.

DETACHMENT

The concept of detachment is a focus in Al-Anon. It means to stop suffering from the actions or reactions of other people, alcoholics in particular. Members of Al-Anon learn how they enable the disease by trying to be helpful. Al-Anon members learn the three C's:

- I didn't cause it.
- I can't control it.
- I can't cure it.

RECOVERY

Al-Anon members learn to be free by focusing on themselves and their own recovery from the effects of alcoholism. By sharing their experience, strength, and hope, they learn to be self-caring and are able to make more intelligent decisions.

LITERATURE

Al-Anon has its own conference-approved literature. Members use meditation books, step-study books, and others by which they learn to work their program.

ALATEEN

Alateen groups are for teenagers affected by alcoholism. They are sponsored by Al-Anon groups. There are over fifteen thousand Al-Anon groups in the United States, and about three thousand of these are Alateen groups. Alatot meetings have sprung up in some places for young children, but the Al-Anon Family Groups headquarters discourages such groups. They believe professionals are best equipped to handle the needs of young children damaged by alcoholism.

OTHER GROUPS

Other support groups have grown out of the ideas developed by Al-Anon. Adult Children of Alcoholics first met as a specialized Al-Anon group, but many are now independent of Al-Anon. Co-Dependents Anonymous is another Twelve-Step group to help people maintain functional relationships.

HEADQUARTERS

Al-Anon has an international service office, their own literature, and functions very much like AA. It is a nonprofit, nonprofessional fellowship. For more information about Al-Anon or Alateen, or to locate a meeting, check your local phone book, an AA intergroup office, or contact:

Al-Anon Family Groups
PO Box 862, Midtown Station
New York, NY 10018-0862
(212) 302-7240 or 800-356-9996 or 800-344-2666.

Al-Anon & Alateen, see also: Adolescents, Alcoholics Anonymous, Alcoholism, Children of addicts, Co-Dependents Anonymous, Enabling, Families Anonymous, History of Twelve-Step groups, Meetings, Other support groups, Steps of AA, Traditions of AA.

Alcohol

Alcohol is by far the most powerful drug you can buy legally without a prescription. It is the most widely used mind-altering substance in the world, known to almost every culture since prehistoric times. It is also a narcotic.

ALCOHOLS

Chemically, an alcohol is any of a class of organic compounds that have hydroxyl (OH) groups. Glycerol, mannitol, and sorbitol are alcohols mentioned elsewhere in this manual. Most people are familiar with rubbing alcohol, which is methyl alcohol. But the word alcohol by itself usually refers to ethyl alcohol, or ethanol, the ingredient in wine, beer, and distilled liquors.

ALCOHOL METABOLISM

From the moment alcohol enters the body, it gets special treatment. While most foods are digested slowly, the tiny alcohol molecule goes to the head of the line. About 20 percent of it enters the bloodstream directly from the walls of the stomach. It can reach the brain in less than a minute after ingestion. If the stomach contains food, there will be some delay before the alcohol enters the small intestine, but once there it will be absorbed quickly whether there is food present or not.

Liver cells are the only ones in the body that can metabolize alcohol at an appreciable rate. Only they produce enough of the enzyme alcohol dehydrogenase (NAD+) and its partner enzyme acetaldehyde dehydrogenase (NALD+), both from the B vitamin niacin. By dropping almost everything else it does, the liver can metabolize about one-half ounce of alcohol each hour. This is the about the amount of alcohol in four ounces of table wine, twelve ounces of beer, or one ounce of 100 proof liquor.

If you are fasting or on a very restrictive diet, there is much less NAD+ available, so the metabolism of alcohol may be reduced to half its normal speed. So drinking alcohol on an empty stomach gets alcohol into the bloodstream faster and it stays there longer.

STRUCTURE

Alcohol has a much simpler chemical structure than other mind-altering substances. Even sugars are complex by comparison. This has led some researchers to suggest that it is not the alcohol that produces addiction, but opiatelike by-products, which occur more often among alcoholics, and even among children of alcoholics.

THIQ

One popular theory involves the neurotransmitter dopamine. The normal metabolism for dopamine requires the same NAD+ enzyme that is in short supply because of the metabolism of large amounts of alcohol. Instead of its normal metabolite, dopamine becomes a compound belonging to a class of chemicals called tetra-hydroisoquinolines (THIQ). These compounds are thought to behave a lot like opiates (Milkman & Sunderwirth, 1987, pp. 68-75).

ENZYMES

These enzymes oxidize alcohol first into acetaldehyde, and then into acetyl co-enzyme A (acetyl CoA), which would normally be used to produce energy. But that process has been suppressed, so the acetyl CoA is changed into fatty acids. After even one night of heavy drinking, these fatty acids can be detected building up in the liver. They also appear as elevated triglyceride levels in the blood.

LIVER DAMAGE

There are three phases of liver damage: fatty liver, fibrosis, and cirrhosis. If the fat buildup in the liver lasts long enough, liver cells die, leaving fibrous scar tissue. Abstinence from alcohol and good nutrition can reverse this damage in the fibrosis stage, but not after it has become cirrhosis.

MEOS

Another mechanism that metabolizes some alcohol is called the MEOS (microsomal ethanol-oxidizing system). It handles about a fifth of the alcohol a person drinks, but its function will expand if repeatedly exposed to alcohol. While it is not very significant from an alcoholism perspective, it is important in relation to other drugs, because it metabolizes various other drugs as well as alcohol.

Suppose an alcoholic starts taking a sedative drug. The enlarged MEOS metabolizes the drug very rapidly, so the sedative wears off. The alcoholic takes a larger dose. This works fine until one day the alcoholic takes the sedative after drinking heavily. The MEOS is now busy metabolizing alcohol, so the alcoholic overdoses on the sedative that, coupled with the depressant effects of the alcohol, can cause death.

OTHER EFFECTS

Alcohol produces many other noxious effects in the body. The body's acid-base balance (pH) shifts toward acid. The fatty liver has trouble making glucose from protein, resulting in ketosis. The liver slows down protein synthesis because it is busy with alcohol, so the immune system is less efficient, weakening the body's defense against infection. The stomach becomes inflamed, producing too much acid, and is likely to develop ulcers. Intestinal cells have trouble absorbing certain vitamins and minerals.

BREATH

About 10 percent of the alcohol leaves the body through the breath and in the urine, making it possible to test the breath or urine for alcohol intoxication. Many alcoholics drink vodka in the mistaken belief that it cannot be detected on their breath.

Alcohol, see also: Blackouts, Drugs, Fetal alcohol syndrome, Heroin, Impaired professionals, Moodifiers, Pregnancy, Tolerance, Withdrawal.

Alcoholics Anonymous (AA)

Alcoholics Anonymous (AA) is the fellowship that has given millions of people the way to recover from alcohol. Its philosophy, principles, and Twelve Steps and Twelve Traditions provide the model and prototype of many self-help groups today. Those who call themselves anonymous fellowships or Twelve-Step programs can look to AA as their original founding father.

BILL W.

There were many factors that influenced AA in the early days, and we will mention a few of the significant ones. Bill Wilson, AA's cofounder, after struggling with alcohol for years was visited by a former drinking buddy, Ebby T., who said he had gotten sober by using religion. Ebby had been helped by Rowland H., who had been told he was a hopeless alcoholic by Carl Jung, the famous Swiss psychiatrist. Dr. Jung, however, said he had occasionally seen such men saved by a miraculous religious conversion.

OXFORD GROUP

Rowland H. joined the Oxford Group, a nondenominational evangelical group that sought the spirit of first century Christianity. He got sober and tried to help other alcoholics by using Oxford Group principles, which became a foundation for the development of AA's Twelve-Step recovery plan. Those principles involved a self-survey, confession, restitution, and the giving of oneself in service to others. See the module on History of Twelve-Step groups for more historical perspective.

DR. BOB

Bill Wilson stayed sober several months, attending Oxford Group meetings and trying to help other alcoholics sober up. It was in Akron, Ohio, in May 1935, that he met Dr. Robert H. Smith, known fondly to AA members as Dr. Bob, AA's cofounder. Bill, that night in May, wanting to drink, called a clergyman looking for another alcoholic to help and was led to Dr. Bob. What was supposed to be a fifteen-minute meeting lasted over four hours. What impressed Dr. Bob was sensing that Bill had suffered just as he had, and more important, that Bill needed him as much as he needed Bill. Dr. Bob had his last drink on June 10, 1935, which is celebrated today as AA's birthday.

CARRYING THE MESSAGE

The key to the success of AA is that an alcoholic who has found a solution to the malady carries the message of recovery to another suffering alcoholic. From that time in Ohio in 1935, the message of recovery has spread to millions of alcoholics throughout the world.

THE BIG BOOK

Alcoholics Anonymous, published in 1939 and known as the Big Book, is the textbook of recovery for alcoholics. An individual learns about AA's Twelve Steps of recovery by reading the Big Book, attending AA meetings, and talking to other alcoholics. The program is a spiritual one, where a person finds a Higher Power to help with their life, and learns to live a life based on spiritual principles. A basic premise is the powerlessness to quit drinking on one's will power. Since alcoholism affects one's whole being, AA says recovery must be physical, mental, and spiritual.

STEPS & TRADITIONS

AA spent its early years struggling to make the program and fellowship most effective. Out of the struggles evolved the Twelve

Steps, the Twelve Traditions, and the Preamble that states what AA is. The Steps tell how individual members get and stay sober, and the Traditions describe how the fellowship stays healthy. These are explained in greater detail in other modules in this manual.

Today AA has over ninety thousand groups, a World Service Office, and a publishing company. Individual members participate for one reason: to stay sober and to carry the message of recovery to those who still suffer. In doing so they put aside personal desire for power and control, prejudice, individual preferences and annoyances, all to share in the gift of the great joy of recovery.

Alcoholics Anonymous, see also: Adolescents, Al-Anon & Alateen, Alcoholism, Community, History of Twelve-Step groups, Meetings, Other support groups, Steps of AA, Traditions of AA.

Alcoholism

Alcoholism has been considered a moral problem since the dawn of recorded history. Around the turn of the century alcoholism began to be treated as a psychiatric illness, although the moral overtones remained. Since most cultures accepted drinking as OK, the attitude was usually not "The drinker is bad," but that "The drunk is bad." People who "disgraced" themselves after drinking too much were assumed to have some kind of moral weakness and lack of will power.

DISEASE CONCEPT
AA's phenomenal success changed public opinion: alcoholism began to be perceived as a disease, and the alcoholic as a sick rather than a bad person. The medical profession had almost given up on treating the alcoholic by 1935, partly because of very poor success rates. Today alcoholism is usually treated as an addictive disease, with generally good results in roughly half the cases.

SIMILARITY TO OTHER ADDICTIONS
Almost everything known about the identification, development, or treatment of alcoholism has its parallel in any other addiction. While each addiction has its differences, they are almost trivial in the long run. Therapists must know the jargon and the painful emotions and circumstances of each specific addiction, but the disease itself seems the same for all addictions.

BIOLOGICAL COMPONENTS

Two trends in the study of addiction stand out. One is the investigation and incorporation of current physical, neurochemical research into the theory of addiction. You may have read articles about biochemistry, opiate receptors, and maybe even the role endorphins, serotonin, and other neurotransmitters play in addictive behavior.

THE FAMILY

The other trend is a growing awareness of the impact that family, especially family of origin, has on people. Concerns about Adult Children of Alcoholics, codependency, abuse, and incest echo this trend in the treatment of addiction.

BIOCHEMISTRY

Alcoholism and chemical dependency treatment have traditionally focused on the substance or drug that is ingested, injected, or otherwise taken into the body from outside. This emphasis has fostered the belief that addiction comes from outside the body.

To understand addiction better, you must also consider addiction to the biochemical changes that occur within the body, whether induced by the drug, by excitement, or by other biological processes.

CODEPENDENCY

Some of these biochemical changes can take place in the bodies of those around the active addict, regardless of whether the addict or the others are using external drugs. These physical effects combine with emotional, mental, and spiritual factors to produce the disease or syndrome known as codependency (see the module on Codependency for more information).

Alcoholism, see also: Addiction, Addiction model (PEMS), Adolescents, Alcohol, Alcoholics Anonymous, Binge history, Bingeing, Biochemistry, Blackouts, Celebrations, Craving, Drugs, Family, History of Twelve-Step groups, Hunger & appetite, Moodifiers, Nutrition, Prevention of addiction, Progression. Next on path A: Drugs.

Allergies

GENERAL ADAPTATION THEORY

Hans Selye, an MD, over forty years ago proposed a theory about allergy that still can be applied to allergy and addiction today. It is too simple to address the medical treatment of allergy, but it is still a useful model of the addictive process. It describes how the body responds to toxic (poisonous) substances or to excessive amounts of almost any substance. The body reacts progressively in these phases:

Alarm phase   This is the body's signal that you have encountered toxic levels of a food or other substance. It can be seen in your first reaction to a cigarette, or in the first time you got sick on too much sugar at Halloween. These are signs that your body is having trouble coping with the onslaught of toxic levels of a substance.

Adaptation phase   Your body's biochemistry can adapt to minimize the effect of most toxins. Some poisons are so toxic that death occurs instead, and other alarm reactions may be so severe that you never touch that substance again. But many warning signs can be ignored, and the adaptation begins. This adaptation may shield you from toxic damage for many years. You quickly adapt to the presence of tobacco smoke or to alcohol or to high levels of sugar in your diet.

Degenerative phase   Eventually, if enough toxins are consumed or produced, the adaptation mechanisms begin to break down, and they can no longer shield you from the effects of the toxin. Examples are the smoker's racking cough, the drinker's hangover or "jitters," and the heavy sugar user's indigestion or daytime drowsiness.

ADAPTIVE STAGE ALLERGY

The body attempts to "take care" of toxic chemicals or toxic levels of ordinarily nontoxic substances for as long as possible, whether they are introduced from the outside or manufactured within.

This is the stage where you can easily delude yourself *and others* into thinking that you really don't have a problem. This adaptation may last for many years. Although you frequently disrupt the balance of your biochemistry, the effects and their damage are minimized by corrective actions your body takes to try to maintain equilibrium.

DEGENERATIVE STAGE ALLERGY

In the middle to late stages of addiction, your body's ability to adapt begins to break down; it can no longer shield you from the toxic effects. Denial or delusion may keep you from seeing that there is a problem, but others will begin to notice it. (Many food addicts, in contrast to most other addicts, enter the degenerative stage of their addiction before or around puberty.) This degeneration may continue for many years.

SYMPTOMS OF ADAPTIVE FAILURE

Just as some people have more athletic ability than others, some people can tolerate biochemical imbalances better than others. These people will endure more abuse, but eventually their adaptive mechanisms are exhausted, and they enter the degenerative stage of the illness.

Obesity   Being excessively overweight is a clear sign that the body is not adapting well to the intake of food, especially fats. This makes obese people the most obvious addicts. The more obese a person is, the higher the probability of addiction to food, with all the physical, emotional, mental, and spiritual consequences of addiction.

Emaciation   This is also easy to see in advanced anorexia nervosa. Relatives and friends who have not seen an anorexic in several years are often deeply shocked by this person's emaciated appearance. Other addicts may become emaciated if they neglect nutrition, or if the drug (such as alcohol) damages vital organs such as the liver or pancreas.

Emotional turmoil   Many addicts experience tremendous emotional chaos from struggling to try to control their drinking, using, eating, purging, weight, or addictive behavior. They also may suffer from intense guilt, poor body image, and low self-esteem.

Cardiovascular   All addictions endanger the heart and other bodily organs. Although normal exercise enhances cardiovascular health, exercise addiction can be dangerous when pushed beyond the body's ability to repair itself.

Susceptibility to other diseases   Poor nutrition can make you more susceptible to other diseases. Heavy drinkers may get sick more often than their coworkers. Food addicts who binge and purge, fast, or follow unhealthy diets may have more viral and bacterial infections, stress-related disorders, and other health problems. Obese food addicts may avoid medical help, or the obesity may mask conditions requiring health care, including pregnancy. Smoking, of course, aggravates virtually every disease known.

Diabetes   It isn't clear whether a high sugar intake *causes* diabetes, but it certainly aggravates it. Many of those who die or suffer blindness or lose fingers or toes do so because of the combination of diabetes and food addiction.

Suicide   We have no idea how many suicides relate to addiction. Most people who commit suicide do not leave a note explaining it, and those who do rarely mention their struggles with alcohol, drugs, food, or whatever their addiction might have been. Many addicts report thoughts of suicide or that they attempted suicide because of their struggles with addiction.

Allergies, see also: Addiction, Alcohol, Binge history, Craving, Food plans, Metabolism, Neurotransmitters, Nicotine, Nutrition, Obesity, Physical aspects, Progression, Sugar, Tolerance, Unmanageability, Withdrawal. Next on path B: Tolerance.

Amends

Amends include anything reasonable you can do to correct the damage and neglect you discover are your responsibility in Step Eight, where you list all the people you have harmed. The harm includes damage, where your actions actually hurt someone, and neglect, where you denied your love, respect, and other resources to family members, friends, employers, and others.

DAMAGE

Damage includes harm through actions, manipulation, gossip, and anything else you do or say.

NEGLECT

Neglect includes the time you spend obsessing about your addictive substance or activity instead of being with your family, the emotional contact that becomes difficult or impossible due to your addiction, and the lower quality job you give to your employers.

You may find that the person you have harmed the most is yourself. Recognizing the need to make amends to yourself can lessen self-pity and self-hatred.

NEED FOR AMENDS

Amends give you a sense of self-worth, which can get lost in addiction. They can relieve your fear of being "found out" as a fake, a gossip, a dishonest person, or an incompetent.

RESISTANCE TO AMENDS

You may have had bad experiences in your family of origin with honesty and with owning up to your mistakes. You may harbor resentments and not want to let them go. "After all, they hurt me worse than I hurt them."

FEARS

You may be afraid of how people will react to your amends, fearing that they will not like you if you tell them what you've done. You may also be afraid of the financial or emotional cost of making amends.

By the time you focus on Step Nine and start making your amends in earnest, you probably have already made some amends and experienced the strength your Higher Power has to offer in working the Steps. Use it.

Addictive behavior results in shame and guilt for many addicts. Making amends is part of the healing process of recovery. You regain a sense of self-worth and self-respect by acknowledging your need for forgiveness for harm you may have caused others. This allows you to feel forgiven by your Higher Power and yourself, whether or not others forgive you. Making amends also eases the way for you to forgive others when necessary. See the module on Forgiveness.

Amends, see also: Forgiveness, Guilt & shame, Incest, Relationships, Resentments, Step Eight, Step Nine, Step Ten. Next on path K: Forgiveness.

Anger

Anger is a perfectly natural human feeling. Like all feelings, it is how you respond to it that determines whether the feeling helps or hurts your recovery.

DENYING ANGER

If you deny or "stuff" your anger, you may have problems with assertiveness, experience internal stress, or miss out on the motivation that healthy anger can produce.

Assertiveness   Many women still believe that expressing anger is not appropriate behavior. Harriet Goldhor Lerner (*The Dance of Anger*, 1985) points out that angry women can be called shrews, bitches, witches, or hags, whereas there is no such unflattering term to describe angry men. People who feel ashamed of their anger often have trouble being assertive anytime there is conflict in a relationship.

Stress   If you deny anger, you will find it hard to deal with stress in your life. A classic pattern for cardiovascular risk is someone who experiences lots of anger but is unable to show it. You can learn the skill of communicating your anger in a way that will reduce stress and make you a more effective person.

Healthy anger   The purpose of anger is to motivate. If you use this energy in a positive way, the anger will not be a negative thing. It can help you to be assertive without being aggressive, move you to take necessary action in relationships, and put energy into good causes.

FEEDING ANGER

The opposite extreme is to cultivate anger actively and to convert other feelings into a perception of anger, or even rage. This intensifies unnecessary conflict in relationships and focuses responsibility (or blame) on others. For some, excessive anger becomes an unconscious or semiconscious way to manipulate others.

Keeping the heat on   Anger, like any other natural feeling, is fleeting. Watch the way a child will be angry one minute, then laughing the next. You may believe that once you have a feeling you should "stick with it." Or you might have a resentful attitude that keeps reminding you that people are out to get you.

Converting other feelings   If anger is acceptable but other feelings are not, you may be experiencing feelings like hurt or fear, but perceive them as anger instead. This is a typical "macho" characteristic that often leads to unnatural, destructive behavior.

Suppose you are a member of a gang. Your subculture frowns on any show of fear. You get into a conflict with another person and both of you feel afraid. Since this is not acceptable, you both inter-pret the fear as anger, and the danger of physical harm increases. This inability to identify feelings accurately probably helps kill several people in the United States every day, in gang warfare or in armed assault.

Poor decisions   Anger clouds judgment. If anger is excessive or if it lasts far longer than its natural course, you may make poor choices. You may say or do things you will later regret.

Unfortunately, some people squelch their anger for fear that they will embarrass themselves or harm others. Eventually the anger builds until they can no longer contain it, and they lash out at someone or something. This strengthens the idea that anger is terrible, and it reinforces the cycle.

Manipulation   Sometimes people learn that when they are an-gry, they get their way. They may encourage anger when they feel it or even fake it to get their own needs met at the expense of others. This is when anger becomes manipulation, and individuals may or may not be consciously aware that they are using anger in a manipu-lative way.

Temper   People who claim they have a "terrible temper" cer-tainly put everyone on notice that they must not be crossed. While they may honestly believe they are powerless over their temper (and might actually be rage addicts), it could also be a kind of manipula-tion or a defense to keep people from getting too close.

Exhausted control   There are others whose control mecha-nisms are so exhausted that all they can do is respond with anger. Addicts who have been trying to control their addiction are not so different from children who are up way past their bedtime and become cranky and irritable because they are tired.

WHAT IS ANGER?

Feelings are biochemical processes that suggest courses of action to us. Anger is essentially a combination of hurt and fear, with neurotransmitters or hormones (like adrenaline) added to prepare us for possible fight or flight.

Hurt   Any perceived hurt can trigger anger. This can be a memory of a painful event in the ancient or recent past, or current pain. If this anger helps you to get out of a painful situation, then it probably worked well.

If you want to get rid of the anger, try to identify the feeling of hurt that may be below the anger. For example, if you often get angry at your boss, see if you can remember some hurt you experienced from this person or another authority figure (like a parent) in the past. Remembering and allowing yourself to feel this hurt (perhaps by crying) may diffuse the anger and allow you to deal more effectively with your boss. Or it may convince you that there is too much pain here and you need to find another job.

Fear   Fear is a physiological (biochemical) reaction that warns that pain or harm is imminent. It is an important survival mechanism that keeps us from exposing ourselves to unnecessary danger. If the danger is unavoidable, biochemical energy is added to make it anger. Some of our ancestors actually defended themselves and their children from saber-toothed tigers through the power of fear and adrenaline, and a stick.

Soldiers throughout history have "psyched themselves up" for a battle by turning their fears into anger, which gave them energy for the ensuing fight. But in modern warfare, where the ability to destroy the enemy may depend on making split-second technical decisions in the cockpit of a jet fighter, anger may actually be counterproductive. In many situations, allowing yourself to experience the fear, and then going on with your challenge, is the best way to deal with anger.

Adrenaline   Intense hurt or fear can trigger the release of norepinephrine (adrenaline) and other neurotransmitters or hormones to mobilize the body for fight or flight. This is the source of the energy in anger.

Rage   An excess of these biochemical agents becomes rage. In all but the most dangerous survival situations, rage produces damage rather than a productive response. Rage often results from hurt or fear that is denied (or "controlled") until it becomes anger, and then further suppressed until it becomes rage.

As anger builds, the neurochemical imbalances within the body may add to the fright, producing more fear, more adrenaline, and more anger. Rage, then, is neurochemically like getting a microphone too close to the speaker—the feedback proceeds rapidly to full volume.

Encountering rage   Dealing with someone who is in a rage can be tricky and potentially dangerous. As with audio feedback, someone needs to turn down the volume or flip off the switch. If you can break off the confrontation, somehow interrupt what may be an "old tape" playing at full volume, or make it safer for the enraged person, you may be able to break the crisis.

PAST EXPERIENCE WITH ANGER

Your family of origin is the best place to begin your search for your problems with anger. If anger was not permitted, you may have used lots of energy throughout your life to avoid becoming aware of it. This is what may be going on if you believe you seldom get angry but feel a knot in your stomach much of the time.

Denying anger   Many adult women who are addicts grew up being "good little girls," and everyone knows that good little girls don't get angry. If this fits, your emotional recovery may include learning to express your anger honestly. This may be frightening at first, but you can learn that sharing your feelings does not have to hurt yourself or anyone else.

Anger, see also: Abuse, Acceptance, Attitudes, Crisis, Dual diagnosis, Emotional aspects, Emotions Anonymous, Energy levels, Excitement, Family of origin, Fear, Feelings, Grief, Intimacy, Panic attacks, Power, Premenstrual syndrome, Relaxation, Serenity, Stress & strain, Survival roles, Tranquilizers, Trust, Visualizations. Next on path C: Craving.

Anonymity

HISTORIC REASONS

The anonymity of Alcoholics Anonymous emerged during a time when alcoholics could be fired from a job or subjected to public scorn if someone found out you were an alcoholic—even a recovering one. The word *stigma* originally meant a mark of identification burned or cut into the flesh of an animal or a slave. It has come to mean a mark of shame. While it is no longer such a stigma for people to find out you are an addict in recovery, it is important that you decide who ought to know about it.

Improvements   Entertainers and public figures are less likely today to be scorned for being a recovering alcoholic. The open admission of Betty Ford and many other addicts has helped the public accept addiction as a disease.

Safe environment   Still, addicts going to meetings need to feel they are in a safe environment. New members especially have enough fear without the worry that their boss will find out they are attending Narcotics Anonymous (or any other addiction-oriented) meetings.

ANONYMITY AND CONFIDENTIALITY

Many people use the word *anonymity* when the word *confidentiality* would be more correct. Anonymity refers to "who" and confidentiality deals more with "what."

For example, if you say, "A friend of mine is having trouble with her husband's drinking," you protect her and her husband's anonymity by not revealing their names or other identifying information. If you are talking to another AA member about a third AA member, whom you both know and care about, anonymity is no problem, but you should be careful not to reveal anything that the third member might not want shared with another. Confidentiality means keeping secret that which someone does not want to be made public.

Using last names   Last names and other identifying information should be avoided at the level of press, radio, films, and other mass media. There is no prohibition about exchanging this information with others in your Twelve-Step group. In fact, Dr. Bob, cofounder of AA, said it was a violation of tradition to withhold last names from other members of AA (see the module on Tradition Eleven).

Outside the meeting rooms anonymity may get a little trickier. Suppose you meet a fellow program member while you are with your family or a friend who later asks, "Where did you meet her?" Try brushing it off with "I met her through friends." Usually simpler is better.

Spirit of anonymity   Recovery offers you the opportunity to share things that shame or embarrass you. The principles of anonymity and confidentiality assure you that others will be sensitive about what you share that is painful. This involves trust.

Secrets   Misuse of anonymity and confidentiality creates paranoia. For example, if you have a problem with your sponsor and want to complain to another group member, you might try to swear the other group member to secrecy rather than being open and honest about your feelings. Fear, suspicion, anger, and gossip can replace the love and trust that characterize relationships in recovery.

Manipulating others   Paranoia can be contagious. Some people get manipulative, using their secrets as weapons against themselves and others. An example is someone who says, "Can I tell you something, and you'll never tell anyone else, ever?" This person may be about to dump their problems on you and also keep you from passing them on to someone else. You could decline, saying you don't like the terms of the agreement. Another response might be, "I will do my best to be discreet and appropriate with everything you share with me." This gives you an out in case you need support or advice from someone else.

Special situations   There are conditions and situations that may require special sensitivity from the people involved. Incest, homosexuality, and illnesses like AIDS are all issues that should be handled with discretion and concern. Many addicts feel very ashamed when sharing past behavior related to the addiction. Examples are stealing, sexual behavior, and being arrested, even when such behavior is the direct result of addiction. Many people find consolation in the phrase, "We are not bad people trying to become good, we are sick people trying to get well."

Burning bridges   The more open and honest you can be, the more freedom and serenity you will experience. Your addiction can use the power of secrets to get you to drink, use, binge, or get off track in your recovery. Sponsors often say, "You are as sick as your secrets." You can eliminate the sinister power of some secrets by the honest use of Steps Four through Nine.

HUMILITY

While newcomers often interpret anonymity as that which keeps secret their membership and what they say, perhaps more important long term is the idea that all members are equal. Here is where humility comes in: an honest understanding of each member's place in the fellowship.

Honesty   Humility includes the ability to look at yourself honestly, neither over- or underselling your capabilities and worth. The spiritual principle of anonymity fits in nicely with this by saying that when it comes to Program activities, all are nonprofessional; each person is as valuable as the next.

Self-image   True humility is a key to improving self-image. If you don't need to put others or yourself down, you can see that everyone has strengths and weaknesses, and appreciate rather than criticize individual differences.

TRADITIONS

The Traditions say that members should remain forever non-professional. Also, the only requirement for membership is a desire to stop the addictive behavior.

No gurus   The Traditions suggest that your activities in the Program focus on sharing your experience, strength, and hope on an equal basis with other members. Although others may try to place you on a pedestal and treat you as a counselor or expert, if you allow that to happen you rob yourself of the spiritual foundation of the program—anonymity.

No status   Anything that creates a caste system in the Fellowship tends to destroy anonymity. If you must have a certain length of abstinence to be a sponsor, doesn't that imply that sponsors are in a higher class than other members? If you know that a certain member is a physician, there is no problem unless she allows or encourages people to treat her as a doctor rather than as a regular addict.

Commercialism   There is also a problem when people go to Twelve-Step meetings and use them to promote their own treatment programs, or even the one where they went to treatment. If a particular treatment experience was critical to your recovery, then it would be somewhat dishonest not to mention that in telling your story, but when it begins to sound like an ad, you become an agent for a treatment program rather than an anonymous Twelve-Step Program member.

Anonymity, see also: Alcoholics Anonymous, Beliefs, Character defects, Defenses, Grace, Gratitude, Half-measures, History of Twelve-Step groups, Humility, Humor & fun, Meetings, Open-mindedness, Priorities, Relapse prevention, Sabotage of recovery, Service & giving, Spirituality, Step Twelve, Traditions of AA, Unity.

Anorexia nervosa

Anorexia nervosa is an eating disorder we describe as addiction to starving. The term is a psychiatric term, and it has the highest fatality rate of all psychiatric disorders—about 20 percent die of the disease. It is usually treated as a psychiatric illness, often focusing on family dysfunction. Usually the addictive aspect is ignored.

Anorexia nervosa is an eating disorder in which the individual struggles to maintain a low food intake, with occasional ventures into what most of the rest of us would call moderate eating. Because of the body image distortions of anorexia nervosa, these fluctuations are viewed by the anorexic as inexcusable, terrible binges, rather than moderate eating, and most anorexics will purge if they can following such a "binge."

DSM III-R

In the *Diagnostic and Statistical Manual* of the American Psychiatric Association, third edition, revised in 1987, the diagnosis for anorexia nervosa is summarized as follows:

• Refusal to maintain body weight over a minimal normal weight for age and height, e.g., weight loss leading to maintenance of body weight 15 percent below that expected; or failure to make expected weight gain during period of growth, leading to body weight 15 percent below that expected.
• Intense fear of gaining weight or becoming fat, even though underweight.
• Disturbance in the way in which one's body weight, size, or shape is experienced, e.g., the person claims to "feel fat" even when emaciated, believes that one area of the body is "too fat" even when obviously underweight.
• In females, absence of at least three consecutive menstrual cycles when otherwise expected to occur (primary or secondary amenorrhea). A woman is considered to have amenorrhea if her periods occur only following hormone, e.g., estrogen, administration.

There is a type of anorexia nervosa that seems much more psychiatric than addictive in nature. In these people there is more dysfunctional thought and behavior, which may involve many areas not directly connected with eating. Often the family is very controlling, overprotective, and may have many problems that cannot be explained by addiction in the family. Roughly half of all anorexics do not respond well to an addiction model, even with good treatment.

Addiction to starvation   Starvation influences many neurotransmitters and other biochemical agents. The anorexic can, of course, become addicted to the body's own chemicals.

Avoiding overeating   Most anorexics have a strong fear that if they begin eating, they will overeat. This fear may come partially from their history of being overweight, or of obesity in the family.

Restricting vs. purging Many anorexics do have binge/purge episodes besides their extremely restrictive eating. You can be anorexic and bulimic simultaneously. In fact, anorexics are often categorized into restricting anorexics and purging anorexics.

STARVATION EFFECTS

Starvation disrupts many bodily functions and changes neurochemical balances. These changes seem most similar to those we see in stimulant drugs.

Ketosis Starvation depletes the glycogen supply, and the body does not have enough blood sugar to metabolize fats properly. Ketone bodies are produced, which supply enough energy to the brain to keep it alive, but they also suppress the appetite and make you smell funny, due to the acetone (like nail polish remover) produced when fats are burned without adequate carbohydrates.

Malnutrition Starvation means an inadequate amount of protein, fat, and other nutrients that produce hormones, especially female hormones. The body shuts down the reproductive system, partly because it is unsafe to bring a child into what seems like a famine outside. Menses (periods) become irregular and stop altogether.

The body needs protein to live and will take it from muscle tissue, like the heart. There is often hair loss, a downy growth of hair all over the body, and loss of sex drive.

STARVATION ADDICTION

The body gets addicted to these biochemical imbalances. To get this high, which resembles an amphetamine or "upper" drug, requires more weight loss as tolerance increases. This may be the most cruel addiction: consuming your own body to get high.

THE "NERVOSA"

The "nervosa" part of anorexia nervosa refers to the mental part of the disease, as obsession and perceptual disturbances become extreme.

Fear of fat The body image becomes distorted to bizarre levels. Even if there is some basis for the fear (like a tendency to overeat), the response to this fear is exaggerated, inappropriate, and destructive. This extreme distortion puzzles and frustrates family members and others trying to help the anorexic.

Control illusion   Most anorexics report a tremendous feeling of power and control, which is usually reinforced by comments (even admiration) from others. Control is an illusion, but this illusion is critical to the functioning of anorexia. It focuses on control of food, eating, fat, weight, and through these, other people.

Anorexia nervosa, see also: Adolescents, Bingeing, Biochemistry, Body image, Bulimia nervosa, Constipation, Control, Crisis, Defenses, Delusion, Dichotomous thinking, Diet mentality, Exercise & activity, Family, Fats, Food addiction, Food plans, Higher Power, Hunger & appetite, Intervention, Magical thinking, Moodifiers, Nutrition, Purging, Sabotage of recovery, Sanity, Self-image, Sex, Stinking thinking, Stress & strain, Therapy & treatment, Unmanageability, Weight. Next on path A: Bulimia nervosa.

Arousal

To classify addictive behavior, we expand on a model suggested by Harvey Milkman and Stanley Sunderwirth (1987). They suggested the addictive states of arousal, satiety, and fantasy. They also mentioned what they called super-reality, though they did not elaborate on it. We call it control, the fourth state or direction for addictive behavior.

AROUSAL

The arousal direction includes all the substances and activities that produce an "up" feeling. Stimulant drugs such as caffeine, amphetamines, or cocaine increase concentrations of the catacholamine neurotransmitters. These include epinephrine (which used to be called adrenaline), norepinephrine, and dopamine. Activities like gambling, risk-taking, high-pressure jobs, and crime stimulate biochemical reactions that can cause powerful mood changes and mind alterations.

Lifestyle   The stronger your addictions point to arousal patterns, the more the obsession for power and activity and doing things. It is no accident that cocaine addicts are more often involved in a fast-paced, performance-oriented lifestyle. The jet set is part of the general addictive process.

Combinations   If you like to combine the arousal state or direction with fantasy, you may be drawn to mystical experiences, where you have both arousal and fantasy. If, instead, you lean toward control, you may like precision excitement, like flying jet planes or very precise sports.

Arousal, see also: Anger, Cocaine, Codependency, Control, Emotional aspects, Fantasy, Satiety.

Assertiveness

Addicts often lack assertiveness; it ties in with their poor self-esteem. But you need to be assertive to take care of yourself and get your needs met. Assertiveness is learned behavior, and many addicts never learned it.

Alberti and Emmons (*Your Perfect Right,* 1982) write: "Assertive behavior enables a person to act in his or her best interests, to stand up for herself or himself without undue anxiety, to express honest feelings comfortably, or to exercise personal rights without denying the rights of others." Behavior that is assertive is self-caring, considerate, courteous, and allows for negotiation.

AGGRESSION
Aggression is a poor example of assertiveness. Aggressive behavior may consider your rights, but no one else's, and may involve being demanding, rude, inconsiderate, and selfish. It is ultimately self-defeating.

PEOPLE PLEASING
At the passive end of the assertiveness spectrum is the nonassertive behavior we call people pleasing. It seems quite common among food addicts and in codependency. People pleasing may have its roots in a desire to feel good about yourself. If you were taught to be self-sacrificing and unselfish, making others happy may help you feel OK. The problem is that you forget to care about yourself. You consider everyone else's needs before your own.

Unfortunately, people pleasing is counterproductive. Ironically, you wind up not pleasing many people. Those who like to use you may benefit, but you don't get much respect from them. Your self-esteem suffers. You may feel like a doormat.

Recovery means learning to care about yourself, including learning assertiveness skills. You may need support or counseling to help you do this.

FAMILY HISTORY

Assertiveness is learned best by having assertive role models and by being reinforced for assertive behavior. Self-worth is built by learning it is OK not only to have needs but to ask that they be met and then to be validated for expressing your feelings and thoughts.

If your role models used people pleasing or aggression to get their needs met, it is not likely you learned assertive behavior.

DYSFUNCTIONAL FAMILIES

Since poor self-esteem and inappropriate ways of trying to get needs met characterize dysfunctional families, it is no surprise that many addicts have a lot to learn about assertiveness.

RECOVERY

Healthy assertiveness is vital for recovery from addiction. You have to value yourself, know how to get your needs met, and be able to negotiate with others and respect their needs also.

Assertiveness, see also: Abuse, Affirmations, Attitudes, Behavior, Character defects, Control, Defenses, Dichotomous thinking, Family, Honesty, Incest, Integrity & values, Intimacy, Inventory, Mental aspects, Perfectionism, Relationships, Slogans, Step Four, Step Five, Step Six, Step Eight, Step Ten, Survival roles, Willingness. Next on path I: Energy levels.

Attitudes

IMPORTANCE

Attitudes may be about yourself, other people, God, institutions, or anything else. They are a critical part of the mental aspects of addiction and recovery. We think of attitudes as habits of thinking, believing, acting, and feeling. For example, if you habitually think of yourself in a negative way, such as, "I can never do anything right," it shows an attitude you have about yourself.

Air Force experiment   In the late 1960s and early 1970s, the United States Air Force conducted an ambitious social experiment in which every Air Force member attended three days of training in race relations. After all that effort and expense, they concluded that little or no change had occurred resulting from education alone.

However, during the same period they also made a simple change in the personnel manual. They inserted a statement that anyone who shows discrimination is unfit to supervise. This meant that you could *be* prejudiced, but you could not *act* prejudiced, if you wanted to be promoted. This demand for behavior change was credited with a significant change in attitudes in the Air Force. Within a few years, it became common to see minority and majority airmen choosing to socialize with each other.

Roots of attitudes   Attitudes are usually established from your family and early childhood experiences. But recent experience changes attitudes more than we realize. If, as a child, you were taught that people from Barkeepia (a fictitious nationality) are inferior, that attitude may change dramatically if you work with several Barkeepians who are very intelligent, industrious, and kind.

NEED TO CHANGE

Long-term recovery requires that we look at negative attitudes that need changing. Some examples we have observed are:

- I have to do this myself (be in control).
- I don't deserve recovery.
- I have to be perfect.
- I shouldn't bother anyone with my problems.

Treatment, meetings, sponsors, therapists, literature, and other influences can help you change your attitudes. Remember that the behavior change precedes the attitude change.

Character defects   Your Fourth Step inventory is one way you can become aware of attitudes that need changing. The Big Book calls them character defects. Some people find it helpful to think of character defects as feelings that have become attitudes. For example, a person who has an attitude of self-pity (a self-pitying person) is different from one who occasionally feels self-pity.

Resistance, defiance   A natural part of addiction is resistance and defiance toward change. But these mental aspects of the disease must change if the promises of recovery and the spiritual awakening are to take place.

Decision (Step Six)   After writing your Fourth Step inventory and sharing it as Step Five, you can change your attitudes by a liberal use of Step Six.

New action (Step Seven)   Step Seven then suggests that you change your behavior, with the help of your Higher Power. This allows your attitudes to follow suit.

Attitudes, see also: Acceptance, Affirmations, Behavior, Beliefs, Character defects, Defenses, Dichotomous thinking, Fear, Grace, Gratitude, Honesty, Integrity & values, Openmindedness, Perfectionism, Prayer & meditation, Self-image, Step Two, Step Three, Surrender, Trust, Willingness. Next on path H: Trust.

B

Behavior

Behavior is what you actually do. In reality there is no such thing as ideal behavior, but you could call normal that range of behavior that is productive, effective, and healthy. You might look at your overall behavior and say that, besides alcohol, drugs, food, weight, or other addictive behavior, your actions are fairly normal. Or, like some addicts, you might take an honest look and see that much of your behavior is outside the normal range.

Addictive behavior is that behavior that supports the continuance and progression of the disease of addiction. You probably can see addictive behavior in every arena of your life—physical, emotional, mental, and spiritual.

The physical includes behavior like excess drinking, using, binge-ing, purging, and starving. You may *feel* physical thirst, hunger, or craving, but there is no direct connection between this feeling and the actions of drinking, using, bingeing, purging, or starving. When you *act* on these feelings, when it is clearly in your best interest not to do so, that is addictive behavior.

Emotional *behavior* may exaggerate mood swings. There is a difference between feeling fear and acting afraid. Anytime you behave as an emotional basket case, or as a depressed person, you increase the likelihood that you will feel like one. This is because your actions cause biochemical changes that affect the production of emotions. If you begin acting as if you are in crisis, your feelings will mirror that. If instead you can take a deep breath, look outside, imagine yourself in a peaceful place, or just count your breaths for a few seconds, your emotions will quiet down considerably.

Behavior that interferes with healthy, productive thinking

degrades judgment. This includes acting on poor choices, misinformation, magical thinking, diet mentality, dichotomous (black-and-white) thinking, and obsession.

Isolation, control, and panic behavior adversely affect your spirituality. Withdrawing from others so you can maintain the illusion of being in control, or avoiding help until you fall apart—these are spiritual consequences of addictive behavior.

BEHAVIOR MODIFICATION

Behavior modification is a therapy technique that rewards desired behavior and withholds rewards for, or even punishes, other behavior. Based on learning theory, it is very effective for certain types of psychological problems, including some substance abuse or eating disorders. With most addicts, however, it stimulates game playing. Because of behavior modification's manipulative nature, addicts often get right into the swing of it without lasting change. We do not usually recommend it as the treatment of choice for addiction.

Behavior, see also: Abuse, Amends, Anger, Assertiveness, Attitudes, Character defects, Control, Defenses, Feelings, Forgiveness, Grief, Incest, Integrity & values, Judgment, Moodifiers, Recovery, Resentments, Responsibility, Step Four, Step Six, Step Seven, Step Nine, Survival roles. Next on path J: Grief.

Beliefs

SOURCES

Where do beliefs come from? Looking at their sources can help in checking out their present validity, and how compatible they are with a good recovery program.

Your earliest beliefs come from your family of origin. Soon after that you begin absorbing beliefs from your society or culture, teachers, peers, and others.

Consciously or not, you are always testing your belief system. Recent experience will strengthen or call into question earlier beliefs. Your strongest beliefs are probably those you've held for a long time *and* have had recently reinforced. This is part of the reason you may like to be around people who echo your beliefs.

EFFECT ON ADDICTION

As your addiction progresses, your beliefs will usually mold to it. For example, if you believe that each person should do what they can without asking for help, your addiction will strengthen that belief, because the addiction is getting mileage out of that isolation and defiance.

Your beliefs probably will change as recovery and understanding grow. Often this change is in the direction of confirming earlier values or in challenging a distorted value system.

Beliefs, see also: Attitudes, Delusion, Habit & structure, Higher Power, Integrity & values, Magical thinking, Openmindedness, Prayer & meditation, Religiosity, Spiritual aspects, Steps of AA, Surrender, Traditions of AA. Next on path E: Integrity & values.

Binge history

PURPOSE
If you are a food addict, a binge history can help you develop an individualized food plan and clarify the idea of abstinence. Other addicts who can relate to bingeing on food may want to review this module to help assess the impact of their involvement with food.

COMMON BINGE FOODS
- Sugar, without significant fat, like jelly beans, hard candies, jello, and any other low-fat sweets.
- Sweet fats, like ice cream, doughnuts, candy bars, most pies, and any other high-fat sweets.
- Flour products without much fat, like plain breads, or plain pasta (perhaps with tomato sauce, but not cheese), plain pretzels, bagels without cream cheese.
- Flour products with fat, like pizza, bread and butter, pasta with meat or cheese, or other combinations of flour and fat.
- Salty fats, like chips and dips, nuts, cream sauces, cheese sauces, gravies, and other salty nonsweet fats.
- Concentrations of wheat, corn, yeast, chocolate, or other foods as possible sensitivities.

Most foods are combination foods, so it is difficult to sort out just what you tend to binge on. A dietitian or nutritionist can help evaluate binge history. If there are only a few specific foods or food components in most of your binges, that tells you to suspect sensitivity for those ingredients. But if your binges seem spread all over a variety of foods, your binge history may suggest quantity with little specific sensitivity.

Binge history, see also: Abstinence, Biochemistry, Craving, Diet mentality, Drugs, Excitement, Food plans, Guilt & shame, Habit & structure, Hitting bottom, Honesty, Moderation, Moodifiers, Obsession, Powerlessness, Purging, Sanity, Sex, Step One, Surrender.

Bingeing

The concept of bingeing fits almost any addiction. We will focus on alcohol and food, and you can broaden the ideas to cover other addictions as well.

What is a binge? Some people call it a binge if there is any excess in drinking or eating. But to give the word any meaning it has to be an excessive quantity, over a somewhat short period. To distinguish a binge from an occasional excess, look at the type and quantity of substance or activity, and how long it takes for that consumption.

QUANTITY

How much would signify a binge for you? Of course, if you believe you are an alcoholic, you probably think any is too much, and we would agree with that. But if you are a food addict who has not decided to stop all drinking you might wonder how much alcohol would be a binge for you.

With food, if you eat a day's worth of food in a single meal, that probably would be a binge. Or, if you eat a week's worth in a day or two, that also could be a binge. A "traditional" Thanksgiving dinner is often a binge.

A half-pint of liquor, a twelve-pack of beer, or a fifth of wine may not be a binge when shared among several nonalcoholics. But this quantity of alcohol consumed at one sitting by one person is probably a binge.

For compulsive gambling, a typical weekend at a casino is a binge. For sex addicts, the weekend might be spent in masturbation while reading pornography, or in illicit sexual activities.

DURATION

How fast (minutes, hours, or days)? For a given quantity of alcohol or food, the faster it is consumed the more likely it would be called a binge. You probably would not be as concerned if you saw someone consume three beers or two pieces of pie in an afternoon as you would if it happened in ten minutes.

TYPES OF SUBSTANCE OR ACTIVITY

Some substances draw more attention than others. In many cultures, distilled liquor seems much more dangerous than beer or wine. Foods with a high sugar content are more easily identified as binge foods. Many people think it is a binge to eat two baked potatoes at a meal, but think nothing of eating an eight-ounce portion of steak.

A binge can be recognized by observing the substance consumed and the feelings associated with that consumption. Take an honest look at how closely it resembles normal, healthy eating or responsible drinking. Is there guilt, panic, a sense of being "out of control"? Is it enough to alter mood or consciousness, either euphoria (a good feeling) or dysphoria (a bad feeling)?

VARIATIONS

With food, there are two main forms of bingeing, and combinations. These same patterns are also common with alcoholism.

Pigging out   Consumption of a large amount of food in a short period could be called "pigging out." This is common with bulimics, a kind of "feeding frenzy." In alcoholism it shows in the fraternity party atmosphere, with "chugging" and drinking contests.

Grazing   With food addiction, "grazing" is clearly excessive amounts of food forming a long, almost continuous meal. "I eat all day long." It often involves a lack of memory or awareness of the amount and kinds of food eaten. This is common with obese people.

Among alcoholics, periodic trips to the decanter for a touch more sherry, or to the refrigerator for another beer, can result in consumption of a lot of alcohol over many hours or days.

Combinations   Often there is a mixture of both patterns. Many alcoholics drink moderately, but daily, during the week, but get smashed on the weekend. It is common with "rollercoaster dieters" to graze sometimes, diet severely at others, and to pig out at other times.

ABSTINENCE

Most definitions of abstinence from any kind of addictive behavior will include, at least, abstinence from obvious bingeing.

If your conceptual understanding of bingeing is clear, it should not be difficult to differentiate bingeing from normal drinking, using, eating, or behaving.

TRIGGERS

A common belief about binges is that there are certain situations, foods, or conditions that "trigger" a binge. While there are sensitive foods that stimulate food cravings, and "slippery" situations, like cocktail parties, where it is easier to start bingeing, we caution against overuse of the idea of a trigger. If you think of a gun, a very slight pressure on the trigger unleashes a tremendous reaction. Once you pull the trigger all the damage is done and there is nothing you can do about it. By giving the idea of a "trigger" too much power, you may be feeding into the stinking thinking that signals the process of relapse. We recommend thinking about slippery places instead, making it clear that you should avoid them if you can, or be careful if you can't.

OTHER ADDICTIONS

With these ideas in mind, you can relate to a compulsive gambler's spree in Las Vegas as a binge. A sex addict may ruin a business trip through uncontrolled sexual activity. These are some examples of binges.

ASKING FOR HELP

Eventually most addicts will encounter a situation in which they have no mental defense against a binge. Then they must be willing to accept help from their Higher Power, the program of recovery, or other people—preferably all of these. It is almost impossible to binge while you are aware that you are in the presence of your Higher Power. You must always convince yourself you are in some sense alone, or have turned your back on God, before you can binge.

Bingeing, see also: Abstinence, Addiction, Alcohol, Behavior, Binge history, Biochemistry, Bulimia nervosa, Craving, Crisis, Dichotomous thinking, Exercise & activity, Fantasy, Fats, Heroin, Marijuana, Obesity, Powerlessness, Progression, Purging, Relapse prevention, Stinking thinking, Sugar, Unmanageability, Withdrawal. Next on path B: Purging.

Biochemistry

Our bodies are incredibly complex chemical factories. Medical science understands only a few of the chemical reactions that continually take place. There are dozens of neurotransmitters thought to be involved in mood, cravings, appetite, and eating.

Biochemical reactions form a system of interactions that regulate and balance body processes. When a certain chemical exceeds the normal range, the body releases another substance that may release another chemical that in turn inhibits production of the first one.

The body reacts to any imbalance with an attempt to restore that balance. These processes affect your physiology, your biochemistry, your psychology, and ultimately, your behavior.

Addiction always involves excess. Most of these excesses upset our biochemical balance. If we perceive that imbalance as increasing pleasure or reducing pain, we tend to repeat it. The body adapts, in its attempt to restore balance, and creates a tolerance. We eventually increase the excess to get the desired effect, and addiction progresses.

DEPRESSANTS

Many drugs, including alcohol, depress bodily functions and relax mood. This suppresses anxiety, pain, fear, and many other emotions that may be viewed as unpleasant. The body detects the artificial suppression of these functions, and begins to increase the arousal signals. As these "negative" sensations build, an addict will naturally tend to reach for the drug that gave relief before.

STIMULANTS

Other drugs suppress the parasympathetic nervous system. This is the part of the central nervous system that signals the body to slow down, relax, enjoy, or sleep. So the result is arousal, being "stimulated." Again, the body detects the imbalance, and increases the parasympathetic signals. The addict takes more stimulants, becomes "wired," and eventually crashes.

HALLUCINOGENS

Drugs like LSD and marijuana distort perceptions and the thinking process. Depending on whether you like the feelings that accompany these distortions, they may or may not be pleasurable. Because these drugs tend to have strange biochemical effects, it is difficult to categorize them as "upper" or "downer" drugs. But the neurochemistry of fantasy is powerful, and many fantasy addicts show a clear progression to stronger fantasy and other addictive substances or activities.

BLOOD SUGAR LEVELS

We usually perceive an increase in blood sugar level as a good feeling. If the increase is very high or very rapid, the body reacts to reduce the blood sugar level, and an addictive cycle can result. This happens to many addicts, whether or not they acknowledge food addiction. A stereotypical representation of an alcoholic in AA includes the image of them having a little coffee with their sugar.

INSULIN, TRYPTOPHAN, SEROTONIN

Rapid increase of blood sugar can produce an excess of insulin released into the blood. The insulin forces glucose and large neutral amino acids (the building blocks of protein) into body tissues, like muscle. The amino acid tryptophan is relatively unaffected by this action of insulin. The lowered competition from these other amino acids allows tryptophan to cross the blood-brain barrier into the brain, where it becomes serotonin, a neurotransmitter that can act as a natural tranquilizer.

PROTEIN, TYROSINE, NOREPINEPHRINE

An excess of protein produces imbalances too. For example, the amino acid tyrosine, one of the building blocks of protein, produces the neurotransmitter norepinephrine in the brain. An excess of norepinephrine has a stimulant effect in many neurochemical circuits.

EXERCISE & ENDORPHINS

Rigorous exercise that lasts more than about thirty minutes triggers the body's release of endorphins, which are natural analgesics (painkillers).

STARVATION

The low blood sugar production of ketone bodies and other biochemical changes that take place in starvation can produce a high that resembles amphetamine use.

FATS

Less is known about the specific role of fats in the biochemistry of food addiction. Yet the prominence of bingeing on fats, especially in combination with sugar or salt, suggests a powerful addictive mechanism.

RELAPSE

Deprivation, especially after the development of a tolerance for a biochemical imbalance, produces cravings and stimulates obsession and compulsive behavior.

Imbalance   In addiction, we train our bodies to expect excess as the norm. If these excess (euphoric) levels are not regularly met, dysphoria (bad feelings) results. Addicts' bodies have learned this expectation so well that neurochemical imbalances feel "right," and moderation feels "flat" or "depressing." These perceptions and attitudes encourage relapse.

Progression   Tolerance to addictive imbalances increases over time, requiring stronger imbalances to produce the desired euphoric effect. This means that the dysphoria and other results of withdrawal also increase over time.

RECOVERY

We have no evidence that the biochemical dynamics of addiction decrease in recovery. In fact, AA experience suggests that something involved with physiological addiction continues to *increase* even during abstinence. Perhaps it has to do with the affected organs getting older and adaptation less efficient.

Still, in good recovery the emotional, mental, and spiritual aspects of recovery counterbalance the biochemistry, decreasing the probability of relapse as time goes on.

In balance—HALT   In the light of the biochemical basis for addiction, it is important for recovering addicts to avoid strong biochemical imbalances, particularly those that affect mood. For years AA has recognized the danger of becoming too hungry, angry, lonely, or tired (HALT).

Functioning as intended   Biochemical imbalances usually wind up degrading the body's ability to perform. If, as the Big Book suggests, your task as a recovering human being is to be of maximum service to God and your fellows, then you will want to take care of your body, your emotions, your mind, and your soul.

Biochemistry, see also: Addiction, Allergies, Craving, Fats, Metabolism, Moodifiers, Neurotransmitters, Nutrition, Physical aspects, Sugar, Tolerance, Withdrawal. Next on path B: Metabolism.

Blackouts

Blackouts are chemically induced periods of amnesia. They are common in alcoholism. In a blackout a person walks, talks, goes about their business, but lacks memory of that time later. Unless something happens to make the alcoholic aware that there is a missing block of time, there will be no knowledge that the blackout occurred at all. Recall of the blacked out events never returns.

FEAR & CONFUSION

Blackouts are not passing out or losing consciousness. Many alcoholics don't even seem drunk in a blackout. This phenomenon is a source of confusion, anger, pain, and fear for both the alcoholic and others. There are reports of alcoholics taking trips, flying airplanes, and even doing surgery in a blackout. Commonly, blackouts last for a few minutes or a couple of hours, but they can last for days.

CAUSE

The exact mechanism of blackouts has not been determined. Some think the drug interferes with the natural transfer of the immediate past events from short-term to long-term memory. In the blackout, you remember events of the past several minutes, but that memory is not being transferred to long-term memory.

There is no indication that the blackout is taking place, so you never know it unless it lasts a long time or something requires you to try to remember it. You may never know you have had a blackout until someone points out a missed appointment, or describes behavior you don't remember.

SYMPTOM OF ALCOHOLISM?

Many consider blackouts to be a sure sign of alcoholism. Varying amounts of alcohol can produce them. Alcoholics may be afraid, defensive, or accusatory about events surrounding a blackout. Even when faced with the awareness that a blackout has occurred, there is so much fear that the memory of the confrontation may itself be repressed.

OTHER DRUGS

Blackouts can occur with drugs other than alcohol. Compulsive eaters report blackoutlike states after a heavy binge, especially on high-sugar, high-fat foods.

EUPHORIC RECALL

Euphoric recall is a distortion of memory that occurs in alcoholism and other addictions. You remember things, but not accurately. Alcohol, other drugs, and possibly even internal neurotransmitter imbalances cause you to feel uninhibited. When the emotions are so affected, you can get the giggles or have crying spells. You may remember feeling good without remembering the embarrassment or other negative effects of the situation. Euphoric recall contributes to the delusional system of addiction.

REPRESSION

Repression is psychologically induced forgetting of unpleasant events or memories. The memory of the pain and shame of addictive behavior can be so great that the conscious mind pushes it out of awareness. It is often a healthy defense to make life bearable, but in addiction it can easily perpetuate the disease. These memories can be triggered by certain stimuli.

ABUSE & INCEST

Children who are victims of abuse or incest may use repression to survive. The repressed fear and anger, lack of trust, and denial of feelings can interfere with their spontaneity and inhibit relationships. Self-searching, experiential therapy, or other stimuli or images may elicit these memories. When memories start to return, you need a safe, supportive environment to work through these memories and feelings.

Blackouts, see also: Addiction, Alcohol, Alcoholism, Bingeing, Biochemistry, Drugs, Flashbacks, Neurotransmitters, Panic attacks, Physical aspects, Progression, Sugar, Tolerance, Unmanageability. Next on path B: Fetal alcohol syndrome.

Body image

Most women and many men in America today would change something about their bodies if they could. Even if you are realistic about how you look, you may be dissatisfied. Issues related to body image are important to many people, but in food addiction body image becomes an integral part of the disease.

Your body image depends on many factors, including physical limitations, how you think and feel about your body, and society's standards. There are also subjective and objective dimensions related to your health, height, fitness, weight, and attractiveness.

WOMEN

Women are particularly affected by gender-specific ideas. Most people think it is more important for a woman to have a "perfect" body than a man. Being a little overweight causes most women to feel undesirable and inadequate. They attempt to diet, conform their bodies to certain expectations, and use all kinds of gimmicks and techniques to transform themselves.

Problems arise when women become obsessed with changing their bodies. Body image disturbances and self-image problems result. These factors contribute to the development of eating disorders and other problems relating to severe body image distortion.

DISTORTIONS

One of the most common body image distortions is feeling fat. Normal weight people can feel fat. This feeling can affect one's sense of self-worth as much as actually being fat. Emaciated anorexics and many overweight or obese people who reach a normal weight report feeling fat.

DENIAL

A survival mechanism related to body image disturbance is denial. As people gain weight they can cut themselves off from bodily feelings and sensations. Many morbidly obese people are out of touch with their actual weight and size. Delusion feeds their addiction. A 550-pound man in a hospital said he saw no problem with his weight except that he was having trouble with his mobility.

SELF-CENTEREDNESS

Body image can become such an obsession that food addicts can spend most of their free time focusing on weight, how they look, whether or not their stomach sticks out, or that their thighs look big. They often hate parts of their bodies or their bodies in general. They can become extremely self-centered. This obsession interferes with their relationships with themselves, others, and a Higher Power.

FAMILY OF ORIGIN

Body image problems often have roots in the family of origin. If you were abused, discounted, or taught you have to look good to get approval, you were set up to have body image problems. Understanding and dealing with those issues will help your recovery.

IMPROVING BODY IMAGE

We suggest that addicts who have body image problems try activities that will improve realistic acceptance of bodily characteristics:

One simple technique is to listen for feedback relating to body image and check out what you hear, either with the person giving the feedback or others you trust.

Group activities that involve writing a letter to your body and writing a letter from your body to you increase awareness and acceptance. Many addiction counselors and most eating disorders counselors can describe techniques for doing this.

Another simple technique for improving body image is to act as if you are attractive. Pretend you are on a stage and people are admiring your body. Walk as if you believe you look great! You may feel much better about yourself.

RECOVERY

Awareness of a distorted body image is an important part of recovery for many addicts. In particular, food addicts with anorexic or bulimic tendencies must learn to tolerate some distortion in body image. You can learn that how you think and feel about your body is inaccurate. It is also helpful to give up the fantasy that one day you can look perfect.

Love & humility   You can nurture a perception of yourself and your body that is loving, tolerant, and realistic. This means being grateful for your assets and accepting your shortcomings. Attitudes free of judgment, envy, or jealousy will open you to healthier relationships. You will feel better about yourself and others.

Recovery from body image problems can be a slow and difficult process. You may have to deal with abuse or incest issues. Whether obsessed with trying to be perfect, cut off from your body, or ignoring it because it seems hopeless, you can learn to love the body you have.

You are body as well as heart, mind, and soul. You can use your Program to give up your obsession, become more self-accepting, less self-centered, and get on with the business of your life. The Twelve Steps of the Program are excellent tools for your journey.

Body image, see also: Abuse, Acceptance, Anorexia nervosa, Attitudes, Bulimia nervosa, Cocaine, Delusion, Dichotomous thinking, Diet mentality, Emotional aspects, Exercise & activity, Family of origin, Feelings, Humility, Obesity, Obsession, Openmindedness, Pregnancy, Priorities, Relaxation, Sabotage of recovery, Sanity, Self-centeredness, Self-image, Service & giving, Spirituality, Sponsorship, Surrender, Trust, Visualizations, Weight, Willingness. Next on path C: Stress & strain.

Bulimia nervosa

The term *bulimia nervosa* is an official diagnostic category in DSM III-R (*Diagnostic and Statistical Manual* of the American Psychiatric Association). Popularly, the word bulimic refers to anyone who binges and purges.

BULIMIC PATTERN

According to psychologist John Lovern's "Unified Eating Disorders Theory (1988)," bulimia is only one of the cyclical eating disorders. The pattern and frequency of cycles from undereating to overeating are most dramatic with bulimia, and most peaks of overeating end with a purge. Typically, most of the eating is excessive, and the typical bulimic would gain weight very rapidly if not for the vomiting or other purging behavior. Bulimics might also have periods of moderate or even undereating, which do not usually involve purging.

BINGEING

The root of the word bulimia means "ox appetite," implying that we are talking about a real "pigging out" kind of binge. Gorging on food is important to this description. It does not include those who nibble (or "graze") throughout the day.

PURGING

Purging is any artificial activity to get rid of binged food or avoid the resulting fat.

The most publicized form of purging behavior is vomiting, though exercise and fasting are probably more common. Bulimics may vomit up to ten or more times a day and spend as much as $50 to $100 a day on junk food.

Another form of purging is using or overusing laxatives in an attempt to get rid of what has been consumed in a binge or to lose weight or "inches." Laxative addicts may use as many as ninety laxatives a day and disrupt their elimination system so that they become dependent on large doses of laxatives.

Some bulimics take diuretics in an attempt to get rid of fat. Weight loss from diuretic use is loss of water, not fat, yet it gives the illusion of quick weight loss.

Excessive exercise to compensate for binges is another form of purging. This may be a supplemental kind of purging or it may be the main way of avoiding weight gain.

Prolonged fasting or near fasting (more than about a day) for rapid weight loss is also a kind of purging.

DIAGNOSIS

The *Diagnostic and Statistical Manual* of the American Psychiatric Association is often used as a set of diagnostic criteria. The 1987 revision attempted to narrow the psychiatric diagnosis of bulimia nervosa. Briefly, to be diagnosed with bulimia nervosa, you must have:

- Recurrent episodes of binge eating (rapid consumption of a large amount of food in a discrete period).
- A feeling of lack of control over eating behavior during the eating binges.
- Regular self-induced vomiting, use of laxatives or diuretics, strict dieting or fasting, or vigorous exercise to prevent weight gain.
- A minimum average of two binge eating episodes a week for at least three months.
- Persistent overconcern with body shape and weight.

THE "NERVOSA" PART

As in anorexia nervosa, the *nervosa* part of the name *bulimia nervosa* has to do with the obsession with body image, weight, fear of fat, and a feeling of loss of control.

VARIATIONS

There are many patterns of bulimic behavior that involve differences in bingeing and purging styles. Most bulimics are at or near normal weight, at least in the earlier stages of the disease. Many later stage bulimics panic when, as often happens, the bulimia "stops working" and they start gaining weight despite continuing to purge.

TREATMENT

Most bulimics respond well to an addiction model for treatment. They may also have substance abuse problems or be in recovery from chemical dependency. Family members may be substance abusers, obese, or have other addiction or codependency problems. Unless there are unusual medical or psychiatric problems, most bulimics do not need inpatient hospitalization.

Special needs   All bulimics need to have special solutions for their special needs, especially those related to cognitive distortions (black-and-white thinking), body image and self-esteem improvement, and learning how to eat in a normal, healthy way.

Food planning   It is important for bulimics to learn to eat enough when not purging—most are used to starving when they don't purge. Many bulimics have not eaten a moderate meal in years, and they need some simple instruction on what constitutes a moderate food plan. They also usually have emotional issues surrounding the meal. Reducing the fear of food is important to recovery.

Social hour   Usually, the hour following meals is the most critical for the bulimic who wants to stop purging. Most bulimics like the feeling of emptiness (and a flat stomach), and learning to tolerate feeling full is essential.

It may help to insure that some supportive person is with the bulimic during the hour following each meal, especially in the first weeks of recovery. The social hour will be effective if they see it as support, not as enforcement.

Dental care   If frequent vomiting has continued for more than a year or two, there is a good chance of damage to the enamel of the teeth. This coating is meant to withstand the weak acid of saliva, not the strong acids of the stomach. Damage is permanent and may require reconstructive dental work. Most other consequences of bulimic behavior will repair themselves in time.

Body image   Most bulimics are obsessed with their bodies and have distorted body images. Feeling fat is usual, even when it is totally unrealistic. Body image improvement is often slow but effective with adequate intervention techniques (see Body image).

Recovery   Recovery involves the restoration of normal eating patterns, elimination of purging, reduction of black-and-white thinking, being honest with feelings, and moving from self-centered obsessions to being able to reach out to others.

Bulimia nervosa, see also: Adolescents, Anorexia nervosa, Binge history, Bingeing, Body image, Constipation, Craving, Diet mentality, Drugs, Exercise & activity, Family, Fats, Food addiction, Food plans, Hunger & appetite, Moodifiers, Nutrition, Purging, Recovery, Therapy & treatment, Unmanageability, Weight. Next on path A: Obesity.

C

Celebrations

Celebrations are a special kind of social event with the expectation that you will have fun or experience joy. They are often very difficult for recovering addicts, especially in early recovery.

EARLY RECOVERY

Sometimes celebrations are hard because the expectations of joy and community are not realistic in early recovery. This adds frustration and fear to an event or gathering that already may contain unfamiliar or stressful circumstances. This is especially true for alcoholics and food addicts. Typically, celebrations include the expectation that people will drink alcohol or eat festive (that is, sweet, salty, fatty) foods in large quantities. This tradition is firmly ingrained in most cultures.

If you are in early recovery, you may want to discuss the following strategies with a sponsor or other Twelve-Step program member before the celebration begins:

- Electing not to go or participate, at least at this time in your recovery.
- Inviting a friend in recovery to go with you, if this is appropriate.
- Making a phone call while you are there, to touch base with some sanity.
- Having an "escape hatch," like your own transportation, so you can leave if you get too uncomfortable.
- Taking your Higher Power with you.
- Asking for ideas in a meeting before you go.

For food addicts, there are special problems. Besides the above, you might want to consider these possibilities:

- Calling ahead to ask about the event. This might include asking what foods will be served. Good friends or family may be willing to accommodate your special needs, if any.
- Eating before or after the celebration, or even leaving, eating at a relatively safe place, and returning.

LATER RECOVERY

With recovery you can learn not to dread celebrations, to enjoy the family, the people, and the original cause for celebration without drinking, using, bingeing, purging, starving, or overeating.

THE AFTERMATH

Be careful afterward. Many people are on guard through the celebration, but have trouble later. They may fall prey to the depression or self-pity that sometimes follows, when remembering how much fun others had drinking or eating. Or, they may relax and "reward themselves." Have appropriate recovery tools available. An excellent strategy is to go to a meeting following the celebration or event.

SPECIFIC EVENTS

Look at birthdays, weddings, Thanksgiving, Christmas, religious holidays, etc. At Thanksgiving even regular people binge, on food if not on alcohol also. Your Twelve-Step group might want to consider an Alcathon, O-Athon, or similar event, where a place, meetings, and/or a phone is available during the day on Christmas, Thanksgiving, or other times.

Celebrations, see also: Abstinence, Aftercare, Crisis, Delusion, Diet mentality, Family, Feelings, Food addiction, Food plans, Gratitude, Habit & structure, Higher Power, Moderation, Prayer & meditation, Priorities, Progression, Relapse prevention, Relaxation, Sabotage of recovery, Sponsorship, Stinking thinking. Next on path O: Relaxation.

Certification

Certification is a process by which addiction professionals are evaluated for their knowledge, experience, and skills in a certain area of addiction. Being certified does not guarantee that a particular counselor is competent. Nor can you be sure that a counselor who is not certified is less qualified than a certified counselor. But it would be wise to ask whether your counselor is certified in the addiction for which you are being treated, and if not, why not.

Academic degrees are also important. These days, a good addiction counselor should have a master's degree in a counseling field, or its equivalent. Counselors without a master's degree in psychology, social work, or other counseling discipline should be willing to tell you how they obtained the knowledge and skills in psychology and human behavior needed to be a good counselor.

There are very few universities that offer degrees in alcoholism, drug abuse, eating disorders, codependency, compulsive gambling, or even in addiction counseling. So the certification supplements academic degrees by telling you, the consumer, that these individuals have specialized in the area for which they are certified, and have met certain experience, knowledge, and skill measurements that suggest that they are qualified to treat the addiction for which they are certified.

STATE LEVEL

Almost every state has at least one organization that certifies alcoholism counselors, drug counselors, or a combined alcohol and drug certification. The name of this dual certification varies widely. Examples are certified alcohol and drug counselor, certified chemical dependency counselor, certified substance abuse counselor, certified counselor/alcohol and other drug abuse, and certified addictions professional. Most state certifying bodies belong to and meet the reciprocity standards of the National Certification Reciprocity Consortium/Alcohol and Other Drug Abuse, Inc. (NCRC/AODA).

NATIONAL LEVEL

The road to a national standard for alcohol and drug counselor certification has been long and arduous. Several professional organizations have worked both with and against each other, and their disagreements are not likely to be fully resolved anytime soon.

NCRC The National Certification Reciprocity Consortium/ Alcohol and Other Drug Abuse, Inc. (NCRC/AODA) developed to help certified counselors who move from one state to another. In the process they created a de facto standard for certification including education, experience, and skill requirements. They developed a Case Presentation Method to measure addiction counseling skills. They also began offering a national level certification to supplement the state level certification.

NAADAC The National Association of Alcohol and Drug Abuse Counselors, Inc. (NAADAC) represents member counselors in most states. They have also developed a similar national level certification.

EAPS

Employee assistance professionals can now be certified by the Employee Assistance Certification Commission of the Employee Assistance Professionals' Association (EAPA).

GAMBLING

Therapists who work with compulsive gambling may be eligible for certification also. For information contact the executive director of the National Council on Problem Gambling.

EATING DISORDERS

The only professional certification directly related to eating disorders are the titles Certified Eating Disorders Counselor and Certified Eating Disorders Therapist. These are granted by the International Association of Eating Disorders Professionals (IAEDP).

OTHERS

Certification is also available for physicians and nurses who specialize in the treatment of addictions. Contact the appropriate professional organization for information.

ADDRESSES

For the addresses of these associations that offer certification, see the module Professional organizations.

Certification, see also: Alcoholism, Core functions, Counseling, Drugs, Dual diagnosis, Employee assistance programs, Impaired professionals, Intervention, Professional organizations, Therapy & treatment.

Character defects

Recovery from addiction using a Twelve-Step model suggests that real freedom requires dealing with character defects that interfere with your relationship with God, your fellow human beings, and yourself.

MORAL INVENTORY

The early members of AA began this process with a moral inventory and confession, adopted from the Oxford Group principles from which AA developed. Today it is done by using Steps Four, Five, Six, and Seven. The purpose is to identify and help eliminate those aspects of character that interfere with one's spiritual growth.

SHORTCOMINGS

The Big Book mentions resentment and fear as character defects that seemed particularly troublesome. By the time *Twelve Steps and Twelve Traditions* was written, AA had the benefit of several more years of experience in identifying problem areas. Bill Wilson began his discussion of character defects with the idea that instinctive drives for security, food, and sex were normal and healthy. Problems occurred when such drives were distorted and exaggerated. He believed that this distortion was often the basis of the drive to drink. So defects had to be faced fearlessly.

RELIEF FROM SHAME

The suggestion that addicts inventory their character defects was never meant to contribute to a person's shame or worthlessness. Quite the contrary. The love, tolerance, and compassion of those who have done so before is witness to the value of the suggested step. In writings on this Step in any fellowship modeling AA you will find an underlying tone of gentleness and encouragement.

SPECIFIC DEFECTS

AA began by talking about the Seven Deadly Sins: pride, greed, lust, anger, gluttony, envy, and sloth. These characteristics, when exaggerated, can easily interfere with your freedom and peace of mind. Others Bill wrote about later were rebellion, self-righteousness, laziness, irresponsibility, foolish rationalizations, outright dishonesty, wrong dependencies, and destructive power-driving.

ATTITUDES

There are also natural feelings that when developed into attitudes can become troublesome. Anger is a natural, normal feeling, but when it becomes an attitude all you see is an angry person. The same can be said of feelings like self-pity, impatience, intolerance, inferiority, guilt, fear, or depression.

It is common for addicts to realize that their disease has resulted in many characteristics that are not useful in recovery. Self-centeredness, dishonesty, and fear can often be seen to underlie many of these problems. An honest self-searching can help you begin to identify those things that will block you from the sunlight of the spirit.

SURVIVAL SKILLS

It is important to mention here that some of your attitudes probably developed as survival mechanisms—for example anger used to protect yourself if your home was not a safe place.

From the start, people in AA were aware that something had motivated them to have a distorted sense of values and worth. You may need to look at the dysfunction in your family of origin to find where some of your values and behaviors came from.

SELF-UNDERSTANDING

The key is to examine your past fearlessly, not for blame but for understanding. See how certain attitudes helped you survive. Give yourself credit for the strengths you have. Be willing to let go of those things you no longer need that will interfere with your ability to have freedom, joy, and meaning in your life.

TURN NEGATIVES INTO POSITIVES

Character defects can be transformed into positive characteristics. Guilt can help you develop a keen sense of honesty and integrity. Fear can be replaced by a healthy caution, courage, and faith. Shyness can be changed into courteous assertiveness. In giving up a resentment you can gain strength and humility, and experience forgiveness.

It is easier to look at the positive benefits of working through your character defects than to focus on how inadequate you are. Also, your imperfections make you human. Changing them shows your courage. After you have worked on your own character defects you can better share with and help others. The use of the Steps, the fellowship, and a Higher Power is the best way we know to do this.

Character defects, see also: Acceptance, Amends, Anger, Assertiveness, Attitudes, Behavior, Body image, Defenses, Fear, Feelings, Forgiveness, Guilt & shame, Inventory, Money, Perfectionism, Resentments, Responsibility, Self-centeredness, Slogans, Spending, Step Four, Step Six, Survival roles. Next on path J: Self-centeredness.

Checklist mentality

"So what do I have to do to recover?" Addiction counselors get a version of that question almost daily. Like many questions, it contains some assumptions, and possibly a hidden agenda or two.

ASSUMPTIONS

The first assumption is that this addict can recover. The second is more subtle. Notice it says, what do *I* have to do? Most seasoned addiction counselors have learned that this means the addict expects the counselor to wave a magic wand, or provide a foolproof recipe, that will allow addicts to gain the power to bring about their own recovery.

DEFIANCE

The counselor will also notice an undercurrent of defiance here. Obviously, if the addict does what the counselor recommends, and does not recover, it will be the counselor's fault, won't it? If the question were asked cleanly, it would be something like, "What is the least I can do (by myself) to guarantee recovery?"

WORKSHEETS

The addict somehow expects to be handed a checklist, a set of instructions, or a prescription that, when followed, will give the addict control over the addictive substance or behavior. In many treatment programs and self-help groups, addicts are given just that, a fill-in-the-blanks worksheet or a list of tasks that must be completed before recovery can take place.

ASSIGNMENTS

Many treatment centers have their patients complete an assignment that relates to the First Step. They may write out a chronology of the progression of their addiction including the consequences that show powerlessness and unmanageability. That may be a very valuable tool to help them learn to use Step One as a tool. Yet we have seen many of them report proudly, "I did my First Step yesterday." This statement implies that they believe they have checked off a box on the ticket to recovery.

FOOD PLANS

Long histories of diets and diet programs have conditioned food addicts to expect to be handed a diet or a food plan. Many will panic and feel "out of control" if they are not told exactly what they can and cannot eat, and when, and how much. The food plan then becomes a checklist that they can either follow (and be in control and in recovery) or "screw up" and feel guilty (and eat more).

DENYING STEPS ONE TO THREE
The problem with the checklist mentality is that it denies the powerlessness and unmanageability of the First Step, the Higher Power and sanity of Step Two, and the surrender of Step Three. Compare the concept of a set of specific directions with the "three pertinent ideas" from the Big Book (p. 60):

THE ABCS
(a) That we were alcoholic and could not manage our own lives.
(b) That probably no human power could have relieved our alcoholism.
(c) That God could and would if He were sought.

EASY DOES IT
If this module eludes you, please don't get discouraged. We are talking about the very heart of the program—ideas that many addicts do not fully comprehend until they have had many months or years of recovery, one day at a time. We are asking you to let go, a little at a time, and follow the guidance of your Higher Power. We are also suggesting that recovery may not come in a simple instruction booklet, or a set of rules.

Checklist mentality, see also: Defenses, Dichotomous thinking, Diet mentality, Disease concept, Judgment, Magical thinking, Mental aspects, Obsession, Priorities, Stinking thinking, Visualiations.

Children of addicts

Even in the early days of AA, there was an acknowledgment of the family disease. The Big Book (p. 122) says, "Cessation of drinking is but the first step away from a highly strained, abnormal condition. A doctor said to us, 'Years of living with an alcoholic is almost sure to make any wife or child neurotic.'" There is even a hint that the family can profit by following the same spiritual program that helps the alcoholic.

AL-ANON

Al-Anon was formed, in 1951, to give family members their own Twelve-Step recovery program. Members of Al-Anon started special meetings for children of alcoholics in 1957. These became known as Alateen. The focus was for teenagers to survive whether the parent was still drinking or not, by using the fellowship and (to some extent) the Steps of Alateen.

Few people considered the needs of adult children of alcoholics until the problem was popularized by family therapists, including Sharon Wegscheider-Cruse, Janet Woititz, and Claudia Black. Chemical dependency programs began treating spouses, children, and adult children of alcoholics along with their addicted patients.

ACA

Special groups began for adult children of alcoholics in 1977 and 1978, some affiliated with Al-Anon and others not. Many of these groups adopted a list of characteristics of adult children, called "The Problem," or "The Laundry List." By 1983 Al-Anon ACOA and independent ACA groups were organized, and the National Association for Children of Alcoholics (NACOA) had been formed.

PROBLEMS

What are the problems of children of addicts (COAs)? Even if they are not victims of abuse or incest, they grow up missing some of the basic tools for interacting with people and the world. The degree of handicap depends on the severity of addiction in the home.

In more extreme cases, COAs grow up with very little structure or consistency in the family. They might be praised and punished for the same behavior on the same day. They get double messages, like "I love you, but go away." They learn to survive by talking back, by acting out, by being overresponsible, by entertaining everyone, by keeping quiet, or by running away or hiding. They are ashamed, afraid, or disgusted at their addicted parent(s), and possibly by their own behavior as well. They may have little basis for understanding what people mean by words like "boundaries," "love," or "joy."

Self-help groups and professional counselors try to help children of addicts learn to express their feelings, validate their experience by sharing with others, learn boundaries and other social skills, get in touch with their natural spontaneity and love (or "inner child"), have fun, be more assertive, and of course, deal with their addictive substances and behaviors.

AFFILIATION

Today it is hard to separate groups and issues relating to children of addicts, and what is being called codependency. Most COA groups are affiliated either with Al-Anon, which has about fifteen hundred ACOA groups among its twenty-seven thousand or more groups, or with ACA (headquartered in California), which has about fourteen hundred groups. ACA seems a little more flexible, allowing any COA literature, while Al-Anon ACOA usually has more stability in membership and tradition. Another group is Co-Dependents Anonymous (CoDA). See the module on Codependency for that information. Look for phone numbers in the white pages of your phone book, or write or call:

> Al-Anon Family Groups
> PO Box 862, Midtown Station
> New York, NY 10018-0862
> 1-800-356-9996
>
> Adult Children of Alcoholics
> PO Box 3216
> Torrance, CA 90510
> (213) 534-1815

Children of addicts, see also: Abuse, Adolescents, Al-Anon & Alateen, Behavior, Codependency, Detachment, Emotional aspects, Enabling, Family of origin, Fetal alcohol syndrome, Forgiveness, Humor & fun, Incest, Intimacy, Prevention of addiction, Relationships, Resentments, Self-image, Survival roles.

Chronic pain

Chronic pain is pain that has continued for more than six months, despite medical attention. It might have an organic cause, such as injury, chronic illness, or arthritis, or there may be no identified cause. It always involves complex physical and psychological components. The psychological factors are more significant if there is no identified cause because the patient is likely to be accused of being a malingerer or a hypochondriac.

TREATMENT

Treatment of chronic pain must consider the interplay of physical and psychological components. The traditional approach to chronic pain is to supply analgesic (painkiller) drugs. These medications work reasonably well for acute or temporary pain, because by the time you develop a tolerance for the drug, the pain may be gone. For chronic pain, however, there is an inherent trap. The relief given by the narcotic diminishes as tolerance builds, and withdrawal of the drug intensifies the perception of the pain beyond what it would have been if the drug were never given. Nonnarcotic analgesics like aspirin provide relief only up to a certain point, and are not very helpful with chronic pain.

People with chronic pain often have below-normal levels of natural analgesic neurotransmitters, like endorphins and enkephalins. Many approaches to chronic pain appear to increase the efficiency of the body's own pain relief system, usually by making available more of the opioid neurotransmitters, or enhancing their use. The following are some strategies that have shown promise in dealing with chronic pain:

Relaxation   Deep relaxation techniques, hypnosis, biofeedback, and meditation can relax muscles and ease anxiety, thereby reducing chronic pain.

TENS   Transcutaneous electrical nerve stimulation (TENS) is a technique using a portable device that produces weak electrical currents near the area of discomfort. The patient feels a mild tingling sensation that blocks the body's pain signals, providing immediate relief.

Acupuncture   The ancient Chinese technique of acupuncture places fine needles into carefully selected points on the body. Studies show pain-relief benefits for 26 to 79 percent of back pain patients. The mechanism for its success is not well understood, and is controversial, but probably affects the opioid neurotransmitter balance, either directly or through placebo effects.

Exercise   Physical activity helps many chronic pain patients. Swimming is especially helpful. Walking and riding a stationary bicycle are commonly used. The exercise can improve overall conditioning, relieve stress, and increase the sense of well-being. If rigorous, it can also release endorphins and enkephalins.

Pain clinics   There are now hundreds of pain clinics across the United States. The best are staffed with multidisciplinary teams that include neurologists, physical therapists, social workers, nurses, psychologists, and others. Their treatment programs include psychological and physical rehabilitative techniques.

Information   The National Chronic Pain Outreach Association (NCPOA) is a nonprofit information clearinghouse for chronic pain and its management. They publish a newsletter and maintain a referral list for treatment and support groups. They offer a catalog with helpful books, audio tapes, and videotapes. Write them at:

> National Chronic Pain Outreach
> 7979 Old Georgetown Rd., Suite 100
> Bethesda, MD 20814
> (301) 652-4948

Addiction   People who become addicted to pain medications need special attention. Regular drug addiction programs seldom deal with chronic pain. Some pain clinics may not be equipped to deal with addiction. Both issues need to be addressed. Even after detox, these patients need to learn to deal with their pain. To deal with the addiction and emotional aspects, try Narcotics Anonymous, Emotions Anonymous, or other Twelve-Step groups. If pain medication is a strong addiction, you may want to contact:

> Pill Addicts Anonymous
> PO Box 278
> Reading, PA 19603
> (215) 372-1128

Chronic pain, see also: Addiction, Alcohol, Biochemistry, Constipation, Drugs, Exercise & activity, Family, Moodifiers, Narcotics Anonymous, Nutrition, Obesity, Prevention of addiction, Stress & strain, Unmanageability. Next on path A: Adolescents.

Cocaine

Coca is a shrub native to the hot, humid valleys east of the Andes mountains. The Indians of South America chew coca leaves as a stimulant, a medicine, and a source of vitamins and minerals, as did the ancient Aztecs.

Various tonics and wines containing coca preparations became popular in Europe and America in the late nineteenth century. Coca-Cola was one of those concoctions. Scientists isolated cocaine from the coca leaves, and doctors began to use it as the first local anesthetic. Its popularity led to its use for all sorts of medical problems, including alcohol and opiate addiction. Soon there were cocaine addicts as well.

In the early 1900s laws made coca leaves and cocaine controlled substances, and Coca-Cola took it out of their soft drink (supposedly, a drug-free extract remained, as flavoring).

ILLEGAL COCAINE

Illegal cocaine is available as cocaine hydrochloride, a white powder. Cut with local anesthetics and all sorts of substances, it is sold in quantities of one gram ($1/28$ ounce), a half gram, or a quarter gram.

Freebase is a purified form of cocaine created by applying ether or other solvents to cocaine powder and then heating it—a particularly dangerous enterprise. Crack cocaine is freebase that comes in chunks or "rocks" that are ready to smoke and easier to carry and use. At $5-10 per rock, crack has unfortunately made cocaine available to the inner city, school kids, and people in all social classes.

Cocaine and its derivatives are the most reinforcing chemicals known. A laboratory rat will press a bar to get a cocaine reward until completely exhausted or convulsing. It will ignore both food and sex while the cocaine is available.

Snorted cocaine peaks in the brain within fifteen minutes. Injected, this shortens to five minutes, while the refined forms of freebase or crack smoked in a water pipe peak in fifteen *seconds*. At low doses sexual desire and perception of performance in all areas of life usually increase. At high doses or after ongoing use, the user may be subjected to all sorts of adverse consequences, from tremors and racing heartbeat, to weight loss and sexual dysfunction, to stroke and respiratory arrest.

HOW IT WORKS

Ordinarily, the excitatory neurotransmitter dopamine (DA) is dumped from vesicles on the presynaptic nerve into the synapse, a tiny gap between nerves. Some of it crosses the synapse to find receptor sites on the postsynaptic nerve, which is fired, passing a message on to the complex neural network. The DA is then pumped back into the presynaptic vesicles in a process called reuptake.

Cocaine works primarily by preventing this reuptake of dopamine (DA) and other neurotransmitters, like norepinephrine (NA) and serotonin (5-HT). These excess chemicals in the synapse produce the pleasure and elation of cocaine intoxication, and physiological symptoms like elevated blood pressure, pulse, and body temperature.

Coke blues   However, these neurotransmitters are not being sucked back into the synaptic vesicles, so they are broken down by enzymes in the synapse, usually within an hour. This means that following a coke run, the DA and some other neurotransmitters are reduced or exhausted, causing the "coke blues." This prompts the addict to find more cocaine or "crack."

Because of the shortness of the cocaine high, coke addicts are likely to turn to other drugs to round out their experience, so they are often polyaddicted. And since cocaine has no trouble crossing the placenta, many premature babies are being born as cocaine addicts, with low birth weight, and in full withdrawal.

Sex addiction   Estimates of sex addiction and sexual dysfunction among cocaine addicts range as high as 70 percent. This is another reason for care in cocaine treatment. See the module on Sex for information about sex and sex addiction.

Self-help   Cocaine addiction presents special problems because of the intense craving and the typical lifestyle of the coke addict. Many addicts have found difficulty relating to Narcotics Anonymous, and AA may help them with their alcoholism but not address their cocaine use. Help for problems with cocaine can be found by contacting:

> Cocaine Anonymous
> 6125 Washington Blvd., Suite 202
> Los Angeles, CA 90230
> (213) 559-5833

Cocaine, see also: Drugs, Exercise & activity, Fantasy, Impaired professionals, Inhalants, Moodifiers, Narcotics Anonymous, Other support groups, Pregnancy, Therapy & treatment, Tolerance.

Codependency

If you are involved in any kind of addiction recovery, you will hear a lot about codependency. *Codependency* is a word used to describe an extremely broad range of behaviors. People who have difficulty with their relationship with themselves (self-esteem) or with other people are likely to be called codependent.

HISTORY

The word began to be used in the 1970s when professionals who saw alcoholism as a family disease began treating family members also, observing the effects of alcoholism on them. Alcoholics and drug addicts were grouped under the name chemical dependency, and family members affected were called codependents. Other terms, such as coalcoholics or paraalcoholics have also been used, but codependency is the term that won out.

HELPING RECOVERY

There is little doubt that many people in our society who are self-searching and looking for ways to grow can find some help in the ideas of the codependency movement. There are many valuable books that can help with such things as self-worth, assertiveness, spontaneity, relationships, intimacy, and feelings. Almost any addict can identify with characteristics of codependency.

ADVANTAGE

Though it may be a misnomer, the word *codependency* has made it easier for people reluctant to seek help for emotional problems. Some people who would have been labeled with a psychiatric diagnosis may now feel comfortable relating to codependency instead.

SYMPTOMS

Pia Mellody (1989) says that codependents have difficulty:

- Experiencing appropriate levels of self-esteem
- Setting functional boundaries
- Owning and expressing their reality
- Taking care of their adult needs and wants
- Experiencing and expressing their reality *moderately*

To see how these develop in a dysfunctional family, look at each of the natural characteristics of a child:

All children are valuable, but when they are abused they survive by acting worse than or better than others. These survival roles in adulthood create difficulty experiencing appropriate levels of self-esteem. To recover means to build self-esteem.

Vulnerable   All children are vulnerable, but surviving abuse usually entails acting either too vulnerable or too good/perfect. Adults then have difficulty setting functional boundaries. Recovery teaches them to be vulnerable, but with protection (functional boundaries).

Imperfect   Children, like other life forms, are imperfect. In dysfunctional families, some play a "bad" or "rebellious" role, while others get trapped in perfectionism. As adults most have difficulty owning and expressing their own reality and imperfections. In recovery, however, they can become accountable for imperfections and can look to a Higher Power for help with these imperfections.

Dependent   Children are dependent, needing, and wanting. If abused they tend to become either too dependent, or antidependent (needless, wantless). These children grow up having difficulty taking care of their adult needs and wants. Recovery allows them to become interdependent and to get their needs and wants met appropriately.

Immature   All children are immature. In response to abuse they usually act extremely immature (chaotic) or overmature (controlling). As adults it is hard for them to experience or express their reality in any moderate fashion. Recovery allows them to gain maturity at their own age level.

FULL CIRCLE

Sharon Wegscheider-Cruse (1989), a pioneer in codependency, defines codependency as: "a toxic relationship to a substance, a person or a behavior that leads to self delusion, emotional repression and compulsive behavior that results in increased shame, low self-worth, relationship problems and medical complications." This definition is compatible with our description of addiction itself. A broader and more inclusive treatment of addiction will cover much of what is now addressed as codependency.

RULING-OUT PRIORITY

We encounter many addicts who identify themselves as struggling with codependency issues and often wonder where they need to put the emphasis in their recovery. We suggest a ruling-out priority system when deciding about treatment, counseling, and recovery.

Primary addiction   First, is there a primary (basic) addiction still rampant? Alcohol, other drugs, food, tobacco, strong excitement, or other primary addictions should be treated as *addiction*, not as a problem resulting from growing up in an addictive family. In fact, some practicing addicts "hide out" in other Twelve-Step groups, like Al-Anon or ACOA, or even codependency treatment.

Addiction conspiracy disorder   If there is no primary addiction that requires attention, you may have what we call an addiction conspiracy disorder. This is the classic Al-Anon type disorder, which is probably the most accurate target for programs for co-dependency. This is a person so enmeshed in others' addictions that they qualify as a coconspirator. If they get rid of the addict (or addicts) in their lives, they will quickly find another.

An interesting description of the dynamics of this disorder can be found in the "Rescue triangle" in which the persecutor, rescuer (enabler), and victim roles are interchangeable, as the system rolls on.

Addiction stress disorder   If not a conspiracy disorder, the stress of living with one or more addicts can result in psychosomatic illness and intense stress and strain. There are people who come from healthy homes who may find themselves married to an addict. This will result in frustration, stress, and other problems. If the person has self-esteem, knows it is not their fault, they may get out of the situation and not choose to get involved with an addict next time. Because they are not a part of the addiction mechanism, they will probably look for a person who shows no signs of active addiction.

Adult Children of Addiction   The following characteristics, from author Janet Woititz, indicate growing up in a strongly addicted family:

- Guessing at normality
- Lacking follow-through
- Lying when truth would be as easy
- Judging oneself without mercy
- Having difficulty having fun
- Taking oneself too seriously
- Difficulty with intimate relationships
- Overreacting to things one can't control
- Constantly seeking approval and affirmation
- Feeling different from other people
- Being either super responsible or super irresponsible
- Being extremely loyal, even when undeserved
- Being very impulsive

(Note: the "Horoscope effect" of such broad statements results in most people being able to relate somewhat to many of them. To require treatment for being an Adult Child of Addiction, you should be able to relate very strongly to most of them.)

DEPENDENCY

Those who are not active addicts and are not reacting strongly to addiction in others may simply have a dependent personality disorder. But watch out for extreme examples of "women who love too much." That disorder might be addiction to excitement or addiction conspiracy disorder somewhat disguised.

OTHER PERSONALITY DISORDERS

Some people being treated for codependency do not have an addictive disorder at all. They have what used to be called neuroses, and their treatment needs to be tailored to their problems.

COMBINATIONS

Few people fit neatly into one of the above categories. Addiction includes many dynamics. For example: a man in recovery from drug addiction marries a woman who is recovering from alcoholism. Both their fathers were alcoholic. After a few years of marriage her eating gets out of control and she becomes obese. He is embarrassed and he shames and criticizes her. She is hurt, defiant, and frustrated. They may have trouble applying what they know about chemical addiction to the present problem of her food addiction and his codependency.

RELATIONSHIPS

Active addiction inhibits the growth of relationships. If you live with an active addict, it may help to review what Al-Anon has learned over the years—that blame and shame are ineffective. While you probably cannot make the other person change, you can work on making your own life more useful to yourself and those around you. Though denial and delusion protect the disease, you can replace control with support, fear with love, and blame with information and understanding.

Codependency, see also: Abuse, Addiction model (PEMS), Al-Anon and Alateen, Amends, Assertiveness, Children of addicts, Control, Crisis, Defenses, Detachment, Emotional aspects, Enabling, Family, Family of origin, Humor & fun, Incest, Intimacy, Love & caring, Power, Psychological problems, Relationships, Resentments, Self-image, Survival roles.

Co-Dependents Anonymous (CoDA)

CoDA wisely ducks the definition of codependency in its leaflet, "What is Co-Dependency." Citing its Eighth Tradition (nonprofessionalism) this Twelve-Step organization says, "We offer no definition or diagnostic criteria for co-dependency, respectfully allowing psychiatric or psychological professionals to accomplish that task."

They go on to describe an honest self-diagnosis based on two destructive patterns of living that interfere with "healthy and nurturing relationships with others and ourselves." These patterns are control (manipulating others) and compliance (pleasing others).

STEPS

CoDA's Step One says, "We admitted we were powerless over others—that our lives had become unmanageable." Alcohol in Step Twelve has been changed to "other co-dependents." All the rest of the Steps are identical to AA's, except that all pronouns for God have been eliminated, a genderless trend that is common in recently developed Twelve-Step groups.

UNIVERSAL

CoDA is perhaps the most universal Twelve-Step program around. "The only requirement for membership is a desire for healthy and fulfilling relationships with others and ourselves." This is not a club that excludes anyone because they don't qualify. You don't even have to come from a very dysfunctional family.

IDENTIFICATION & HOPE

Healing in CoDA comes about through the twin messages of identification and hope. Members who share are encouraged to identify their codependency, sharing how it developed in their lives and how they have carried it into adulthood. The hope is sharing how they are using the Steps, the fellowship, and other tools in recovery. Eliminating self-defeating lifestyles, affirmations, nurturing the inner child, learning boundaries, and assertiveness are typical results of working the Steps.

A GENTLER WAY

Melody Beattie (1990) describes codependency recovery as a way to learn a "gentler, more loving approach to self," compared with the "hard line" approach that may be needed for alcohol or sex addiction. The fact that so many people belong to several Twelve-Step groups simultaneously shows that they may need both the close identification with very similar addicts and a place where they feel free to deal with much broader issues. CoDA seems to be such a place.

Co-Dependents Anonymous
PO Box 33577
Phoenix, AZ 85067-3577
(602) 277-7991

Co-Dependents Anonymous, see also: Adolescents, Al-Anon & Alateen, Children of addicts, Enabling, Families Anonymous, Meetings, Other support groups, Steps of AA.

Community

Community is a concept closely related to unity. It is a sense of feeling connected with other people when prejudice, the need to control, and the need to fix and heal have been put aside.

STAGES OF COMMUNITY

Scott Peck (1987) teaches and describes a process he calls "community making." A group of people together for some reason will go through the following stages:

Pseudocommunity Pseudocommunity is where people avoid disagreement, ignore individual differences, and avoid conflict. There is no honesty, individuality, or intimacy.

Chaos Chaos is when people begin to express their differences openly. Someone will try to get things organized. There is fighting and despair. Leaders emerge and there is struggling. The chaos results from those things members must let go of in the next stage, called emptiness.

Emptiness Emptiness is the stage the group enters in which individuals empty themselves of barriers to community. These barriers are expectations, prejudices, solutions, the need to control, and the need to fix, heal, or convert. This stage requires sacrifice before the group can move into community.

Community Community is where members talk honestly about themselves and allow themselves to be vulnerable. People accept each other, feel comfortable with their differences, and are free to pursue the task that binds them together. Intimacy is then possible.

SHARED STORY

The sense of community in Twelve-Step groups is created by a shared story, by the unity that binds members together. Spirituality involves this sense of connection. A criterion for spirituality is seeking out "the company of saints" in the words of Ignatius (AD 95). By this he meant those who were also seeking spirituality.

Individual also   In the same vein, an individual Twelve Stepper will need to go through a similar process in his or her recovery. By working the Steps one can participate fully and freely in that sense of community. Until you have put aside your prejudice and the need to control and organize, and have shared yourself honestly and openly, it is unlikely that you will benefit from the spiritual sense of community the Twelve-Step fellowships have to offer.

Organization incompatible   One reason that some groups do not provide this spirit could be the failure of members to understand the need to give up rules, regulations, and formalities. Addicts often have difficulty giving up their need to organize and control. Peck says, "organization and community are also incompatible." (1987, p. 93)

Community, see also: Alcoholics Anonymous, Anonymity, History of Twelve-Step groups, Meetings, Service & giving, Spirituality, Step Twelve, Traditions of AA, Unity.

Constipation

The infrequent or difficult passing of hard, dry feces is called constipation. It refers to slowing of the bowels. Usually it is harmless, but occasionally it may be a symptom of another disorder, including drug abuse (like heroin) or bulimia. In severe cases, it may be called *obstipation*, where the bowels are not moving at all.

The most common cause of constipation is a lack of dietary fiber. Eating more fruit and fiber-containing vegetables is the best solution for most people.

LAXATIVES

If you have been taking laxatives, especially large quantities of laxatives to purge, your body may have become dependent on laxatives. Depending on the severity, you may need to work with a physician to gradually restore proper bowel function. The problem may take many months to resolve.

Laxatives disturb the body's natural balance. Some laxatives can cause abdominal cramps, while others can cause chemical imbalances in the blood. Lubricant laxatives like mineral oil may coat the intestines and prevent absorption of vitamins.

For normal constipation, try to ride it out and gradually increase your fiber intake to avoid the problem in the future.

MEDICAL HELP

If there is significant lower abdominal pain, if you do not have a bowel movement for three days or more, or the constipation lasts more than two weeks, seek medical help.

See your family physician. If you have a long history of laxative use, you need to find a doctor who knows about eating disorders (and addiction) and will help with withdrawal.

Constipation, see also: Addiction, Alcoholism, Biochemistry, Bulimia nervosa, Drugs, Edema, Exercise & activity, Metabolism, Nutrition, Obesity, Physical aspects, Purging, Unmanageability, Withdrawal. Next on path B: Edema.

Control

The idea of control is one of the greatest obstacles to recovery for any addict. Loss of control, struggling to control, resistance to control—all are frequent topics at Twelve-Step meetings, and often produce lots of confusion.

CONTROL AS ILLUSION

No one really has control over people, or of major situations or events, or ever will. History has demonstrated that the harder dictators try to maintain control of a nation, the more violently they will be overthrown. The more one tries to control another's addiction, the greater the likelihood that addiction will disrupt their relationship. When you look at how impossible it is to control your own or someone else's behavior or beliefs, you may begin to see that control is nothing but an illusion.

Obstacle to Step One This illusion is a real obstacle to the acceptance of Step One, which says that you are powerless over your addiction, and your life has become unmanageable. The addict tries to hold up this mask of control, saying "Hell no! I can handle it!" As long as addicts hang on to this idea of control, they will be stuck on Step One, unable to progress in recovery.

Most addicts can understand when others say, "The harder I tried, the worse it became." Why is it so hard to discard this destructive model? Perhaps because abandoning it is so threatening to the disease of addiction. Another major reason, for most addicts, is their history with authority figures, terror at feeling out of control, and the intoxication that comes with the illusion of power.

Dysfunctional families   Those who come from dysfunctional families usually have a great deal of difficulty surrendering control. If they grew up in a family where they learned to survive by taking "control" of situations, by developing survival skills to cope, then they are likely to experience intense fear at the thought of somebody else, even a Higher Power, running the show. In fact, the skills that kept them alive, emotionally if not physically, are the very skills that could be interfering with their recovery today.

Influence   Another problem with letting go of the illusion of control may be not having an alternative model to understand ordinary life situations. If you do not have control, then what do you have?

A good alternate concept is influence. While you cannot control anyone else, you can and will influence the lives of everyone you meet. The idea of influence is more accurate, and is easy to understand in terms of a broad spectrum from almost negligible influence (over a casual acquaintance) to very profound (such as a spouse or child). It also relieves you of some of the expectation that you are responsible for those over whom you have some influence (rather than control).

Responsibility   Using the model of influence instead of control also makes it easier to understand responsibility. Certainly you have responsibilities to others in your life—your parents, spouse, children, employees or employer, friends, and others. You may legitimately accept some responsibility to influence their lives in a positive way. Responsibility becomes almost deadly when you assume that you can *control* others. This is a setup for frustration, fear, excessive guilt, and a sense of failure. For an addict, it can also provide a wonderful excuse to drink, to use, to gamble, or to eat compulsively.

CONTROL AS ADDICTION

Extreme obsession with control can easily become a compulsion or even an addiction. Many people who are treated for codependency are suffering from this obsession with the illusion of control. There is probably even a biochemistry associated with it that normally balances the addictive state of fantasy. An extreme version of this state or direction of addiction can be seen in people with obsessive-compulsive disorder (OCD).

Obsessive compulsive disorder (OCD)   This is a true personality disorder that is far beyond the usual compulsion and obsession of addiction. Compulsive handwashers, stove-checkers, and crack-avoiders are examples. Many researchers believe that OCD is caused by neurochemical imbalances.

Codependency   From what we know of addiction, it makes sense that addicts could produce these imbalances out of their addictive behavior. Codependency and other family illness often involve obsessive, compulsive behavior.

Checklist mindset   Many addicts ask, "What can I do?" and expect a pat answer, or a checklist. There is a subtle expectation that if they follow instructions carefully they will gain control. Also it is then not their responsibility if it fails. This kind of expectation is not compatible with the First Step, or with spirituality, which includes the awareness that you will *never* be God.

LETTING GO

The good news is that you do not have to let go of control, only the illusion of control. You never had control anyway. And you have to let go to experience the transformation that happens in recovery. The ultimate solution to the issue of control is Step Three, turning your will and your life over to the care of your Higher Power—whatever you understand that Higher Power to be.

Control, see also: Anger, Codependency, Emotional aspects, Enabling, Step Three, Surrender.

Coping skills

Recovery offers you the opportunity to live without the harmful effects of addiction. You will then be required to face life's challenges like everyone else. How well you do this will depend on your coping skills—those abilities and attitudes that help you deal effectively with whatever comes your way.

HOW YOU TAKE IT

Someone said that life is 10 percent how you make it and 90 percent how you take it. You don't have to consider yourself a victim of life. There are many resources to help you develop the power to deal with any situation.

COPING WITH TEMPTATION

You first have to cope with the temptations that lure you back toward addictive behavior. Fortunately, the tools and skills necessary to avoid relapse are readily available. Powerful help is found in the fellowships of the Twelve-Step groups and in using the Steps as principles in your daily life.

LIVING SOBER

In 1975 AA World Services published a book called *Living Sober*, which is filled with solid Twelve-Step program information. It contains practical experience of recovering alcoholics, with useful tools to avoid drinking. It also helps with other things, like self-pity and insomnia. It is easy to adapt those suggestions for other addictions.

HELP FROM OTHERS

Most addicts find that the best assistance for coping comes from other people who have had similar experiences. That is a benefit of having friends in recovery, a sponsor, and regular meetings.

DEALING WITH LIFE

Your recovery may require dealing with the consequences of addiction. You may have to live with decisions you made while in active disease. You may have relationships that need healing. Other family members may be active addicts. You may discover your family of origin was very dysfunctional, and you lack self-esteem or social skills to make life click for you. Fortunately help is available for all these problems.

EARLY AND LATER RECOVERY

You need coping skills to deal with addiction itself, especially if you are in early recovery. Addictive behavior does not die an easy death. After your recovery is established, and you get some sobriety or abstinence under your belt, you may simply need skills to cope with your job or career, relationships with family and friends, illness or natural disasters, and the other challenges of life. The good news is that your Twelve-Step program is a design for living. It comes from practicing the Steps in your daily life.

BLESSINGS OF RECOVERY

Recovery can open you to many new and wonderful opportunities. Simple blessings, like a day without the pain of addiction, provide simple joy. Being grateful, using the Steps, the slogans, the

Serenity Prayer, and your Higher Power should give you a solid basis for living. Then you can pursue tools for stress management, biofeedback, meditation, therapy, or whatever you need to enhance your recovery and provide you with the coping skills for life.

Coping skills, see also: Celebrations, Exercise & activity, Hunger & appetite, Moderation, Nutrition, Stress & strain, Therapy & treatment, Tools of recovery, Visualizations.

Core functions

The National Certification Reciprocity Consortium / Alcohol and Other Drug Abuse, Inc., established a set of twelve "core functions" necessary for addictions counselors. This list became the de facto standard of skills required for certification of alcohol and drug counselors. The International Association of Eating Disorders Professionals, Inc., has (with permission) implemented this concept for certification of eating disorders counselors and therapists as well.

Definitions

These twelve core functions and their official definitions are:

1. *Screening* The process by which a client is determined appropriate and eligible for admission to a particular program.

2. *Intake* The administrative and initial assessment procedures for admission to a program.

3. *Orientation* Describing to the client
    • general nature and goals of the program
    • rules governing client conduct and infractions that can lead to disciplinary action or discharge from the program
    • in a nonresidential program, the hours during which services are available
    • treatment costs to be borne by the client, if any
    • client's rights

4. *Assessment* Those procedures by which a counselor/program identifies and evaluates an individual's strengths, weaknesses, problems, and needs for the development of the treatment plan.

5. *Treatment planning*   Process by which the counselor and the client:
   - identify and rank problems needing resolution
   - establish agreed-upon immediate and long-term goals
   - decide on the treatment methods and resources to be used

6. *Counseling*   (Individual, group, and significant others) The utilization of special skills to assist individuals, families, or groups in achieving objectives through:
   - exploration of a problem and its ramifications
   - examination of attitudes and feelings
   - consideration of alternative solutions
   - decision making

7. *Case management*   Activities that bring services, agencies, resources, or people together within a planned framework of action toward the achievement of established goals. It may involve liaison activities and collateral contacts.

8. *Crisis intervention*   Those services that respond to a client's needs during acute emotional or physical distress.

9. *Client education*   Provision of information to individuals and groups concerning addiction and the available services and resources.

10. *Referral*   Identifying the needs of the client that cannot be met by the counselor or agency and assisting the client to utilize the support systems and community resources available.

11. *Reports and recordkeeping*   Charting the results of the assessment and treatment plan; writing reports, progress notes, discharge summaries, and other client-related data.

12. *Consultation*   Relating with counselors and other professionals in regard to treatment (services) to assure comprehensive, quality care for the client.

Core functions, see also: Certification, Counseling, Disease concept, Dual diagnosis, Employee assistance programs, Impaired professionals, Intervention, Professional organizations, Psychological problems, Therapy & treatment.

Counseling

Counseling is a profession that uses a specific body of knowledge and skills to assist others (clients) to reach certain goals. Counselors help clients mobilize resources to solve problems and modify attitudes and values. Most people go to a counselor with a specific problem they can't seem to solve without help.

In your recovery you may need counseling at times for specific problems. Some of these are: you can't stay sober or abstinent, you have trouble with relationships, you become aware of abuse or incest issues, or you may want to do more intensive self-searching and growing.

CHOOSING A COUNSELOR

How do you decide whom to see? Try to identify what you need as best you can. Talk to others who have had similar experiences. They can steer you in the right direction. To help with prioritizing, see the module on Codependency.

Counselors should have models and techniques they are skilled in using. See if their ideas fit and are comfortable for you. Don't hesitate to say so if they are not. See the module on Models and concepts.

Addictions counseling   If you are involved in addictive behavior, you need someone trained and skilled (and preferably certified) to work with that addiction. If you are abstinent from your primary addiction, any addiction counselor or other mental health professional may be fine if they have the skills to help you with your specific problems.

Credentials   When shopping for a counselor, feel free to ask about credentials and experience. Remember that you are the employer. Have an initial interview, even if you have to pay for it, to see if a counselor seems right for you. Many addicts with low self-esteem may feel they have no right to choose their therapist. The counselor is selling you their skills. You are the one who must live with the results of your mutual work.

Remember that a counselor should be a professional. You may feel more comfortable with an addictions counselor who is in recovery, but that is not why you are hiring them. Many people who are not in recovery themselves are excellent counselors. Also, being in recovery does not make one a counselor. Choose a counselor for their skills and a sponsor for their recovery.

DEFINITION

The National Certification Reciprocity Consortium/Alcohol and Other Drug Abuse (NCRC) defines counseling as: The utilization of special skills to assist individuals, families, or groups in achieving objectives through:

- exploration of a problem and its ramifications
- examination of attitudes and feelings
- consideration of alternative solutions
- decision making

Techniques   Counseling is a relationship in which the counselor helps the client mobilize resources to resolve problems and/or modify attitudes and values. Counselors should be familiar with various counseling techniques and methods, like Reality Therapy, Rational Emotive Therapy, Behavior Therapy, Systemic Counseling, Transactional Analysis, Client-centered Therapy, etc.

Mastering several   It may be unrealistic to expect a counselor to be highly skilled in many different approaches to counseling. Each may take several years to master. It is important, however, that counselors have a high level of skill in more than one technique. Craig Johnson, a noted authority on eating disorders, reminds us that if a hammer is the only tool in our tool belt, everything we meet is in danger of being treated as a nail.

Aware of limitations   It is equally important that counselors be aware of and be able to admit their limitations. Many counseling techniques are very powerful and potentially dangerous. The Health Care Professions (note that the middle name is Care) owe much to the noble ideas that have been passed down since the time of Hippocrates. Part of that tradition states that first, do no harm.

Counseling, see also: Aftercare, Certification, Core functions, Disease concept, Dual diagnosis, Employee assistance programs, Impaired professionals, Intervention, Professional organizations, Psychological problems, Sponsorship, Therapy & treatment, Withdrawal.

Craving

In addiction, craving is a strong emotional response to a physical, allergic, addictive withdrawal.

PHYSICAL
The actual allergy or addictive imbalance produces biochemical signals that are interpreted as craving.

EMOTIONAL
The feelings that occur with craving can upset you and frighten you that you might binge or use. This in turn can produce more neurochemical response.

AVOIDING
It will help reduce craving if you avoid sensitive foods or any environmental factors that resemble the addictive substance or activity. Also, by avoiding getting too hungry, angry, lonely, or tired (HALT) you can help avoid the conditions that feed the cravings.

GETTING THROUGH IT
What is important to realize is that having cravings does not mean you have to binge. If we believe that addiction is a disease, craving does not mean something is necessarily wrong with your recovery, either.

You don't have to fight cravings alone. You can talk with someone, read literature, or make contact with your Higher Power. It is important to reject drinking, using, smoking, bingeing, purging, starving, gambling, spending, or other addictive behaviors as options to deal with the craving.

One way of dealing with craving is to visualize the binge, in the most vivid details possible, all the way through using the substance or participating in the activity to the feelings you will experience afterward. The delusional pleasure of addictive behavior can be dissipated by remembering the pain, guilt, and shame that follow the behavior. This visualization can be done alone, on the phone with someone in your Twelve-Step program, or with your Higher Power.

Craving, see also: Allergies, Biochemistry, Bulimia nervosa, Cocaine, Emotional aspects, Excitement, Feelings, Heroin, Hunger & appetite, Obsession, Premenstrual syndrome, Pregnancy, Sweeteners, Withdrawal. Next on path C: Body image.

Crisis

A crisis is any situation that interrupts normal events of daily living. Ferguson's Precept (a relative of Murphy's Law) says a crisis is when you can't say, "Let's just forget the whole thing."

Examples include deaths, jail, wrecks, bankruptcy, acute illness, and relapse.

We are told that in the Chinese language, there are two characters that together mean "crisis." Individually those two characters mean "danger" and "opportunity." Many people report that out of a crisis came a gift for learning or spiritual growth. If you focus on the negative, you will miss the blessings.

Whatever the crisis, your responsibility to recovery is to keep your abstinence from addictive substances or behaviors. This does not mean that your recovery plan can't change temporarily, for good reason.

If you are in the hospital, do the best you can while still following sound medical advice. If you are taken hostage by a terrorist group, you don't need to refuse wine or donuts if that is all they are willing to feed you. However, most crises are less extreme.

ADDICTION CAN MAKE IT WORSE

No matter how bad a situation gets, retreating into addiction will make it worse. Remember that your addiction will probably try to make use of the crisis to give you an excuse to drink, use, binge, starve, or otherwise get into addictive behavior.

Not every problem is a crisis. Recognize when you have a tendency to be dramatic, making big deals out of less important problems. Recovery from histrionics might include learning that a flat tire on the road suggests a call to AAA, not to the suicide prevention hotline. Focusing on the negative and hopeless views of the problem can turn everything into a catastrophe. Histrionics and catastrophizing are related.

GETTING HELP

Ask for help. People are generally more willing to help during a crisis than under normal conditions.

It is very important to be careful of the let-down after the crisis is over. You might tend to relax, become complacent, and become vulnerable to relapse. More people report relapse after a crisis than during it.

Crisis, see also: Abstinence, Acceptance, Behavior, Bingeing, Codependency, Control, Coping skills, Defenses, Feelings, Hitting bottom, Intervention, Judgment, Obsession, Powerlessness, Priorities, Relapse prevention, Sponsorship, Step One, Steps of AA, Surrender, Survival roles, Telephone, Therapy & treatment, Unmanageability, Withdrawal. Next on path F: Delusion.

D

Debtors Anonymous

It is not surprising that so many addicts get involved in compulsive spending. Especially since the proliferation of credit cards, it is easy to go overboard. There is a sense of power in being able to gratify instantly a desire to have something you want, even if you don't have the money or can't afford it. Buy now, pay later—this is part of the American dream, isn't it?

From the psychology of designing a shopping mall to the magazine and TV ads enticing you to charge it, a large segment of the business world seems intent on helping you overextend yourself. About the time you notice one credit card has reached its limit, you get a brand new one, unsolicited, in the mail. After all, banks and other financial institutions are making a healthy profit from money, and they are trying to sell you some of the most expensive money around.

BIOCHEMISTRY

Like the compulsive gambler, the compulsive debtor can get a "high" from the biochemical changes that accompany the purchase of goods or services. Also like for the gambler, these neurochemical imbalances are likely to be stronger on the "downside," when they are driven by the fear of not being able to pay, or of losing everything.

ABSTINENCE

New members at Debtors Anonymous are advised to avoid incurring any unsecured debt, including credit cards, personal loans, or educational loans. This avoids compulsive spending one day at a time.

PRESSURE GROUP

After several meetings, the new member is encouraged to set up a "pressure group." Its purpose is to *relieve* pressure (remember the neurochemistry of fear we just mentioned). Two other DA members who have been abstinent from compulsive spending for a while meet several times with the new member for support and to develop a spending plan and a debt repayment plan. They also focus on any pressure that could lead to more debt.

DEPRIVATION

Many debtors use deprivation as part of the disease, alternately bingeing and fasting like a bulimic. DA helps them learn to put legitimate personal and family needs first. As their financial and emotional condition improves, they can pay off their debts. DA does not advocate bankruptcy. Repaying debts is seen as part of Steps Eight and Nine.

For more information, contact one of the two hundred or so DA groups listed in the white pages of your phone book, or call or write:

Debtors Anonymous
PO Box 20322
New York, NY 10025-9992
(212) 642-8222

Debtors Anonymous, see also: Enabling, Gambling, Meetings, Money, Other support groups, Spending, Steps of AA, Traditions of AA.

Defenses

In mental health, defenses have gotten a "bad rap." You may have been led to believe that you should not have any. There is a healthy purpose for defenses under ordinary circumstances.

EXAMPLES OF DEFENSES

Some psychological defenses can operate at healthy or at unhealthy levels. Most happen unconsciously, although part of the awareness can be conscious. The purpose of defenses is to cushion us from emotional shocks. Too little shock protection and you might be an emotional basket case. Too much and you might be very isolated from others and reality.

Addiction can result in an exaggeration of defenses to protect itself. Most of the following defenses may be seen in addicts' psychological makeup.

Compensation   You try to make up for real or fancied deficiencies in your physical, mental, or emotional abilities.

Denial   You disavow thoughts, feelings, needs, or other realities that are consciously intolerable.

Displacement   You transfer your emotions or ideas from their original object to a more acceptable substitute.

Dissociation   You detach your feelings from an idea, situation, or object.

Identification   You pattern yourself after another person.

Intellectualization   You use reason and logic to avoid stressful emotions.

Isolation   You separate an unacceptable impulse, idea, or act from a memory, making the memory less emotional.

Projection   You attribute (project) to others what is emotionally unacceptable in yourself.

Rationalization   You try to justify feelings, behavior, or motives that otherwise would be intolerable.

Repression   You keep unacceptable ideas, fantasies, feelings, or impulses from becoming conscious.

Sublimation   You divert instinctual drives that are consciously unacceptable into acceptable channels.

Substitution   You replace an unattainable or unacceptable goal, emotion, or object with one that is more attainable or acceptable.

Undoing   You symbolically (and usually repetitiously) act out the reverse of something unacceptable and already done, in hopes of relieving anxiety.

NATURAL USE

A moderate level of defenses is healthy. You have to be able to detach from things. Defenses can fall on a continuum. For example, people react to death in varying degrees; some act as if they'll never die, while others may be preoccupied with death.

Need in family of origin   In the addictive family, the survival roles its members adopt are defenses that allow them to continue to function. However, they may not be realistic, and they may be carried on into situations where they are no longer necessary or may be detrimental. (See the Survival roles module.)

Need today People need a certain level of defensiveness to function in the world on a daily basis. You may need to guard yourself against the "thirteenth step" where someone takes advantage of your new recovery and vulnerability, sexually or otherwise.

ADJUSTING LEVEL

You have some choices in recovery relating to the defenses you use. Gaining balance is the key to success in using defenses. Most people find they can be comfortable with more vulnerability as their recovery becomes more stable.

Defenses, see also: Affirmations, Assertiveness, Behavior, Character defects, Control, Dichotomous thinking, Family of origin, Honesty, Intimacy, Inventory, Mental aspects, Perfectionism, Psychological problems, Step Four, Step Six, Step Ten, Surrender, Survival roles. Next on path I: Perfectionism.

Delusion

DENIAL

In order for addiction to exist and to progress, there must be some mechanism for keeping the addict from seeing or acknowledging reality in an undistorted form. Many addiction counselors call this *denial*. While that term is useful, we prefer to use *delusion*.

Consciously aware? There is a danger in using the term *denial*, which implies a conscious refusal to see the truth. For most addicts, seeing how addiction affects them is almost, by definition, beyond the person's conscious awareness. If you know you ate a half-gallon of ice cream and lie about it, that is certainly denial in everyday terminology. But if you are unable to see how much you nibble during the day, delusion seems a better description.

ILLUSION

An illusionist is a magician who specializes in making your senses fool you. A mirage looks like a lake, and it may reflect other objects that make it appear even more real.

Illusions in addiction can appear so real that you start to believe them. This becomes delusion.

Examples   You start to believe that your sweetheart is the answer to all your dreams, and fail to see his or her considerable faults. You continue to think of beer or sweets as harmless, even wholesome and healthy.

RECOGNIZING

Addiction works by turning illusion into delusion. You start to believe you really have no trouble with your eating, drinking, or smoking. When you accuse someone else of eating the ice cream, it may be a manipulative tactic to shift suspicion from yourself. When you begin to believe, or half-believe, that you really didn't do it, it is delusion.

Dispelling   Honesty dispels delusion. Addicts in recovery need to be as honest as possible with others, and be openminded to feedback so they can get more honest with themselves. This inherent inability to see themselves accurately is a primary reason addicts need other addicts to help with their recovery.

Delusion, see also: Acceptance, Beliefs, Body image, Defenses, Half-measures, Honesty, Judgment, Mental aspects, Obsession, Openmindedness, Paradoxes in addiction, Sanity, Steps of AA, Stinking thinking, Unmanageability. Next on path F: Half-measures.

Detachment

People who are family or friends of active addicts often find themselves involved in the disease process. Trying to help may be enabling, which means the addictive patterns are being supported. Enablers end up frustrated, angry, guilty, frightened, and lonely. Patterns of behavior are adopted to survive the confusion and chaos. The addictions field has been flooded with information, treatment options, and support groups to help these people deal with their feelings and behavior.

AL-ANON

Al-Anon, the first support group for family and friends of alcoholics, understands the value of detachment. Detachment means that through education about addiction, you can separate yourself from the feelings and behaviors you developed to try to control the addict or deal with the situation. You learn you didn't cause the problem, and you can't cure it.

FOCUS

People learn to detach by taking the focus off the addict and concentrating on their own behavior. They use the same Twelve Steps of recovery to do this, and get help and support in meetings from others who share the same problems.

SUPPORT GROUPS

As Twelve-Step support groups for other addictions were founded, so were support groups for families and friends of compulsive gamblers (Gam-Anon), compulsive overeaters (O-Anon), and sex addicts (S-Anon).

LET GO

Experience has shown that it is rare for a person today to find himself with only one identity that has to do with addiction. Addicts are married to other addicts, have parents or children who are addicts, and have friends who suffer. So it makes sense that everyone can benefit from learning the tool of detachment. The slogan, "Let go and let God," best describes it:

To "let go" does not mean to stop caring, it means I can't do it for someone else.

To "let go" is not to cut myself off, it's the realization I can't control another.

To "let go" is not to enable, but to allow learning from natural consequences.

To "let go" is to admit powerlessness, which means the outcome is not in my hands.

To "let go" is not to try to change or blame another, it's to make the most of myself.

To "let go" is not to care for, but to care about.

To "let go" is not to fix, but to be supportive.

To "let go" is not to judge, but to allow another to be a human being.

To "let go" is not to be in the middle arranging all the outcomes, but to allow others to affect their own destinies.

To "let go" is not to be protective, it's to permit another to face reality.

To "let go" is not to deny, but to accept.

To "let go" is not to nag, scold, or argue, but instead to search out my own shortcomings and correct them.

To "let go" is not to adjust everything to my desires but to take each day as it comes, and cherish myself in it.

To "let go" is not to regret the past, but to grow and live for the future.

To "let go" is to fear less and love more.

—AUTHOR UNKNOWN

Detachment, see also: Al-Anon & Alateen, Control, Coping skills, Intervention, Love & caring, Meetings, Priorities, Service & giving, Slogans, Sponsorship, Telephone, Tools of recovery, Trust.

Dichotomous thinking

Dichotomous, or black-and-white, or all-or-nothing, thinking is very characteristic of the thought processes of addicts. Recognizing this distortion in thinking enhances recovery.

DESCRIPTION

Black-and-white thinking is characterized by the tendency to see oneself and the world in extremes. When you think in terms of success or failure, perfect abstinence or total relapse, or any other extremes, you are engaged in dichotomous thinking.

Once you become aware of the tendency for dichotomous thinking, you can recognize it in the thinking of many facets of your life. How much it pervades an addict's thinking seems to fall on a continuum. For some, it may be related primarily to drinking, using, eating, or other addictive behavior, whereas for others it may permeate many areas of their life.

FOOD AND DIETING

For food addicts, the most obvious kind of dichotomous thinking is food, diets, weight, and other eating-related thoughts. Diet mentality sets you up for this kind of all-or-nothing thinking. You are either on or off a diet. You absolutely avoid all sugar or you eat huge quantities of it. Whether or not you have been good or bad, a success or a failure, is dependent on your eating. Even food is considered good or bad for you. You are either at goal weight or you are overweight. You have to have a rigid food plan or you are not abstinent.

Dichotomous thinking exists in other addictions. For alcoholics, dichotomous thinking shows in the philosophy that if you are not drinking, you are in recovery. Or, you are either in recovery or relapse. It leads some to the erroneous belief that any use of prescription psychiatric drugs is a relapse.

You may find black-or-white thinking in other areas of your life. Someone loves you or does not. You are a success or failure at your job. You are a good or bad spouse, child, or parent. You do trust others or you don't. Whatever form dichotomous thinking takes, it doesn't allow for the middle ground.

LABELS

Having to label something or someone can be dichotomous thinking. Someone is an addict or is not. Your family is dysfunctional or normal.

THE PROBLEM

Whenever you think in extremes, you are using a model of thinking that does not fit reality. Most characteristics and experiences fall on a spectrum. To be able to see and relate to a more realistic, flexible way of thinking is necessary for good mental health.

PERFECTIONISM

Perfectionism is related to dichotomous thinking. It is a distortion of perception that interferes with the grace the Program has to offer. You have to have perfect recovery, perfect abstinence from all addictive behaviors or even thoughts. You have to look a certain perfect way, weigh a perfect (goal) weight, or you are not OK and therefore a failure. In reality everyone is imperfect and it is that imperfection and need for each other that is an essential element in a community of recovering addicts. You accept not only your own imperfections but everyone else's as well.

TIE WITH ADDICTION

Addictive thinking (the mental part of PEMS) easily uses dichotomous thinking to encourage continuation of the disease. For example, your abstinence is perfect or you are a failure. Ironically, this kind of thinking can be a prime setup for relapse. It can make recovery miserable, cause more obsession, and set such standards that any hint of deviance suggests you might as well drink, use, binge, purge, or starve, since you cannot do everything perfectly anyway.

RECOVERY

Recovery involves identifying where dichotomous thinking is causing you problems. Thinking realistically means seeing moderate alternatives, more options, and intermediate choices. It means seeing that you do not have to be perfect to be acceptable and lovable. You can understand that you are simply a human being with a variety of characteristics that make up who you are. Being human is good enough.

Recovery means using the program to accept who and what you are so you can start a journey toward the person you would like to become. And remember, recovery is the journey, not the destination.

Dichotomous thinking, see also: Affirmations, Body image, Character defects, Defenses, Delusion, Diet mentality, Habit & structure, Judgment, Magical thinking, Mental aspects, Obsession, Paradoxes in addiction, Sabotage of recovery, Slogans, Stinking thinking, Therapy & treatment, Trust, Visualizations. Next on path D: Diet mentality.

Diet mentality

Diet mentality refers to the thought processes that are a carryover from old ideas and old tapes related to dieting behavior and dichotomous thinking. These attitudes have a lot of power. Diet mentality is primarily applicable to food addicts, although many other addicts will recognize it or the related idea of deprivation as a potential problem in their recovery.

HOW TO IDENTIFY IT
Some key phrases in diet mentality are:

- Squeaky-clean abstinence
- Perfect abstinence
- Stick to the food plan
- I cheated
- Legal foods
- Good and bad foods

The feelings associated with diet mentality are guilt, the illusion of control, and "I have to do it right."

BREAKING OUT OF IT
Recognize it! Watch for phrases like, "must do," and "have to." The solution is to use Step Three. Use a Higher Power and the Steps of recovery.

Diet mentality, see also: Attitudes, Body image, Checklist mentality, Delusion, Dichotomous thinking, Food plans, Habit & structure, Judgment, Magical thinking, Mental aspects, Metabolism, Nutrition, Obsession, Paradoxes in addiction, Sanity, Therapy & treatment, Visualizations. Next on path D: Magical thinking.

Disease concept

DEFINITION OF DISEASE

Is addiction really a disease? *Webster's Medical Desk Dictionary* (1986) defines a disease as:

> **disease** *n* : an impairment of the normal state of the living animal or plant body or of any of its components that interrupts or modifies the performance of the vital functions and is a response to environmental factors (as malnutrition, industrial hazards, or climate), to specific infective agents (as worms, bacteria, or viruses), to inherent defects of the organism (as various genetic anomalies), or to combinations of these factors: SICKNESS, ILLNESS. . . .

Depending on whether you strictly or broadly employ this definition, you could either argue that addiction has or has not been shown to be a disease. As an either/or question, it becomes an academic exercise.

First generation: lab testable   Lab testable disease includes the physical kinds of diseases that can be clearly identified by lab test or trained physical observation. Stanton Peele, in his book *Diseasing of America* (1989), lists malaria, tuberculosis, cancer, and AIDS as examples. He says these diseases are defined by their measurable physical effects. These are the diseases that are least contested by medical insurance. They represent conditions that are easier to pin down.

Second generation: mental illness   Emotional disorders are not currently measured by blood or urine tests but by the thoughts, feelings, and behaviors of those who suffer from them. Schizophrenia, clinical depression, and autism may respond to drug therapy, but diagnosis depends much more on what a person says and does than anything as objective as a brain scan.

Third generation: addiction   Peele says that addiction is one step farther from a lab testable disease. While schizophrenics can be identified from their disordered thinking process, we cannot tell an addict in the absence of the ongoing addictive behavior—the drinking, using, eating, smoking, gambling, etc.

Fourth generation: dysfunctions   Although Peele lumps codependency, adult children of addiction or dysfunctional families, and other trauma or addiction-related conditions in with second and third generation disease, we are inclined to extend his model to include these in a fourth generation of disease. These are all those character and personality characteristics that are generally dysfunctional for the individual, and may be related to addiction, trauma, or other problems in the family of origin, present family, career, etc.

Multiple categories   Most diseases do not fit in only one category. Diabetes, for example, clearly fits in the first generation description. You can measure the high blood sugar on a test paper or a meter. It can be very dangerous, even with a careful nutritional regimen, frequent monitoring, and insulin therapy. But most people who suffer severe consequences have not followed their diet carefully. Most people who have fatal heart attacks increased their risk factor by smoking, poor nutrition, lack of exercise, or by ignoring signs of danger. How many other "physical" diseases are in some sense self-induced?

Bulimics may have dangerously low electrolyte levels or other life-threatening "lab testable" medical conditions resulting from their bulimia (first generation disease). They may also have severe depression (second generation) following or preceding their binge/purge episodes. Their eating pattern may almost exactly match their alcoholism before they stopped drinking (third generation), and they may be unable to establish or maintain healthy relationships (fourth generation) because of unresolved family issues. They may need immediate medical attention, an antidepressant drug, bulimia treatment, and ongoing counseling to deal with all levels of their recovery.

CHARACTERISTICS
We find it works to treat addiction with a disease model. A disease has signs and symptoms, a predictable course of progression, a causative agent (though it may not be identified), and it is primary, not a result of something else.

RESPONSIBILITY
Labeling addictions "disease" does not absolve you of responsibility for your behavior, for decisions that affect your life, or for the consequences of over- or undertreating yourself. You must make the best decisions you can, whether the question is buying a new car, changing jobs, getting married, deciding whether you need treatment, and when you need help.

Disease concept, see also: Addiction model (PEMS), Binge history, Dual diagnosis, Intervention, PEMS model, Paradoxes in addiction, Powerlessness, Psychological problems, Therapy & treatment, Unmanageability. Next on path D: Obsession.

Drugs

In this module we focus on psychiatric prescription drugs. For others of interest to addiction, see the module on Moodifiers. These drugs are listed by their most common psychiatric use.

ANTIDEPRESSANTS

These drugs, introduced in the early 1960s, are used to treat long-term clinical depression. The most common are called tricyclic antidepressants (TCA). Unless otherwise noted, they increase norepinephrine (NE) or serotonin (5-HT) or both, and they are used most often to treat depression.

First generation TCAs   Elavil (amitriptyline) and Tofranil (imipramine) are used for depression, especially of a biological origin, and sleep disorders.

Second generation TCAs   Introduced in the early 1970s, these drugs generally have fewer side effects than the older TCAs. Norpramin (desipramine) and Pamelor (nortriptyline) are used like the older TCAs. Asendin (amoxapine) is used for psychotic depression and anxiety also. Sinequan (doxepin) is often used with anxiety or depression with alcoholism. Wellbutrin (bupropion) is also used to stabilize manic-depression.

Serotonin reuptake blockers   The newest TCAs are more specific, usually affecting only the serotonergic system. They are often used with substance abuse or eating disorders. By blocking the reuptake of serotonin in the synapse, they make more of it available to the serotonin receptors. Desyrel (trazodone), Prozac (fluoxetine), and Anafranil (clomipramine) are examples.

MAO inhibitors   By inhibiting the enzyme monoamine oxidase (MAO), these drugs increase those neurotransmitters that produce emotional stability. A major adverse effect of monoamine oxidase inhibitors is that certain foods contain the amino acid tyramine, which requires MAO for its metabolism. If someone on these drugs ingests hot dogs, cheese, alcoholic beverages, or certain other foods and medications, the tyramine will remain active and release excess norepinephrine (NE). This causes severe headaches, nausea, vomiting, and heart palpitations. A stroke or even death is possible.

Because of these and other side effects, MAO inhibitors are usually used only when other antidepressants do not work. Examples are Nardil (phenelzin), Marplan (isocarboxazid), and Parnate (tranylcypromine).

ANTIPSYCHOTICS

These drugs block the dopamine (DA) receptors in the brain, correcting the imbalance of nerve impulse transmission that seems to play a role in certain psychiatric disorders. They are often effective with severe anxiety, delusions, and hallucinations associated with psychosis. They are also called the major tranquilizers.

Low potency examples are Thorazine (chlorpromazine) and Mellaril (thioridazine). Higher potency is found in Haldol (haloperidol), Stelazine (trifluoperazine), Navane (thiothixene), Prolixin (fluphenazine), Moban (molindone), and Compazine (prochlorperazine), which also blocks acetylcholine (ACh), relieving severe nausea and vomiting.

HYPNOTICS

Hypnotics do not hypnotize people. The Greek word *hypnos* means sleep. So these are sedatives, or sleeping potions. Some work by decreasing norepinephrine, some by action on the sleep center of the brain, and some on the limbic system. In general, their action is not well understood. They are highly addicting, producing tolerance in about three or four weeks of prescribed dosages. They are very dangerous when combined with alcohol.

Barbiturates   Examples are Amytal (amobarbital), Seconal (secobarbital), and Nembutal (pentobarbital).

Nonbarbiturates   These include Placidyl (ethchlorvynol), Doriden (glutethimide), and Paral (paraldehyde).

Benzodiazepines   Some benzodiazepines used for sleep are Dalmane (flurazepam) and Halcion (triazolam).

ANTIHISTAMINES

These drugs are used primarily to reduce histamine, which is released in allergic reactions. They are chemically related to the antipsychotics or major tranquilizers such as Thorazine, and they produce a sedative effect, causing concern for driving or any activity where drowsiness is unsafe.

Examples of antihistamines are Benadryl (diphenhydramine) and Phenergan (promethazine), also used for motion sickness, and Atarax or Vistaril (hydroxyzine), also used for skin problems including itching.

STIMULANTS

In the past these drugs were used as antidepressants and to suppress appetite. Today they are prescribed mostly for hyperactive children, for narcolepsy, and to augment the treatment of depression. They cause release of the neurotransmitter norepinephrine (NE).

Common stimulants are Dexedrine (dextroamphetamine), Ritalin (methylphenidate), Cylert (pemoline), and Pondimin (fenfluramine), which is still used for weight reduction.

ANTIANXIETY DRUGS

These are also called the minor tranquilizers. Most of them depress the limbic system and the gaba-benzodiazepine complex of the brain, reducing anxiety. Once thought to be nonaddicting, the benzodiazepine (BZP) drugs account for the majority of prescription drug addiction in the United States.

Long-acting BZPs   Long-acting benzodiazepines include Valium (diazepam) and Librium (chlordiazepoxide).

Pro drugs   Pro drugs (from Latin *pro* meaning before) have no pharmaceutical action themselves, but break down into active ingredients after entering the body. It was thought this would make them less addicting but it does not. Examples are Tranxene (chlorazepate), Centrax (prazepam), and Paxipam (halazepam).

Short-acting BZPs   These short-acting benzodiazepines were thought to be less addicting because they act quickly and leave the body quickly. Actually, they have a greater chance of dependency than the longer acting BZPs. This may be similar to the high addiction potential of quick-acting drugs like tobacco and cocaine. Examples of short-acting BZPs are Xanax (alprazolam), Atavan (lorazepam), and Serax (oxazepam).

Short-acting nonspecific   Other antianxiety drugs include Inderal (propranolol), which also lowers blood pressure and the likelihood of migraine headaches, Catapres (clonidine), which slows norepinephrine centers, lowers blood pressure, and is used in alcohol and opiate withdrawal, and Buspar (buspirone), which interacts with dopamine (DA), norepinephrine (NE), and serotonin (5-HT) neurotransmitters to relieve anxiety.

MOOD STABILIZERS

These drugs are used to control the mood swings of conditions like manic-depression. Lithium carbonate alters the metabolism of norepinephrine (NE) and serotonin (5-HT). Its levels in the bloodstream must be closely monitored, and there are often side effects. Tegretol (carbamazepine) reduces seizures and manic attacks.

DANGERS OF RX

The medical profession has a sad history of using drugs to treat addiction. In the late nineteenth century opium was prescribed to cure alcoholism. Shortly after the turn of the century, they tried using heroin to treat opium addiction. As late as ten years ago, many physicians believed that Valium, at one time the most prescribed drug in the United States, was nonaddicting. It is clear that no addict, especially those with a history of chemical dependency, should take any kind of drug without careful consideration.

PAA   Members of Pill Addicts Anonymous (PAA) take an especially hard-line stand on prescription drugs. Their Step One says, "We admitted we were powerless over mood-changing, mind-bending pills and drugs—that our lives had become unmanageable." They report that treatment centers and addictionologists are often pleased to learn that they include prescription and over-the-counter (OTC) drugs in that category, as well as alcohol. They then get the door slammed in their faces when those same counselors and doctors learn that they also abstain from antidepressants. PAA members tell how they were instilled with terror by physicians who told them if they did not take some mood-altering drug they would die. If taking a hard line on prescription and OTC drugs appeals to you, write or call:

> Pill Addicts Anonymous
> PO Box 278
> Reading, PA 19603
> (215) 372-1128

If you need a slightly more liberal approach, or if you have difficulty finding a PAA meeting, contact Narcotics Anonymous (see that module).

Drugs, see also: Addiction, Alcohol, Arousal, Binge history, Biochemistry, Blackouts, Chronic pain, Craving, Flashbacks, Moodifiers, Narcotics Anonymous, Neurotransmitters. Next on path A: Food addiction.

Dual diagnosis

The term dual diagnosis in the addictions field usually means that a person is chemically dependent and also has a psychiatric disorder. The most common of these disorders are schizophrenia, major depression, and manic-depression. Patients are often called MICAs (mentally ill chemical abuser). No doubt the dual diagnosis phenomenon is as old as alcoholism and mental illness. But the treatment programs of the past few decades have noted that these clients are unsuccessful when treated with either a substance abuse or a mental illness model alone.

SYMPTOMS

The symptoms of each disorder can mask or mimic the other. In the past chemical dependency programs would miss the mental illness, while psychiatric and mental health workers might miss the substance abuse.

Chronic relapse, medication abuse, failure to progress, disruptive behaviors, criminal behavior, and incarceration all pointed to the need for better treatment for these patients. Therapists needed a lot more training.

PROGRAMS

There are many programs available for the patient who is chemically dependent and schizophrenic. They are more obvious than other combinations. Some states have specialized programs and groups for the dual diagnosed client.

TRAINING

Counselors, social workers, psychiatrists, and nurses need special training to deal with this population. Dual diagnosis programs must have an integrated approach, combining all the knowledge and skills needed to treat each problem individually, with special strategies for dual diagnoses.

TREATMENT

Interventions for this patient population are different from conventional chemical dependency treatment. Patients' thinking may be fragmented and egos may be fragile. Traditional methods of education and confrontation may be ineffective. A New Hampshire model reported in *Addiction and Recovery* magazine ("Integrated Services for the Dually-Diagnosed Client," June 1990) addresses the special vulnerabilities and slow progress of these clients. There are four stages to the process:

- Engagement. Patients must be convinced of the need to become involved.
- Persuasion. Clients must learn to want long-term abstinence.
- Active treatment. Teaching skills and attitudes to maintain abstinence, often linked with NA and AA.
- Relapse prevention. These clients are relapse prone, need daily reinforcement for clean time, and benefit from monitoring abstinence.

Depression   People with chronic depression and chemical dependence may have a chemical imbalance that suggests antidepressants. They may not appear disoriented or be disruptive, but they will find little joy in their recovery unless the depression is treated. For these patients, the depression is not related to what is going on their lives, and the Steps or gratitude lists do not help much. This condition should be diagnosed by a psychiatrist who knows about addiction.

Manic-depression   This disorder is more than the dramatic mood swings that occur with addiction. They can wreak havoc for a person in treatment or trying to recover. If there is a history of it in your family, or symptoms continue months into recovery, see a psychiatrist.

Borderlines   A person with a borderline personality may have trouble recovering from addiction. Craig Johnson (1987) has done a lot of work with borderline bulimics and anorexics. He does not call bulimia an addictive disorder, but his suggestions are applicable when working with a borderline addict of any kind.

Borderlines do not know how to make effective use of human contact. Early caretakers were often perceived as trying to injure them. This sets up a harsh, punitive, sadomasochistic inner world, which they act out in relationships most of their lives. Borderline addicts will probably have more serious illnesses, suicide attempts, self-mutilating behavior, and more substance abuse accompanying other addictions.

These clients wear out both counselors and friends. You have to know how to avoid getting hooked into what Johnson calls projective identification. They try to set up an empathic link with you and carry you along with whatever rage or impulsivity they are feeling. With borderlines you feel "damned if you do and damned if you don't." Borderlines are best treated by teams. Johnson warns that they can make progress if you are willing to have a client for life.

Note that this psychological approach to the treatment of borderlines sounds a lot like some popular descriptions of codependency. It may be that Johnson is treating severe codependency, or that some people who are identifying with the codependency movement are indeed borderline. Either way, professional treatment of these individuals requires skilled diagnostics and therapy.

MPD

Multiple personality disorder (MPD) may also coexist with addiction. For more details refer to the Psychological problems module. When severe, this mental illness is likely to take priority over a person's recovery. Many MPDs who are chemically dependent end up in prison. This disorder should be treated by programs with highly trained professionals.

MEDICATION

Many hard-line AA members tell everyone they know that any use of a drug is relapse. This can cause problems for vulnerable, sensitive addicts who have dual diagnoses. Even Bill and Dr. Bob were aware of their limitations in the medical and psychiatric area, and they sought to work with doctors and psychiatrists for mutual understanding about alcoholism. The right answer for one addict can be the wrong solution for another.

Dual diagnosis, see also: Anorexia nervosa, Codependency, Core functions, Counseling, Disease concept, Employee assistance programs, Energy levels, Impaired professionals, Intervention, Progression, Psychological problems, Therapy & treatment.

E

Edema

Edema is an abnormal accumulation of water in the body. Generalized edema used to be called dropsy.

About three-fifths of normal body weight is water, and this water is constantly being exchanged between the blood and the tissues.

Water is forced into the tissues by the pressure of blood being pumped around the body. Thanks to the water-drawing power of the proteins in the blood, water is reabsorbed from the tissues to maintain a balance.

POSSIBLE CAUSES

Various disorders, including renal failure and cirrhosis of the liver, can interfere with the reabsorption of water and cause swelling. Certain drugs and insufficient protein in the diet can also cause edema.

Up to about 15 percent excess fluid will normally only increase weight. After that, edema will show itself as swelling, usually in the lower parts of the body, like the lower back and around the ankles.

STRATEGIES

If possible, remove the cause of the edema. Make sure your protein intake is adequate. Avoid salt. Drink more water—this will usually reduce salt in the body.

When to get medical help   If swelling is painful or long-lasting or unusual, get a medical opinion. Avoid taking diuretic drugs (water pills) unless directed by a physician.

123

Edema, see also: Allergies, Biochemistry, Constipation, Exercise & activity, Fats, Metabolism, Nutrition, Obesity, Physical aspects, Premenstrual syndrome, Purging, Sugar, Weight. Next on path B: Blackouts.

Emotional aspects

The basic PEMS model we use to look at addiction includes emotional aspects. These are all the things that affect your feelings and emotional state.

SOBRIETY OR ABSTINENCE

Physical sobriety or abstinence is a prerequisite for dealing with most emotional issues. Many people, even professionals, point to feelings as causing addiction. We think emotional factors affect addiction, not cause it. You may learn and grow emotionally while using, but somewhere you will probably get stuck until you abstain from the addictive substance or behavior.

IN ADDICTION

Emotions while addicted are tumultuous, erratic, often uncontrolled, and painful. Fear, loneliness, self-pity, anger, shame, and guilt are pervasive. You feel in bondage to them. Recovery frees you for joy, spontaneity, and freedom.

Since feelings are biochemical, they are affected by your physical state, such as fatigue, hormone problems, hunger, and stress. You won't always feel good in recovery, but if you are lucky, you will always be able to feel.

Emotional aspects, see also: Abuse, Anger, Body image, Craving, Crisis, Dual diagnosis, Emotions Anonymous, Energy levels, Family of origin, Fear, Feelings, Grief, Obsession, Panic attacks, Premenstrual syndrome, Pregnancy, Relaxation, Stress & strain, Tranquilizers. Next on path C: Feelings.

Emotions Anonymous (EA)

Most EA members suffer from anger, depression, grief, anxiety, phobias, low self-esteem, shame, or any other strong emotions. By using the fellowship and working the Steps and other tools of the Program, they develop the ability to detach from their problems. "Part of our serenity comes from being able to live at peace with unsolved problems." (*Emotions Anonymous*, 1978, p. 244.)

IDENTIFICATION

This branch of the Twelve-Step tree, applying the Twelve Steps to problems that do not directly involve addiction, has not reached as many people as the AA and Al-Anon style groups. EA is over twenty years old, and has about sixteen hundred groups worldwide. That is much larger than most self-help organizations, which usually have about five hundred groups or less. But it does not begin to compare to AA, with ninety thousand groups, or Al-Anon, with twenty-seven thousand groups. One reality is that once you leave a specific addiction orientation, there are many groups open to you. People who could benefit from EA may already be in almost any other Twelve-Step group.

TRY EA

For more information on EA check the white pages of your phone book, or call:

Emotions Anonymous
PO Box 4245
St. Paul, MN 55104
(612) 647-9712

Emotions Anonymous, see also: History of Twelve-Step groups, Meetings, Other support groups, Steps of AA, Traditions of AA.

Employee assistance programs (EAPs)

When chemical dependency treatment programs sprang up all over the United States in the last half of the 1970s, recovering alcoholics and other concerned people tried to bring the concepts of intervention and aftercare support into the workplace. The idea was to help employees get into treatment, and then to support their recovery afterward. The alcoholism contacts or the offices responsible became known as employee assistance programs (EAPs).

INTERNAL AND EXTERNAL EAPS

There are two major approaches to implementing an employee assistance program. One is for the EAP to be an office within the company, an internal EAP. Often this kind of EAP is attached to the medical or personnel department. Here the EAP usually works closely with other internal departments and with the worker's supervisors. The other major approach is to use an EAP service that is outside and relatively independent of the company. These EAPs have contracts to provide services to a number of companies.

TEAM APPROACH

The better employee assistance programs have a multidisciplinary team including certified employee assistance professionals to evaluate and refer the employees and their families to counseling or treatment. Most of these programs offer a "broad brush" service where they are prepared to deal with any problem that might affect an employee's job performance, from alcoholism and drug addiction to financial trouble, marital problems, and personality conflicts with supervisors or coworkers.

AFTERCARE

Many EAPs conduct aftercare group sessions, or refer their clients to counselors who have aftercare programs. The EAP idea has become a valuable employee benefit, and we hope the current environment of cost consciousness will not reduce the involvement of good EAP services.

Employee assistance programs, see also: Aftercare, Anorexia nervosa, Certification, Codependency, Core functions, Counseling, Dual diagnosis, Halfway house, Impaired professionals, Intervention, Professional organizations, Psychological problems, Therapy & treatment, Withdrawal.

Enabling

As addiction progresses it is likely that an afflicted person will experience more of the physical, emotional, mental, and spiritual symptoms and consequences of the disease. It has been observed for some years now that family members and friends can also become involved in the disease process, and one of the ways this happens is by something called enabling.

HELP PERSON, OR DISEASE?

In everyday language, to enable means to help, to assist, to support. Those who care about or love addicts attempt to help, but they inadvertently end up helping the disease rather than the person. This happens because of their own denial, confusion, or lack of understanding. They might cover up, ignore symptoms, and even develop a series of defenses and symptoms themselves.

CODEPENDENCY

The involvement of others in the addictive disease process is as old as addiction itself, but it got particular attention in the 1970s and 1980s when an emphasis on chemical dependency as a family illness became prevalent. There was much study and writing on how family members, who became known as codependents, were affected. This has even mushroomed into an industry of its own today (see the module on Codependency).

SELF-HELP

Enablers now have available information and support groups, such as Al-Anon and Co-Dependents Anonymous (CoDA), that can be helpful and powerful. There are also groups for families and friends that involve other addictions, like gambling, overeating, or sex and love addiction.

HOW TO STOP

To stop enabling requires a gentleness with yourself and an understanding that with addictive disease, you didn't cause it, you can't control it, and you can't cure it. You can get support from others, learn to focus on yourself, and learn to be self-loving and self-caring.

Enabling, see also: Abuse, Adolescents, Al-Anon & Alateen, Behavior, Children of addicts, Codependency, Control, Detachment, Disease concept, Family, Incest, Intimacy, Prevention of addiction, Relationships, Sabotage of recovery, Self-image, Survival roles.

Energy levels

Most addictive drugs and behaviors wind up elevating or depressing the mood. Many addicts become confused about whether they are chronically depressed, or why they do not seem as "up" as someone else.

NATURAL OR OPERANT LEVEL

We like using the term "energy level" to describe how people seem to have different amounts of energy at different times. Sometimes you feel like going out and tackling the adventure of life, and other times you may wish you could just stay in bed.

Different people have different average levels of energy, and different extremes, ranging from very depressed to extremely manic. There are lots of individual differences in these natural patterns.

DRUG EFFECTS

All kinds of drugs, whether external or internal in origin, affect the mood, but usually the body tries to adjust back to its natural balance.

Danger of adjustment   The danger is that a tolerance will develop, bringing the balance back to near normal, and that you will increase the dosage or become dependent on that drug.

When to adjust   Only if the natural level of energy is so depressed or so manic that normal living and recovery are impossible, should you try to adjust this level.

How to adjust   If you have a genuine abnormality in your energy level, you need to find a doctor who has some appreciation for the dynamics of addiction, and work with that doctor along with sponsors and others in the program to insure that you neither neglect nor overdo the medication.

SAD

Seasonal Affective Disorder (SAD) is a condition in which people experience significantly more depression in winter than in summer months. Treating this disorder can be as simple as increasing your exposure to indirect sunlight to a half hour or more per day in the winter months.

If this is impossible, any light that is several times brighter than normal room light will do—bright fluorescent light, for example. You do not need sunburn or eye strain to produce enough light to do the trick.

MODERATION IN RECOVERY

You may have to be satisfied with less dramatic highs to avoid terrible lows. Life is a dynamic balance, with large, medium, and small waves at various times in our lives, but usually changing.

Excitement

We suspect that one of the most common addictive processes is also the most ignored. It is the addiction to excitement, to the neurochemistry associated with arousal.

BIOCHEMISTRY

Think about a time when you were suddenly terrified, either purposely—as in a movie—or against your will. To your biochemistry, there is not much difference whether you were driving normally and someone pulled in front of you, or you were heading down the first steep plunge of the rollercoaster. Your mind recognizes the danger, real or imagined, and begins the biochemical reactions necessary for flight or fight. The surge in epinephrine (adrenaline) increases your pulse, your blood pressure, and puts your body on alert, within fractions of a second. Meanwhile the norepinephrine (NE) almost instantly clears your mind of any sad feelings, other preoccupations, or drowsiness.

REINFORCEMENT

If you swerve and miss the other car, or stomp on the brakes in time, within a few minutes other neurotransmitters will restore the balance and you will be back almost to the place you were before the near miss. But suppose, consciously or unconsciously, you liked the arousal state produced by all that excitement. You might find yourself gradually developing a tendency to drive fast, paying less attention to your driving, and getting into a dangerous driving situation several times a week.

Some people do just that. They may joke about being accident-prone. Or they may choose exciting or dangerous sports and hobbies and play them obsessively. Just a few examples are football, hockey, rugby, boxing, skydiving, skindiving, caving, cave diving, whitewater rafting, car or airplane racing, rollercoaster riding, surfboarding, and paint pellet war.

OTHER ADDICTIONS

These examples are probably similar to the biochemistry involved in compulsive gambling, compulsive spending, fierce competition, and frequent rage. And excitement plays at least some part in sex, love, romance, drug use, abuse, incest, violence, power trips, anorexia, and arguments.

TOLERANCE

If you are doing any of these things often, your body will sense the chemical imbalances. If there is an excess of norepinephrine, your body can shift the balance in any of several ways. The result is a tolerance to the excitement, and everyday life will seem really boring. You will need more excitement to reach the same highs.

WITHDRAWAL

Eventually, you have to stop the exciting activity, and you begin to go through withdrawal—a sense of depression, boredom, and lack of purpose. So it's off to get excited again, or try some cocaine, or maybe see a doctor about an antidepressant.

RECOVERY

If you are in a recovery program and you recognize excitement as a secondary addiction for you, there is a good chance you can simply broaden your use of the Twelve Steps to include your addiction to excitement. If you think excitement is your primary addiction, it will be hard to find a specific Twelve-Step program. You might even need to start one. See the Meetings module for some suggestions.

Excitement, see also: Addiction, Adolescents, Arousal, Binge history, Biochemistry, Celebrations, Drugs, Exercise & activity, Families Anonymous, Family, Moodifiers, Sex, Spending, Stress & strain. Next on path A: Gambling.

Exercise & activity

Anyone needs a fair amount of exercise to give the body a decent chance to feel good.

If you are getting little or no exercise, your body will adjust, efficiently, to what it assumes is your preparation for death. For all human history, until the last century or so, slowing down of physical activity meant getting ready to die, and that is how the body reacts: the metabolism slows down, the muscles atrophy, and life loses its zest.

HEALTHY EXERCISE

A healthy amount of exercise or physical activity tells the body that we are very much alive and part of life. Activity decreases depression and many negative feelings. For weight management, exercise alone is far more effective than diet alone.

CATEGORIES OF ACTIVITY

Catharine Stewart-Roache and Marvel Harrison (1989) have written a delightful book on physical fitness that can give you many helpful suggestions. They integrate emotional and spiritual factors into the ideas they present. They provide many helpful guidelines for developing your personal activity program. They give four categories of activities you might consider pursuing:

Flexibility   Flexibility exercises include activities like stretching and dance. These are relaxing, improve balance and posture, and help with back and joint difficulties.

Strengthening   Strengthening exercises are anaerobic (not aerobic). Lifting weights and calisthenics are examples. Pushing or pulling against resistance increases muscle tone, causing you to feel better. If you are out of shape, increasing muscle mass will also make weight management easier, because muscle tissue uses more energy than fat does.

Skill building   Sports, such as tennis, football, skiing, bowling, and other recreational activities, build skills. They help with coordination and balance, offer the opportunity to be sociable, and are fun!

Aerobic   Cycling, swimming, walking, running, and aerobic dance classes are important for developing a healthy heart and lungs. When your pulse increases and you breathe faster than usual, you are exercising your respiratory and circulatory system. Aerobic activities are continuous (not stop-and-start), have rhythm, use large muscle groups, and can be done by a healthy person for at least twenty minutes. They also burn more fat than other activities.

Exercise increases metabolism, allowing you to burn more carbohydrates and to feel better. Many recent studies suggest that this increase in metabolism persists for hours after the exercise is done.

EXERCISE AS ADDICTION

Unfortunately, even a good thing can be done to excess, and addicts are great at doing things to excess. The chemicals the brain manufactures during heavy exercise can become addictive. Professionals speculate that with the emphasis on looking robust and healthy, exercise addiction will become more common in the years ahead.

There are no recognized diagnostic criteria for exercise abuse. William Rader, MD, (in an article by Bill Dobbins, "Exercise Addicts," *Muscle and Fitness,* September 1988, pp. 110–12, 200–2) indicated some possible signs of exercise addiction:

- You exercise while injured or ill.
- Exercise comes ahead of family and friends.
- You exercise when it isn't fun anymore.
- You exercise even when you don't want to.

One of the authors recalls a friend who wouldn't take a job unless he could continue his triathlon training during work hours. He had withdrawals when he had knee surgery. He eventually lost a managerial job because of his exercising, and took a job in an athletic store.

When it is part of bulimia   When there is a clear attempt to lose weight or burn calories or fat through lots of exercise, there is a good chance of exercise addiction. This will often be combined with the "runner's high" kind of phenomenon, when endorphins (painkillers) are produced after about thirty minutes of rigorous exercise.

THE THERMIC EFFECT OF EXERCISE

Most approaches to weight loss include some form of exercise, to burn some (not too many) calories, and more important, to "stoke the metabolic furnace" and to improve physical and psychological health. Exercise is a key to long-term weight management.

WEIGHT GAIN

Some people actually gain weight when they exercise. Start-stop, largely anaerobic activities like calisthenics, some aerobic dance, racket sports, power lifting, and other sports that require sprinting burn about 60-70 percent carbohydrate and about 30-40 percent fat. So if in an hour of tennis you burn five hundred calories, about three hundred fifty of those will be carbohydrate and one hundred fifty from fat. If you are still eating a high-fat diet (about 40 percent of the calories from fat and 45 percent from carbohydrate), you will probably eat about three hundred ten fat calories with the three hundred fifty carbohydrate calories you eat to restore your previous glycogen level. You will have eaten one hundred sixty more calories of fat than you burned in the exercise!

With aerobic activity, on the other hand, if you walk briskly (four miles per hour) for an hour, you will burn 50-60 percent fat and 40-50 percent carbohydrate. If you expend four hundred calories, you will burn around two hundred forty fat calories and one hundred sixty carbohydrate calories. Replacing your glycogen, if you are on a low-fat diet of about 20 percent fat and 65 percent carbohydrate, you will consume only about sixty calories of fat with the one hundred sixty calories of carbohydrate.

Also, the more fit you become, the more fat you can burn, up to five times as much as when you start exercising. Continuous, aerobic activity, which does not leave you winded, is best, in a range of about thirty minutes to an hour. Anyone who needs to gain weight might try anaerobic exercise and increasing fats in the diet rather than trying to force down vast amounts of carbohydrate foods.

KEEPING A BALANCE

Something in the range of thirty minutes of vigorous exercise, or an hour of slightly less strenuous activity, is not too much. In general, a lifestyle that includes physical activity is preferable to an exercise regimen, but anything is better than either nothing or too much.

Start slow   If you have been fairly inactive physically, it is best to begin with something very light, like walking or swimming, and avoid the temptation to start out at an advanced level. If you are obese, middle-aged or older, or have any reason to question your health, you should see a physician before any significant change in your activity level. A very gradual increase is much better than an abrupt change, and it is more likely to last.

Other benefits   Finding an exercise or activity you enjoy and can do regularly can greatly enhance your recovery. It is great for stress and depression and contributes to your physical health and self-esteem. Activity is most beneficial if you can see it as adding play, fun, and even joy to your life.

Exercise & activity, see also: Addiction, Adolescents, Anorexia nervosa, Arousal, Bingeing, Biochemistry, Body image, Bulimia nervosa, Chronic pain, Diet mentality, Energy levels, Excitement, Hunger & appetite, Moodifiers, Nutrition, Obesity, Prevention of addiction, Purging, Relaxation, Sleep. Next on path A: Excitement.

F

Families Anonymous

Families Anonymous is a Twelve-Step group for people concerned about their children or others with drug abuse or behavioral problems. They admit they are powerless over drugs and other people's lives.

FA is patterned after Al-Anon and helps its members cope with family disruption. Most FA members are parents, but even teens are welcome if they are concerned about their reaction to a sibling's drug or behavioral problems. They have published a book called *Alternative to Enabling,* which describes the constructive use of tough love.

There are about five hundred groups worldwide, and meetings usually last one and a half to two hours. For information write or call:

Families Anonymous
PO Box 528
Van Nuys, CA 91408
1-800-736-9805

Families Anonymous, see also: Adolescents, Al-Anon & Alateen, Co-Dependents Anonymous, Enabling, History of Twelve-Step groups, Meetings, Other support groups, Steps of AA, Traditions of AA.

Family

RELATIONSHIPS

As you learn to use the principles of recovery, most of the Steps suggest that you look at relationships with others. Family members are certain to be included. The changes required for a spiritual awakening encourage taking a close look at how you developed habits, beliefs, and behaviors.

Healthy family   There have been many models to describe the characteristics of a healthy, functioning family. The following are some examples:

- Each person, big or little, is valued and nurtured for who they are.
- Appropriate, spontaneous feelings are affirmed, not discounted or prohibited.
- Independent thinking and awareness are encouraged.
- Rules are flexible, spoken, and negotiable.
- Love, care, and respect for each individual exists.
- Integrity, honesty, openness, and trust are valued and modeled.
- It is OK to make mistakes and learn.
- Blame and fault-finding are rare.
- Individual differences are acknowledged and encouraged.
- Values are modeled and taught that are conducive to the well-being of each person involved.

Ernest Kurtz   Ernest Kurtz, a noted alcoholism historian and author, says a dysfunctional family is where techniques to survive in your family interfere with your ability to survive in the world. The less you can relate to the characteristics of a healthy family, and the more Kurtz's description fits, the more likely you may need to work on family issues.

Kurtz also says that in your family is where you suffered your first wounds and it is the most appropriate place to experience forgiveness and healing. Part of the purpose of a family is to give you a feeling of belonging, of connectedness. If you can work through family issues with your family of origin, you are lucky. Many addicts have to process these issues in treatment groups, aftercare, Twelve-Step group meetings, or with therapists or friends. Present family members can either support or complicate this process.

Belonging   Many addicts turned to alcohol, other drugs, food, or other substances or behaviors in part because they never felt they belonged. These chemicals may originally have given the illusion of belonging, but eventually they only made the isolation worse.

After suffering the pain of addiction, many do feel at home in the rooms of Twelve-Step programs like AA, NA, and OA. Members often report that out of this sense of belonging, true healing begins.

ENMESHMENT

Much of the current work in families looks at enmeshment in relationships. If we look at the basic intergenerational tasks, we see that many people misunderstand them:

Parents' job   The parents' major job is to make themselves unnecessary. They must help their kids feel secure and give them a good set of tools for living their own lives. Then let them fly on their own. It has been said that parents should give their children roots and wings.

This is the message we see throughout the animal kingdom— parents care for young only long enough for the children to become independent. In some species, parents and children may remain part of the same "family," but as equals. Besides human beings, where do you see the parent-child relationship continuing into adulthood?

Kids' job   The kids' major job is to rebel. This rebellion may be in token ways, like wearing their hair in a certain way or getting their ears pierced. But if parents try to keep their children dependent on them, then the children will eventually have to rebel more violently.

Failing at these tasks produces an enmeshed, unhealthy family. Parents often try to make their children fill needs that should be filled by a spouse or peers, and kids delay establishing their unique personalities, often until the break must come violently or painfully. Unfortunately, sometimes it never happens, and you have a forty-year-old who is still financially and emotionally dependent on the parents.

Martyrdom   Parents who become martyrs for their children seldom think what they are modeling for their kids: don't grow up— it's no fun to be an adult. It is normal to want to give your children more than you had, but taking that to extremes robs them of self-respect. Ironically, they lose respect for you, too.

HEALING IN THE FAMILY

Few parents are perfect, or even close to it. Parents are almost by definition amateurs. Most have done the best they knew how. It has been suggested that the last stage of growing up is forgiving your parents, which you do for yourself, not them.

If you can find nothing positive about your family of origin, you may find it difficult to hope. Healing involves forgiveness, for others and for yourself, and paves the way for gratitude and joy.

THERAPY

Whenever you have family problems that don't seem to get better, it is a good idea to seek some professional help.

It is important to find a qualified family therapist who understands or at least tolerates addiction recovery in the family.

Family recovery   IF everyone in the family who is clearly addicted is recovering from those addictions, THEN the family itself can begin the recovery process. Like each individual, the family may need help to overcome its dysfunctions as a unit.

Family, see also: Abuse, Addiction, Adolescents, Al-Anon & Alateen, Amends, Behavior, Beliefs, Celebrations, Children of addicts, Codependency, Control, Defenses, Detachment, Enabling, Family of origin, Forgiveness, Humor & fun, Incest, Intervention, Intimacy, PEMS model, Prevention of addiction, Relationships, Responsibility, Sabotage of recovery, Self-image, Survival roles.

Family of origin

To look at your family of origin—the family into which you were born—it is interesting to draw a genogram, a family chart. Place the names of your parents, their parents, your siblings, yourself, and any relatives who were close enough that you considered them your immediate family. Then identify addiction (alcohol, drugs, food, work, excitement, sex, or others) in each member. Include codependency and children of addicts. Looking at the patterns of addiction in your family can help you understand how you got it.

DYSFUNCTIONAL

If your family of origin was abusive or dysfunctional, you may have work to do. John Bradshaw's ideas (1988) on toxic shame are about healing the pain of an abusive childhood. You may need to do that, dealing with all the shame, guilt, and anger, before moving on with your recovery.

CHANGES
Most addicts find positive and negative in their families of origin. You can use your Program to let go of what you don't need, change what you don't like, and be grateful for your gifts. For more information, see the module on Family.

INVENTORY
The module on the PEMS model can give you more ideas for looking at your family of origin. Your Fourth Step is a good time to do this. If needed, pursue any insights or problems further with reading, workshops, or counseling.

Family of origin, see also: Abuse, Adolescents, Al-Anon & Alateen, Amends, Children of addicts, Codependency, Control, Detachment, Emotional aspects, Enabling, Family, Incest, Intimacy, PEMS model, Relationships, Resentments, Sabotage of recovery, Self-image, Survival roles.

Fantasy

Imagination and myth are important parts of our identity as a species. As far as we know, we are the only species on earth capable of imagining our own death, and creating stories to try to make sense of it. We love to play with images, to make literary and artistic connections, and to create models to describe our world, and even alternate universes.

BIOCHEMISTRY
There is a biochemistry associated with imagination and fantasy. It probably involves the neurotransmitter dopamine (DA). Schizophrenics have either too much DA, or too many DA receptors. They may also have a deficiency of the enzyme dopamine B-hydroxylase. This would decrease the rate at which DA is converted into its next metabolite, which happens to be norepinephrine (NA).

HALLUCINOGENS
Those addicts whose drugs of choice are LSD, marijuana, or other hallucinogens use them to produce a fantasy state. But they

are not the only fantasy addicts. There are people who become addicted to television, books, role-playing games (like Dungeons and Dragons), movies, or video or computer games. Fantasy is a place that everybody visits. Those who take up residence are either psychotic or fantasy addicts.

RECOVERY

If your primary addiction is not hallucinogens but other fantasy not involving drugs, you will have to piece together your own recovery program. You are not likely to find a TV Anonymous meeting near you. If you use hallucinogenic drugs, you will probably find support at Narcotics Anonymous. If you just recognize that fantasy is part of your total addictive pattern, you can probably take it into account in your other Twelve-Step programs.

Fantasy, see also: Arousal, Control, Emotional aspects, Marijuana, Satiety.

Fats

It is important that you understand something about fat and fats if you are a food addict, because most food addicts are concerned with weight management. Because of the tendency to overdo anything, many other addicts should know about these substances so they can manage their weight without resorting to diets and gimmicks that might interfere with their recovery.

Fats and oils provide the body with its most concentrated form of energy. They are compounds of carbon and hydrogen with very little oxygen. Most consist of fatty acids combined with glycerol, an oily alcohol.

TRIGLYCERIDES

The fats called triglycerides are the main form of structural fat in the body. They are composed of glycerol with three fatty acids. The three fatty acids may be of different types; for example, saturated, monounsaturated, or polyunsaturated.

FATS VS. OILS

The only difference between a fat and an oil is consistency. Oils are liquid at room temperature, and fats are solid or semisolid. The more saturated a fat is, and the longer the carbon chains, the harder it will be. The word "fat" is often used to include both fats and oils.

CHOLESTEROL

While cholesterol, a kind of fat, has had bad press lately, it is necessary in the body for a variety of functions, including being converted into hormones or vitamins. It is only an excess of cholesterol that is a problem, and while there is a controversy about the role of dietary cholesterol in the development of circulatory diseases, most authorities agree that people should avoid too many high cholesterol food sources, like whole eggs and foods high in saturated fats.

SATURATED FATS

If the fatty acids contain as much hydrogen as possible, they are called saturated fats. These are usually solid at room temperature. Animal fats are usually high in saturated fats, but some vegetable sources, like coconut and palm oils, are also very high. They are liquid because they have short carbon chains. Saturated fats tend to raise cholesterol levels, presenting a danger to the cardiovascular system.

LOW-DENSITY LIPOPROTEINS (LDLS)

Since fats (lipids) are not water soluble, they are carried around the bloodstream in little packages, encased in protein, called lipoproteins. Saturated fats tend to produce low-density lipoproteins (LDLs), which carry large amounts of cholesterol to the cells. If these are excessive, fat may be deposited on the linings of blood vessels, causing atherosclerosis.

POLYUNSATURATED FATS

If there are multiple double-bonds between carbon atoms, leaving several vacant sites on the carbon atoms remaining for hydrogen, that fatty acid molecule is called polyunsaturated. These fats are liquid at room temperature. Vegetable oils usually contain a high proportion of polyunsaturated fats.

MONOUNSATURATED FATS

Fats that still have a single double-bond between two carbon atoms, leaving only one "hole" where otherwise two hydrogen atoms would attach, are called monounsaturated. Found in a high concentration in certain vegetables like olives and peanuts, these oils are thought to lower cholesterol in the blood. This health benefit occurs only if they *replace* saturated fats in the diet.

HIGH-DENSITY LIPOPROTEINS (HDLS)

High-density lipoproteins (HDLs) have a higher percentage of protein, and a lower percentage of fat. Their function is to pick up cholesterol from the tissues around the body, and carry it back to the liver where it is then processed and turned into bile, or excreted. Thus the higher the ratio of HDLs to LDLs in your body, the lower is your risk of heart attack.

HOW BAD IS FAT?

From a nutritional point of view, most Americans should be eating less total fat. Since almost all food addicts, and many other addicts, are concerned about weight management, those who are obese should be limiting fats to about 20 to 40 grams a day, those who are near normal weight should still be using a food plan fairly low in fats, and those who are underweight should be eating more fats to gradually approach a healthy weight.

PREFERENCE FOR FAT

One reason you may prefer foods that are high in fat has to do with flavor. Most flavors and aromatic substances in foods are fat soluble, rather than water soluble. Some vitamins are also. It is fairly easy for the food industry to put back the vitamins that are removed with the fat (nonfat milk is "fortified" with vitamins A and D), but the flavor is a different story. The key is to avoid the diet mentality of eliminating all fats, while also developing the ability to enjoy the more subtle tastes of lower fat foods.

CARBOHYDRATE–FAT CONNECTION

Although it has not yet been scientifically studied, we see a strong connection between carbohydrates and fats in food addiction. If we look at binge foods, sweet fats are most common, probably followed by salty fats. Bingeing on sugar alone is not rare, but certainly not nearly as common as bingeing on sweet or salty fats.

THE T-FACTOR

Martin Katahn, author of *The T-Factor* (1989), has helped make people aware of the influence of dietary fat and the dynamics of conversion of fat into energy (thermogenesis, or the "T-factor"). Much of the following information is discussed at length in that book.

Lost energy (calories)   It takes energy for the body to convert one kind of fuel to another. If we eat more fat than we burn, it takes only about 3 percent of the energy in the fat to store it as fat in our bodies. When we eat excess carbohydrates, however, the body must expend about 25 percent of the carbohydrate's energy just to convert it to fat. This means that about a quarter of any excess carbohydrate is lost, even if the body decides to convert it to fat.

Conversion resistance   However, it seems that the body resists converting carbohydrate to fat. It will do everything it can to store carbohydrates (sugars and starches) as glycogen in the liver and muscles, rather than convert them to fat. In fact, under normal circumstances only about 4 percent of your daily intake of carbohydrates is converted to fat. When research subjects ate a whopping 2,000 calories of carbohydrates in a single meal, only 81 of those calories were converted to fat!

Carbohydrates are not very fattening   If you are intent on gaining weight by eating carbohydrates, you would have to overeat by hundreds or even thousands of calories every day for many days. According to the T-Factor theory, gaining weight by an excess of carbohydrates would require an unusual eating pattern, even for someone with an eating disorder.

Glycogen storage   Most of the carbohydrate we eat is converted to glycogen, for short-term storage of energy. About 400 calories can be stored in the liver, and another 1,200 to 1,600 can be stored in muscle tissue. This amount can be increased by regular exercise. The glycogen is stored in a solution with water, about a pound of water for each 500 calories.

Quick-loss diets   This is the secret of many quick-loss miracle diets; if you severely restrict carbohydrates, you can lose three or four pounds very rapidly, just by depleting your glycogen and its associated water. It will, of course, come back just as rapidly when you eat again. And you will experience the symptoms of low blood sugar: hunger, weakness, etc.

Storage ratios   Fat is stored in a ratio of four parts fat to one part water, almost the opposite of the ratio of carbohydrate to water. So it takes a fat restriction of 3,500 calories to lose a pound (of 80 percent fat, 20 percent water), compared with a restriction of only 500 calories of carbohydrates to lose a pound (of 70 percent water, 30 percent glycogen).

Water weight loss   You can lose only three or four pounds from carbohydrate restriction, and several more from dehydration, and these are unhealthy and illusory. After the first week or two of rapid weight loss, you have depleted the glycogen stores and your weight loss will slow to about a seventh of what it was. The discouragement many feel is only matched by the amazement with how fast it is regained.

Fat intake is key   What all this means is simply that the amount of carbohydrate and protein you eat makes much less difference in your weight management compared with the fats you eat. Whether you need to lose, gain, or maintain weight, the trick is in adjusting your fat intake, not total calories.

ADAPTIVE THERMOGENESIS

Adaptive thermogenesis is the idea that the body can adapt to either conserve or waste a certain amount of energy, depending on the circumstances.

Weight cycling   Much has been written lately about the way we "train" our bodies to conserve fat, by alternating between rapid gain and rapid loss of weight. Something in that process signals the body that we are in a famine situation and we must store all we can while we're eating and conserve all we can when the food supply dries up.

Metabolic reduction   With fasting or a low-calorie formula diet, there is an average metabolic reduction of about 25 percent, and it can approach 40 percent. This means that your body is burning less fuel than normal, trying to conserve energy. Many people may not return to normal metabolism for a long time after the diet is over.

Rebound effect   Also, after several weeks on a low-calorie diet, there is a rebound effect that increases the fat-incorporating enzyme, adipose tissue lipoprotein lipase. This enzyme controls the rate at which fat enters your fat cells, and it may be elevated 300 to 400 percent above normal after you start eating again. Katahn says, "It's as though the fat is being sucked right out of the bloodstream and soaked up by your fat cells." This may continue for a year after the diet, and may stop only after you have regained all your weight.

Set point theory   The ability of your body to adapt to different food patterns is probably a key to understanding, and getting around, the concept of set point. While there are definite genetic factors in predisposition toward body shape and preferences for fatty foods, you can change the odds simply by changing the proportion of fat in your diet.

Exercise benefit   You can increase your preference for high-carbohydrate, low-fat foods by beginning a program of regular exercise and other physical activity. This will deplete glycogen below the levels of most sedentary people, and call for carbohydrate rather than fat.

Fat gram counters   We recommend that you get some kind of guide that shows the grams of fat in each food. This should NOT be used to "count grams" for each meal, as many food addicts used to count calories. But spot checks will help you learn how to keep fats within the desired range. If you need to lose weight, fat intake should be about 20-40 grams a day for women and 30-60 grams a day for men.

Not overdoing it   For food addicts or those who have a problem with food, remember that diet mentality is an enemy of recovery. Avoid the temptation to eliminate all possible fats from your food plan. Anorexia nervosa is a lousy alternative to bulimia or obesity.

Fats, see also: Binge history, Craving, Diet mentality, Exercise & activity, Feelings, Food addiction, Food plan, Metabolism, Moodifiers, Nutrition, Stinking thinking, Sweeteners.

Fear

Fear is a familiar feeling for most addicts. Although it may be covered by a wall of defenses, it is always there. The Big Book (p. 62) states that alcoholics suffer from a hundred forms of fear.

It is no surprise that addicts are fearful in the face of self-destructive behavior they are unable to control. Delusion and denial often prevent the fear from surfacing. If it does, addictive behavior can assuage it, or it may come out as anger.

In *Twelve Steps and Twelve Traditions* (p. 49) Bill suggests that the debilitating fear alcoholics (addicts) experience is a soul-sickness from instincts gone wild. There is fear that excessive ambition, lust, and power needs will not be satisfied. In recovery these fears are replaced by a different set of values and a spiritual life. Losing the fear of people and of economic insecurity is one of the promises of the program.

Abstinence and the use of Steps Two and Three can help eliminate the fear from the addiction itself. Steps Four through Nine help with other fears related to addiction. Then addicts have to face fears like everyone else.

NATURAL FEAR
Fear is a biochemical event to warn you of danger and prepare you for flight or fight. It is a basic survival response. Since flight or

fight is not usually an option to dissipate the energy associated with fears these days, anxiety results. Much of this anxiety involves the fear of losing love, control, or self-esteem.

When you live life on a spiritual basis you learn tools to free you from anxiety and debilitating fear. You will continue to experience fear, but with faith and living in concord with what you believe is the will of your Higher Power, you can have the freedom and joy you deserve.

PTSD

Abuse can traumatize a child and carry over into adulthood. Fear, anger, lack of trust, and withdrawal from people or attempts to control them may have been ways to deal with the abuse. Survivors may experience posttraumatic stress disorder (PTSD). This often includes sleep disturbances, nightmares, overalertness, difficulty concentrating, numbed emotions, and underlying terror. If this is your experience, please get counseling or treatment, and join a specialized support group to help you deal with your past. There you can experience the love and healing you need to continue with your recovery.

EXTREMES

There are extremes of fear that are characteristic of mental illness or serious psychological problems. Paranoid schizophrenia and chronic anxiety states are examples that require professional help.

Fear, see also: Abuse, Anger, Codependency, Crisis, Emotional aspects, Emotions Anonymous, Excitement, Family of origin, Feelings, Neurotransmitters, Obsession, Panic attacks, Self-image, Serenity, Sleep, Stress & strain, Tranquilizers, Trust, Visualizations. Next on path C: Anger.

Feelings

• Feelings are predictable and easily understood.

That statement may be hard to believe for someone who has learned to deny feelings, suffered rollercoaster tumultuous feelings, or has thought feelings were mysterious and enigmatic. Many things you read or hear about emotions tend to be philosophical or poetic instead of therapeutic and practical, and they may leave you confused or mystified.

BELIEFS ABOUT FEELINGS

Until a few hundred years ago, the human body was shrouded in mystery. Even the best scientists had little idea of the function of bodily organs. Our feelings-language developed when medical research on the human body might result in imprisonment or execution. People interpreted their feelings through their superficial knowledge of their bodies. They began to think that fear comes from the gut, because that is where you feel somatic reactions to your fear. Love comes from the heart. Why not—touching your left upper abdomen feels warm and the rhythmic thump elicits memories of being cared for, possibly even while still in the womb. Being "in your head" is less emotional, because you are farther from the visceral sensations that accompany most feelings.

FEELINGS PHRASES

Phrases like "dealing with your feelings," "getting in touch with your feelings," and "stuffing your feelings" are common in treatment programs and therapy situations designed to help addicts recover. We find that many people hear these phrases and acknowledge them because they "sound right," without understanding what they mean.

"Deal with your feelings" and "get in touch with your feelings" mean to identify and communicate the emotions you are experiencing. "Stuff your feelings" means to block the memory associated with the feeling and to avoid the thoughts and expression of that feeling. There is no organ in the body where feelings are known to be stored—all feelings are here-and-now, although they may be in response to stored memories.

BASIC DRIVES

Feelings or emotions are biochemical messengers that tell us we should consider doing something. They evolved as chemical bodily processes to get our attention. Originally these signals occurred as a suggestion to act on basic drives, such as fight, flight, feed, or flirt. Simple emotions like anger or hunger were directly linked to behavior that enhanced survival of the species.

A helpful model for understanding feeling is the triune brain (Sagan, 1977). The human brain evolved over millions of years. The oldest part is the R-complex, which is about all the brain a reptile has. This complex supports the basic drives for survival: fight, flight, flirt, and feed. This pretty well covers an alligator's needs.

LIMBIC SYSTEM

Later, when we became mammals (milk drinkers), the mother had to care for her babies or they would die. This limbic system is the seat of our higher-level emotions and feelings.

NEOCORTEX

Most recently, we developed a large neocortex, which is used to think, reason, and organize thoughts into ideas or models and language.

This helps explain why you may hate someone (R-complex), yet care for them (limbic system), and intellectually believe both feelings are unreasonable (neocortex).

FEELINGS & BEHAVIOR

The problem is that our civilization and technology have advanced more rapidly than our bodily chemistry, and it is no longer always necessary or even advantageous to link our feelings with a behavior. Sometimes we need to behave contrary to our feelings. For example, if you feel angry with your boss, it is certainly not appropriate to hit her or him, and it may not even be wise to express your anger at that time.

EMOTIONAL HEALTH

What does it mean to be emotionally healthy? Human beings are born with a natural capacity for spontaneity, the ability to have and express a wide range of feelings in response to events occurring in life.

Most children, if nurtured properly, have no difficulty with this skill. Watch a small child, before it has been taught that once you have a feeling, you ought to hang on to it for a long time. Children naturally laugh when happy, cry when sad or hurt, and are angry when frustrated, sometimes all within a few minutes. These feelings do not last long if no one interferes.

FAMILY HISTORY

In many families, however, this natural expression may be stifled by authority figures. A child learns that the expression of all or certain feelings may incur disapproval. The child learns to substitute another feeling for the natural one. Each family may have certain feelings that are discounted or prohibited, while others are encouraged or rewarded. For example, you may have gotten the message that anger was not allowed in your family, but it was fine to be sad. Or you might have been taught that anger was OK but you should not show any signs of weakness. These messages may be direct, or your parents or others may have modeled them for you.

SETUP FOR ADDICTION

As you matured you may then have used a lot of energy to avoid the expression of the natural feeling. When you continue this behavior for many years, you may feel as if you have a knot in your stomach. This is a perfect scenario to set you up for the relief that some kind of mood-altering drug or behavior will provide. It is not surprising that many addicts use feelings as an excuse to drink, use, gamble, spend, binge, purge, or starve.

LINK WITH ADDICTION

Addiction takes all kinds of feelings and uses them as excuses for addictive behavior. It gets much mileage out of confusion over feelings. We hear people saying, "I used to drink over that," or "It's what's eating you rather than what you're eating," and we suspect they are buying into the addiction's excuse system.

The human body can produce real, honest-to-goodness pain to get drugs. We see this often in drug addicts who have chronic pain. If the body can produce pain to get drugs, why not *other* feelings to use as an excuse for addictive behavior?

COMPULSION

A compulsion is an obsession that produces impulses to do something, like binge. If you do not act on that impulse you will feel anxiety. This is, of course, part of the emotional aspect of the disease. But if you *do* act on the impulse, you will feel guilt or other emotions. The addiction says, "Since you are craving it, you have to drink, use, eat, or do it." Recovery simply answers, "Whatever happens, you do not have to binge. Your choice is either to talk about that craving and get some relief, or to 'grin and bear it,' and let it pass. Either way, your Higher Power can help you through it if you will let Him/Her/It."

NO DIRECT LINK

The addict tries to create a direct link between the impulse and the binge. There is no such direct link. You can insert your better judgment (augmented by your recovery) and your Higher Power between the compulsion and the binge.

HALT

AA has recommended for years that you do not get too *h*ungry, too *a*ngry, too *l*onely, or *t*ired. This is a simple acknowledgment of the power of feelings to work for or against your recovery.

IDEAS FOR RECOVERY

Here are some simple ideas for emotional health. Remember the triune brain when considering these ideas.

- Feelings are not right or wrong, they just are.
- Specific feelings are natural to certain perceptions.
- You need not be controlled by your feelings.
- Communicate feelings for healthy relationships.

Not right or wrong   A feeling is a natural biochemical response to an event, a thought, a memory, or even other bodily processes. Feelings are not right or wrong, good or bad. Of course, there are feelings that we perceive as pleasurable and others as uncomfortable. If someone discounted or disapproved of your feelings, you probably placed a value judgment on that feeling.

Feelings & perceptions   For every perception, whether of an external event, a memory, or biochemical changes within your body, there are specific emotions that are triggered. If you remember a time when you were hurt, you will probably feel the same kind of hurt that you experienced at the time, although perhaps not as intensely. If that perception is strong enough, your body may also release adrenaline or other neurotransmitters that prepare your body for flight or fight. So you experience anger in the here-and-now in response to an old memory.

Also, if your hormones are out of balance through PMS or pregnancy, you may experience feelings that seem to have no cause. If you look around, you can always find something going on in your present world that could have triggered that feeling, so then your perceptions begin to strengthen the feelings, and you become convinced that your feelings, even happy feelings, are caused by somebody or something in your present life.

The point is that your feelings may or may not be related to something that is going on right now, but they are always related to your perception of your entire world, past, present, and your expectations of the future. It may help to identify the target or targets of your feelings, with the understanding that it is easy to misdirect those emotions, and to over- or underrate the significance of them. In any case, they will change soon if you don't invest energy into hanging on to them.

Feelings need not control you   Resentment is a feeling (the refeeling of an anger associated with a hurt or loss) that can consume a person and make life miserable. Other negative feelings, like fear, guilt, or self-pity, can do the same. Your feelings are associated with your thoughts and perceptions, and it is possible to replace negative thoughts or perceptions with positive ones.

Addiction thrives on negative feelings, and many addicts think that they drink, use, binge, purge, or starve because of them. This is usually an excuse, because you can have negative feelings and not act on them if you have a Higher Power. It is, however, reasonable to say that your recovery will not provide much joy or serenity if negative feelings predominate.

So what can you do? Change your thinking and perceptions! You do not need to deny your feelings, but when you are suffering feelings related to negative thoughts, ask yourself, "Will this kind of thinking be worthwhile to me or to anyone else? Is this thinking inspiring, encouraging, or beneficial to anyone?" How else could you perceive the same situation? Is the glass half empty or half full? You can use affirmations, inspirational readings, and gratitude lists to help you.

To dwell in guilt about the past or fear about the future will prevent you from appreciating the gifts recovery has to offer you today. Today you have a choice.

Communicate feelings   Being aware of what you are feeling helps you to live spontaneously. This awareness also allows you to examine your thoughts and perceptions and to change them if necessary. At times you may need to experience your hurt, anger, or sadness so you can move on to the positive feelings of life, like gratitude, love, hope, and joy. Once you have learned to be aware of what you are feeling, you can tell this to someone else and enhance relationships and intimacy.

You might have picked up the idea that when someone loves you, that person should be able to guess what is going on with you and what you need. This idea will almost guarantee that you will be unsatisfied with the important relationships in your life. If you take the risk to share what you think and feel, you will alleviate the loneliness and isolation of active addiction.

If you share an uncomfortable feeling, it may not go away, but it will lose its power to control you. It will tend to become less intense each time you talk about the event or circumstance that may be associated with the feeling. You might communicate it at a meeting, with friends, or with family members. Communication of feelings is essential to the honesty and openness required for an intimate relationship.

Feelings, see also: Abuse, Anger, Body image, Craving, Defenses, Emotional aspects, Emotions Anonymous, Energy levels, Excitement, Fear, Gratitude, Grief, Guilt & shame, Habit & structure, Humor & fun, Hunger & appetite, Incest, Intimacy, Love & caring, Obsession, Panic attacks, Premenstrual syndrome, Pregnancy, Relaxation, Serenity, Stress & strain, Tranquilizers, Trust. Next on path C: Fear.

Fetal alcohol syndrome

Alcohol and many other mood-altering, mind-bending substances cross the placenta easily, so the unborn child uses anytime the mother does. More has been written about alcohol's effect on the fetus than about other drugs, so we will begin by considering alcohol only.

Fetal alcohol syndrome (FAS) can cause:

- Retarded growth before and after birth
- Impaired brain and nerves
- Mental retardation
- Poor coordination
- Hyperactivity
- Face and skull abnormalities
- Birth defects
- Spontaneous abortion

About one in seven hundred fifty babies are born with clear symptoms of FAS, but about one in seventy-five have some effects from the alcohol consumed during pregnancy.

HOW MUCH ALCOHOL?

How much alcohol does it take to cause FAS? There are no clear answers to that question. When alcohol crosses the placenta, the blood-alcohol level of the fetus rises until it matches the mother's. This may not seem to be a problem if the mother does not get drunk, but remember that the fetus is much smaller and its detoxification system is not well developed. Because of this the blood-alcohol levels drop more slowly in the fetus and alcohol can be detected in the fetus after it has disappeared from maternal blood.

FATHER'S PART

There is also evidence from animal studies that drinking by the father before conception can affect birth weight, learning ability, and other factors. It is not yet known whether and how much this may contribute to FAS.

NO ALCOHOL

The Surgeon General has said that pregnant women should drink absolutely no alcohol, and the editors of the *Journal of the American Medical Association* have said that women should stop drinking as soon as they plan to become pregnant. Most documented cases of FAS show that mothers drank an average of five or more drinks a day throughout their pregnancy. Even those physicians who do not advise total abstinence during pregnancy suggest no more than two drinks a day.

Powerlessness   There is an irony here. Nonalcoholic women have no difficulty giving up alcohol throughout their pregnancy, because FAS is the one birth defect that is totally preventable. But alcoholic women may be unable to stop, and for them their guilt and shame about drinking during pregnancy may add to their pain. The addiction will, of course, use this pain as an excuse to drink. That's why alcoholics need a First Step.

OTHER DRUGS

Other drugs also affect the fetus. Cocaine babies are common enough in many parts of the United States that there is a crisis in the availability of critical care neonatal units to deal with them. Caffeine intake of two or more cups of coffee a day has been linked to increased risk of spontaneous abortion. Tobacco use during pregnancy stunts fetal growth, increasing risk of retarded development, low birth weight, and other birth complications. One study showed smoking during pregnancy doubles the risk of cancer and leukemia in children.

DIETING

Even dieting during pregnancy is hazardous. Low-carbohydrate diets or fasts that cause ketosis deprive the fetal brain of glucose needed for proper development. Such diets may also prevent proper nutrition of the fetus.

FREEDOM FROM GUILT

If you feel guilty for drinking, smoking, starving, or using during a past pregnancy, look to Steps Eight and Nine and the love of your Higher Power for forgiveness. If you are thinking of a present or future pregnancy, go directly to Step One, and the available Twelve-Step fellowships, and treatment, if necessary, to help save two or more lives.

Fetal alcohol syndrome, see also: Addiction, Alcohol, Alcoholism, Physical aspects, Responsibility, Unmanageability, Withdrawal. Next on path B: Flashbacks.

Flashbacks

People who have taken hallucinogens, especially stronger ones like LSD, often have flashbacks—brief recurrences of psychedelic symptoms that include visual images, "spaced-out" feelings, or other similarities to the hallucinogenic experience. It is entirely possible that even normal people have occasional little episodes like this, where memories or emotions suddenly appear from somewhere in the brain. A common occurrence is the *déjà vu* experience, where you feel strongly that you have lived this experience before, and can *almost* predict what is going to happen next.

PSYCHEDELICS
How powerful hallucinogens like LSD work is still mostly unknown. LSD (lysergic acid diethylamide) is related to other psychedelics, including DMT (dimethyltryptamine) and psilocybin (4-phosphoryl-DMT). They affect serotonin (5-HT) and dopamine (DA) receptor sites in specialized parts of the brain. LSD somehow triggers an unusual response, opening some kind of floodgate for DA activity. It is possible that the psychedelic drug enables this floodgate to open in response to more normal neurochemistry, and that is perceived as a flashback.

FREE RIDE
Counselors who have treated many hallucinogen addicts or abusers have reported that most flashbacks in people who have no history of psychiatric problems are brief, not necessarily frightening, and can be turned off if necessary. Some LSD "freaks" welcome them, as a free ride. There are flashbacks that are bad trips, but they seem to occur mostly in people who are not too mentally stable.

DON'T PANIC
Since flashbacks seem to involve runaway DA activity, the most important thing to do with a flashback is to avoid panic. Intense fear

would only increase the available DA and reinforce the process. It would also give you a bad attitude or "set" for the experience, further insuring a bad trip. If you recognize it as harmless, it probably will be.

SUPPORT

Support, understanding, and helpful experience can be found in any of the Twelve-Step groups that deal with drugs other than alcohol. Narcotics Anonymous is the one prevalent group.

Flashbacks, see also: Addiction, Alcohol, Alcoholism, Biochemistry, Blackouts, Narcotics Anonymous, Panic attacks, Physical aspects, Withdrawal. Next on path B: Panic attacks.

Food addiction

What causes bulimia, anorexia, or obesity? Specialists in the eating disorders field agree that social, genetic, psychological, and biological factors all play a part. Many psychiatrists, psychologists, and social workers contend that eating disorders have nothing to do with addiction. We have found that many people with eating problems respond well to an addiction model when it is applied using a physical, emotional, mental, and spiritual (PEMS) approach.

UNIFIED THEORY

John Lovern, a psychologist who works with eating disorders, has developed what he calls a Unified Eating Disorders Theory. In it he describes all eating disorders as cyclical. The graph on page 155 can represent any eating disorder, which he calls food addiction.

According to the Unified Theory of Eating Disorders, any variety of eating disorder has periods of overeating and periods of undereating. What distinguishes them is the duration of the cycle—hours, days, weeks, or months, and relative intensity of the bingeing or restricting. For bulimics, the binge-purge cycle may occur many times a day or only a couple of times a week. In obesity months of overeating may alternate with months of restrictive dieting (undereating). In anorexia, weeks of restriction may be broken by brief binges (and usually purges), although what anorexics consider a binge, their family may celebrate as their first normal meal in a long time.

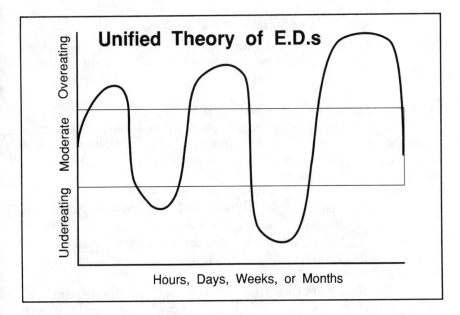

Food addiction means addiction to the biochemical imbalances that result from bingeing, food sensitivities, purging, starving, etc.

There are many foods that seem to do no harm in small or moderate quantities, but invite a spiral of binges or excess eating when large quantities are eaten. For some food addicts, it seems to matter very little what they eat, as long as they eat a lot of it. Some people do binge on salad items, and it is possible that a full stomach may cause release of some neurotransmitters that affect mood.

STARVING

Starving (fasting) or very low calorie diets cause biochemical changes that resemble stimulants. Excessive amounts of these neurochemicals seem addicting, especially to those with addictive tendencies.

PURGING

Vomiting, laxative abuse, excessive exercise, and other purging techniques all produce biochemical reactions in addition to the above, which may be part of the physical addiction.

PHYSICAL ASPECTS

The physical aspects include your behavior (what you actually eat and do), and all the biochemistry associated with food and eating, bingeing, purging, and starving.

EMOTIONAL ASPECTS

The emotional aspects include your feelings or mood responses to food and to the conditions surrounding your eating and your addiction.

MENTAL ASPECTS

The mental aspects include all your obsession and mental mismanagement as you try to maintain the illusion that you are in control of your eating, or are just about to regain control.

SPIRITUAL ASPECTS

The spiritual aspects include your isolation from God (or your Higher Power) and other people, including your family. They also include the characterological conflict as you find yourself behaving in self-centered ways that are at odds with your own values, beliefs, and ethics.

In rollercoaster dieting the variations are similar to those of dietary chaos, but over a much longer period. There are cycles of overeating, alternating with periods of dieting or undereating.

STYLES

We identify five styles of food addiction—anorexia, bulimia, dietary chaos, rollercoaster dieting, and obesity. This is just another model, so food addicts may relate to more than one style. We often find people who have experienced all five during the course of their food addiction.

Anorexia   Food addicts who are addicted to starving may fit the psychiatric diagnosis anorexia nervosa. Their eating pattern is primarily fasting or restricting, with extreme distortion of body image. Most anorexics also binge and purge. Abstinence for anorexics includes abstinence from starving. For more on anorexia, see the module Anorexia nervosa.

Bulimia   The most prominent feature of bulimia nervosa is the binge and purge. Purging may include vomiting, laxatives, fasting, or exercise. Feelings of loss of control, fear of fat, and distorted body image distinguish the bulimic style. For further information, see the module Bulimia nervosa.

Dietary chaos   What we call dietary chaos is a pattern of eating and attempts to control food and weight. It makes food addicts feel crazy. You may use lots of fad diets and do crazy things to control food intake or weight to give the illusion of control. Dietary chaos may have elements of bulimic behavior, like eating a diet meal followed by a pint of ice cream followed by more dieting to compensate. It spans the gap between rollercoaster dieting and bulimia.

In this style of food addiction, there is a craziness that comes with the obsession with eating or not eating. It can be identified by the amount of energy spent focused on food, weight, diet, and appearance. With dietary chaos, healthy relationships are difficult because of the obsession, insane thinking and behavior. It adversely affects significant others.

Some other mental illnesses, like schizophrenia, can look like dietary chaos, but in these there are usually bizarre thinking patterns not directly related to the food, weight, or body image.

Giving up the illusion of control is especially important with dietary chaos. Abstinence based on a rigid food plan will make "recovery" look a lot like the disease, only with a shift in obsession from food to food plan.

Rollercoaster dieting   Rollercoaster dieting is our term for a style of food addiction that is probably the most common. It consists of weight cycling, with periods of bingeing or other compulsive overeating, followed by attempts to diet or cut back. Many call it the "yo-yo syndrome." Even if you do not consider yourself a food addict, you may be able to relate to this pattern with your weight.

With rollercoaster dieting, the variations in eating (and then in weight) will be substantial. You may be down to 130 pounds, then up to 180, then back down to 140, within a calendar year. If you average your weight over several years, however, there is usually a "creep" up the scale. Each time you diet, and then gain weight, you are teaching your body how to better conserve fat as you are trying to diet, and then how to put it back on faster when you go off your diet.

The physical dangers increase with the difference between the high and low weights, and the frequency of cycling. For rollercoaster dieting, there is probably more harm to your body than if you just stayed at your maximum weight.

Of course, the driving fear is that you will NOT stay at any upper limit, but will continue to increase. In fact, that is what usually happens, so the weight fluctuations tend to be like going backward up a rollercoaster, with each maximum being a little higher.

Since this is the most familiar form of food addiction, the needs are those common to all food addiction: to stop the dieting mentality and focus on abstinence from compulsive eating. Weight management is a secondary issue, with emphasis on adjusting fat intake and getting adequate carbohydrates to support a reasonable amount of exercise or other physical activity.

At times, the rollercoaster dieter will experience many of the characteristics and difficulties we describe in the module on Obesity, while at other times their lives may resemble those of the dietary chaos style.

Obesity   Many food addicts gain excess weight from their overeating. Some have never seriously tried to control it, but most have tried dozens of diets, gimmicks, spas, and weight loss programs. The module Obesity explains many of the issues involved with this disorder.

OA

Most food addicts will find support and hope in Overeaters Anonymous (OA). There are other support groups that address eating disorders, some using the Twelve Steps and others who don't, but none are nearly as large and universally available as OA. See the module Overeaters Anonymous.

Food addiction, see also: Addiction, Alcoholism, Anorexia nervosa, Binge history, Bingeing, Biochemistry, Blackouts, Bulimia nervosa, Craving, Diet mentality, Exercise & activity, Food plans, Hunger & appetite, Moodifiers, Nutrition, Obesity, Purging, Weight. Next on path A: Anorexia nervosa.

Food plans

Issues around food plans are the most controversial aspect of eating disorders. Approaches range from seeing diets and food plans as the major *cause* of eating disorders to saying that no one is in recovery unless they are following a rigid food plan. Even addicts who do not recognize an addiction to food struggle with diets or food plans.

EVERYBODY HAS ONE

We maintain that everyone has a food plan. It is how people decide when, what, and how much to eat. A food addict who is bingeing may be using a food plan that says, "I'll eat everything I want to eat anytime I want it." So not every food plan is healthy.

Reasonable vs. unreasonable   Essentially, a food plan that works is probably reasonable, and one that doesn't may be pretty unreasonable. We will talk generally about food plans, and then make some suggestions about the goal of any food plan, which is to help you eat moderate meals.

Degree of structure   How much structure do you need? You may find that you like some definite guidelines about your meals, or you may be able to eat moderate meals by guessing and asking your Higher Power to help. Your particular compromise may fall anywhere between a very rigid food plan and very general guidelines.

If the plan is too lenient, there is not enough guidance to gradually manage weight, to avoid mood alteration or cravings caused by food, or to avoid obsession caused by these things. Also, if you are a food addict, you should have enough structure to know, and say, that you are abstinent.

If the plan is too rigid, the excessive concentration on food and fear of losing control will produce obsession about food, diet, and other things in life.

Following a food plan   To be effective, a food plan must be seen as a tool rather than a restriction. It should make your recovery easier, not harder. Ultimately, the strength to follow the food plan must come from a Higher Power instead of will power.

Individual differences   Different people have different needs. There are far too many variables in human bodies and in nutrition to suggest that a "one size fits all" food plan will work for most food addicts, much less other addicts.

Staying on it   A rigid food plan, especially if you equate it with abstinence, is a setup to fail. Any deviation is translated by your diet mentality into a perception of failure. And every addict knows that failure is ample justification for a binge.

What if you get off?   The dichotomous thinking of success or failure may work in the short run to keep you out of trouble, but it breaks down in the long haul. We like to talk about a lapse (like a near miss), a relapse (a minor accident), and a collapse (a tragic accident). This analogy makes it more apparent that the quicker you can reverse a relapse process, the better. See the module on Relapse prevention.

For food addicts, if you find yourself straying from your food plan, get back into it solidly, and start talking with others in OA. Don't try to figure out whether it was a relapse until after you have gotten back solidly into recovery.

FOOD PREPARATION

For food addicts some of these common patterns of compulsive eating relate to food preparation:

- Not thinking ahead
- Impulsive shopping or eating
- High-sugar or high-fat foods
- Fast foods
- Nibbling while preparing food
- Reading/watching TV while eating
- Cooking and eating alone

Planning   Food planning and food preparation are related. You need to plan to buy what you are going to prepare. We have heard of people who are required to plan and "call in their food" to another OA member every day. Some people plan for a whole week. Others plan just a few hours or even minutes ahead of time. Do whatever fits your lifestyle and helps free you for living, if it actually works.

Planning can be a great aid, if you don't go to the opposite extreme of obsession and fear. Having reasonable guidelines and a reasonable food plan are important. You should be neither too much nor too little involved in food preparation, and there is a wide range in this, according to your situation.

HEALTHY PATTERNS

You need some flexibility in how you plan and prepare meals. Work on getting some kind of balance. You may need to make significant changes in how you cook or prepare meals, or they may be minor changes. Remember that nutrition is important in food preparation. Most food addicts, and other addicts concerned about their weight, should avoid deep-fat fried food, gravies, and fatty sauces. Even underweight anorexics should be encouraged to make good nutritional choices, choosing, for example, less *saturated* fats.

You can prepare tasty foods without spending too much time, if you have a realistic food plan.

Food plans, see also: Abstinence, Allergies, Binge history, Biochemistry, Control, Craving, Delusion, Fats, Food addiction, Habit & structure, Judgment, Metabolism, Moderation, Moodifiers, Nutrition, Obsession, Physical aspects, Step One, Sugar, Weight.

Forgiveness

Being forgiven by other people feels good, but it is not really part of your program. It may be a part of the *other* person's program to forgive, just as it is your responsibility to forgive others. If you nurture your resentments and avoid forgiving, you block the awareness of forgiveness that comes from your Higher Power. And like so many other things in the Program, you may not be able to forgive through will power; you will probably need the help of a Higher Power.

LEWIS SMEDES

Lewis Smedes (1984) offers a model of forgiveness that many addicts might find useful if they find themselves snarled in resentments. He describes forgiveness as a process that involves hurt, hate, healing, and coming together. You may need to work at deeper levels of forgiveness if you have experienced severe hurts, especially as a child. Until you can forgive, you will miss much of the peace, joy, and love recovery has to offer.

ABUSE & INCEST

Forgiving has nothing to do with blocking the memory of what happened to you. If you experienced incest or abuse, or have been victimized in any way, you should consider therapy to get in touch with and desensitize those memories without having to repress them. You may have to get very angry for a while, and let the forgiveness come when it is natural. These are skeletons that cause trouble while they stay in the closet.

Nor does forgiving mean placing yourself in harm's way. You can forgive the uncle who molested you without leaving your children alone with him. You can forgive and still choose to have nothing to do with a dysfunctional family.

ASSERTIVENESS

You can develop the skills to know where forgiveness ends and assertiveness begins. This is a common confusion among children of addiction or codependents.

For example, a relative or close friend borrows your new shorts, and goes swimming with them in a pool. When they return they are noticeably faded. Compare these three responses:

• You say nothing, though you feel angry and hurt that the

other person didn't even try to take care of them, and didn't offer to replace them.

- "You're always careless with my clothes. I'll never let you wear anything of mine again. You really ought to pay for them, too."
- "That's all right; our friendship is more important than pants. But maybe we would both be more comfortable if we didn't exchange clothes. We don't want to risk bad feelings coming between us."

The first response shows no forgiveness, and no honesty about your feelings. The second protects your interests, but also keeps you stuck in blame. The third shows both forgiveness and a willingness to be assertive.

Some addicts, and one story in the Big Book (p. 552), suggest praying for someone you resent. This even works if your prayer is, "Give that S.O.B. what he deserves," as long as you do not presume to *tell* your Higher Power what the S.O.B. deserves.

Who's hurting?   It may be easier to simply realize who is doing the hurting. *You* are suffering from your inability to forgive much more than the resented person is. Also, you may see that judging others is in some respects playing God, and that will inhibit your recovery.

It may be helpful to understand why someone hurt you, but that is not essential for forgiveness. Forgiveness has more to do with discovering that you, a finite imperfect human (like all others), do not have to suffer from the harsh role of judge or vigilante.

To expect unconditional forgiveness is to deny that human beings are limited and not God. It also tells the person you are forgiving that anything they do to you doesn't matter. Assertiveness must be part of the equation.

Not forgetting   If you "forgive and *forget*," you will waste the learning potential of the experience. A major lesson from AA is that we should learn from our past rather than forget it.

HIGHER POWER

Remember that forgiving, or not being forgiven, like everything else in the program, is not something you have to do alone. Nor can you make it happen. It comes as grace, a gift from your Higher Power, usually a while *after* you are ready for it. You have a Higher Power if you will simply make some contact.

Forgiveness, see also: Amends, Anger, Assertiveness, Attitudes, Behavior, Character defects, Control, Defenses, Family, Gratitude, Guilt & shame, Higher Power, Humility, Incest, Inventory, Love & caring, Relationships, Resentments, Step Three, Step Eight, Step Nine, Trust. End of path K. Next on path L: Step Ten.

Freedoms

RECOVERY

Many people in recovery from addiction call freedom one of the greatest gifts of the Program. What does it mean to be free?

Hostages can be released by their captors. Depending on what they do after release, they may or may not experience freedom. They may also have to fight to maintain their freedom.

RELEASE VS. FREEDOM

You are released from compulsive drinking, using, eating, and other effects of addiction by your Higher Power. You turn this release into freedom by using the Steps of the Program.

Often it is good to think about the freedoms you have gained, or will gain, through working a Twelve-Step program.

Physical aspects   Recovery will allow freedom from the physical aspects of the addiction.

The addictive behavior includes the intoxication of mood-altering substances, extremes of eating, spending, sexual behavior, and other addictive actions.

Addicts in recovery gain freedom from their physical addiction, including drunkenness, liver damage, obesity, purging, high blood pressure, and other medical, legal, financial, social, or other serious problems created by the addiction.

The physical craving for alcohol, other drugs, food, or other external or internal substances is reduced and often absent in recovery.

Emotional aspects   In recovery, you can expect a lot of freedom from the emotional aspects of the disease as well.

The fear of losing control, fear of others' accusations, and other fears diminish.

You gain freedom from the rapid mood swings and emotional turmoil of food addiction.

Remember the hopelessness? You get the good feeling that maybe this will work for you.

Mental aspects   The mental mismanagement of addiction begins to disappear in recovery, and you gain freedom for better decision making.

You get some relaxation of the constant or frequent obsession with drinking, using, spending, sex, gambling, excitement, food, eating, weight, and/or purging.

Recovery brings relief from the severe black-and-white thinking that feeds so well into the disease.

Many addicts agree that they used to be their own worst enemies. In recovery they start to work for themselves rather than against themselves.

Judgment, not just about the addictive substances or behaviors, improves with recovery.

Spiritual aspects   Finally, the freedom of recovery allows you to develop the spiritual aspects of your life.

Addiction promotes isolation, loneliness, lies, half-lies, delusions, and general dishonesty, especially with yourself.

Addicts' obsession with maintaining the illusion of control over their addiction makes them "play God" with their lives and their disease. You may have pushed your Higher Power out of the driver's seat and worn yourself out trying to miss the bumps in the road.

Addicts learn through recovery that freedom of choice was taken away by the addiction long ago, leaving in its place only an illusion that hides pain. Paradoxically, a major defense that addiction uses is that recovery requires giving up the freedom to drink, eat, use, or do the addictive behaviors, or as much as you want. In reality, recovery gives you the freedom from the bondage of addiction. That captivity was far more terrible than not having something like a drink or a dessert today.

Freedoms, see also: Abstinence, Acceptance, Addiction model (PEMS), Affirmations, Behavior, Craving, Feelings, Honesty, Judgment, Moderation, Obsession, Openmindedness, Powerlessness, Prayer & meditation, Recovery, Sanity, Serenity, Spirituality, Step One, Stress & strain.

G

Gamblers Anonymous (GA)

Gamblers Anonymous was the fourth Twelve-Step organization, founded in September 1957. There are about eight hundred groups in the United States.

GA made minor changes to most of AA's steps. These modifications do not change the essential meaning, but they do tend to soften the emphasis on a Higher Power. For example, their Step Six reads, "Were entirely ready to have these defects of character removed."

PRESSURE GROUPS

Another innovation in GA was what they call a "pressure group." This actually means a group to relieve pressure, not to apply it. A meeting is set up to which a GA member brings financial data about income, debts, and expenses. The other GA members give support and advice to help with employment, financial, legal, and personal problems. The advice is not professional but offers support, common sense, and a wealth of personal experience.

For information about GA, consult the white pages of your phone directory, or write or call:

> Gamblers Anonymous
> PO Box 17173
> Los Angeles, CA 90017
> (213) 386-8789

For the family and friends of compulsive gamblers:

Gam-Anon Family Groups
PO Box 157
Whitestone, NY 11357
(718) 352-1671

Gambling

Compulsive gambling is an addiction. It has been recognized as an alcoholismlike condition since before the founding of AA. Until very recently addiction-oriented counselors and programs did not know exactly how to deal with it because there was no substance ingested or introduced from outside the body. Recent research into neurotransmitters and endogenous drugs has given us the handle we need to place it squarely in the framework of an addiction.

The National Council on Problem Gambling was organized similarly to the National Council on Alcoholism to distribute information and education on compulsive gambling as an illness and public health problem. They estimate that 10 percent of Americans risk more money than they can afford on gambling activities, from lotteries to casinos. Many become pathological gamblers and some resort to crime when all credit resources are gone.

Gamblers Anonymous (*Sharing Recovery through Gamblers Anonymous*, 1984) defines gambling for the compulsive gambler: "Any betting or wagering, for self or other, whether for money or not, no matter how slight or insignificant, where the outcome is uncertain or depends on chance or 'skill' constitutes gambling. Compulsive gambling, very simply, is gambling which is beyond the emotional control of the gambler."

Common activities for compulsive gamblers include horse racing, sports betting, card games, casinos, dice, slot machines, lotteries, and bingo. Damage includes loss of time and financial resources, illegal connections and activities, prison, and embezzlement. As with alcoholism, there are also physical and psychiatric illnesses that are caused by or aggravated by the compulsive gambling.

PHASES OF COMPULSIVE GAMBLING

Robert L. Custer, MD, is the prominent pioneer in the treatment of compulsive gambling. He has identified three phases in the progression of compulsive gambling.

In the search for action, the winning phase, the gambler wins, loses, and breaks even often. Borrowing is common, but at this point usually does not hurt.

In the chase, or the losing phase, there are many losses and frantic attempts to win them back. Self-esteem erodes and guilt intensifies. Lies, fraud, forgery, job problems, and family problems increase. This phase can last for decades.

In the desperation phase, the gambler is totally obsessed. Losses and indebtedness are heavier. Often illegal options are sought and rationalized. Family, vocation, and social life are devastated. At this point gamblers may see only four options: suicide, prison, running away, or seeking help.

TREATMENT

Until recently there were only a handful of treatment programs outside the Veterans' Administration system. There are now dozens of treatment programs for compulsive gamblers. Many of these are chemical dependency programs that have initiated a compulsive gambling track. Most use a Twelve-Step model and recommend Gamblers Anonymous.

Many are alcoholic   Jim W., the founder of GA, was also an alcoholic. Estimates of alcoholism among compulsive gamblers range from 8 percent in an early study, to 49 percent in a more recent estimate from a treatment program that deals with both addictions.

The percentage of compulsive gamblers who are female is at least as high as the percentage of alcoholics who are female. This seems parallel to the change in AA as the female component went from about 1 percent to more than a third.

For general information about compulsive gambling, write or call:

National Council on Problem Gambling
445 W. 59th St.
New York, NY 10019
(212) 765-3833 or 1-800-522-4700

Gambling, see also: Addiction, Alcoholism, Arousal, Binge history, Debtors Anonymous, Excitement, Family, Gamblers Anonymous, Money, Moodifiers, Sanity, Spending, Unmanageability. Next on path A: Sex.

Grace

Grace means gifts given by your Higher Power that you need not (in fact cannot) earn. Many addicts have tried to "become worthy" of recovery, bargaining with God. "If you will just let me stop drinking (or stop using, or lose weight, or whatever) I promise I will . . ." Most have found that this didn't work. Turning this logic around, they felt that their Higher Power was somehow displeased with them, and that's why they were still struggling with addiction. This kind of shame feeds directly into the disease.

For people who are used to paying through the nose for treatment, counseling, or diet clinics, there is a powerful urge to think "there must be a catch." It seems as if recovery can't really be a gift from God.

The "old tapes" of control, do-it-yourself, and try harder don't get erased; you must make new tapes as alternatives. For a long while, it may be very easy to start beating your head against the wall again.

ATTAINING GRACE

Simply stop fighting the gift and let it happen. If you believe in a traditional God, just say "thanks, God." If not you can appreciate the wonder and life-giving qualities of life or whatever you can vaguely identify as a Higher Power.

Grace, see also: Abstinence, Acceptance, Beliefs, Gratitude, Guilt & shame, Higher Power, History of Twelve-Step groups, Humility, Magical thinking, Prayer & meditation, Sanity, Serenity, Service & giving, Spiritual aspects, Spirituality, Step Eleven, Surrender, Trust. Next on path M: Gratitude.

Gratitude

It is hard to get to spirituality without being grateful. The way is easy: grace presents the recovery program, and all you have to do is stop fighting it. Gratitude is the natural response to this gift. A thankful attitude helps you to surrender.

Gratitude is an effective cure for self-pity. It is hard to dwell on fear and disappointment that the glass is half empty if you are grateful that it is half full.

NOT STUFFING FEELINGS

We are not suggesting that you deny your feelings. Far from it. Honest sharing of feelings is a major advantage of Twelve-Step fellowships. The problem is getting stuck in negative feelings. Many people struggling with codependency do not understand the difference between feelings and attitudes. So when someone suggests they change a negative attitude, they think the suggestion is to stuff their feelings.

REASONS FOR GRATITUDE

If you are in a grateful state of mind, you are closer to spirituality and more advanced in your recovery. Paraphrasing Father Joe Martin, a well-known lecturer on alcoholism, gratitude is the hinge on which the gate to recovery swings.

TURNING IT AROUND

A favorite solution for self-pity in the Twelve-Step programs is to make a gratitude list.

Think of ten things you can be grateful about right now. How does that change your attitude? After you have listed everything you can think of, add three things each day. You might find yourself grateful for paper clips and toilet paper.

TELLING YOUR STORY

The recommended format for telling your story at a Twelve-Step meeting (or most anywhere) is:

- What it was like
- What happened
- What it's like now

By sharing that in a meeting or with a suffering addict, it will be hard to avoid feeling gratitude and to hold onto self-pity.

LITERATURE

Reading the Big Book, *As Bill Sees It,* or other Program literature can increase gratitude. Most meditation books have an index where you can look up specific selections on gratitude.

Read the "Promises" in the Big Book (pp. 83-84).

HELPING OTHERS

Reaching out to others who are struggling with recovery is a good way to get back in touch with gratitude. We get out of ourselves when we share with others.

Gratitude, see also: Acceptance, Attitudes, Feelings, Forgiveness, Freedoms, Grace, Guilt & shame, Higher Power, History of Twelve-Step groups, Love & caring, Prayer & meditation, Recovery, Serenity, Spirituality, Step Nine, Step Eleven, Step Twelve, Surrender. Next on path M: Serenity.

Grief

Grief is a normal, healthy process by which a person works through losses. It involves experiencing the painful feelings associated with the loss, and leads to its resolution.

Most people have experienced losses that result in grief. Death, illness, divorce, and the loss of a job are some obvious losses. But moving to a new town and leaving friends behind, or moving into a new home and giving up an old one with happy memories can also result in grief. The meaning you attach to the loss will determine its impact on you.

Addiction exacerbates losses for individuals, families, and friends, so information about grief issues is important for addicts.

STAGES OF GRIEF

Physicians, mental health workers, and religious leaders have studied and written about the process of grief. These writings have a common thread with only minor variations in descriptions of the process. The following model of the stages of grief is typical:

Shock   This is nature's way of protecting you from feeling the devastating impact of a significant loss all at once. "I can't believe it" is shock. Things don't seem real. You feel as though you are in a daze. Normal feelings and existence are suspended.

Denial   This is a continuation of shock, where at one level you go through the motions but at a deeper level, you have not experienced the impact of the loss. There may be tears, but real despair is yet to come.

Anger   Since anger is a natural response to a hurt or loss, it also occurs during grief. There may be no rationale for the target of the anger—it is just discharged. It may be extended or brief, accompanied by tears or not, according to individual differences. Some people express more anger than others. There is no right or wrong way to do it.

Bargaining   This is a psychological, usually subconscious attempt to minimize the loss. A feeling of guilt may be involved. "If only I had . . ." is a common sign of bargaining.

Depression   A deep sadness and reality about the loss sets in. The loss is real and forever. This stage is eased by allowing floods of tears, nurturing yourself, and letting others console you. It is painful, but it doesn't last forever, as acceptance begins to replace it.

Acceptance   Acceptance means to integrate the loss and go on with your life. It is learning to live again, and being grateful for the memories you want to keep of what you lost. Acceptance occurs as a gift of not fighting the grieving process.

PROCESS
The feelings in grief do not move in order from one stage to the next, but seem to cycle back and forth. When you don't try to force or deny them, they flow naturally. Knowing that your feelings are natural is important. Allow yourself to feel and do not ridicule, judge, or rationalize away your feelings.

UNRESOLVED
Since grief involves feelings, many addicts have difficulty with it. The use of mood-altering chemicals and behaviors, as well as prohibitive injunctions from your family about feelings, may have prevented you from healthy grieving. If this is true, your recovery may involve dealing with unresolved grief. We encourage you to be open to that possibility.

ADDICTION LOSSES
Joseph Kellerman (*Grief: A Basic Reaction to Alcoholism*, 1977) identified several significant losses for alcoholics and their family members. Attention to these ideas makes it easy to see the losses any addict could experience as the disease progresses. Some typical losses are:

- Loss of control over a once pleasant behavior
- Loss of memory (alcoholic blackouts)
- Loss of the ability to choose not to indulge in behavior that has negative consequences
- Loss of self-esteem
- Loss of the respect of others
- Loss of employment or ability to do a job effectively
- Loss of health

Losses families may experience are:

- Loss of order and security in life replaced by chaos and confusion
- Loss of proper roles for parents and children

- Loss of trust, honesty, and even love
- Loss of the sense of family

CHILDREN OF ADDICTS

Children who grow up in families where there is active addiction may need to grieve the loss of the opportunity for a happy childhood. Some work done with children of alcoholics suggests that part of the healing process involves grief work.

HEALING

The damage and injury experienced from addiction can best be healed by participating with others who have similar experiences. That is the basis for Twelve-Step recovery groups: a shared story. As you open your heart and share your pain, others will be there for you, and your grief can be transformed by grace into God's healing love.

As your wounds are healed, you are then able to be there for others when they need you. You then share the power of a wounded healer, and the process of recovery is passed on.

Grief, see also: Abuse, Acceptance, Affirmations, Anger, Attitudes, Behavior, Control, Family, Fear, Feelings, Grace, Guilt & shame, Higher Power, Incest, Inventory, Love & caring, Magical thinking, Prayer & meditation, Resentments, Responsibility, Self-centeredness, Slogans, Step Three, Step Eleven, Surrender. Next on path J: Guilt & shame.

Guilt & shame

GUILT

In recovery from any addiction, abstinence from the addictive substance or behavior is only the beginning of the process. As you begin to use the Steps as principles for living, you will inevitably have to confront guilt and shame. In Steps Four to Nine, you take an inventory of yourself, assess aspects of your character that need changing, and make amends for the harm you have done to others. In learning to use these Steps you will most likely need a way of looking at guilt and shame that will be beneficial and healing.

GUILT VS. SHAME

In its very simplest form, guilt refers to how you feel about what you **did,** and shame refers to how you feel about who you **are.**

As a practicing addict you may have done many things you regret. When you violate some rule you have for yourself you are likely to feel guilty. This relates to your behavior. Shame relates to how you feel about yourself. You are less than perfect, you fall short, and you may feel a sense of failure about what you are.

Steps as therapy   The Steps provide therapy for guilt and shame. The two can be thought of as different, but one affects the other. You make mistakes (guilt) because you are imperfect. You make a list of people you hurt and make amends to them. That is what you do for guilt. Step Ten provides a way to continue to make amends when you make a mistake, which you are likely to do since you are imperfect.

"I am _____ and I am an alcoholic (or addict or compulsive overeater)." This simple introduction acknowledges the shame you may have felt, and provides, through the fellowship of the Program and the love of a Higher Power, the transcendence of that shame into acceptance and a bonding with others.

Fourth Step inventory   In your Inventory it is helpful to think about how you feel about **yourself**, and maybe examine where those feelings come from. Self-image and self-worth are related to shame.

SHARING SHAME
Please note that to identify yourself as an addict, you are saying something about what you are. That is an essential element for the recovery process. Healing comes from fellowship with other addicts. The therapy for shame is to share it.

Healing   The intuitive wisdom of the Twelve Steps includes healing for both guilt and shame resulting from addiction. It is easy to see where guilt is treated (Steps Eight, Nine, and Ten). Members of the fellowship with experience report the freedom that comes from being able to be honest about human errors and mistakes, and say simply, "I'm sorry."

Honesty   By being honest with yourself and others, admitting your need for those with kindred spirits, and being open to the need for the give and take of recovery, you experience healing through caring. Every time you say, "I am _____ and I am an addict," you connect with others and help heal shame.

The shame factor   The information in this module is a simplified explanation to help you begin to understand guilt and shame. There are mental health and addiction professionals who have done extensive work and investigation into these ideas, and some make it the most important factor to be considered in recovery and healing. It is obvious that the part shame plays in your life will certainly be a factor to consider.

Further investigation   There are recovering people who find it necessary to investigate deeper into the nature of their feelings about themselves, to identify where some of the problems originated. Most addicts can relate to having some degree of dysfunction in their family of origin. No doubt this is a factor in the maladaptive and disruptive patterns adopted by the individual to survive.

The addictive spiral   These factors also contribute to the emotional, mental, and spiritual difficulties that may predispose you to addictive behavior. Then the addictive behavior compounds the guilt and shame, and addicts find themselves in a self-defeating downward spiral of addictive behavior, remorse, self-deprecating thoughts, shame, and more addictive behavior.

RECOVERY

Recovery often involves more than a superficial acknowledgment of how you became the way you are. It involves the courage to honestly face your past, giving up the role of victim, persecutor, or rescuer, and learning to take responsibility for your life. The beauty of recovery is that you do not have to do it alone.

Guilt & shame, see also: Abuse, Affirmations, Amends, Anger, Assertiveness, Attitudes, Behavior, Body image, Character defects, Codependency, Family, Feelings, Forgiveness, Grief, Incest, Inventory, Perfectionism, Resentments, Responsibility, Self-centeredness, Self-image, Spirituality, Step Four, Step Six, Step Eight, Survival roles. Next on path J: Resentments.

Habit & structure

A habit is something repeated enough that it is done easily and automatically with little effort or even conscious thought.

BAD HABITS

Most people have some bad habits. Some simple examples of habits or habitual behaviors are:

- Tics. Nervous twitches might be neurological, but they also may be psychological and habitual.
- Affectations. Habitual behaviors, like saying "You know?" after you speak, are very common.
- Addictive behaviors. Drug addiction used to be called a "habit." Actually, addiction has only a little to do with habit. The model of habit is inadequate to describe the constellation of behaviors we see in addiction.

However, you may have addictive behaviors that continue into recovery largely from habit. Examples include heading to the bar or refrigerator as soon as you get home, or eating in front of the TV.

HELPFUL HABITS

Many habits are actually beneficial. Here are some examples of how habits can work against or for you:

- Tying shoes. Have you ever tried to explain how to tie a shoe to a child? Unless you are an experienced elementary school teacher, it may be difficult. Tying shoes is habitual for most people, so you have forgotten exactly how you do it; you just do it out of habit. Try making the first loop with your other hand sometime!

- Driving to work. Things we do habitually, if they are helpful things, save energy because we don't have to think about them. If you drive the same way to work each day, you probably don't have to put much effort into remembering where to turn. You may even surprise yourself sometimes by realizing that you weren't aware of much while you were driving—perhaps your mind was on something else.

  You can become so "automatic" while driving that you become unsafe. Some people describe this type of situation as a "blackout," which it *might* be. More likely it is normal (though perhaps somewhat reckless) concentration on something else (or even nothing—a trance state) while your habits try to take care of you.

EXTINGUISHING THEM

Habits aren't that difficult to change, if you have no vested interest in maintaining them. For example, suppose you change jobs. For ten years, you drove to a certain intersection and turned left. Now you have to go to the same intersection but you must turn right to get to the new work place.

For a month or so it will take a conscious effort when you get to that intersection to turn right instead of left. But before long, you will find that your automatic reaction will increasingly be right instead of left. The old habit is dying through lack of use, and a new habit is taking its place.

Many months after the habit is extinguished, you may find that out of the clear blue, you suddenly turned left instead of right. This is a normal phenomenon, which can be demonstrated by laboratory rats. It just means that new habits will replace old habits fairly quickly, but the old habit will not die finally until after many months of disuse.

If you are a food addict, you might have a habit of accepting snacks offered unexpectedly, whether at a party or at a grocery store. This habit will work against you for several weeks, and you must be conscious of it. It is not unusual to pop something in your mouth before you even realize it, and then have to find a discreet way to spit it out. Yet after several months of not eating between meals you may find you have declined an offer without even consciously considering it. A new habit has begun to work in your favor.

STRUCTURE

Like habits, structure can work for you or against you. In recovery, structure is the framework of habits, rules, beliefs, attitudes, and other factors that anchor experience and give it meaning.

Many addicts are defiant if they don't get their way. They respond to too much structure with rebellion. This is why AA makes such a point of emphasizing that the Steps are suggestions only. Try to stuff them down an addict's throat, and you will quickly discover how much energy the disease can muster.

On the other hand, without enough structure, there are too many decisions. You could become overwhelmed and exhausted, with a "lost" feeling.

BALANCE FOR YOU

The important thing is to find a balance that you can live with, that works for you. This will be somewhere between excessive structure and not enough. Examples might include a food plan or other moderation plan, meetings, and sponsor involvement.

Food plan   Some food addicts find success in more structure in a food plan, while others need less. Too much rigidity encourages obsession and rebellion, while too little may be inadequate guidance for moderate eating, and might lead to increased cravings and poor weight management.

Meetings   What types, how many meetings a week do you need? Again it depends on your particular needs. Generally, we would recommend one or two too many rather than a meeting or two not enough. It is possible, however, for people to overdo even meeting attendance.

Sponsor involvement   Some people prefer a sponsor that gets very directive and very involved in their lives; others like one that gives very gentle suggestions and does more listening. Recovery will do best with a compromise that works for you.

Habit & structure, see also: Affirmations, Behavior, Character defects, Control, Defenses, Dichotomous thinking, Diet mentality, Food plans, Half-measures, Halfway house, Meetings, Mental aspects, Priorities, Psychological problems, Relapse prevention, Service & giving, Sponsorship, Therapy & treatment. Next on path D: Paradoxes in addiction.

Half-measures

The term "half-measures" is familiar to most recovering addicts, if only because it is mentioned in the first part of chapter 5 of the

Big Book (*Alcoholics Anonymous*, 1976), which is read before many Twelve-Step meetings. It says, "Half-measures availed us nothing" (p. 59).

The concept of half-measures does *not* mean doing half what is theoretically possible. Recovery requires some kind of compromise in most areas. This includes, for example, how much time you spend "working the program." It *is* possible to spend too much time on recovery activities, like meetings. More often, addicts try to recover with an inadequate amount of time or effort.

Your attitude may be that you just need a technique for controlling your drinking, stopping drug-related arrests, succeeding in weight loss, or you simply need to be rid of the inconvenience of excessive use, bingeing, or purging so you can get on with your life. If so you are not likely to follow through with all you need for recovery. The Twelve-Step programs were designed for those who have decided that recovery is *vital*, not just something nice to have.

Half-measures are more than just not quite doing enough. They represent a delusion that a totally inadequate effort is OK.

FOLLOWING THROUGH
With recovery, follow-through is important. The addiction wants you to give lip service to recovery tasks, so you should be sure your effort is enough to get you into good recovery, one day at a time.

Half-measures, see also: Abstinence, Acceptance, Codependency, Crisis, Defenses, Delusion, Habit & structure, Hitting bottom, Honesty, Intervention, Meetings, Paradoxes in addiction, Powerlessness, Priorities, Progression, Relapse prevention, Step One, Step Three, Stinking thinking, Surrender, Unmanageability. Next on path F: Hitting bottom.

Halfway house

A halfway house is a therapeutic community to help with recovery after primary treatment (the inpatient, residential, or outpatient program where the individual gets started on recovery). A halfway house is sometimes called a secondary treatment program or extended treatment.

EXTENDED TREATMENT
A quarter-way house, sometimes called extended treatment, is close to the structure of primary treatment. Usually residents are in full-time treatment and cannot work during the day.

HALFWAY HOUSE

A true halfway house is about midway between the intensity of primary treatment and the "real world" following treatment. Often residents work during the day and have some group therapy and other therapeutic activities in the evenings, but not necessarily every evening of the week.

THERAPEUTIC COMMUNITY

A three-quarter-way house, sometimes simply called a therapeutic community, is closer to ordinary living. The residents can usually work, have more freedom, and have little or no professional counseling.

WHEN NEEDED

Halfway houses are excellent follow-up treatment for those who have significant obstacles for recovery after a primary care program. These obstacles may include inadequate family support, difficult job or social situation, youth, physical handicaps, poor response to previous treatment, or other factors that make recovery difficult in the everyday world.

Most programs range from about three months to over a year, depending on the individual's needs. Often there is no set length of stay.

It is not difficult to find chemical dependency or even mental illness halfway houses. Unfortunately, halfway houses that specialize in other addictions are far less common. Contact a reputable private practice counselor or primary treatment program for a referral.

Halfway house, see also: Aftercare, Anorexia nervosa, Core functions, Counseling, Dual diagnosis, Employee assistance programs, Half-measures, Impaired professionals, Incest, Intervention, Priorities, Progression, Psychological problems, Relapse prevention, Responsibility, Therapy & treatment, Trust.

Heroin

To many people, heroin is the prototype of the illegal or street drug. Its image fits their stereotype of the drug addict: lower class, dirty needles, AIDS, and a state of war with tough cops. These are the images that come from dozens of action movies like *The Man with the Golden Arm* (1955) to media coverage from just a few years ago when cocaine edged out heroin as the "baddest" drug in town.

OPIATES

Heroin is a derivative of opium, like morphine, codeine, hydromorphine (Dilaudid), and oxycodone (Percodan). These drugs fit the same receptors as the natural painkillers, the endorphins, enkephalins, and dymorphins. It makes sense that they would be effective at reducing anxiety, increasing tolerance to pain, and promoting a feeling of well-being.

There are still many older, higher class, more responsible heroin addicts. Many who burn out on cocaine, other stimulants, and "life in the fast lane" have overtaxed their body's natural neurochemical balances. When they try heroin, they may find a satisfaction they have been missing for a long time. They begin by using heroin or another opiate in the classic sense of a medication, to soothe the abnormal "dis-ease" caused by years of substance abuse and other excesses.

SELF-MEDICATION

Edward J. Khantzian, a psychiatrist with Harvard Medical School, has interviewed hundreds of addicts. He is convinced that opiate addicts' life histories are filled with uncontrolled rage and anger, and that they use the opiate as medication. As Milkman and Sunderwirth (1987) point out, however, "The doctor who treats himself has a fool for a patient." As we have mentioned in the module on Chronic pain, prolonged use of analgesic drugs, like heroin, causes the body to produce less of its own natural opiates, and to reduce sensitivity to any opiate neurotransmitter.

The drug "works" until a tolerance develops, and then the addictive cycle takes over. The drug is progressively less successful, and eventually the addict is using the drug to keep from feeling terrible. It is in the later, degenerative stage that the addict experiences most of the consequences of drug addiction.

THERAPEUTIC COMMUNITIES

Therapeutic communities provide an alternative to typical chemical dependency programs. Scattered around the United States are groups of people, often self-managed, who provide a drug-free therapeutic community for addicts who are willing to tough it out. They are based more or less on the highly confrontive programs like Synanon and Daytop Village that developed in the late 1960s.

BOOT CAMP

These programs are like a boot camp for recovery. Confrontation and honesty are major tools. Residents learn to stay straight, learn a skill (if necessary), and to carry their own weight. The programs claim five-year success rates of up to 92 percent for graduates (although many leave without completing, and some of those come back later). Most programs advocate Twelve-Step program membership for support after treatment. There is often a small professional staff, augmented by graduates supervised or trained by more experienced staff.

A residence of two to four years is common, with adolescents making up most of the longer stays. Most are nonprofit, and some are true communes, where the only cost is your entire productive labor for the time you are there.

Others operate on a sliding scale. They are an option for those with lots of desire for recovery and few financial resources. Two of the larger therapeutic communities are Daytop Village with sixteen facilities in New York, two in California, and one in Texas; and Delancey Street, with a facility in San Francisco, one in New York, one in South Carolina, and one in New Mexico that also accepts adolescents.

Daytop Village
54 West 40th St.
New York, NY 10018
(212) 354-6000

Delancey Street
2563 Divisadero St.
San Francisco, CA 94115
(415) 882-5427

For an excellent self-help program for heroin addicts, see the module on Narcotics Anonymous.

Heroin, see also: Alcohol, Blackouts, Drugs, Fantasy, Impaired professionals, Inhalants, Moodifiers, Narcotics Anonymous, Nicotine, Pregnancy, Tolerance.

Higher Power

TRADITIONAL GOD

There are many different ideas of a Higher Power. The chapter on Step Two in *Twelve Steps and Twelve Traditions* describes several types of experiences with God before getting into a recovery program. Some are what one might call a traditional idea of God and some are very nontraditional.

All that seems to be required is that the Higher Power be someone or something that you can relate to that is more powerful than your addiction. It helps if you can believe that this Higher Power is God or has some kind of intelligence, even if it is not something mortals can understand, and that in some way it is more benevolent than vengeful.

PEOPLE AND THE PROGRAM
It might be that the best you can do for now is to understand that people in recovery, and the things that make sense in the recovery program, seem to have some power that you are lacking. If so, that will do. Many people have gotten into recovery with no more than that seed of faith at first.

VAGUE IDEAS
You may have only vague ideas about God or a Higher Power. That is OK too. For people in recovery, either vague notions of God seem to get much sharper, or they become comfortable with God remaining vague. Some people have such negative reactions to traditional ideas that for a while they have to think of "GOD" as Good Orderly Direction, from wherever it comes. Some even say their Higher Power was just a Group Of Drunks.

DIRECT LINE TO GOD
There are people who believe they have a very strong spirituality—that they have a "direct line" to God. They talk to this God several times a day and ask for help with their addiction. While they may be on the right track for spirituality, a possible danger in this way of thinking is that they envision God as a kind of supernatural servant whose job it is to grant favors. Sometimes people who believe they have a direct link to God close their ears to feedback from others, and ironically, perhaps from their God in the certainty that they know what their Higher Power wants them to do. See Step Eleven in *Twelve Steps and Twelve Traditions* (pp. 103–104).

TEMPORARY
Sometimes just a single person, like a sponsor, is the only Higher Power you can relate to. That is fine for the moment, but eventually you will begin to see that all humans have feet of clay, and you will

need to refocus your idea of a Higher Power on something more spiritual, even if that is the people in a Twelve-Step program, collectively, and the spirit that unites them.

Higher Power, see also: Acceptance, Beliefs, Character defects, Control, Grace, Honesty, Humility, Magical thinking, Openmindedness, Power, Powerlessness, Prayer & meditation, Religiosity, Sanity, Self-centeredness, Spirituality, Step One, Step Two, Step Three, Step Eleven, Trust, Willingness. Next on path G: Openmindedness.

History of Twelve-Step Groups

The history of Twelve-Step groups is mostly the history of Alcoholics Anonymous. There is not enough space here to give more than a simple chronology as an overview. A study of the history will help with the spirituality of recovery.

BEFORE AA

1879—Robert Holbrook Smith is born August 8, in Vermont.

1895—William Griffith Wilson is born November 26, also in Vermont.

1910—Bob Smith earns his MD at Rush University. He will become a proctologist.

1915—Dr. Bob marries Anne Ripley, on January 25.

1918—January 24, Bill marries Lois Burnham. Lois and Anne will become vital to the development of the Twelve-Step programs, from the support they give their husbands and their contributions to the movement that will become Al-Anon for recovery of the family.

1933—Dr. Bob begins going to Oxford Group meetings to cope with his alcoholism. In spite of the strong spiritual orientation of this nondenominational Christian movement, Dr. Bob continues to drink. Bill enters Towns Hospital in New York for the first time, where Dr. William Silkworth tells him that alcoholism is like an allergy to alcohol. Bill thinks he has been cured.

1934—December 11, Bill takes his last drink. He enters Towns Hospital again, but this time he has a spiritual experience. Dr. Silkworth tells him to hang onto it. Bill and Lois start attending Oxford Group meetings. Bill works with dozens of other alcoholics in the next five months, and none of them get sober—but Bill stays sober!

BIRTH OF AA

1935—May 12, a "fifteen minute" meeting in Akron, Ohio, between Bill and Dr. Bob turns into five hours. June 10 is Bob's last drink. Dr. Bob later says an important part of this meeting was the sense that Bill needed him as much as he needed Bill. June 10 is later recognized as the birthday of AA.

1939—April, *Alcoholics Anonymous*, known as the Big Book, is published, distilling the practical experience of the first hundred (actually ninety-six) members of AA. Two days later Hitler's Germany invades Poland, inhibiting the early development of AA while the world prepares for war.

1941—Alcoholics Anonymous is written up by Jack Anderson in the *Saturday Evening Post*. The interest in AA and the growth from this publicity threaten the fledgling organization.

1944—Bill begins a bout with depression, which will last about thirteen years.

1949—June 1, Anne Smith dies.

1950—July, at the First International AA Convention (in Cleveland, Ohio) the Twelve Traditions are accepted. November 16, Dr. Bob dies of cancer.

OTHER GROUPS

1951—Al-Anon is founded.

1953—July, Narcotics Anonymous begins. AA's *Twelve Steps and Twelve Traditions*, written by Bill, is published.

1955—July, at the St. Louis Convention, Bill gives AA its "formal release into maturity."

1957—Friday, September 13, first Gamblers Anonymous meeting. Alateen begins as an integral part of Al-Anon.

1960—January 19, Overeaters Anonymous begins.

1971—January 24, Bill dies of emphysema. July 6, Emotions Anonymous begins.

1988—October 5, Lois dies.

STORYTELLING

A vital link between the history of Twelve-Step groups and spirituality is the AA-style personal story. When addicts tell "what we used to be like, what happened, and what we are like now," (from *Alcoholics Anonymous*, 1976, p. 58) they carry the wisdom of recovery in the time-honored tradition of all the great spiritual leaders.

Why tell your story   Visitors to AA often comment that it is hard to understand why alcoholics would want to remember the pain of their life before recovery. Without this storytelling, alcoholics would quickly lose the benefit of what is usually the most expensive education they have ever had.

Kierkegaard said that life must be lived forward but it can only be understood backward. The wisdom of the journey from addiction into recovery makes possible a spiritual awakening, not only for the listener, but for the storyteller as well.

The addict's story is not an untruth (like the "story" we got punished for telling as a child) or even a myth, which has a kind of universal truth but does not come from one person's real life. It is not a "drunkalog." The best kind of story is one that comes from the heart, with humility and gratitude.

History of Twelve-Step groups, see also: Abstinence, Al-Anon & Alateen, Alcoholics Anonymous, Alcoholism, Children of addicts, Co-Dependents Anonymous, Community, Debtors Anonymous, Emotions Anonymous, Families Anonymous, Gamblers Anonymous, Humility, Meetings, Narcotics Anonymous, Other support groups, Overeaters Anonymous, Paradoxes in addiction, Service & giving, Sex addiction groups, Sponsorship, Steps of AA, Tools of recovery, Traditions of AA, Unity.

Hitting bottom

The phrase "hitting bottom" originated in the early days of AA, although it is not found in the text of the Big Book. Bill Wilson does use the term in Step One of *Twelve Steps and Twelve Traditions* where he talks about "low bottom cases," "raise the bottom," and the idea that alcoholics must feel they have hit bottom before they will sincerely try to work the Program.

JELLINEK CURVE

Since Bill's writing, some have described the progression of addiction and recovery, using a U-shaped curve based on the developmental model of E. M. Jellinek (1960). People try to fit themselves and others into such a model, describing how they can raise the bottom to avoid having to go all the way down.

LIMITS OF THE MODEL

The concept of hitting bottom made more sense in the early days of AA when most members were very late stage alcoholics. You don't have to have a sense of hitting bottom in all areas of your life—physical, emotional, mental, and spiritual—to use the First Step as a tool.

We do think to get full use of Step One you have to believe you have exhausted all your own resources to control your addiction. With this sincere attitude you can go on to use the rest of the Steps to recover.

Hitting bottom, see also: Abstinence, Acceptance, Bingeing, Crisis, Delusion, Half-measures, Honesty, Judgment, Obsession, Paradoxes in addiction, Powerlessness, Step One, Step Two, Unmanageability. Next on path F: Honesty.

Honesty

Honesty is very important in addiction recovery because of the power of dishonesty with others and delusion of self. These are major mechanisms for perpetuating the disease. The major weapon for fighting delusion is honesty.

NEED IN ADDICTION

Especially with addiction, dishonesty fuels delusion and promotes dysfunctional behavior and relationships. Honesty, with self and others, is a cornerstone of recovery.

Like most things, honesty may appear to be black and white, but it isn't. We can place ourselves roughly on a scale from pathological liar to brutally honest. Also, we may fall at different places on the scale in our business lives, our personal lives, or in particular situations.

Pathological lying   This is a level of dishonesty that is truly crazy. Pathological liars weave fantastic stories about who they are and what they have done. It is symptomatic of a genuine character disorder, if not a psychosis.

Fraud and theft   In the extreme, fraud and theft also suggest character disorders, but on the near end, they may be more related to the addictive behaviors. Many addicts find themselves involved in these situations, largely due to their addiction.

Minor cheating   A more common level of dishonesty is cheating. Examples include:

- Adultery or infidelity in relationships
- "Borrowing" that never gets returned
- Copying books, tapes, or computer software we have not paid for
- Lying on an income tax return
- Stealing supplies from an employer

Cash register   This is a level of honesty where you would not "take money from the register." Here you have an idea of things that are theft or cheating, and would avoid doing anything that is clearly dishonest.

Guarded truth   At this level, what you say is usually true, but you might not feel any requirement to correct misinterpretations by others. Dishonesty is by omission rather than by commission. Asked the right questions you might tell the truth. Politicians are notorious for this level of honesty.

Essentially honest   Then we move into an area where honesty is the norm, although you may make exceptions for good reasons. You might not worry too much about "little white lies," especially if they don't seem to be told for your personal gain, and don't hurt anyone.

If you are engaged in addictive behavior, it is very difficult to be this honest.

Rigorously honest   The Big Book talks about rigorous honesty. This does not mean perfect honesty, but it is striving in that direction. If someone does rigorous exercise, they work up a sweat. Rigorous honesty implies that you make a conscientious effort to be honest with yourself and others in all your affairs.

Brutally honest   It is possible for an addict to overdo almost anything. Meeting someone and saying, "You sure are ugly," may be honest, but it may totally ignore any sensitivity to the other person's feelings about something over which they may have no control. There is a hidden dishonesty in brutal honesty, having to do with motives.

With any of these levels of honesty, you may need to make a value judgment about what is brutal and what is rigorous. Again, the program suggests progress, not perfection.

Somehow, children and older people, especially those who are "characters," can get away with a lot more brutality in their honesty than most others. We seem to make allowances for them, and there is not as much sting to what they say.

DEALING WITH CONSEQUENCES

People often experience consequences of dishonesty, even if they are not "caught." If you decide to lie, you immediately double or triple what you have to remember; you have to *try* to remember the truth so you can use the information, and you must also remember the lie, so you won't accidentally get caught in it. And often, the same lie won't do for everyone. So you may have to remember the truth, lie "A" and whom you told it to, lie "B" and whom you told it to, and so on. You may wind up expending more energy and paying more consequences than if you had just told the truth. Honesty makes living, and recovery, easier.

TAKING RISKS

Sometimes people tell the truth, and do in fact get into trouble. Usually the trouble is not nearly as bad as they imagined it would be, but even if it is, they have the freedom of not having to dread the possibility that someone might find out, and they can feel good about their honesty and integrity. Honesty often gets lots of support from others.

Honesty, see also: Acceptance, Amends, Behavior, Beliefs, Character defects, Control, Defenses, Delusion, Forgiveness, Half-measures, Higher Power, Humility, Integrity & values, Judgment, Obsession, Relationships, Responsibility, Step One, Step Four, Step Five, Stinking thinking, Trust. Next on path F: Powerlessnes.

Humility

Twelve Steps and Twelve Traditions (1952, p. 58) describes humility as "a clear recognition of what and who we really are, followed by a sincere attempt to become what we could be." Having humility means you are teachable, and that you are prone neither to toot your own horn nor to put yourself down.

If honesty is the cornerstone of recovery, humility is the mortar that holds it in place. Bill Wilson said thousands of times that alcoholics are all-or-nothing people. Humility means accepting that all people are both beast and angel, that being a human being is good enough. Without this acceptance, without humility, it is all too easy to slip into playing God.

MISCONCEPTIONS

There are some myths and misconceptions about humility, in the general population as well as in addiction recovery.

The appearance of humility that is not genuine is called false humility. Suppose you have good public speaking skills. You give a talk at a Twelve-Step meeting and someone says, "That was great. I got a lot out of it." You reply, "It was nothing, really." Not only have you put yourself down, you have also rejected the compliment, the gift, that the other person wanted to give.

Low self-esteem   Often, addicts miss the mark of humility, not by being arrogant and overconfident, but by failing to recognize their strengths. Ironically, arrogant people are often people who also have low self-esteem, but try to cover up for it with their audacity.

REAL HUMILITY

Real humility includes gratitude for your strengths and honesty about your weaknesses. The truth is that everyone has strengths and gifts, weaknesses and shortcomings. Those that cause you trouble can be overcome using the Program, one day at a time. In the last analysis, you and every other human being will remain imperfect, limited, both beast and angel.

Humility, see also: Acceptance, Anonymity, Attitudes, Character defects, Grace, Gratitude, Honesty, Humor & fun, Inventory, Love & caring, Openmindedness, Prayer & meditation, Self-image, Service & giving, Slogans, Spirituality, Step Ten, Step Eleven, Surrender, Unity, Willingness. End of path L. Next on path M: Step Eleven.

Humor & fun

ACOA LEGACIES

At least half of all addicts come from addictive families or other dysfunctional families. Often their survival roles within those families included either a preoccupation with the serious side of life, or else a clown role, laughing on the outside while crying on the inside. We have known several recovering adult children of alcoholics who wore T-shirts that said, "Are we having fun yet?" They called it their ACOA T-shirt.

USE IN AA

Humor is important in AA. The Big Book (p. 132) suggests that if newcomers could not see that AA members' lives are full of fun and joy, they would not want recovery.

Lack in some groups   Some Twelve-Step groups are oppressive with their seriousness and self-pity. Perhaps it is due to a poor ratio of recovering to struggling members in these groups.

Creative humor   One very practical aspect of humor is the relief of boredom. All addicts need to hear the same basic messages of recovery repeatedly, but it can get boring. Humor adds spice, and allows addicts to take their "medicine" with real enjoyment.

Health benefits   Scientists are investigating the effect of laughter on health. Laughing stimulates the heart, lungs, upper body, and back much like exercise. A hundred hearty laughs a day can be as beneficial as ten minutes on a rowing machine. Laughing causes release of catecholamines that aid blood flow and healing.

FUN IN RECOVERY

Recovery should involve fun and joy. Often addicts need to learn how to enjoy themselves. Instead of focusing on what they had to give up (alcohol, bingeing, certain foods, etc.), they can feel the freedom of recovery and see the variety of experiences that were not open to them before.

Humor & fun, see also: Attitudes, Codependency, Control, Family, Grace, Humility, Inventory, Meetings, Obsession, Open-mindedness, Recovery, Self-image, Slogans, Step Eleven, Surrender, Willingness. Next on path L: Humility.

Hunger & appetite

"Lose 20 pounds in one month *without being hungry!*" How many claims like that have you heard? The message many of us have picked up over the years is that success at weight management depends on somehow losing weight without being hungry.

WEIGHT CYCLING

The reason for this is simple. Many addicts, especially food addicts, have been cycling for years, between bingeing on high-fat foods, thereby gaining weight, then going on very restrictive diets, which told their bodies that there was a famine outside. When the body produced hunger and feelings of panic, this became a good excuse for breaking the diet. Then the cycle started all over.

Don't restrict carbs   The first suggestion to avoid problems with physical hunger, then, is almost too simple: don't ever restrict your carbohydrate intake enough to produce hunger much before time to eat another moderate meal. In fact, while you **could** gain weight with very excessive carbohydrates, you should never try to lose weight by cutting back on carbohydrates, unless that intake was excessive to begin with.

If you feel hungry more than an hour or two before the next regular mealtime, you should check to see if you are eating enough carbohydrates. If you are sure you are, then you might see if something you are eating is causing cravings that you are interpreting as hunger.

Food addicts probably cannot rely on hunger or lack of hunger to tell them when to eat, how much to eat, or when to stop eating. The addiction can cause hunger feelings, or you may have hormone or other biochemical functions somewhat out of adjustment, and you may just be hungry for no reason.

Look at other aspects   We must then leave the physical aspect of the Program and look at the emotional, mental, and spiritual. If you have a hunger or appetite, you don't *have* to eat! The addiction tries hard to make a link between hunger and binge, but there simply is no direct link there. If you believe there is a direct link, then you will have no mental defense against a binge, your emotions probably will start running wild, and you may not have the spiritual contact to calm all that down.

COPING WITH A FOOD ADDICTION

If you are fighting hunger, then, you can look at your carbohydrate intake and sensitive foods, but now:

- Make contact with your Higher Power and (if possible) someone else in recovery. This will give you guidance to put the hunger in perspective.
- Share your fear, anger, or other feelings with both your

Higher Power and the other person. This will help you deal with the emotional aspects.

• Realize that hunger does not have any direct link with binge- ing, or even eating between meals. This will get your mental aspects into line.

• Remember that the next meal will come along eventually, and you will feel so much better that you waited for it. Abstinence tastes great, doesn't it?

Hunger & appetite, see also: Abstinence, Affirmations, Aller- gies, Behavior, Celebrations, Craving, Diet mentality, Food addic- tion, Food plans, Moderation, Prayer & meditation, Relapse prevention, Sabotage of recovery, Sanity, Sponsorship, Stress & strain, Tools of recovery, Visualizations.

I

Impaired professionals

The term "impaired professionals" refers to members of the medical, legal, social service, or other professions who have been disabled to some degree by alcohol or drug addiction. There are now many resources for these people, but there are few if any support or advocacy groups that serve professionals suffering from other addictions, such as food, gambling, or sexual addiction.

The development of groups for impaired professionals has grown out of an awareness of the prevalence of this problem.

Before the 1980s there was a lack of awareness of the early signs of addiction and a conspiracy of silence among colleagues reluctant to confront each other's problems. Intervention was provided or help sought only after significant damage had occurred to a person's self, family, and possibly even their clients or patients.

SELF-HELP

Programs for impaired professionals grew out of the interest of many who had suffered from the disease of addiction themselves. This, combined with a medical community better informed about addiction and recovery, has led to help for many who previously lacked such opportunities.

COOPERATION

There has been a cooperative effort by professional organizations, advocacy committees for the addicts, and the licensure authorities designed to protect the public. There are avenues for the addicts to get confidential help, and there are intervention techniques available for families, friends, and other concerned professionals. A professional may seek help herself. Family and friends can intervene. A noncoercive advocacy group of colleagues and peers may approach an addict. Employee assistance programs can help. A state professional society's committee formed for such a task can intervene. As a last resort, a person could be reported to a state's licensing board.

The impaired professional movement is designed to provide education, support, and protection for both the consumer and the addict. Referral and treatment are confidential, and there are usually recovering professionals available on treatment staffs and in advocacy and support committees and groups.

NETWORKS

There are informal networks in many states composed of dedicated professionals to provide education, intervention, referrals, and aftercare support. They also may help members who have lost their license to practice. Some professions for which support is available are doctors, nurses, dentists, anesthetists, nuns and priests, pharmacists, lawyers, social workers, and airline pilots. For details of what is available in your area, contact your state professional organization, professional regulatory board, or an employee assistance program.

Impaired professionals, see also: Aftercare, Certification, Co-dependency, Core functions, Counseling, Disease concept, Dual diagnosis, Employee assistance programs, Energy levels, Half-measures, Halfway house, Incest, Intervention, Professional organizations, Progression, Psychological problems, Therapy & treatment, Tolerance, Withdrawal.

Incest

Incest is just one kind of abuse. For information about the general topic of abuse, see the module Abuse.

Awareness of incest and child sexual abuse is increasing as more people are sharing what has been a shameful secret. The actual incidence is unknown, and results of studies to determine its prevalence vary, sometimes because of the definition of incest. It is common enough in addicts that it should be considered essential in any assessment. It is important to have skilled, trained therapists who know the right questions to ask their clients, and have at their disposal options for recovery.

At one time, incest referred to sexual activity or intercourse between close blood relatives. In the work done with incest survivors, a more useful definition has emerged that helps explain the trauma and its effects.

The elements that are significant are that there has been a violation of trust between a caregiver and a child. It is abusive because of the power an adult has over the child. It involves sexually inappropriate acts or those with sexual overtones involving a child and a person who has authority by virtue of an ongoing emotional bond.

DENIAL

While it is possible to look too hard for incest, it is much more likely for incest victims to deny it or try to explain it away. Survivors of Incest Anonymous (SIA) defines incest very broadly to include any sexual abuse by a family member, extended family member, or other person known to them whom they were led to trust.

Blume (1990) has developed an Incest Survivors Aftereffects Checklist, not considered exhaustive, that can assist in the assessment of incest or child abuse. Some characteristics are fear of the dark, alienation from one's body, covering one's body excessively, eating disorders, alcohol and drug abuse, self-mutilating behaviors, perfectionism, depression, rigidity, serious trust issues, boundary issues, shame and guilt, patterns of being a victim, not meeting one's own needs, abandonment issues, blocking out memories of a period of early years, feeling crazy or different, denial, sexual issues and problems, serious problems of intimacy, the desire to change one's name, difficulty in tolerating or seeking happiness, stealing, and multiple personality disorder.

Blume makes the point that incest frequently coincides with an alcoholic environment, and many ACOA (adult children of alcoholics) characteristics overlap with those of incest survivors. Blume believes that studies on incest should not assume that incest caused all the trauma.

Recovery from incest is essential if addicts are to experience the emotional, mental, and spiritual freedom of recovery. It may be a major piece of the work many have to do. Since it affects the very essence of who you are, it interferes with sanity, joy, relationships, self-esteem, and spirituality.

Bass and Davis (1988) offer a helpful guide for the recovery process. It involves getting in touch with reality about what happened, as best you can—remembering, feeling, believing, and grieving about what happened. Survivors need to learn to trust themselves and to express their anger. Healing from the shame and guilt (knowing it was not your fault), and reaching forgiveness at your pace, are all part of the process.

TRAUMA

Incest is a major trauma. Personality disorders, dissociation, and other dramatic survival mechanisms may result. Recent research is finding that victims often develop multiple personalities as a coping mechanism. Survivors generally need competent professional treatment.

SELF-HELP

Many incest victims find themselves in AA or in other Twelve-Step recovery programs. There they are often told to focus only on the alcohol, or food, or addictive behavior, to make amends to others they have hurt, and to forgive. They may be told that they could not be hurt unless they allowed it to happen. Especially for incest victims in early recovery, the strategies that worked for many people in alcohol or drug recovery simply reinforce the shame, guilt, and denial of the incest and the victim's feelings.

SIA

Members of Survivors of Incest Anonymous learn that the anger they feel is part of the healthy process of recovery. They are innocent victims, they did not seduce their abuser, and they are survivors. They learn that stuffing the feelings does not bring healing. They confront the abuser without necessarily reaching a reconciliation. They rock the boat. "In SIA, we learn we can lose our families and still recover," says an excellent SIA pamphlet called *Bittersweet: For Those in Other Twelve Step Programs.* SIA also strongly suggests that members see a professional counselor while attending SIA.

FORGIVENESS

SIA says that acceptance is necessary but forgiveness is optional. We still believe that forgiveness is necessary for healing from any addictive process, but we do agree with SIA that forgiveness cannot be forced. It must come about through contact with a Higher Power and working the Steps of the Program, one day at a time. A support group like SIA, along with professional therapy, can help that process happen gradually.

Survivors of Incest Anonymous
PO Box 21817
Baltimore, MD 21222-6817
(301) 282-3400

Incest Survivors Anonymous
Box 5613
Long Beach, CA 90805-0613
(213) 428-5599

Incest, see also: Abuse, Adolescents, Al-Anon & Alateen, Amends, Anorexia nervosa, Behavior, Children of addicts, Codependency, Control, Detachment, Enabling, Family, Family of origin, Forgiveness, Grief, Intimacy, Other support groups, Power, Relationships, Resentments, Self-image, Survival roles.

Inhalants

What drugs are easiest for young children to find around the house? Probably some kind of organic solvent or aerosol. Examples are gasoline, benzene, and toluene. They are common in household products.

EPIDEMIC

Gasoline, glue, and other inhalants are epidemic among kids. Cans of toluene-based spray paint are also popular in the general population. Abusers spray the paint into an empty soda can or onto rags or into bags, then sniff the vapors until they become intoxicated. Hexane, found in paint thinner, and trichlorethylene, in aerosol sprays, are often used as well.

NITRITES

Older adolescents may find amyl nitrite, a drug used to relieve symptoms of angina pectoris. It comes in cloth-covered glass capsules that pop when they are crushed—hence the street name "poppers." Butyl nitrite is often sold as a room deodorizer, and is known as Locker Room or Rush.

These substances produce dizziness, lightheadedness, and disorientation. Nitrous oxide, used by dentists as "laughing gas" and sometimes in cans of whipped cream, can also produce giddiness when inhaled.

Besides the danger of suffocation or accident, long-term toxic effects of inhalants include memory loss, liver and kidney damage, seizures, cardiac problems, and respiratory arrest.

Inhalants, see also: Blackouts, Cocaine, Drugs, Fantasy, Heroin, Impaired professionals, Marijuana, Moodifiers, Narcotics Anonymous, Nicotine, Pregnancy, Tolerance.

Integrity & values

The word *integral* means whole. You acquire and maintain integrity when your behavior generally matches your values. In considering your integrity, look at your values, those things you find worthwhile or desirable. If you value honesty, the dishonesty of your addictive behavior will cause you pain. The Twelve Steps work for people who value honesty and living life on a spiritual basis.

LOSING INTEGRITY

Addictive behavior is often incompatible with integrity. You may find yourself stealing booze, drugs, or food, lying about what you drink, use, or eat, blaming others because you broke your sobriety, your diet, or your abstinence, and doing other things that may violate your value system.

A subtle erosion of integrity happens with attitudes like entitlement. This means that you believe you are *entitled* to certain things. If you go to a restaurant that has high prices, you may think you deserve to steal things from the table. In recovery you will find freedom as your sense of honesty becomes more keen. It has to do with doing what is right.

REGAINING INTEGRITY

Working the Steps restores your integrity, through being honest with yourself and others, working on your character defects, making amends, and improving the contact with your Higher Power.

IMPORTANCE IN RECOVERY

You feel better about yourself when you are honest, when you show you care about others, and when your behavior generally matches your values. This integrity is the foundation for the freedom and spontaneity that recovery offers.

Integrity & values, see also: Attitudes, Behavior, Beliefs, Delusion, Half-measures, Higher Power, Honesty, Humility, Inventory, Judgment, Power, Prayer & meditation, Recovery, Self-centeredness, Spiritual aspects, Spirituality, Steps of AA. Next on path E: Spirituality.

Intervention

When AA began, there was a strong idea that you shouldn't push alcoholics into recovery until they want it. In the 1960s and early 1970s people began to realize that was fine for the one in thirty-five who got sober in AA, but what about the other thirty-four, who just suffered and eventually died? The process that developed, popularized by Vern Johnson (1980), was called intervention.

Intervention is a technique of breaking into a delusional system. It works very well with addiction. The delusion of addiction effectively prevents most addicts from seeing the reality of their disease. Examples:

- I don't have a problem.
- Nothing is wrong.
- It's no big thing.

TYPES OF INTERVENTION

Intervention can be a formal process that happens infrequently or an informal technique used every day.

Formal   A formal intervention is a planned, even choreographed, event designed to create a crisis in the life of an addict. Concerned family, friends, employers, or others closely involved in the individual's life meet, share information, and prepare for the intervention. A trained professional may instruct the participants and even lead the intervention, in which all concerned share data and feelings about specific events in the person's addictive behavior. The goal is usually immediate entry into a treatment program.

Informal   An informal intervention takes advantage of one of the many crises that abound in the life of an addict. It often involves being prepared, and "striking while the iron is hot." An informal intervention may take place without the participant(s) or the addict ever knowing it is an intervention.

ELEMENTS OF INTERVENTION

Whatever the style of the intervention, there are some elements that increase the chance of success:

Specific data   The more specific the data you share with the addict, the more it hits home, and the harder it is to defend against. Compare these two items:

- "You get mean and argumentative when you are drinking, and you make me so embarrassed."
- "On my birthday last year you came in yelling and screaming and slurring your speech, and my guests all left early. I told you I was embarrassed and hurt and you insulted me. That's not like you."

Love and concern If you, the participant(s), can show genuine love and concern for the addict, the addict is much less likely to see it as an attack. If you share how you feel, they will find it hard to argue with you.

Alternatives for recovery You have to give the addict some alternatives for recovery. Will power hasn't worked in the past, so you need to have a solution that doesn't just say, "try harder."

A what-if clause If you have decided what you will do if the addict refuses the options for recovery you have offered, you have an edge. If you can honestly say, "I love you, but I can't and won't stay here and watch your addiction destroy both our lives," you have a much more powerful bottom-line tool. It helps if family members are already in Al-Anon or committed to family treatment. The intervention can then be an invitation to join them in recovery.

It is important to carry through with your what-if clause, or the addiction will be enabled to continue. Unfortunately, many family members do not pursue their own recovery if the addict refuses help.

The worry over whether the intervention will be successful assumes that if the individual does not choose to enter treatment immediately, there has been a failure. In our experience, even an intervention that does not seem satisfactory to the interveners has probably raised the awareness of the problem and provides relief that it is finally out in the open. Most of these will eventually result either in the addict getting some help later, or in positive benefits to the family for getting honest about it.

REWARDS

An intervention is one of the few opportunities an ordinary person can have to save a life. The risks are considerable; you may lose a friend—but if the addiction is rampant, how long would you keep the friendship anyway? Most addicts who get into recovery are very grateful to those who cared enough to take that risk.

Intervention, see also: Acceptance, Addiction model (PEMS), Behavior, Crisis, Delusion, Disease concept, Employee assistance programs, Enabling, Gratitude, Inventory, Love & caring, Recovery, Responsibility, Self-centeredness, Service & giving, Sponsorship, Step One, Step Twelve, Therapy & treatment, Tools of recovery. Next on path N: Service & giving.

Intimacy

Intimacy is one way people relate to each other that involves honesty, openness, and trust. It is one of the riskiest things you can do with another person and one of the most rewarding.

At its best an intimate relationship is an opportunity to give and receive unconditional love, to experience the dissolution of the illusion of separation we feel from other people, and to have what John Powell, in *Why Am I Afraid to Tell You Who I Am?* (1969), calls "peak communication" with another person. He describes it as "a complete emotional and personal communion," where "the two persons will feel an almost perfect mutual empathy." This is an experience that occurs at times, but is not permanent.

DEVELOPING INTIMACY

Because of all sorts of injunctions from your dysfunctional family, unfavorable experiences with other people, and the strength of your addiction, intimacy may be something you have never experienced or have no idea how to develop.

Knot of yarn   Intimacy would be difficult and confusing even without the complications of addiction. As an illustration, imagine trying to untie a huge knot made of several pounds of yarn. Can you feel the frustration of trying to loosen and unravel it without damaging the yarn? Now think about trying to untie the same knot while under about thirty feet of sea water! This gives you an idea of what addiction does to complicate ordinary life problems.

Abandonment   Human beings have a natural ability and need to feel OK while separate from others, and also to be very close to others. If your experience includes emotional abandonment, then you may either cling too closely to others or avoid getting close because of the real or imagined risk of loss.

Enmeshment Clinging because of fear is called "enmeshment." A good common word for it is to smother. Inability to get close results in feeling isolated and in not being able to get interpersonal needs met.

INTIMACY IS DYNAMIC

Intimacy is a dynamic thing. It involves the movement of getting close and getting separate. The closeness feels safe and comfortable, but the separation is not threatening. To be separate and OK has to do with your self-esteem and sense of your place in the world. It does not depend on another person.

When you have this sense, it makes risking closeness easier. You can allow yourself to be vulnerable because you know that no other person has the power to damage your spiritual center.

Any model to describe intimacy could involve many dimensions; for example, honesty, trust, need, satisfaction, commitment, and choice. You can be honest and trusting with many people, but because of normal human limitations you probably will experience real intimacy, including commitment and meeting each other's intimacy needs, with only a few. So the choices you make for friends and lovers are very important.

ADDICTION AND INTIMACY

Addictive disease, whether in your family, your friends, or yourself, makes intimacy difficult. Fear, dishonesty, mistrust, and poor self-esteem all tend to crush intimacy. So if you want to experience intimacy, one of the most rewarding human adventures, you must put recovery from addiction as your priority.

Even then you may need special work to learn how to be intimate. Professional help is sometimes appropriate, as are self-help books and workshops.

Intimacy requires time, energy, and other personal investment. You have to risk admitting your needs and feeling vulnerable. But the rewards are well worth the risk. To feel secure, to be truly honest, to share thoughts, feelings and dreams, to laugh and cry with another human being, and to love and be loved, is a spiritual experience of the highest order.

A realistic look at the way the deck is stacked against intimacy, especially for addicts in the disease or in early recovery, shows that intimacy cannot be forced. Like a fawn in the forest, it will not come to you if you rush after it. You will need to work on your recovery and develop an appreciation for the grace that will present opportunities for intimacy in your life.

Intimacy, see also: Aftercare, Assertiveness, Codependency, Community, Control, Coping skills, Family, Feelings, Forgiveness, Freedoms, Honesty, Humor & fun, Integrity & values, Intervention, Love & caring, Recovery, Relationships, Self-image, Surrender, Unity.

Inventory

Steps Four and Five talk about a thorough inventory, and Step Ten asks you to conduct a continuing, daily inventory.

THOROUGH & SEARCHING

The Fourth Step inventory is a major assessment of strengths and weaknesses. Its purpose is to gain information that will be used in Steps Five through Nine.

When you share with God and another person the inventory you have prepared, and get their feedback, that is Step Five.

Purpose   The purpose of an inventory is to see what you have, what you need to keep, and what you need to discard. The Twelve-Step program suggests you don't need those things that interfere with your ability to be of maximum service to your Higher Power and other people.

Step guides   There are many guides to doing the Fourth Step, including booklets from various publishers and some brief instructions in chapter 5 of the Big Book. Some people write things chronologically, following logical blocks of time.

With whom?   The inventory can be shared with someone in the clergy, a sponsor, or someone else in a Twelve-Step program. They should understand what the Fifth Step is about, and you should be willing to share your most sensitive information with them.

Confession?   The Fifth Step is more than what most people think of as confession. In some denominations, confession is a sacrament of the Church. Early AA history talks about the benefits of confession and links that to the Fifth Step. Indeed, some things you discover in your inventory may need to be confessed, but the primary purpose of the Fourth Step inventory is to discover the information that will be needed to use all the later Steps.

Cleaning house   The inventory (Step Four) and sharing it (Step Five) both lead directly into Step Six, becoming ready to have God remove the shortcomings you have identified in Steps Four and Five.

Step Seven is when you humbly ask your Higher Power to remove these defects of character.

Step Eight asks you to list all you have harmed. Your inventory gave you some ideas about that and helped you decide what harm means.

Step Nine is where you make direct amends to these people.

DAILY INVENTORY

For the daily inventory that Step Ten mentions, some people like inventory sheets to fill out. Others like to write in a diary or journal. Still others just like to go over the day's activities and lessons learned just before retiring. One recovering addict says she likes to keep her Tenth Step handy because she never knows when she might need it. Anything that works is OK.

Inventory, see also: Abuse, Acceptance, Addiction, Affirmations, Amends, Anger, Assertiveness, Attitudes, Behavior, Beliefs, Body image, Character defects, Codependency, Control, Coping skills, Crisis, Defenses, Delusion, Detachment, Dichotomous thinking, Enabling, Energy levels, Excitement, Exercise & activity, Family, Family of origin, Fantasy, Fear, Feelings, Forgiveness, Grace, Gratitude, Grief, Guilt & shame, Habit & structure, Half-measures, Higher Power, Honesty, Humility, Humor & fun, Hunger & appetite, Incest, Integrity & values, Judgment, Love & caring, Moderation, Money, Nutrition, Obsession, Openmindedness, Perfectionism, Power, Prayer & meditation, Priorities, Psychological problems, Relationships, Relaxation, Resentments, Responsibility, Satiety, Self-centeredness, Self-image, Serenity, Service & giving, Sex, Sleep, Spending, Spirituality, Step Three, Step Four, Step Five, Step Six, Step Eight, Step Ten, Stinking thinking, Stress & strain, Surrender, Survival roles, Telephone, Therapy & treatment, Trust, Willingness. End of path I. Next on path J: Step Six.

J

Judgment

CRITICAL FUNCTION

The word *judgment* is one of the most powerful words we know. It affects everything we do in life. This one word has a tremendous influence on our success, our happiness, our choices, and ultimately our very lives.

Having good judgment and being judgmental are two very different things. Judgment here means wisdom, and judgmental implies morally evaluating someone else or their actions.

Affected by addiction Judgment, or lack of it, is a powerful mental aspect of the disease. However good your judgment was before the development of addiction, we can safely bet that addiction has degraded your judgment. As the addiction progresses, most addicts will rely on older, more dysfunctional tapes for decision making.

REMEDY

Certain types of brain damage can impair judgment. Some people are able to believe that they have experienced that damage, and frequently check out their judgment with others to be sure they don't make any serious mistakes. Others stubbornly suffer from such mistakes, often tragically.

It might be helpful to think of addiction in that way. As the disease progresses, judgment is gradually affected. At first, the judgment becomes questionable surrounding the food or other addictive substance. Gradually, it worsens, affecting an ever-increasing part of the addict's life.

The answer for addicts is not to totally abandon their judgment, but to learn not to rely on it without outside feedback. This means accepting the guidance of a Higher Power, which often comes through the experience, strength, and hope of others.

RECOVERY

Usually, judgment improves dramatically as addicts in recovery learn to use this guidance from their Higher Power.

Judgment, see also: Affirmations, Behavior, Defenses, Delusion, Dichotomous thinking, Diet mentality, Habit & structure, Integrity & values, Magical thinking, Mental aspects, Moodifiers, Obsession, Openmindedness, Paradoxes in addiction, Priorities, Step Three, Stinking thinking, Therapy & treatment, Visualizations. Next on path D: Habit & structure.

L

Love & caring

LOVE IS . . .

Love is something that people write books about, compose songs about, make movies about, etc. We won't attempt to cover all aspects of love, but we will, in this section, look at a few basic ideas we think may be helpful to you in your recovery.

Greek words   It is interesting that in English we have only one four-letter word used many ways for somewhat different things. "I love to smell roses" doesn't have the same meaning as "I love my children." The Greeks had at least three words to describe love — *eros,* which means erotic or sexual love; *philia,* which means brotherly love; and *agape,* which is love for all things.

Probably the most common way the word love is understood is to think of it as just a feeling. We find something or someone that we find attractive, desirable, appealing, and that probably makes us "feel good." So we say "I love it/him/her."

Scott Peck, in *The Road Less Traveled: A New Psychology of Love, Traditional Values and Spiritual Growth* (1978), describes this process as a cathexis in which we somehow incorporate the object or person into our own understanding of ourselves. We reach out beyond ourselves in a loving way. This kind of love may enrich our lives, but the good feelings are transitory.

Act of will   Peck goes on to describe love as not a feeling but an act of the will. The definition of love that he finds useful is, "The will to extend oneself for the purpose of nurturing one's own or another's spiritual growth" (Peck, 1978, p. 119).

Loving acts   Parents have the unpleasant task of having to act in a loving way that may not result in a child's feeling good. The act is in the child's best interest and motivated by a genuine desire for the child's best welfare. Though the act is loving, the child's immediate feelings may be painful. This does not, of course, mean that loving acts cannot result in positive feelings that can be delightful.

Tough love   Tough love is a phrase that describes behavior to stop enabling addiction. When you refuse to cover up for an addict, to rescue them, or to prevent them from experiencing consequences of their addiction, that is tough love. It is loving of the person but tough on the disease.

ADDICTION AND LOVE

Addictive disease, however, is a process that does a good job of interfering with your ability to be loving to yourself, to others, or to anything that matters to you. And loving plays a very important role in your recovery.

Caring for others   When you become involved with others in the Program, you get a sense of compassion and caring that comes from having shared a common suffering. Often that sense makes you feel not so alone and gives you some hope. That mystical bond is the foundation of the Twelve-Step recovery programs. It is commonly called caring.

Your history   People in Twelve-Step groups have a wide diversity of backgrounds with many reporting they never felt cared for or loved, or had to earn love by self-sacrifice and always placing others first.

Self-worth   Fellowship rooms are filled with people struggling with problems with self-worth and self-esteem. These negative feelings could easily have contributed to the attempt to find good feelings from addictive substances or behavior.

In early recovery you find yourself with no pleasure from the addiction while experiencing feelings of isolation, self-deprecating thoughts, and a worse sense of self-worth than you started with.

WHERE TO START

So, where do you start? Recognize that your self-worth is not zero, or you would never have been interested in recovery at all. Give yourself credit for having some love for yourself. Notice that you do have some capacity to care for other people. Probably there are people who mean a great deal to you and that you truly love.

In any relationship, the greatest gift you have to offer is yourself. And you don't want to give junk, do you? So don't put yourself down or treat yourself like junk.

Generosity   It is not difficult to think of people you know who seem to have taken care of themselves enough to have plenty to offer other people. Maybe in early recovery you need to devote lots of time to caring for yourself and letting other people share their Program with you. Recovery is such a gift that you don't just "give it away to keep it," you give it away because generosity is the natural response of a grateful heart.

Energy   Try to keep it simple when you think of love and caring. Remember that addiction thrives on self-pity and isolation. Love is the energy that makes the Program work; the sooner you open yourself up to it the sooner you will feel better.

Love & caring, see also: Beliefs, Coping skills, Family, Feelings, Gratitude, Higher Power, Honesty, Humility, Integrity & values, Intimacy, Openmindedness, Recovery, Relationships, Service & giving, Sponsorship, Step Twelve, Trust, Unity.

M

Magical thinking

Dichotomous thinking and addictive thinking processes play directly into the disease of addiction. Magical thinking may simply distract or confuse issues relating to recovery. Magical thinking is that style of thinking in which you believe that you or others can control reality in magic, supernatural, unrealistic, or mysterious ways.

Some of these beliefs result from childhood trauma, when they helped you make sense out of nonsense. For example, if your alcoholic parent hit you and told you they were forced to hit you because of your behavior, you may have believed you had that kind of power. These beliefs may have enabled you to survive an impossible situation. But now they're obsolete, more hurtful than helpful.

Magical thinking includes the belief that your attitudes or even your actions can cause reactions in the real world that are far out of reasonable proportions.

Some addicts believe that everything good (or bad) that happens to them is the direct result of their behavior, beliefs, attitudes, or efforts.

GOD

Some addicts may also believe that God is their supernatural servant. You may believe that God is available to cater to your whims and desires, that if somehow you are in God's favor, you will be granted whatever you ask.

Others may not believe in God as a benign servant, but that somehow God "has it in for you," and has nothing better to do than thwart your every plan. Even if you believe that God is making bad things happen so you can learn a spiritual lesson, it is still magical thinking.

Divine cure   Believing that you can pray to God to magically remove the obsession, while you're still drinking, bingeing, or continuing addictive behavior and not doing what you can for yourself, is magical thinking.

Faith   Having faith is the essence of the program, both a key to and a gift of recovery. But presuming that faith literally gives you magical powers is magical thinking.

VISUALIZATION AND AFFIRMATIONS

There is still a place for positive thinking, visualizing what you would like to happen, and making affirmations. Suppose you have a dream—of recovery or of anything else. You can do all the footwork to make it happen. You can visualize it and repeat affirmations to adjust your attitudes. These actions can remove all mental blocks that might interfere with its coming true. Ultimately the Serenity Prayer applies here: there are some things you can do, some you can't, and the Program or a Higher Power will help you know which is which.

Step Three   You might need to ask your sponsor or counselor to help you differentiate between magical thinking and Step Three, which says, "Made a decision to turn our will and our lives over to the care of God *as we understood Him.*" Proper use of Step Three is not magical thinking.

Gurus   When you begin to believe that another person—a sponsor, a therapist, or an author—can magically cure you or heal you, this is magical thinking.

Magical thinking, see also: Attitudes, Beliefs, Control, Defenses, Delusion, Dichotomous thinking, Diet mentality, Mental aspects, Obsession, Paradoxes in addiction, Step Three, Stinking thinking, Visualizations. Next on path D: Judgment.

Marijuana

For years we have heard people argue about whether marijuana is as bad as or worse than alcohol. It is easy for users to build a case that marijuana is less dangerous than alcohol. Marijuana users are much less likely to have traffic fatalities, die of liver disease, or commit violent crimes while under the influence. But these arguments do not begin to prove that marijuana is harmless. It is something like trying to argue that the drug dealer on the street is harmless compared with the leader of a major drug cartel.

HEMP

Marijuana comes from the hemp plant, *Cannabis sativa,* which has provided an important fiber, an edible seed, an oil, and a medicine since prehistoric times. The active ingredient, delta-9-tetrahydrocannabinol (THC), comes from a sticky resin concentrated in the flowering tops of the plant, especially the female plant. This resin is collected and pressed into lumps or cakes called hashish. A solvent can be used to extract the resin into a concentrated, thick oil known as hash oil.

Users can smoke or eat any of these forms of marijuana. First-time users often experience mild effects. Usually the pulse rate increases, the mouth dries out, and the whites of the eyes become reddened. Though not as powerful as other hallucinogens, marijuana produces a characteristic distortion of space and time, and everything seems funny. Appetite increases, causing the "munchies." As tolerance develops, these effects often give way to a relaxed sensation and a long-term habit.

EFFECTS

Marijuana is fat soluble, so about half the THC ingested builds up in the fatty tissues of the body. About half the stored THC is released each week, causing long-lasting effects. Its actual action is not well understood, although there is some release of dopamine (DA), possibly accounting for some thought distortion. There is usually impairment of short-term memory.

Chronic use also depresses the body's immune system, making it more dangerous for AIDS patients and causing some doctors to question its use to calm the nausea of chemotherapy in cancer patients. There is still some support for its use to suppress muscle spasms with multiple sclerosis and to relieve the symptoms of glaucoma.

MORE POTENT, MORE MONEY

Marijuana typically contains about 8 to 14 percent THC today, compared with 1 to 4 percent in the 1960s, when most of the marijuana studies were done. It has also increased in price, leading to the observation that marijuana has switched places with cocaine, which was the drug of the rich but is getting cheaper.

HARMLESS?

Probably the most dangerous thing about marijuana is the perception that it is harmless. There are people who believe it is less harmful than tobacco. Again, the comparison is with an extremely destructive drug, and produces some disturbing results for the three million or so daily pot smokers. There is good evidence that smoking marijuana causes bronchitis, emphysema, and lung cancer. A few joints a day subject the user to the lung damage usually associated with smoking more than a pack of cigarettes a day. Lung problems can develop in a year of heavy use, compared to ten to twenty years for tobacco.

Pregnant and nursing mothers who smoke pot put their children at risk, because THC will accumulate in the baby also. The effects are similar to the information in the module Fetal alcohol syndrome.

POT ADDICTION

Finally, marijuana addiction is a drug addiction with all the physical, emotional, mental, and spiritual consequences of other addictions. There is tolerance and withdrawal, and an easy route to other addictive substances and behaviors. For self-help information, contact Narcotics Anonymous. There are also several small organizations, mostly in California or New York, with the names Marijuana Anonymous, Marijuana Addicts Anonymous, or Marijuana Smokers Anonymous. See the module Other support groups for information on how to network with smaller support groups.

Marijuana, see also: Drugs, Fantasy, Impaired professionals, Inhalants, Moodifiers, Narcotics Anonymous, Nicotine, Other support groups, Pregnancy, Tolerance, Withdrawal.

Meetings

WHY GO?

Regular Twelve-Step group meeting attendance is the best way you can reinforce your recovery. You benefit by hearing other people share their experiences, you are reminded of who and what you are, you share and celebrate your recovery with others as they do with you, and you can get lots of physical or emotional hugs and good fellowship.

How many?   Some people recommend that newcomers or those having trouble attend ninety meetings in ninety days. This is a carryover from a traditional recommendation in AA. You may need two meetings a day or two a week, depending on how solid your recovery is and what is going on in your life. Almost all addicts need more than one Twelve-Step meeting a week, and only those brand new or struggling with recovery should go daily, with most finding two to four meetings a week to be comfortable and effective.

Attending meetings regularly is putting Step One into practice, every time you go. Regularity is important. Those who go only when they are in trouble insure that they will continue to be in trouble. We suggest that you use meetings as insurance rather than as crisis management.

No guarantee   It would be wonderful if as a newcomer to Twelve-Step groups you could walk into any meeting and find understanding and encouragement coupled with hope that you can live the rest of your life without all the crazy behavior associated with addictive using or behavior. Unfortunately, there is no guarantee that you will find good fellowship and recovery in all Twelve-Step groups in your area.

Some meetings (other than AA) even wind up enabling the addiction by taking relapse for granted and by slighting the spiritual or physical aspects of recovery.

DEVIATION FROM AA

All Twelve-Step groups are modeled after Alcoholics Anonymous. However, from the very start, some deviated from AA in some very significant ways, and we believe this is one reason their rate of recovery may not compare favorably with AA.

Laughter   In most AA meetings you will find lots of laughter, people sharing about weeks to decades of solid recovery, and you hear people comfortably using the Twelve Steps to avoid drinking so they can live happy, joyous, and free.

Recovery   While almost every AA group will have some people who are struggling with their recovery, you will find the vast majority to be sober (for months or years), saying that their lives are tremendously improved since coming into the Program. For most, these claims would be backed up by their family, friends, and co-workers.

We do not mean to imply that over 90 percent of AA members are "cured" of all addictive behaviors—a visit to a typical meeting will quickly show excessive use of coffee, sweets, and tobacco. But they came to stop their addictive use of alcohol, and for most, they have. Incidentally, in the last few years, there are more nonsmoking meetings and sensitivity and openmindedness about other addictive tendencies.

Spirituality vs. rules   AA began with spirituality as the cornerstone. This was natural for a group growing out of the Oxford Group, a nondenominational, theologically conservative, evangelical movement designed to recapture the spirit of first century Christianity. Some other Twelve-Step groups were founded in the heyday of pop psychology. Thus they began with a predominantly psychological bent, which may continue to this day. Many of these meetings are far more organized and "controlled" than AA, with even more tendency to be run by old-timers. In some places these leaders may not even be abstinent from the substance or addictive behavior themselves! There are more rules about who can speak, how long you can speak, and what you can or can't speak about. Some meetings of OA, for example, prohibit mentioning the names of foods.

CROSSTALK

Crosstalk in a Twelve-Step group meeting means answering or responding directly to another's question or statement. A clear example would be if someone said, "I just can't stay sober," and somebody else replied, "Well, if you'd just go to ninety meetings in ninety days like I told you last week, you might keep off the sauce!"

This is a natural way of speaking, and the second person's reply may actually come out of a deep caring for the alcoholic in trouble. There are several problems with this kind of crosstalk. First, it violates the spirit of AA's Twelfth Tradition, which says, "Anonymity is the spiritual foundation of all our traditions, ever reminding us to place principles before personalities." The person responding claims to know how the slipping alcoholic can get sober, subtly elevating the responder to a position of authority.

Second, we know that most addicts react with defiance to advice. Spoken or unspoken, the reaction is likely to be, "Who are you to tell me how to recover!"

Third, the struggling alcoholic may defiantly accept the advice, only to blame the advice-giver when it doesn't work. "See, I went to ninety meetings in ninety days and still got drunk." We call this "checklist mentality."

In typical discussion meetings where crosstalk is avoided, it is still common for a newcomer to ask a specific question. The chairperson or leader might say, "You probably have lots of questions about our program. If you'll stick around after the meeting, I'm sure some of our members will be glad to answer them, and give you their phone numbers and information about other meetings." Then they may return to the meeting topic or even switch to another subject. A good Twelve-Step meeting teaches the idea of avoiding crosstalk by example.

RECOVERY ATTRACTS

A good yardstick for the quality of a meeting is to ask yourself, "If I had been a newcomer, would I have been attracted by the recovery here? Would I have sensed that this was not just another fellowship, support group, diet club, or social gathering? Would I have been turned off by the intolerant attitudes I heard?"

TYPES OF MEETINGS

Speaker meetings are where one or more individuals tell their story, sharing their experience, strength, and hope in some detail with the whole group. In a larger group there is usually a podium and a lecture seating arrangement. There are combinations, where a group may have a speaker meeting once a month and discussion the other weeks, or where part of the meeting has a speaker, or where the chairperson for that week "qualifies" with a brief telling of their story before the discussion begins.

Pitch meetings are meetings where each speaker talks for three to five minutes, either with or without a stated topic. Usually the moderator encourages them to be upbeat and positive, and allows no crosstalk between members.

Discussion meetings devote most of the time available to discussion on one or more topics relating to the addiction. Members try to keep their sharing brief enough that many or most of those wishing to speak have an opportunity to do so. The topic is usually selected by the chairperson or suggested by members on the spot.

Step meetings are where a Step or Tradition is read or discussed each week, often including some reading from *Twelve Steps and Twelve Traditions*.

Big Book study meetings include reading and discussion from parts of the Big Book of AA *(Alcoholics Anonymous)*.

Newcomers' meetings are those designed especially for newcomers, usually led by more experienced volunteers. Although these meetings can help answer newcomers' questions, the leaders are often the same ones each week, and this often casts them in a guru role. Sometimes people volunteer to lead newcomers' meetings largely for their own ego trips. In other newcomers' meetings there is a healthy balance of members with more recovery to share their experience, strength, and hope.

Combination meetings may include parts of the above or other styles at different times in the same meeting, or rotating over time. For example, a group may have a speaker meeting once a month, and for the rest of the month have discussion meetings.

Special, occasional meetings, like marathons, retreats, and conventions, are announced in regular meetings or can be found in the group's journal, like the *Grapevine* or *Lifeline*.

Meetings, see also: Al-Anon & Alateen, Alcoholics Anonymous, Assertiveness, Co-Dependents Anonymous, Community, Debtors Anonymous, Emotions Anonymous, Families Anonymous, Gamblers Anonymous, History of Twelve-Step groups, Humor & fun, Narcotics Anonymous, Other support groups, Overeaters Anonymous, Priorities, Service & giving, Sex addiction groups, Sponsorship, Telephone, Tools of recovery, Traditions of AA, Unity.

Mental aspects

The basic PEMS model we use to describe addiction includes mental aspects. Dr. William Silkworth was the first to tell Bill Wilson that alcoholism is a mental obsession coupled with a physical allergy. We still see this obsession with the substance or addictive behavior as a major symptom of addiction. It may also occur in other areas of your mental life.

MISMANAGEMENT
Dichotomous (black-and-white) thinking and poor judgment also characterize addiction. These and other varieties of mental mismanagement support the continuance of addictive disease.

RECOVERY
Some mental attitudes and habits may interfere with recovery:

- Looking for a checklist so you can get control.
- Thinking of models as reality that you have to fit into.
- Using magical thinking.
- Being confused by paradoxes.

These mental aspects are each covered in separate modules in this manual.

Recovery from the mental aspects of addiction allows you serenity and peace of mind. Identify areas where you have trouble and use the Steps as tools to change.

Mental aspects, see also: Addiction model (PEMS), Beliefs, Defenses, Delusion, Dichotomous thinking, Diet mentality, Disease concept, Habit & structure, Judgment, Magical thinking, Obsession, PEMS model, Paradoxes in addiction, Priorities, Psychological problems, Stinking thinking, Visualizations. Next on path D: Disease concept.

Metabolism

The word *metabolism* means all the chemical processes that take place in the body. One type of metabolism is the breaking down of complex substances into simpler ones, like the "burning" of glucose (sugar) in the cells to produce energy, heat, carbon dioxide, and water. The other type of metabolism builds complex substances from simpler ones, like turning amino acids into proteins.

The way the body uses nutrients depends on many factors. Among these are whether you are in an absorptive state (you are still digesting nutrients), in a postabsorptive state (following digestion), or in a fasting state (ready energy is depleted). The situation is also changed if you have a large deficiency or excess of any major nutrient.

ABSORPTIVE STATE

Shortly after you begin an adequate, balanced meal, and for up to about four hours after you have finished, your digestion is supplying and replenishing your body's reserves. Here is what happens to the major nutrients during this time:

Carbohydrates   Enzymes in the small intestine break up starches into individual glucose molecules, and break disaccharides (sucrose, lactose, and maltose) into glucose, fructose, and galactose. These sugars are transported to the liver, where glucose enters the bloodstream, and fructose and galactose are converted to glucose and then enter the bloodstream.

If blood sugar is high enough, insulin is released so glucose is converted to glycogen (animal starch) to fill the reserves in the liver and other body tissue. After glycogen reserves are filled, excess glucose can be stored as fat.

Protein   Dietary protein is broken down into its amino acids in the stomach and small intestine. The amino acids are delivered to the liver, which keeps some and releases the rest into the bloodstream, where cells throughout the body use them to rebuild cells, make hormones and neurotransmitters, and so on.

An excess of protein will trigger the release of insulin also. If blood sugar is low (there was not enough carbohydrate ingested), then the amino acid will be converted to glucose. If there is enough glucose, excess protein will be changed to fat and stored.

Fats   Since fats are not soluble in water, they do not circulate freely in the bloodstream. Instead, the liver packs them into little packages called lipoproteins, which transport them to fat cells for storage. Some triglycerides (fats) are always being used for energy. Resting skeletal muscles and the liver itself actually prefer using fat as an energy source, if there is enough oxygen present.

If there is not enough glucose (blood sugar) present, a small part of each triglyceride (the glycerol part) can be converted to glycogen, but the fatty acids cannot.

POSTABSORPTIVE STATE

When most of the food is gone from the digestive tract, three or four hours after a normal meal, the body must shift gears into using its reserve supplies. These needs include energy from glucose and fats, and amino acids.

The main sources of energy in the body are glucose (blood sugar) and fats. Under normal conditions both are used.

Glucose   When the digestive tract stops supplying sugars, the blood sugar level will start to drop. This triggers the release of the hormone glucagon, which causes conversion of glycogen to glucose. If the glycogen reserves were filled, you will have up to about four more hours before they are depleted. This means you can go up to four hours in the absorptive state, and about four in the postabsorptive state, before things start to get critical.

Protein   The body cannot exist without amino acids. They are the building blocks for many structures and processes of the body. There is no actual storage site for amino acids, so in less than a day the free amino acids will be used up, and the body has to begin breaking down muscle and other tissues to supply the protein it needs.

Fats   For most people, fat supplies are adequate to provide energy for a long time. Fats are energy-dense: about nine calories per gram, compared with carbohydrates and protein, which each supply about four calories per gram. Fats need both oxygen and glucose to be "burned" properly. When the stored glycogen runs out, the body begins to enter an emergency mode in the postabsorptive state that amounts to fasting.

FASTING

What happens when the glycogen is used up and the glucose has stopped coming in or is inadequate? Most of your body can switch to burning fat to stay alive, but brain cells require glucose and will get what is available first. And the brain uses a lot of it. Though the brain is only about 2 percent of your weight, it uses about 20 percent of your glucose!

Glucose sparing   With reduced glucose available, the body starts adapting to conserve all the glucose it can for the brain's use. Almost every other organ can switch to using fats for its major energy needs. Protein can also be converted to glucose through a process called gluconeogenesis. This means loss of lean muscle mass, which in the long run conserves more glucose (and fat).

To meet this need, in the first week of fasting, up to a pound of muscle may be lost each day, in addition to a half-pound of fat. Obese people will lose about ten to thirty pounds of fluid, while nonobese people will lose about four to six pounds of fluid during this time.

Ketosis   Fortunately there is an emergency process that can help keep the brain alive. Without glucose, the fats are burned improperly, and ketone bodies (usually acids) are produced. After four or five days of fasting, the brain will begin to use these along with what glucose is available, cannibalizing less tissue protein. After the first week or so, weight loss falls to about one-quarter pound of muscle and about one-third to one-half pound of fat a day.

METABOLIC ADAPTATION

When you fast or go on a low-calorie diet, you are signaling your body that there is a famine outside. The body slips into a survival mode, in which it tries to conserve all the energy it can. The body can slow its energy consumption to about half its normal rate. If this is done repeatedly, the body "learns" how to store fat more efficiently, and to resist losing it.

Stoking the furnace   We can "fire up the furnace" by increasing exercise (supplying more oxygen to help burn fats) and increasing carbohydrate consumption. Both actions tell the body that the famine is gone, it does not need to spare glucose or adapt its metabolism to conserve energy, and it is OK to reduce its fat stores.

Metabolism, see also: Alcohol, Allergies, Bingeing, Biochemistry, Exercise & activity, Fats, Nutrition, Obesity, Physical aspects, Purging, Sugar, Tolerance, Withdrawal. Next on path B: Bingeing.

Models & concepts

MODELS VS. REALITY

People like to have ways to organize, understand, and explain information. This is done by using a model (or theory or concept). Many people operate as if theories were reality. A theory or concept is only a model of reality, a "portrait" of reality that may be more or less accurate.

Looking at the process   A good model will explain what really happens in as simple a way as possible, while still predicting what may happen.

Example   A table can be seen as a solid object. Most of the time this model is sufficient. We can set things on it and they don't fall through. But there are alternatives:

- If we were looking at the chemistry of the table, we might need to think of the chemical bonds and interactions that are going on all the time.
- Biologically, we might see the table as a platform for all kinds of microscopic plant and animal life.
- A nuclear physicist might see it as composed of atoms and subatomic particles separated by lots of empty space, or even as mathematical formulas of quantum physics.

Which is correct? It depends on your needs. Actually, we don't know the reality of a table at all, only several models, each of which serves a particular purpose. The models help us *approach* an understanding of the table.

All or none?   We create models to represent reality. They are not reality themselves. Addicts with dichotomous thinking often accept or reject all parts of a model. They may also try to fit themselves into a model rather than seeing what parts of the model fit their experience.

As an illustration, adult children of alcoholics often think they have to fit into one of Sharon Wegscheider-Cruse's survival roles—hero, scapegoat, lost child, or mascot. While you may have a tendency toward one role, you probably have characteristics of more than one of them.

Openmindedness   Understanding models can help you avoid a closed mind, dogma, and attitudes that resemble cultism. Here are a few examples of models that are very helpful when used to describe addicts' experience, but may be confusing and limiting if you think they apply universally:

- Alcoholics need the Twelve Steps to stop drinking.
- Children of alcoholics don't think, don't trust, and don't feel.
- Addiction fits into certain stages of progression.
- Shame causes addictive behavior.

MODELS FOR RECOVERY

There are many models for recovering addicts. In this manual we have tried to present some of the most useful. An example is the PEMS (physical, emotional, mental, and spiritual) model to describe addiction and recovery.

You have the opportunity to choose what you can use from the models available. Even the suggested Steps are a model for recovery. We recommend them because they are so effective for so many.

Models & concepts, see also: Addiction model (PEMS), Affirmations, Attitudes, Beliefs, Disease concept, Mental aspects, PEMS model, Paradoxes in addiction, Steps of AA, Visualizations.

Moderation

All addiction involves excess. Alcoholics drink too much. Drug addicts use too much. Compulsive gamblers gamble too much. Most food addicts eat too much, but anorexics starve too much. Sex addicts lust too much.

Some of these addictions have an advantage. Because alcohol is not needed for a healthy life, alcoholics do not have to moderate alcohol consumption—they can totally stop drinking. Drug addicts can quit using illegal drugs. Gamblers can stop betting.

NECESSARY FOR LIVING

Other substances and activities require moderation instead of abstinence. Food, necessary medications, spending, exercise, work, sex, love, relationships, excitement, and religion are all examples of substances or activities that may be necessary parts of your life, and recovery from addiction to them requires a moderation model instead of total abstinence.

No Twelve-Step program that we know of uses a total abstinence model without also a moderation model. Almost everyone in AA is familiar with the term dry drunk. It means an alcoholic who is not drinking, but also not using the Program to moderate their emotions, attitudes, and behavior.

BOUNDARY LIMITS

Part of the moderation model involves boundaries and buffer zones. In any kind of addiction, you can define limits of behavior that represent unacceptable danger or damage to yourself and others. If you are a sex addict, you may decide that paid sex, extramarital affairs, or use of pornography would violate those limits. If you are a workaholic, you might set a limit on the maximum number of hours you will spend at work. If you are an anorexic, you could decide that you will not skip meals. Almost anyone using a Twelve-Step approach could find some kind of boundary behavior—some dangerous behavior that it would be better to avoid entirely.

The moderation model also gives you a way to look at Abstinence and Relapse prevention. Refer to modules for more details.

ABSTINENCE

These boundaries give you at least part of the abstinence model as a tool against addictive or destructive behavior. A few examples from everyday life: There may be a red line on your car's tachometer that represents the maximum allowable RPM. There might be a certain temperature, above which you would whisk your child off to the doctor or emergency room. The smoke detector on your ceiling will squawk when the number of particles in the air exceeds a certain concentration. These boundaries give you a set do-not-exceed point to protect against catastrophic damage.

PUSHING LIMITS

Recovery will be chaos if you push yourself right up to that red line on a daily basis. It would not be good recovery for a sex addict to make frequent contact with prostitutes, but back out at the last minute. Workaholics who have committed to working no more than ten hours a day are obsessing a lot about work if they work nine hours and fifty-eight minutes each day. An alcoholic who often orders drinks, looks at them for a while, and then gives them away is not very sober.

BUFFER ZONES

Buffer zones represent a range of normal behavior. They acknowledge another reality of moderation: that moderation is dynamic rather than static. Almost everything in life changes. It cycles between a normal minimum through an average to a normal maximum. Your body temperature does not stay at 98.6 degrees Fahrenheit—it varies within a range that would be considered normal. Outside that range you are still not in trouble—you may just have a touch of fever or a subnormal temperature, either of which could indicate an illness. There is a buffer zone on either end of the normal range that says, "Pay attention, this is not normal," before you go to the emergency room.

Moderette to moderose   For almost any addiction or addictive process, you can look at a normal range of actions and identify those patterns of behavior that are OK and acceptable as normal recovery (moderate). Depending on the addiction, it might be helpful to call the lower end of that range "moderette" and the upper end "moderose." Then there should be a buffer zone that would signal a problem with your recovery requiring attention (call a sponsor, talk about it in a meeting, or make closer contact with your Higher Power). Finally, there may be boundaries that would indicate a relapse, and an immediate priority to get back into recovery.

FOOD ADDICTION
Addiction has no better example of the use of abstinence and moderation models than in food addiction. The ideas presented will apply very closely to sex addiction and many other addictive behaviors. See the modules Abstinence and Food plans for a detailed description.

Moderation, see also: Abstinence, Addiction, Addiction model (PEMS), Allergies, Arousal, Binge history, Biochemistry, Chronic pain, Drugs, Excitement, Food plans, Freedoms, Moodifiers, Neurotransmitters, PEMS model, Recovery, Sex, Weight.

Money

MONEY MISMANAGEMENT
Addicts often have trouble with money. They spend money on alcohol, drugs, fad diets or diet aids, sex or romance, legal or medical consequences of their addiction. Drug addicts may spend hundreds of dollars a day on illegal drugs. Bulimics report spending up to $100 a day or more on food. Anorexics or their families may spend $30,000 or more on their treatment.

COMPULSIVE SPENDING
Compulsive spending on other things may complicate the problem. Addicts commonly report times in their lives when compulsive

spending seemed more of a problem than their identified addiction, as if the addiction would migrate back and forth to and from compulsive spending. Others say they did both at the same time. For more information, see the module on Spending.

FINANCIAL PROBLEMS

Many addicts in recovery have to deal with problems with money and money management even after active addiction has been arrested. In *As Bill Sees It* (1967), Financial Problems appears in the index, and several selections are offered. It suggests that recovery depends on placing priority on spiritual matters rather than on the material. In the Big Book (p. 127) it says, "For us, material well-being always follows spiritual progress, it never precedes it."

In today's world it is quite a spiritual challenge to experience the promise that "Fear . . . of economic insecurity will leave us" (*Alcoholics Anonymous*, 1976, p. 84). There are bills to pay, obligations to be met, and the desire for comforts that we have taken for granted as necessary.

MONEY AS ENERGY

It helps to understand the purpose of money. It is easier to use than trying to find chickens or manufactured goods to exchange for whatever you have to trade. You can diffuse some of the emphasis placed on money itself by seeing it as energy rather than a thing. This energy is limitless—to see it as limitless energy rather than as something to be hoarded can help remove your fear of not having it.

Seeing money as a thing of value is a trap. If you have it and others don't, you can feel guilty. If others have it and you don't, you may feel resentful.

SPIRITUAL FOUNDATION

You do need enough money coming in and going out to meet your needs, but it is most important to build your recovery on a solid foundation of spiritual principles. Things accumulated with money can always be taken from you. You can lose jobs, possessions, and investments, but no one can take your faith from you.

Money, see also: Acceptance, Affirmations, Attitudes, Behavior, Character defects, Control, Defenses, Feelings, Inventory, Perfectionism, Power, Recovery, Resentments, Responsibility, Self-centeredness, Spending, Step Four, Step Six, Step Eight, Surrender, Survival roles, Trust. Next on path J: Affirmations.

Moodifiers

We have coined the word *moodifier* to mean any substance or drug capable of causing strong mood swings. Moodifiers may be ingested or otherwise taken into the body, or manufactured by the body itself.

To understand moodifiers, it is important to understand the basic mechanism of all thinking and feeling, which occurs at the synapse, a microscopic gap between nerve cells. It is here, in various parts of the brain and throughout the body, that decisions are made, sensations are interpreted, thoughts are recorded, and communication between cells of vital organs takes place.

A NERVE CELL

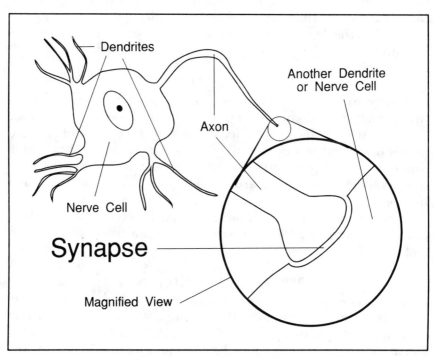

When a nerve cell is stimulated by another nerve cell or a sensory receptor, the message is conducted to the end of its axon(s) by a cascading electrochemical process. There tiny sacs called synaptic vesicles each release thousands of neurotransmitter molecules into the synapse. The synapse is about a millionth of an inch wide. The neurotransmitters cross the synapse, and some may fit, like keys in keyholes, into receptor sites in the dendrites or (sometimes) cell body of the next nerve cell. If enough of them find receptor sites, the next nerve cell will fire, and so on.

EXOGENOUS DRUGS

When a moodifier, like heroin, is eaten or smoked or injected, it is called exogenous, meaning coming from outside the body. Heroin in the body breaks down into morphine, and the morphine winds up crossing many billions of synapses between brain and other nerve cells in your body. Its drug effect comes when lots of these molecules find certain kinds of receptors, like the μ (or mu, for morphine) receptor. These signals alter the perception of suffering caused by pain. This is why morphine (and its synthetic imitators) are used following major surgery.

ENDOGENOUS DRUGS

Morphine is derived from the opium poppy, which for many centuries has been known to alleviate pain. But why would the body have receptors just for the product of this one plant? The answer is very important to the study of addiction. If you find a key on the sidewalk and try it in enough locks, you will eventually find one it will open. It will probably not be the lock it was designed for. It is just close enough that it works. In the body, morphine is the "accidental" key; the natural one is a class of neurotransmitters called endorphins. These are "drugs" that are manufactured within the body, and their actions are very similar to morphine. They are called endogenous, meaning that they come from within the body itself.

This bombshell has far-reaching implications for the treatment of addiction. It means that people can become addicted not only to powerful neurochemical imbalances induced by drugs like heroin and alcohol but also from drugs created within the body. All that an addict must do is find some way to produce quantities of these endogenous drugs that are well above the natural levels the body needs for proper functioning.

RATING MOODIFIERS

Even when only alcohol, narcotics, and certain other drugs were considered mood-altering, it was difficult to compare drugs based on their addictive potential. Now that even common caffeine is recognized as having a moodifying effect, we need some model to get a handle on how we view these various drugs, whether administered from outside the body or produced by the body itself.

We will borrow a rating scale familiar to almost everyone: the motion picture rating scale. Just as with movies, this will be a judgment call; your experience may differ considerably. And due to individual differences, any certain drug might be more accurately placed in a different rating when it is present in **your** body.

X-rated drugs   These are moodifiers that usually have a high potential for addiction and are generally not needed to maintain good health. In fact, they may be connected with severe health costs, to the individual and to society. We believe that this rating includes alcohol, heroin, cocaine, tobacco, marijuana, and many other illegal drugs.

R-rated drugs   Moodifiers that have a high potential for addiction but also have legitimate uses for health care include analgesics (painkillers), tranquilizers, depressants, stimulants, and many other prescription drugs that are known for their mood-altering properties. People with known addictive tendencies should use these drugs only if genuinely medically needed, with no fooling, and then they should take measures to insure they are used only as necessary.

PG-rated drugs   There are many drugs and other substances that are generally not thought to have extreme mood-altering properties, but often do wind up being abused by addicts and sometimes by other people. We would include here sugar, caffeine, antidepressants, laxatives, diuretics, and many over-the-counter (OTC) medications, and the body's response to activity like sex, gambling, or high risk.

G-rated drugs   Finally, even those substances that are often considered natural and even healthy, when abused and incorporated into the addictive cycle can become addictive moodifiers. This might include the chemistry your body produces in response to exercise, excitement, hunger, romance, and even religious behavior.

DEPRESSANTS
Some drugs depress the sympathetic nervous system. This is the part of the central nervous system that tells the body it is time to be alert, to do things, and to be concerned or worry. A depressant drug dulls or reduces those signals.

Alcohol   This is the moodifier that most people relate directly to when you mention addiction, treatment, and recovery. It is a very powerful and dangerous drug.

Alcohol is exempt from control by the Food and Drug Administration; it is controlled by the Bureau of Alcohol, Tobacco and

Firearms. If the FDA had jurisdiction, it would be available only by prescription.

Sleeping potions   Barbiturates (like Seconal, Tuinal, and Nembutal) and other medications commonly used as sleeping pills (like Quaalude, Placidyl, and Dalmane) have a depressant effect similar to alcohol.

Heroin   Many analgesics (painkillers) are depressant drugs. Heroin is refined from morphine. In fact, heroin was once promised as a cure for morphine addiction because it was thought not to be addicting. While morphine and other opiates are still used as painkillers, heroin has no approved medical use in the United States.

TRANQUILIZERS
The "major tranquilizers" often have a beneficial effect on people with severe mental disorders. The "minor tranquilizers," on the other hand, are usually unnecessary, and highly addicting. When someone tells you they are not addictive, remind them that it was only a few years ago when almost all physicians thought that Valium was not an addictive drug, and it was the most prescribed drug in the United States. We would rate tranquilizers as PG, with more legitimate uses for the major ones.

Sugar   As a mood-altering drug, sugar seems to most resemble tranquilizers. When used in quantities or concentrations high enough to produce even a mild moodifying effect, we would rate it at least PG, or higher depending on the individual's sensitivity to it.

STIMULANTS
Stimulant drugs actually depress the parasympathetic nervous system—that part of the central nervous system that works in balance with the sympathetic system. While the sympathetic nervous system tells the body to get up and do things, the parasympathetic system says slow down, relax, and enjoy. If this parasympathetic system is depressed, the sympathetic system has less competition, so you feel more awake, alert, and ready to go.

Ironically, the more you do, the less you will be pleased with it, owing to the depression of the parasympathetic system.

Caffeine   The most common powerful stimulant is caffeine. It is not only addictive but its withdrawal produces headaches, lethargy, and other discomfort.

Cocaine   This is a stimulant that also has the capacity to distort sensual perception, and is also highly addicting.

Diet pills   Diet pills, like the over-the-counter drugs based on propanolamine, can produce addictive responses.

Nicotine   The drugs in tobacco, including nicotine, share with cocaine the dubious distinction of being the most addicting drugs known to humankind.

Excess protein   Eating too much protein also produces a stimulant effect, and frequent bingeing on protein can produce an addictive sensitivity to it.

ANTIDEPRESSANTS

These are drugs that often have a positive effect on clinical depression. Examples are Elavil, Sinequan, and Prozac. They are not often abused, and they are very useful if depression is severe. They are also sometimes prescribed when they are not needed, and they should be used with caution, especially for people with an addiction history.

HALLUCINOGENS

These include marijuana, LSD, and any other drugs whose major action is to distort the perceptions or the thinking process.

Moodifiers, see also: Abstinence, Addiction, Alcohol, Binge history, Biochemistry, Chronic pain, Cocaine, Crisis, Drugs, Excitement, Heroin, Inhalants, Judgment, Marijuana, Moderation, Neurotransmitters, PEMS model, Physical aspects, Powerlessness, Progression, Purging, Relapse prevention, Sex, Sugar, Tolerance, Weight, Withdrawal.

N

Narcotics Anonymous (NA)

Narcotics Anonymous is the third largest self-help organization, behind only AA and Al-Anon. According to their World Service Office, there are about eighteen thousand groups in the United States, and about two thousand more worldwide. It is also the third oldest Twelve-Step group, founded in July 1953.

NA's translation of AA's Steps and Traditions is straightforward. Its members admit they are powerless over their addiction, and the only requirement for membership is a desire to stop using. It is one of the few Twelve-Step groups that does not use AA's Big Book, having its own basic text, *Narcotics Anonymous*. It incorporates a description of the program including discussion of the Twelve Steps and Twelve Traditions of NA, followed by a section of stories from NA members.

To make contact with NA, consult the white pages of your phone book or write or call:

> Narcotics Anonymous
> PO Box 9999
> Van Nuys, CA 91409
> (818) 780-3951

Narcotics Anonymous, see also: Adolescents, Alcoholics Anonymous, Enabling, Families Anonymous, History of Twelve-Step groups, Meetings, Other support groups, Steps of AA.

Neurotransmitters

Your brain has about 100 billion nerve cells, or neurons, and many of those receive information from hundreds or thousands of its connections, called dendrites. Each neuron usually sends its own message down a single path, called an axon, where if the information is to be passed on, chemical messengers must be dropped into a tiny gap called a synapse, which separates nerves by about a millionth of an inch. The messengers that cross this synapse are called neurotransmitters. They play a major role in our every thought, memory, feeling, sensation, bodily function, action, and behavior.

SCOPE

A thorough explanation of neurochemistry is beyond the scope of this manual and the skills of its authors. Our intent is to give you an overview and some hints to help you understand articles and discussions that mention some of these vital chemicals.

First, you will be disappointed if you try to discover which neurotransmitter is responsible for alcoholism or cocaine addiction or addiction itself. Neurochemistry is easier to appreciate if you can envision extremely complex patterns of chemical interactions, rather than individual, sequential actions. There may be over a hundred different neurotransmitters, and at least the common ones seem to cause different things to happen depending on what part of the brain or the body they concentrate in, and with what other chemicals.

Here are some common neurotransmitters, and some generalizations about their action:

ACETYLCHOLINE

Acetylcholine (ACh) is involved in the body's quiet attention and preparation for action, memory, aggression, thirst, sexual behavior, play, and REM sleep. The nicotine from tobacco will increase or decrease ACh, depending on dosage.

CATECHOLAMINES

The three common catecholamine neurotransmitters are dopamine, norepinephrine, and epinephrine. Enzymes convert the amino acid tyrosine into each of these catecholamines.

Dopamine Dopamine (DA) is associated with appetite and reward-seeking activities. There is normally a kind of balance between ACh and DA in various parts of the brain and body. An oversensitivity to DA in the frontal cortex of the brain is thought to be involved in schizophrenia, while Parkinson's disease is caused by gradual loss of DA neurons until less than 20 percent remain.

In 1984, an underground chemist tried to produce a new "designer drug" called MPPP. Through an error, a chemical called MPTP was produced instead. This drug caused severe, irreversible parkinsonism in dozens of users, after as little as a single dose. The drug destroyed DA cells.

Norepinephrine Norepinephrine (NE) has an alerting, attention-focusing effect. Learning, memory, and awareness are mobilized by NE. In some ways NE is the opposite of serotonin (5-HT). Many antidepressant medications directly or indirectly increase the availability of NE.

Epinephrine Epinephrine (E) used to be called adrenaline. It has a general activating function and increases heart and respiratory rate.

SEROTONIN

Serotonin chemically is 5-hydroxytryptamine (5-HT). It inhibits activity and behavior, including feeding, aggression, play, and sexual activity. It increases sleep and has a connection to the body's "clock" for daily, lunar, and seasonal cycles.

ENDORPHINS

Endogenous opioid peptides (endorphins) decrease suffering, the perception of pain. They also affect mood and thinking in other ways that are only beginning to be understood. Morphine and other opiates mimic the effect of these natural narcotics. Enkephalins and dymorphins are other natural opioids.

There are reports that people who have a high tolerance to pain have more endorphins available in their bodies. Endorphins may also increase as a result of long-distance running, acupuncture, hypnosis, or even placebos.

TOLERANCE

A characteristic of all these neurotransmitters is that the body usually counteracts any external manipulation of its chemical balance. For example, if too much serotonin is reaching the serotonin receptors, the body will start decreasing the number of serotonin receptors. So whatever you were doing to increase your serotonin will not only become less effective but you may become dependent on that "solution," and it becomes the next "problem."

Neurotransmitters, see also: Abstinence, Addiction, Arousal, Biochemistry, Drugs, Excitement, Moderation, Moodifiers, Physical aspects, Sex.

Nicotine

Nicotine and the other active ingredients in tobacco probably kill more Americans each year than all other addictions combined. Some 50 million Americans still smoke, and another 12 million or so chew or dip tobacco. Many users of "smokeless" tobacco mistakenly think it is harmless. While 80 to 90 percent of all smokers say they would like to quit, less than 3 percent quit each year. Smokers are persistent quitters, however, and there are about 40 million former smokers in the United States. Most of these stopped without using any formal program, though not usually on the first try.

LIKE COCAINE?

Nicotine is similar to cocaine in many ways. It reaches the brain within seven seconds of each drag on the cigarette, and the nicotine level in the brain peaks by the end of the cigarette. After about thirty minutes the level has fallen enough that craving begins to set in. This rapid intoxication followed by rapid detoxification is very similar to cocaine. No one doubts that the mood and mind alterations caused by cocaine are more powerful, but it may be mostly a matter of degree.

FATAL ADDICTION

We believe the perception that nicotine is less harmful than alcohol or other drugs also inhibits nicotine recovery for many alcoholics and other addicts. While only about 28 percent of adults smoke, about 80 percent of sober alcoholics smoke. Until recently it was hard to find a nonsmoking AA meeting. Bill Wilson, cofounder of AA, and Marty Mann, founder of the National Council on Alcoholism, both died of their nicotine addictions.

CRAVINGS

Recovering smokers stress that you will continue to have cravings for some time. No other addiction develops such strong habit patterns. If you smoke two and a half packs a day and take ten drags off each cigarette, that is 500 immediate reinforcements of the nicotine habit each day. A Nicotine Anonymous member said, "When I smoke I want to quit, and when I quit I want to smoke." Although your biochemistry may not know it, the craving will go in the same length of time whether you smoke or not. For more help, write or call:

> Nicotine Anonymous
> [formerly Smokers Anonymous]
> 2118 Greenwich St.
> San Francisco, CA 94123
> (415) 922-8575

Nicotine, see also: Arousal, Drugs, Enabling, Inhalants, Moodifiers, Other support groups, Physical aspects, Pregnancy, Tolerance, Tranquilizers, Withdrawal.

Nutrition

This module describes basic human nutrition without relating it specifically to any addiction. These things are true for everyone, addicted or not. For the relationship between metabolism and addiction, see the module on Metabolism.

DEFINITION
Nutrition is the science or study of a proper, balanced diet to promote health.

NUTRITION BASICS
You do not need to be an expert on nutrition to recover from food or any other kind of addiction, but you do need enough sound nutritional information to make wise food choices. No matter how flexible or structured your food plan is, you should know the basis for what you are including or excluding.

Humans meet their nutritional needs by eating food. The two major sources of food are plants and animals. From these we get what are commonly referred to as the food groups.

FOOD GROUPS
Fruits, vegetables, and **grains** are from plants, and **meats** and **dairy products** are from animals. Some people include **fats** as a food group because some foods (like butter and cooking oils) are almost pure fat, which may come from animals or from plants.

Food choices   From these choices, we decide where we are going to get our carbohydrates, protein, and fat. It is inaccurate to call a food choice "a protein" since almost all protein sources (like meats) include a considerable amount of fat also, and some (like beans) are also good sources of complex carbohydrates.

Problems can occur when you choose "a protein" for a food choice that is also high in fat, like nuts or peanut butter, and many red meats. We suggest that you learn in very broad terms an appreciation of the carbohydrate, protein, and fat content of common foods so you can make wise choices and still have effective weight management.

Fruits   Most fruits are sources of simple carbohydrates, which are actually sugars. They are useful for energy, vitamins, minerals, and fiber.

Vegetables   Vegetables are sources of energy, vitamins, minerals, and fiber also. Some, especially those we call starchy vegetables, are good sources of complex carbohydrates (starch). Examples are potatoes, yams, and legumes (starchy beans). Many legumes are also good sources of protein.

Grains   Grains are a category of food that are often ground into flour to make breads, cereals, and pasta, though some are eaten in a less processed form (like corn and rice). Their major use is to provide complex carbohydrates for fuel, as well as vitamins and minerals, and sometimes fiber.

The more common grains are wheat, corn, oats, barley, rice, rye, and millet. Products such as rice bran and oat bran have received much press about possible cholesterol-lowering qualities.

Whole grains   In whole grain flour the entire grain is ground up, retaining the higher levels of vitamins and other nutrients in the bran and germ. White flour is only the endosperm (which generally has better baking characteristics), but some 80 percent of the trace nutrients are lost. These flours are usually "enriched" to restore the iron, niacin, thiamine, and riboflavin, but not the zinc, copper, and other minerals or fiber. Whole grain products are more nourishing.

Meats   Meats include parts of various animals, such as cows, pigs, birds, and fish. We usually eat the fleshy part of the animal, but sometimes organs are eaten, such as the liver and heart.

Meat from cows (beef) and pigs (pork) is usually higher in fat than the meat from fish and birds (poultry). Most recommendations for healthy eating are to reduce the intake of high-fat meat for cardiovascular health as well as for weight management.

All meat is high in protein and it takes very little meat when combined with other sources of protein to fulfill your daily requirements. A woman whose healthy weight is about 130 pounds can usually get more than half her daily requirement for protein in one three and a half-ounce portion of meat.

Dairy products   Dairy products are good sources of protein as well as calcium and other vitamins and minerals. Low-fat and nonfat products are usually the best choices for overweight or normal weight people. Anorexics may need to include higher fat dairy products to help gain weight without feeling they have to eat too much extra food.

Fats   Some dietitians include fats as a food group. Products like margarine, oils, mayonnaise, nuts, and most salad dressings are primarily fat. You do need some dietary fat each day, but overweight or normal weight individuals will easily get enough in all but the most restrictive food plans.

CARBOHYDRATES

The above food groups relate mainly to sources. The rest of this module considers the nutrients themselves, regardless of their source. Carbohydrates are the basic fuels (with fats) used by the body for heat and energy. They are of two types: sugar (including sugars naturally found in fruit, milk, and many other foods) and long chains of sugars called starches (found in grains and other vegetables). Unrefined carbohydrates, like whole grains and fruit, are higher in fiber and natural nutrients than refined carbohydrates, like table sugar and white flour. Carbohydrates should make up at least half our food energy (calories).

When broken down into glucose (blood sugar), carbohydrates form the preferred fuel for the body. An excess of glucose can easily be converted to glycogen, which is stored in the liver, muscles, and other tissues for short-term energy.

Simple carbohydrates (sugars)   Simple carbohydrates are monosaccharides (one sugar molecule) and disaccharides (combinations of two sugar molecules). There are also trisaccharides (three) and tetrasaccharides (four sugar molecules), but they are rare and less important.

Sugars are found naturally in fruits, vegetables (including cane, beets, and corn), and other foods like milk. Many processed foods have added amounts of sucrose, fructose, or other sugars.

Complex carbohydrates (starches)   Complex carbohydrates are long chains of sugar molecules. They are found in most vegetables, especially starchy ones like potatoes and beans, and cereal grains like wheat, rice, oats, and corn. Cellulose is actually another carbohydrate, but we do not have the enzymes to break it down, so it passes through the body virtually unchanged, and we call it fiber rather than a sugar or starch.

Starches must be broken down into monosaccharides before the body can use them as fuel. This process begins with enzymes in the saliva, but digestion is not completed until the sugars and starches reach the small intestine.

Hunger   What most people report as hunger (physical, not emotional) is actually an awareness by the body that blood sugar and glycogen stores are low, and the body needs fuel. The fuel the body needs is best supplied by ample quantities of complex carbohydrates.

PROTEIN

About 60 percent of our bodies is water, but about half the rest is protein. Known as building blocks of muscle and other tissues, as well as various important chemical substances used by the body, every protein is made up of hundreds or thousands of units called amino acids. Of the twenty or twenty-two kinds of amino acids found in the body, eight or nine are considered essential amino acids, because the body cannot make them out of other amino acids. These essential proteins must come from a well-balanced diet.

Protein makes muscle tissue, hormones, neurotransmitters, and other products vital for life. If too little protein is eaten, the body must take protein from tissues in the body. If too much protein is consumed, the excess is likely to be converted to fat.

When people think of protein, they usually think of meat, eggs, and dairy products. But all those farm animals got *their* protein from vegetable sources. Good legumes for protein include soybeans, black-eyed peas, kidney beans, chick-peas, navy beans, pinto beans, lentils, split peas, and lima beans.

Effects of deficiency   If the body does not get enough protein, as in the starvation associated with anorexia nervosa or in very low calorie diets, the body will rob protein from tissues in the body, including lean muscle, like the heart. Singer Karen Carpenter's death has been attributed to heart failure caused by a combination of starvation and ipecac poisoning.

Effects of excess   Most Americans eat too much protein, perhaps with the idea that it is better to have too much than too little. The recommended dietary allowance (RDA) for protein (which includes a 45 percent safety margin) depends on your ideal body weight.

Requirements   At birth, your RDA for protein is the highest it will ever be, at one gram daily per pound of body weight. It gradually declines to adults nineteen and over, at a third of a gram per pound. However, pregnant women should have about two-thirds gram per pound, and nursing women should have a half gram per pound of ideal weight. A simple rule of thumb for most adults is to divide your healthy weight by 3 and get about that number of grams of protein each day.

This means that a woman whose ideal weight is about 120 pounds should only get about 40 grams of protein a day, or less than 15 per meal. For example, a breakfast might be two-thirds cup cooked oatmeal (4.6 grams), eight ounces skim milk (8.8 grams), and a medium banana (1.2 grams). This would give you 14.6 grams of protein.

Excess fat   All natural protein sources include fat, so an excess of protein usually means a high-fat diet. If, as part of your recovery, you are trying to lose weight gradually, the excess fat with the protein can be an obstacle to that weight loss. With good choices you can have adequate protein and still lose weight—the breakfast above only contains 2.9 grams of fat.

Tyrosine/Norepinephrine   Finally, an excess of protein can produce a mood-altering effect. Tyrosine is not one of the essential amino acids, but it is common in most protein sources, especially cheese (including cottage cheese) and milk chocolate. Tyrosine in the brain becomes norepinephrine, a neurotransmitter that acts like an "upper," increasing alertness and stimulating bodily functions.

FATS

Foods called fats are for long-term storage of energy, and also to electrically insulate nerves and to thermally insulate the body. There are three kinds of dietary fats: saturated fats (found mostly in meat and dairy products), monounsaturated fats (as in avocados and olives), and polyunsaturated fats (found in fish and many vegetable oils). Most people in the United States eat too many fats, especially saturated fats.

Dietary fats are dissolved by bile salts and then broken down into fatty acids and glycerol (an oily alcohol) by lipase, a pancreatic enzyme. They are absorbed into the lymphatic system before entering the bloodstream. All this means that fat takes longer to digest than carbohydrates.

Fats are used with carbohydrates as a fuel source. Ordinarily, if more fat is consumed than burned as fuel, you will gain weight. Like a bucket with a hole in the bottom, if you take in less fat than you burn up, the fat stored in your body will be used up, gradually.

FIBER

The indigestible structural materials from plants are called fiber. Fiber is found in unprocessed foods, like fruits, raw vegetables, and whole grains. There are two kinds of fiber, and both are usually present in many whole foods, but to differing degrees.

Insoluble fibers   Insoluble fibers provide bulk for proper operation of the elimination system. They aid in preventing constipation and are a positive factor in decreasing the risk of colon cancer. Wheat bran and many legumes are good sources of insoluble fibers.

Soluble fibers   Soluble fibers slow the digestion of certain foods, including glucose. Therefore, it is probably important for those sensitive to sugars to get adequate amounts of soluble fibers. Oat bran, barley bran, and many fruits are good sources of soluble fiber.

WATER

Our bodies are about 60 percent water. Water is required for most bodily functions, and more is needed if you are losing weight and having to flush out the toxic substances that result from the metabolism of stored fat.

VITAMINS

Substances that regulate metabolism, vitamins are necessary for the healthy functioning of the brain, nerves, muscles, skin, and bones. They do not provide energy themselves, but some are necessary to produce energy from foods.

A reasonably balanced diet contains all the vitamins we need, so supplements are not usually necessary. In fact, some vitamins, especially A, D, E, and K, are dangerous in excess amounts, and others may imbalance the biochemical balances in our metabolism. If you are concerned about your vitamin intake, you can take an ordinary daily multivitamin, but anything stronger should be taken only on medical advice.

MINERALS

Also, a healthy diet will provide enough calcium for maintaining our bones, zinc and magnesium for controlling cell metabolism, and sodium and potassium to maintain fluid and electrolyte balances. Women who have heavy periods may need additional iron, and women need adequate calcium to help avoid osteoporosis in later years.

We human beings (not just addicts) have survived because our bodies can obtain all we need from a varied diet of natural, relatively unprocessed foods.

Unrealistic promises   All the overt or veiled promises made by the pharmaceutical and food industries cannot gloss over the fact that we do not know enough about human nutrition to be able to supply all the vitamins, minerals, and other nutrients in a pill form. We simply don't know how much of what nutrients we need, and how much is detrimental.

Danger of megadoses   A common American idea is that if some is good, more must be better. With vitamins and minerals, this reasoning can get you in a lot of trouble. Ingesting more than the RDA of any vitamin or mineral may actually deplete other vitamins or minerals, preventing the proper proportions from being absorbed. This can lead to actual poisoning or malnutrition much worse than a slight deficiency of a vitamin or mineral.

Herbs are drugs   Before you begin taking large amounts of some herbal tea or other herbal concoction, remember that many herbs are drugs, even in relatively small quantities. In fact, they were among the only drugs we had for many centuries.

Useful in some circumstances   Nature's way to provide vitamins and minerals is in natural foods, eaten with a large variety of other foods. The danger of taking extra vitamins is twofold: you might actually take too much of a particular vitamin or mineral, and even if you don't, you might be lulled into a false sense of security by thinking you don't need to eat a varied, natural diet since you're taking a daily multivitamin pill.

While a normal multivitamin probably doesn't hurt, the only people who need added vitamins or minerals are:

- Pregnant or nursing mothers (when advised)
- Women who have heavy periods (may need iron)
- Others when recommended by their physician

BALANCE

Everything needs a balance. Anytime we are not giving the body the nutrients it needs, in reasonable (neither too high nor too low) quantities, we will experience some kind of malnutrition.

FOOD LABELS

Learn to read food labels when shopping so you can make wise choices. You may have special needs to consider, such as the need to restrict salt. Books listing food values, like Pennington (1989), can help you get a better idea of the actual nutritional components of common foods.

Nutrition, see also: Biochemistry, Celebrations, Constipation, Diet mentality, Edema, Exercise & activity, Fats, Food addiction, Food plans, Hunger & appetite, Metabolism, Moderation, Overeaters Anonymous, Sugar, Sweeteners.

O

Obesity

DESCRIPTION

Obesity means significantly overweight, usually a body mass index (see definition later in this module) of about 32 or more, or more than about 30 percent above ideal weight. It is possible to be obese without being a food addict, but the more severe the obesity, the harder it is to explain the phenomenon without suspecting that addiction is involved.

Using John Lovern's Unified Eating Disorders Theory we can describe obesity as a cyclical eating disorder in which the cycles gravitate toward the overeating side of moderate. Over time, the cycles get much longer, and obese people may eventually give up trying to manage their weight at all. There may be long periods of time on rigid, very low calorie diets that are nearly fasting, alternating with steady overeating for months or years at a time.

Risk factors   There are strong genetic links with obesity, so the best single predictor of whether a person wil become obese is to look at obesity in the family. This does not mean that having overweight parents and grandparents dooms you to be obese, however. It simply means there is a tendency.

Cultural factors   Some cultures tolerate obesity, and some even encourage a fair amount of obesity. These cultures usually include more fat in their diets, and fat is often a sign of wealth rather than something shameful.

ADOLESCENT PAIN

Obesity is especially tragic in adolescents. Poor self-image often starts there. Many obese people cannot remember a time in their lives when they were not significantly heavier than their peers, when they were not the brunt of jokes and insensitive comments from family, friends, and strangers alike.

Obese children are discriminated against in all sorts of ways. Usually self-image is distorted at a young age, and these children grow up with lots of deficits in interpersonal skills. Sometimes there has been no healthy bonding with others, and this may be aggravated by emotional or even physical abuse from others.

Some people who have been obese since childhood may develop serious personality disorders. Sometimes their shame, fear, and lack of trust are like that of abused children. Because they did not know how to stop the abuse (ridicule, threats, and others' obsession about their fatness), they developed a pattern of eating to soothe this pain, which only aggravated the problem.

ADULT PAIN

Adults are also targets of discrimination, in jobs and social situations. They are often bombarded by family and friends who say, "That's all in your head. You can get a job if you try." The reality is that they have a terrific handicap. It is also true than many fat people will not take advantage of the opportunities they do have. The pain is tremendous.

Most obese people have already tried so many things to lose weight that it is difficult to hope anymore. They are vulnerable to any scam that comes along that promises a cure, which is usually followed by severe discouragement and depression.

MEASUREMENTS

The traditional measure of obesity has been weight. This measurement is very misleading. For example, 154 pounds might be in the anorexic range for a person 6 feet 6 inches tall, but obese for someone who is 4 feet 10 inches.

Body mass index   In the last few years the eating disorders profession has begun using a measurement called the body mass index. This is weight (in kilograms) divided by height (in meters) squared. See the Weight module for an easy way to calculate it. There are at least two advantages to using it compared with ordinary weight. First, it does consider height, so there is some comparison between people of different heights. Also, the numbers that result are unfamiliar to most people and may produce less obsession.

Waist/hip ratio   This determines whether the person is more apple- or pear-shaped, or whether they carry their weight more in their abdomen or their thighs. Pear shapes are healthier for any given weight because the weight puts less stress on the spinal column and the internal organs.

PROBLEMS IN TREATMENT

It is very difficult to break the diet mentality for obese people. There is so much pressure from family, friends, and the culture itself, and there are many old assumptions about being fat, dieting, and failure.

Factors in recovery   Focus must be shifted to the process (now) rather than what it will be like when you have lost all the weight. If you are eating moderately and losing weight, even very gradually, you will feel great! Obese people are weight-lifters; your muscles are toned to lifting a heavier person, so you will feel like doing more each week.

Many obese people also have work to do on their emotional, mental, and spiritual recovery. Self-esteem, assertiveness, social skills, codependency, and control issues are all areas obese people may need to address in recovery. Many find individual and group counseling helpful. It is best if counselors have experience in food addiction treatment. Of course, the ultimate solution involves use of the Twelve Steps.

Obesity, see also: Addiction, Adolescents, Anorexia nervosa, Binge history, Bingeing, Biochemistry, Bulimia nervosa, Constipation, Craving, Diet mentality, Edema, Exercise & activity, Fats, Feelings, Food addiction, Food plans, Hunger & appetite, Nutrition, Physical aspects, Recovery, Sex, Therapy & treatment, Unmanageability, Weight. Next on path A: Exercise & activity.

Obsession

Obsession is intense focus or a mental lock on a particular thought or thought pattern. It is something like a tune you can't get out of your mind. For most of us it is an occasional nuisance. In people with obsessive-compulsive disorder (OCD) it seems to be a severe thinking disorder that can make normal living almost impossible.

For most addicts, obsession falls somewhere between normal and the kind of abnormality we find in OCD. Obsession is only part of the addictive process, and whatever level of obsession (about alcohol, other drugs, cigarettes, food, diets, weight, body shape, etc.) you experience is magnified by the other elements of addiction to create the mental mismanagement characteristic of addiction.

This distortion of thinking can lead to mental fatigue, perceptual errors, and very poor judgment. In the earlier stages of addiction, it tends to be concentrated around the addictive substance and behavior directly involved with it. But later it seems to spill over into other areas of life.

COMPULSION

Compulsion is the seemingly uncontrollable urge to do something. The combination of obsession and compulsion forms a very powerful part of the disease of addiction.

The key to understanding and coping with obsession and compulsion is to realize that there is no direct link between them and the behavior they seem to demand. The addiction keeps wanting to put a link between the obsession/compulsion and the behavior. The feeling is, "I just have to do it." You don't.

The trouble lies in remembering that when the obsession or compulsion is very strong. Pain does not require the application of drugs, but when you are in considerable pain it is hard to remember that you don't need the drug to survive. When you are very angry, even enraged, you don't have to attack anyone, although it is not always easy to remember that. When you are very hungry, you don't have to eat right then. When you crave a drink, you don't have to drink alcohol. And when you experience strong obsession and compulsion, you still have healthy options.

Because of the mental distortion that happens in addiction, do not rely on only your own thinking process for your decisions and action. This is where a Higher Power comes in. By being willing to listen to other addicts, to the literature of the Program, and to God (or your Higher Power), you defuse the power of the obsession and compulsion, and get past the crisis without damaging your recovery.

BODY IMAGE OBSESSION

A special burden for many addicts is obsession about body image. This obsession may be strong in any addiction (or even in people who are not addicted), but it is more common among women addicts, and especially in food addiction. See the Body image module for more information.

PREOCCUPATION

Preoccupation is almost the same as obsession, but it implies decisions and acting on those decisions rather than just thoughts running through the head. Preoccupation usually distorts your priority system because it decreases judgment in a larger area of your life. Obsession may be very isolated, like frequent, powerful thoughts about alcohol, drugs, cigarettes, or your weight. Following are some examples of preoccupation:

Living in the future   Worry is a preoccupation that short-circuits decisions and action in the present in favor of living in the future. Self-help for worrying a lot may involve: reexamining your priorities, sharing your fears with someone else in the Program, trying to help someone who is struggling, reading some Twelve-Step literature, and making contact with your Higher Power.

Disconnected with people   Loneliness is a preoccupation that magnifies the feeling of separateness from others. It is often teamed up with self-pity. Almost by definition, the only way to get out of loneliness is to take a risk to get close to others.

Disconnected with life   Boredom is a preoccupation that signals lack of meaning in life. It is a clear sign that you do not have an adequate contact with a Higher Power. A good way to develop better contact is to reach out to others.

When the "committee in the head" is in session, the way out is to use a Higher Power and get out of your preoccupation with yourself. In most cases, that involves other people.

Obsession, see also: Addiction model (PEMS), Affirmations, Beliefs, Body image, Character defects, Control, Craving, Defenses, Delusion, Dichotomous thinking, Diet mentality, Dual diagnosis, Emotions Anonymous, Gambling, Habit & structure, Mental aspects, Psychological problems, Relaxation, Religiosity, Serenity, Service & giving, Sleep, Slogans, Sponsorship, Telephone, Therapy & treatment, Visualizations. Next on path D: Dichotomous thinking.

Openmindedness

The Big Book (pp. 550, 570) suggests that honesty, openmindedness, and willingness are needed for recovery. It also describes how the disease of addiction fights openmindedness.

First you need to be openminded about what might help you. If you have suffered enough from addiction, an open mind is easier. You need to be openminded about the Steps, meetings, a Higher Power, and the experience of others.

OPENING THE MIND

A simple technique for becoming more openminded is to tell yourself, "In spite of how crazy that sounds, if even part of it is true, it would explain how I am feeling and what is happening to me."

Another suggestion, when it is hard to accept feedback or other awareness, is to ask yourself, "Would I be willing to consider the possibility that . . ."

It is good to remind yourself that you have a lot to gain by being openminded and much to lose if you are not. You or your disease may be threatened by the truth, but denial or ignorance will hurt more in the long run. Remember that the truth will set you free (even if you have doubts at the moment).

Opportunities   As you recover, openmindedness can help you take advantage of many opportunities. If you are stuck, you can become open to new ideas, such as a need for counseling, assertiveness training, body image work, codependency treatment, incest or abuse therapy, or the identification of other addictions.

Contempt prior to investigation   Looking at a closed mind may help describe openmindedness. "There is a principle which is a bar against all information, which is proof against all arguments and which cannot fail to keep a man in everlasting ignorance—that principle is contempt prior to investigation" (Herbert Spencer, *Alcoholics Anonymous*, 1976, p. 570).

SPIRITUAL OPENMINDEDNESS

The Big Book (p. 48) explains how, faced with the destruction of addiction, you can learn to be openminded about spiritual matters.

Openmindedness, see also: Acceptance, Attitudes, Beliefs, Control, Delusion, Dichotomous thinking, Higher Power, Honesty, Humility, Magical thinking, Paradoxes in addiction, Powerlessness, Prayer & meditation, Step One, Step Two, Step Three, Step Eleven, Trust, Willingness. End of path G. Next on path H: Step Three.

Other support groups

Most of the large Twelve-Step organizations, and some representative smaller ones, are in this manual under their own modules, or under the addiction or disorder they serve. In this module we discuss the types of support groups, and briefly list some other examples.

TWELVE STEP

These are support groups that closely follow the Twelve Steps and Twelve Traditions originated by Alcoholics Anonymous. This is not meant to be a complete list; it is to give you an idea of the kinds of groups available.

Compulsive Stutterers Anonymous
Box 1406
Park Ridge, IL 60068
(815) 895-9848

Drugs Anonymous
PO Box 473, Ansonia Station
New York, NY 10023
(212) 874-0700

Emotional Health Anonymous
PO Box 429
Glendale, CA 91209
(818) 240-3215

HIVIES (HIV positives)
610 Greenwood
Glenview, IL 60025
(708) 724-3832

Obsessive-Compulsive Anonymous
PO Box 215
New Hyde Park, NY 11040
(516) 741-4901

Workaholics Anonymous
PO Box 661501
Los Angeles, CA 90066
(310) 859-5804

ADAPTED

There are also self-help groups who have adapted the ideas pioneered by AA, but do not follow the Twelve Steps and Twelve Traditions exactly. For example, Incest Survivors Anonymous (listed in the Incest module) has a person who is a lifetime head, a clear violation of AA's traditions. Another example is a group for Christian support for addictions, sharing Twelve Steps through the Bible:

Overcomers Outreach
2290 W. Whittier Blvd., Suite A/D
La Habra, CA 90631
(213) 697-3994

OTHER "ANONYMOUS"

There are support groups that use the word *anonymous* in their name, but do not appear to be Twelve-Step groups at all. Fundamentalists Anonymous does not use a Higher Power, and Parents Anonymous, for people who want to avoid abusing their children, uses volunteer professionals as a resource.

Fundamentalists Anonymous
PO Box 20324, Greeley Square Station
New York, NY 10001
(212) 696-0420

Parents Anonymous
6733 S. Sepulveda Blvd., #270
Los Angeles, CA 90045
(800) 421-0353

OTHERS

There are also plenty of support groups, for everything from Alzheimer's syndrome to Zellweger syndrome. Some of them have local chapters, while others simply provide written materials, referrals, and telephone support. There are also councils that provide information and other services.

CLEARINGHOUSES

There are several national clearinghouses that try to keep up with all the self-help groups, and provide what information they can about them. One of them, the American Self-Help Clearinghouse, even publishes a biannual book listing all the self-help organizations in its files. For current information, write or call:

American Self-Help Clearinghouse
Saint Clares-Riverside Medical Center
Denville, NJ 07834
(201) 625-7101

National Self-Help Clearinghouse
CUNY Graduate Center
25 West 43rd St., Room 620
New York, NY 10036
(212) 642-2944

Other support groups, see also: Adolescents, Al-Anon & Alateen, Alcoholics Anonymous, Children of addicts, Co-Dependents Anonymous, Debtors Anonymous, Emotions Anonymous, Families Anonymous, Gamblers Anonymous, History of Twelve-Step groups, Meetings, Narcotics Anonymous, Overeaters Anonymous, Sex addiction groups, Steps of AA, Traditions of AA.

Overeaters Anonymous (OA)

Overeaters Anonymous is the largest Twelve-Step organization for food addicts (compulsive overeaters) in the world. It has over eleven thousand groups registered worldwide, a World Service Office, a monthly recovery journal (*Lifeline*), and it publishes books, tapes, and pamphlets.

Rozanne S. founded OA in January, 1960, in Los Angeles. The early OA members did not see their problem as addiction, and they were not looking for a spiritual solution. Originally, they removed most references to God or a Higher Power from their Twelve Steps, though they were soon changed back to match AA's. Early members were more inclined to use psychological means for recovery than spiritual tools. It was more like a self-help diet club. Experience has shown that abstinence from compulsive eating and the use of the Twelve Steps is the way members get and maintain lasting recovery.

OA's unity has suffered from controversy about what to do about food, food plans, and abstinence. For many years OA provided members with food plans, though they were always officially optional. The first such plan was a restrictive, low-carbohydrate diet. It was called the "gray sheet" because it happened to be printed on gray paper. Alternatives were offered later. In 1986 food plans were declared an outside issue and discontinued, leaving choices about food plans to individuals and their Higher Power.

Subgroups   One of the results of not having an official definition of abstinence was a polarization within OA. Some members don't think abstinence is critical, while others adhere to a specific, highly restrictive food plan. There are subgroups in OA including HOW and Westminster groups, who have made such food plans the focus of their abstinence, sometimes equating sugar and white flour (and maybe other foods) with alcohol for the alcoholic. There is also a moderate course—members who find that an individualized food plan and using the Steps work well to empower them to recover from compulsive eating.

What's in a name?   Some treatment centers for food addiction teach their patients to call themselves food addicts. It is actually just another name, probably more accurate, for compulsive overeater.

For information, look for OA in the white pages of your phone book, or write or call:

> Overeaters Anonymous
> Box 92870
> Los Angeles, CA 90009
> (800) 743-8703

Overeaters Anonymous, see also: Alcoholics Anonymous, Community, Food addiction, Food plans, History of Twelve-Step groups, Meetings, Other support groups, Steps of AA, Traditions of AA.

P

Panic attacks

A usually short but extreme experience of anxiety without an obvious cause is called a panic attack. Panic attacks are accompanied by physical and emotional symptoms such as chest pain, rapid heartbeat, sweating, and feelings of numbness, unreality, or impending doom.

Panic attacks have been linked to addiction in a couple of ways. Some people medicate themselves with alcohol or drugs when anxious. Panic attacks are also seen in withdrawal from addictions, especially those involving drugs (including alcohol).

KINDLING THEORY

One theory to explain panic attacks is called the *kindling* phenomenon. James Cocores, MD, in *The 800-Cocaine Book of Drug and Alcohol Recovery* (1990), says it occurs after repeated stimulation of areas of the brain. This can happen with cocaine or other drug use, or from alcoholic withdrawal (the shakes). The brain has a panic threshold and repeated stimulation appears to lower it. Lower levels of neural activity can then produce a panic reaction. When these kindled reactions are repeated frequently, the brain may become so sensitive that little or no stimulation can cause a panic attack.

RECOVERY

Panic disorders in the general population usually respond to medication and psychotherapy. Study of the complex relationship between panic disorders and addiction is in its infancy. When panic disorders occur in sobriety or abstinence we recommend alternatives to drug therapy, including psychotherapy, relaxation, meditation, or contact with your Higher Power.

Paradoxes in addiction

ROOT OF PARADOXES

A paradox is a statement that seems contradictory or absurd but may be true, or else a statement that is self-contradictory and therefore false. This gives a hint that the root of paradox is inadequacies in the language or models being used.

Language/concept assumptions   A simple example is the question, "If God is all powerful, can God make a rock bigger than God can lift?" There is no answer to this question because the question itself is a paradox; it contains its own negation. The assumptions of the concept or model must be examined if we are to make anything useful out of a paradox. For example, in the question above, the critical points are not God's capabilities, but your assumptions about the ability of human beings to understand God.

PARADOXES IN ADDICTION

The reason we talk about paradoxes is that the world of addiction seems to invite paradox, and it leads to much confusion in recovery.

A phrase that is used often in recovery, "Surrender to win," seems paradoxical. We assume that surrender means defeat. The key is that the war is within you, so unless you surrender you will inflict further damage on yourself. Surrender means accepting your disease and giving in to the process of recovery.

You may also be told that you have to give to receive. Giving and receiving seem opposites, but in relationships both are aspects of caring. You receive satisfaction and joy when you give of yourself. In receiving, you provide others with the opportunity for the joy of giving.

Is sponsorship for the sponsor or the sponsee? Sponsorship is based on the simple idea that by helping others you help yourself. "To keep it [recovery] you have to give it away." Bill W.'s first talk with Dr. Bob came about because Bill was fighting the urge to drink. Many had tried to help Dr. Bob, but it was important to Dr. Bob that Bill needed him, too.

You may also hear someone say this is a selfish program. That sounds greedy, but if you understand it as meaning that you must take responsibility for your own recovery, it makes more sense. You must focus on yourself in recovery as you turn loose your self-centeredness.

Sometimes you will hear people say that alcohol or drugs or food or addictive behavior is not the issue, and other times that it is the issue. The truth is that in addiction, the addictive substance or behavior is an issue, but only part of the physical aspect of the disease.

You will hear people say, "You have to do it yourself." Others will say, "You can't do it by yourself." Actually, you can't change yourself without help. Nor can you expect anyone else to do your legwork. And you certainly have no business trying to change or control someone else. Another way to say it is, "Only you can do it, but you can't do it alone."

DANGER OF PARADOX

The danger of not recognizing and working around paradoxes is that you will get yourself confused and tied up in the language you or others are using.

Spiritual matters often invite paradox. Bill W. quoted a prayer in *Twelve Steps and Twelve Traditions* (p. 99) that ends with paradoxes. "For it is by self-forgetting that one finds. It is by forgiving that one is forgiven. It is by dying that one awakens to eternal life."

As long as you are trapped in the wrong questions, like "How can I get control of my eating?" you are not likely to find the solutions. Ask instead, "How can my eating be controlled?" and the answer is more obvious: by a Higher Power.

Paradoxes in addiction, see also: Affirmations, Beliefs, Control, Delusion, Dichotomous thinking, Disease concept, Mental aspects, Openmindedness, Priorities, Sabotage of recovery, Serenity, Stinking thinking, Visualizations. Next on path D: Psychological problems.

PEMS model

The most powerful model we know for understanding addiction, except for the Twelve Steps, is looking at the physical, emotional, mental, and spiritual aspects of the disease—PEMS, for short. These are explained briefly under the module Addiction model.

The model can be expanded to relate not only to the individual but to the family, relationships, and occupation as well. While we do that, we will also describe how this expanded PEMS model could be used in a Step Four inventory.

PHYSICAL ASPECTS

The physical aspect includes all the facts and realities of the physical world, and of your addiction.

Family level   Family here refers primarily to family of origin, and all your early education. It includes things that make up your legacy from your parents and family of origin.

Individual level   This includes your physical appearance as well as your addiction and addictive behaviors.

Relationship level   Friends, in and out of the program, and any family members that serve as friends are physical realities of the relationship level.

Occupation level   The word *occupation* describes not only your job or career but your hobbies, avocations, and your "life work," whatever that is.

EMOTIONAL ASPECTS

The emotions are biochemical messengers that try to motivate us to speed up, to slow down, to sleep, to have sex, to eat, etc. They speak no verbal language, but we try to label them and to "understand" them.

Family level   We develop patterns of responding to feelings while we are very young.

Individual level   Feelings do not cause addiction, but they contribute to it. Also, addiction does not generate all your emotions, but it has a progressively adverse effect on your feeling life.

Relationship level   Healthy relationships have a positive effect on our emotions, while unhealthy relationships develop addictive dynamics.

Occupation level   Addiction tends to destroy careers and spoil your feeling that life is worthwhile. Recovery, on the other hand, can enhance your career and hobbies, and strengthen the feeling of meaning in your life.

MENTAL ASPECTS

The mental aspects include your attitudes, beliefs, and ability to solve problems.

Family level   Some of your ideas came from your family of origin; they may be anywhere from very useful to extremely destructive.

Individual level   These ideas and others have become assets or liabilities in your ability to think clearly or have good judgment about your addiction, your self-concept, and your daily living.

Relationship level   Your friends and family may be very helpful with solutions to your problems. Friends in Twelve-Step groups, especially, can help your recovery if you let them.

Occupation level   Much of your success in your career, your hobbies, your interests, or your "life work" will depend on your ability to make contact with other people and share information with them.

SPIRITUAL ASPECTS

The spiritual aspects include your relationship with a Higher Power, with your religious or philosophical orientation, with other people on a deeper level, and with yourself as a spiritual being.

Family level   Your first contact with spirituality, or lack of it, was in your family of origin.

Individual level   All those things that make up the core of your being—your integrity, your love of others, your belief in some sort of Higher Power—determine who you are.

Relationship level   Many people believe that God (of their understanding) speaks through other people. Certainly the tradition of all major world religions has religious and spiritual communication going on primarily from one person to another, rather than directly from some sort of god.

Occupation level   Not everyone chooses a career that reflects their purpose of being of maximum service to God and their fellow humans. But for good recovery, your job, your hobbies, and your other activities must all be reasonably well attuned to your idea of what your Higher Power wants you to do with your life.

PEMS model, see also: Addiction model (PEMS), Delusion, Disease concept, Emotional aspects, Family, Mental aspects, Physical aspects, Spiritual aspects.

Perfectionism

Perfectionism is a character trait known to many addicts. It can be found in all areas of an addict's life. Examples are thinking and feeling that you must not make any mistakes, that everything you do must be in order, and that you must not be caught doing acts or showing feelings that make you look bad.

The biggest problem with perfectionism is that it sets impossible goals. People are human, and not perfect (God). You can never be perfectly loving, honest, noble, unselfish, or anything else. To consciously or unconsciously think you can be perfect is an illusion that is bound to give you trouble.

Any job you do could be done better. Any meal you fix could be tastier and more nutritious. Any interaction with other people could have been smoother or more productive. The real problem is the all-or-nothing attitude that if it is not perfect, it is no good.

Perfectionism is usually an attempt to cover up or make up for perceived inadequacies, poor self-esteem, fear, or lack of trust in yourself or others. It is a close companion to all the attempts, including addictive behavior, to try to make yourself feel OK.

Many recovering addicts once took pride in their perfectionism. They would say, "You know what a perfectionist I am." They did not see how this isolated them from others, or that they were playing God. Recovery allows them to laugh at themselves. In working the Steps, addicts can identify with others, relax and accept their humanity, and even be comfortable with imperfection.

STEP ONE

The First Step, admitting powerlessness, is an acknowledgment of imperfection and limitations. It is a vital link with the millions of other imperfect addicts in their spiritual journey. The essence of the Twelve-Step community is the spiritual bond of people who need each other *because of* their imperfections and weakness. In that bond lies their strength.

STEP FOUR

As you do your Fourth Step inventory, look for perfectionism. A simple test is to ask yourself whether you are trying to do a *perfect Fourth Step.*

LIGHTEN UP

If you find that perfectionism is one of your problems, you can learn to be more comfortable with imperfection. Try to say, "I made a mistake," rather than making an excuse. Volunteer to do something you know you can't do really well. Share your feelings of inadequacy in meetings or with friends, and try to accept their feedback without overreacting. Don't take yourself so damned seriously. Laugh at the everyday examples that simply show that human beings are not God.

Perfectionism, see also: Affirmations, Assertiveness, Character defects, Defenses, Dichotomous thinking, Humility, Inventory, Mental aspects, Psychological problems, Step Three, Step Four, Step Six, Step Eight, Step Ten, Survival roles. Next on path I: Inventory.

Physical aspects

The physical aspects of any addiction include all those factors from the physical world that play a part in the addiction, including sensitivity to certain substances, intoxication, tolerance, and withdrawal. Many of these factors overlap the emotional, mental, and spiritual aspects. This is an overview; each of these factors is discussed in more detail in a module under its own name.

ALLERGIES

The term *allergy*, in a broad sense, means your body will react to the presence of an excess of almost any substance with an alarm reaction first, to try to get your attention, and later with an attempt to adapt to the presence of the substance. If you continue to use or produce an excess of this drug or chemical, the adaptation mechanism will break down and fail to protect you from the substance. This model can explain many physical effects of addiction.

BEHAVIOR

All your actions affect your world, which includes yourself. When you seek drugs or sex, argue with others, abuse people close to you, binge, purge, gamble, or do almost anything to excess, these behaviors form a major part of the addiction.

BINGEING

Most addicts binge, but some relate to it more than others. Any period of intense use of a drug, food, or other substance is a binge. A concentrated period of any other addictive behavior, like gambling or sex, is also a binge. Even family members may relate to a particular time of intense enabling as a binge.

BIOCHEMISTRY

Imbalances in particular hormones and neurotransmitters are integral to our model of addiction. This neurochemistry is also a strong factor in the emotional and mental aspects of the disease.

PURGING

If you use a broad definition of purging, it is a common companion to bingeing. It is not just bulimics who binge and then try to purge themselves of the effects of that binge. Overeaters diet, alcoholics and gamblers swear off or go on the wagon, debtors cut up credit cards, and even codependents may hurt themselves in some attempt to atone for their behavior.

TOLERANCE

The fantastic adaptation mechanisms of the human body insure that almost any excessive behavior or chemical or neurochemical imbalance will lead to adjustments that will decrease their effect. Since all addictive behavior or substance abuse produced pleasure or relieved suffering in some way, at least in the beginning, this tolerance keeps the emotional and mental aspects of the addiction busy producing excuses to use more, use more often, or switch drugs or addictions.

WITHDRAWAL

The flip side of tolerance is withdrawal. Whatever physical effects the substance or activity produced must have given pleasure or relieved suffering, or you would not have continued them long enough for a tolerance to develop. Withdrawal means losing the pleasure or a return of the suffering you sought to escape. When more addictive use or activity follows withdrawal, you establish a strong addictive cycle.

PHYSICAL CHARACTERISTICS

It is mostly the physical aspects and their emotional and social consequences that distinguish one addiction from others. Different substances or activities cause some differences in the biochemical imbalances that result. Also the physical circumstances of how you obtain the substance or activity vary.

Drugs   Because of the vast differences in drugs and how you get them, drug addiction (including alcohol) produces a wide variety of physical aspects. This is probably why there are so many Twelve-Step groups that address drug problems. An alcoholic who drinks in bars may find it hard to relate to heroin addiction. Many cocaine addicts have trouble identifying with the users of sedative hypnotics. The emotional, mental, and physical aspects of addiction are much the same, but the physical aspects are different in many respects.

Food   The differences between styles of food addiction are also mostly physical. Most food addicts overeat and then undereat, but the degree of overeating and undereating, and the duration of that cycle, is very different for an anorexic and for someone who is morbidly obese. Especially in early recovery they might find little in common.

Gambling   The environments of legal or illegal betting, horse and dog races, sports betting, card games, lotteries, dice, casino gambling, and other wagering mean that the compulsive gambler has a disease with physical aspects different from other addictions.

Sex   A sex addict may have a lot in common with a food addict, but the illicit sex, pornography, prostitution, masturbation, casual sex, and other manifestations are a lot different. They might be disgusted at the physical aspects of each other's stories, but they could relate to the emotional, mental, and spiritual aspects, especially if they are both in good recovery.

RECOVERY

Whatever the addiction, the physical aspects are more critical in early recovery. Medical or other professional services may be needed for detoxification, withdrawal, and other physical aspects of the disease. Abstinence may be difficult to achieve, or even to understand. After the physical aspects of the disease are brought into balance (addictive use or addictive behavior stops), the emotional, mental, and spiritual aspects of the addiction become at least as important as the physical.

Physical aspects, see also: Addiction, Alcoholism, Allergies, Behavior, Bingeing, Biochemistry, Blackouts, Constipation, Craving, Edema, Exercise & activity, Fetal alcohol syndrome, Flashbacks, Metabolism, Neurotransmitters, Nutrition, Premenstrual syndrome, Purging, Tolerance, Weight, Withdrawal. Next on path B: Allergies.

Power

Understanding power and powerlessness is useful to your recovery. You are told you are powerless over your addiction. You may hear talk of being powerless over people, places, and things. You hear you have to have a Higher Power to recover. Therefore it may take some attention on your part to make sense of these ideas.

FIRST STEP

The First Step simply means admitting powerlessness over your addictive substance of choice. This is not so difficult if you see it as simply a way of stating that trying to control and use will power have not worked. Numerous commitments, plans, diets, gimmicks, and even psychological improvement don't quite provide the relief you need from the struggle. So part of the First Step is giving up the idea that there is a magical solution that will give you control.

ILLUSION OF CONTROL

The Twelve-Step programs are full of people who struggle with trying to control their lives. No one really has any control over most things, although they may be deluded into thinking they do (see the module Control). Giving up that delusion is what Step Three is all about. There is, however, a use of the energy we call power that is beneficial in recovery and in life in general.

TYPES OF POWER

Rollo May (1972) says, "Power is the ability to cause or prevent change." He describes five kinds of power.

Exploitative power   This is a simple and **destructive** kind of power that is identified with force. Violence or the threat of violence is usually involved and allows for no choice or spontaneity by the victims. Dictatorships and child abuse are examples of exploitative power.

Manipulation   This is power **over** another person that capital-izes on the victim's weakness, desperation, or anxiety. Hitler began his reign of terror by manipulation of the German people. Con artists use manipulation. Again, victims in this type of interaction are robbed of conscious and voluntary participation, and are robbed of their power to make decisions.

Competitive power   This is power **against** another. In pure competition one succeeds only because another fails. One wins and the other loses. Severe competition causes a lack of community among people. Friendly competition, however, gives zest and vitality to human relations, and can be constructive.

Nutrient power   This is power **for** the other. Parents use power for their children and politicians can use their power for the people.

Integrative power   This is power **with** the other person. Two people can combine their power for a better product or service than one alone could do. One example of integrative power is demon-strated every time a Shuttle lifts off from Kennedy Space Center. Thousands of people have combined efforts to make it happen, and many of us are still thrilled as we participate in feeling that power.
The Twelve-Step fellowships are good examples of integrative power.

IN ADDICTION
Addiction may give you the illusion of power, and some people may appear addicted to power. This may actually be a form of excitement addiction.
There is no doubt that people do help effect changes in others, and it might be more useful to think of this as influence. This avoids the trap of the control illusion.

HEALTHY USE
Because so many addicts and codependents may have learned meekness and compliance that no longer serve them, claiming the ability to have some influence in your life can be quite healthy. Sharon Wegscheider-Cruse (1985) states this as her "ninth step for

healing" for codependents: to assume healthy power in your personal life.

Power, see also: Abuse, Acceptance, Amends, Behavior, Codependency, Control, Defenses, Forgiveness, Higher Power, Honesty, Incest, Magical thinking, Openmindedness, Powerlessness, Prayer & meditation, Religiosity, Sanity, Self-centeredness, Step One, Step Two, Step Three, Step Four, Step Six, Step Eleven, Surrender, Trust. Next on path G: Higher Power.

Powerlessness

Admitting powerlessness over your addictive behavior is essential to the use of Step One, the beginning of recovery.

DIFFICULT TO ADMIT
Powerlessness is not the easiest thing to admit. Most addicts tend to hang onto the illusion that they are in control, long after it becomes obvious that control is not working.

Loss of control, or the devotion of too much energy to maintain control can happen in many aspects of addiction:

- Drinking, gambling, or using
- Staying late at bars or parties
- Concealing addiction
- Obsession with appearance or weight
- Bingeing, purging, exercise, or spending
- Relationships with family or others
- Memory of abuse or incest
- Emotions and behavior
- Promises to self or others

POWERLESSNESS AND UNMANAGEABILITY
One trick the addiction uses is to try to block (through delusion) your awareness of powerlessness or unmanageability. If you are not fully aware of both, you are not likely to do what you need to recover. For example, if you realize that your life is unmanageable, but you don't really think you are powerless, then you can ease your mind, since obviously you will get control soon. "I'll quit smoking when I finish this carton," or, "I can stop anytime I *really* want to."

If you admit powerlessness, but not unmanageability, then the disease can convince you that while you have not been able to control it, the situation isn't that bad. This leads to all sorts of rationalizations, like "I can't stop eating, but if I had to do without the foods I like I wouldn't really want to live anyway," or "Anytime my family tries to control my drinking, I drink more just to show that it's my body and my life."

ACCEPTANCE AND SURRENDER

When you get tired of trying to hold everything together, tired of playing God (or the director of your whole world), you are ready to accept that you are powerless over your addiction, and that your life has become unmanageable. This is the necessary preparation for the spiritual awakening that will insure your recovery on a daily basis. It leads directly to Step Two.

Powerlessness, see also: Acceptance, Bingeing, Codependency, Crisis, Delusion, Detachment, Half-measures, Hitting bottom, Honesty, Humility, Judgment, Obsession, Paradoxes in addiction, Power, Step One, Step Two, Step Five, Steps of AA, Stinking thinking, Surrender, Telephone, Unmanageability. Next on path F: Unmanageability.

Prayer & meditation

PRAYER

Many people believe that praying means asking God for things or to intervene on behalf of other people. We will not try to argue that this is wrong, but we will point out the suggestion in the Eleventh Step: "Sought through prayer and meditation to improve our conscious contact with God *as we understood Him,* praying only for knowledge of His will for us and the power to carry that out."

Listen to the will of God   This suggests that the praying you do for your recovery consists mainly of listening to the will of God. That can be in a formal prayer, or very informally, in a conversation with that Higher Power, in which your role is that of listener and learner, rather than instructor.

If you can't listen, you must feel   A clergyman friend, also a recovering addict, said that those who do not listen will learn by feel instead. The child who ignores the warning not to touch the hot stove learns through the pain of touching it. Like a child, you can learn through hearing the word of your Higher Power, or through the pain that results from not listening.

It is hard for many of us to accept that a loving God could use pain as an instrument of learning. But it seems to be the way of life. To turn the negative into a positive, it is also true that people in recovery almost universally gain a greater ability to learn from prayer and from others' experience without getting into painful situations.

Many addicts even feel better when they realize how much they have learned from the pain of their past. Occasionally an addict grateful for recovery will say, "I wouldn't take ten million dollars for that experience—nor to repeat it, for that matter."

Discipline means ordered learning. A disciple is the follower of a teacher. In spiritual matters, then, you become a disciple by following the discipline necessary to receive the will of your Higher Power.

MEDITATION

To some people, prayer and meditation are essentially the same, while to others they are totally different. The difference, if any, seems to do mostly with how active your Higher Power is in the process. An atheist may not relate to the word prayer at all, and see meditation as an inner searching. Someone with a strong faith in God may see little difference between the two, unless prayer has somewhat more to do with talking to God and meditation a little more with listening to the will of God.

Discipline of solitude   You must get away from the hectic demands of your everyday life if you are to meditate to learn the will of your Higher Power, or to learn more about your relationship with your world.

Think of getting your car stuck in the snow. Stepping on the gas, trying to go faster, won't help you—in fact it might make it worse. Meditation is like getting out of the car and finding some sticks to slip under the drive wheels.

To make meditation a part of your life, make yourself a space of retreat, where you are unlikely to be interrupted. It can be a walk in a park, a quiet part of your house, or whatever you can find. Set time, if possible, as well as a definite length of time, starting perhaps with ten minutes. As you begin to realize the benefit of this meditation, you may wish to increase it.

Discipline of community   In a spiritual community, such as a church, a temple, or even a Twelve-Step fellowship, you can share what you have learned in solitude. Those who only parrot what they have heard in community, such as Twelve-Step meetings, may have little recovery to share. It is the discipline of solitude combined with the discipline of community that produces the strongest spiritual experiences.

Other meditation ideas   There are schools for specific techniques for meditation based on Eastern philosophies like Buddhism that believe meditation is a key to enlightenment. Ideas from these models can be found in popular tools for spiritual growth, stress management, and relaxation techniques.

It will help your recovery to learn to quiet your mind, to stop obsessive thinking, and to concentrate without distraction. You may wish to try classes in prayer, yoga, progressive muscle relaxation, or other meditation or relaxation techniques.

Meditation books and other program literature can be helpful for meditation. You might look for a subject in the index and then meditate on that reading.

A church or other spiritual group might provide useful ideas on meditation. Daily devotional books or magazines often give positive affirmative readings and guidelines for meditation.

Tangents   The main danger with any meditation discipline is that you might get "off track," concentrating so much on the particular discipline that you might ignore the rest of your recovery.

Prayer & meditation, see also: Affirmations, Beliefs, Grace, Gratitude, Habit & structure, Higher Power, Magical thinking, Relapse prevention, Relaxation, Serenity, Sleep, Spiritual aspects, Spirituality, Step Six, Step Eight, Step Eleven, Step Twelve, Surrender. Next on path M: Grace.

Pregnancy

Pregnancy is a state that may present weight, food, and emotional problems for any woman, so it is natural that women with addiction or eating disorders may have exaggerated stress because of it. Nutritional needs, which of course involve food, a changing body, and a flood of unpredictable emotions are major factors for consideration.

It should be obvious that if you have a good recovery program, a healthy food plan, self-esteem, and especially if you want a baby, the stress need not be debilitating.

FEELINGS

In pregnancy, however, biochemical changes do occur that affect feelings, and you need supportive friends or family members with whom you feel free to share your feelings. You may wonder if you are unselfish enough to be a parent or fear you will do things to your child that were done to you. You may worry that your child will inherit strong addictive traits and feel pressure to break the chain of addictive patterns. Fatigue may affect your emotions.

Especially for bulimics and other food addicts, obsession about body image can return during pregnancy, and weight may become an issue. You may worry that you will never get your figure back or be able to wear your clothes again. Pregnancy is an opportunity for your addiction to grab hold of you.

FOOD PLAN MODIFICATIONS

If you are following a particular food plan as part of your recovery (even if you are not a food addict), you should share it with your doctor and nutritionist, and of course be willing to make appropriate modifications as needed for your health and the health of the baby. If you have been on a rigid food plan, the need to make modifications can be a mixed blessing. You may find variations that work well. You also have to be willing to eat more food, especially protein.

Remember that alcohol, drugs, and tobacco all affect an unborn child. See the module Fetal alcohol syndrome for more information.

MORNING SICKNESS

Morning sickness may be a problem and require some changes in how you eat. Especially if you are a bulimic or have bulimic tendencies, stick as closely as you can to your food plan and talk to others in the Program about deviations that may be necessary so you don't feel alone or guilty.

LOOKING AHEAD

Having kids will bring out the best and the worst in you. You may find yourself doing things you had vowed not to do, and things you weren't sure you could do. You may find more understanding, love, gratitude, or forgiveness for your own parents as you learn the stress of parenthood. These experiences can be major milestones in your recovery.

HIGHER POWER

Throughout the pregnancy and parenthood, don't forget you have a Higher Power. We have seen many addicts cope, and even grow in their spirituality and recovery, if they used this special time to gain closer contact with their God and the Program.

Pregnancy, see also: Aftercare, Assertiveness, Attitudes, Biochemistry, Body image, Chronic pain, Counseling, Craving, Crisis, Drugs, Edema, Emotional aspects, Exercise & activity, Family, Feelings, Fetal alcohol syndrome, Food addiction, Gratitude, Intimacy, Love & caring, Moderation, Nicotine, Nutrition, Premenstrual syndrome, Priorities, Relapse prevention, Relaxation, Sabotage of recovery, Sex, Stinking thinking. Next on path O: Premenstrual syndrome.

Premenstrual syndrome (PMS)

CONTROVERSY
Premenstrual syndrome (PMS) is a condition that is still shrouded in a lot of mystery, misunderstanding, and controversy. Experts disagree about its prevalence, but the consensus is that it does exist.

PMS AND ADDICTION
An addict with PMS may experience most of her food or other cravings in the week before her period. She may also experience very profound mood swings, bloating, and lack of concentration during this time. These symptoms are thought to be the result of hormone cycles and imbalances that affect and are affected by the emotions.

Women suffering from PMS need to have their feelings validated, and they need as much information as is available to treat the symptoms. PMS does occur before menses, and is alleviated at or a day or two after the beginning of menses.

NUTRITION
Women who are active addicts usually do things that aggravate the condition, and it may be hard to separate the PMS symptoms from those of addiction. Because of the interaction with nutrition and the emotions, PMS may disappear or be reduced with the onset of sobriety, recovery, or abstinence from compulsive eating, and with the relief many women feel when they find out this craziness is not just "in their heads."

RECOMMENDATIONS
The good news is that the most common recommendations for dealing with PMS are also compatible with recovery from any

addiction. MacMahon, in *Women and Hormones* (1990), says symptoms can often be alleviated if you:

- Eliminate alcohol, smoking, and caffeine
- Cut down on salt and sugar
- Exercise regularly
- Learn relaxation and stress reduction techniques
- Eat a diet high in complex carbohydrates

Other suggestions include eliminating artificial sweeteners and getting plenty of rest.

Though PMS symptoms are unpleasant, it is helpful to know that your hormones are responsible and you are not crazy or emotionally unstable. Continue to use your Higher Power and your recovery program to help you.

Premenstrual syndrome, see also: Abstinence, Acceptance, Aftercare, Crisis, Delusion, Dichotomous thinking, Edema, Family, Food addiction, Moderation, Nutrition, Pregnancy, Priorities, Progression, Relapse prevention, Relaxation, Sabotage of recovery, Sponsorship, Step Three, Step Eleven, Stinking thinking, Surrender, Therapy & treatment, Tranquilizers. Next on path O: Prevention of addiction.

Prevention of addiction

RISK FACTORS

If you are an addict, chances are that you are not the only addict in your family of origin. Addiction definitely seems to run in families, and typically there are several varieties of addiction present. Eventually, addicts start to worry about the prospect of passing their addiction on to their own kids and grandkids.

Genetics　We know that there seems to be a genetic component to alcoholism and obesity, and we can guess that genetics play a part in all addictions. Short of deciding not to have children, there is little you can do to determine what genes your kids inherit.

Addiction education　One area that you may be able to help with is providing a good role model and information about addiction. Because of your children's increased chance for addiction, you can gently educate them about addiction and recovery.

The key word here is *gently*. Forcing addiction education down kids' throats is not the best way to give them a positive attitude toward recovery. You can share your feelings honestly and be willing to listen to theirs. What you can give them is the positive role model of seeing you work your own recovery program.

Build self-esteem tools   You can also help them develop their self-esteem. Try to give them messages that they are important, that they have good skills and talents, that they are worthwhile people. There are lots of parenting books and classes that have practical suggestions on how to do this.

Self-esteem will not necessarily keep children from developing an addiction, but it will make it much easier for them to recover if they do.

Since addiction is not just physical, the healthier the family environment the less likely a person will be emotionally, mentally, and spiritually vulnerable to addiction.

EARLY RECOGNITION

One thing we do know about children who come from homes where there is addiction recovery is that their problems, not just with addiction, are more likely to be identified and treated at an earlier age.

Children can be the focus of a formal or informal intervention (see the Intervention module). With kids it is especially important to find the appropriate kind of treatment, whether the problem is addiction, behavioral problems, or learning disabilities.

However, it is almost as dangerous to send your children to treatment too soon as too late. Often families who are not in recovery wait long after the problem has become very serious, and many addicted children have even died of addiction. But sometimes recovery families go overboard in the other direction, sending their kids off to inpatient treatment before there are good signs that the problem is addiction, and before there is any clue that the child is ready for recovery.

The danger of too-early treatment is that the children become treatment wise, and alienated from their "fanatic" parents, and it leaves few options to follow if the treatment does not take on the first attempt.

Family involvement   If possible, start with something less extreme. Outpatient treatment, especially family counseling, may produce good results for much less money, and leave the option of an inpatient program in case it is needed later.

3 C's   Organizations like Al-Anon and other self-help groups can be very helpful. Al-Anon talks about the three C's, which have helped many parents to hang onto their sanity:

- I didn't cause it.
- I can't control it.
- I can't cure it.

Prevention of addiction, see also: Abstinence, Acceptance, Addiction, Adolescents, Aftercare, Codependency, Counseling, Crisis, Family, Food addiction, Habit & structure, Honesty, Intervention, Moderation, Pregnancy, Priorities, Progression, Recovery, Sabotage of recovery, Serenity, Stinking thinking. Next on path O: Priorities.

Priorities

Recovery from addiction requires the ability to rank crisis situations, recovery actions, and daily activities so that you give adequate attention to each day's priorities. Remember "first things first."

For many people, crisis is fun, and balance is boring. This means that you might be getting an excitement high from screwing up the priorities. Addicted people should follow priorities that take addiction into account.

REAL CRISIS

A real crisis is a condition that clearly interrupts the ordinary schedule of life, like a fire, a hurricane, a death in the family, or other critical situation that everyone would agree is a crisis. If you have a heart attack on the way to a Twelve-Step meeting, go to the emergency room, not the meeting.

This does not mean that addiction recovery (even meeting attendance) should be abandoned during a crisis, but the situation may dictate that some things be suspended for a brief period.

If the crisis is genuine, and you are doing what you honestly can for your recovery during the crisis, your Higher Power will carry you through the crisis itself (but not necessarily through the aftermath).

MEDICAL PRIMARY

If there is a real medical problem, like surgery or diabetes or other serious physical necessity, that may take precedence over certain (not all) aspects of your recovery. For example, if you have to fast until noon to take a medical test, that is not a break of your abstinence from compulsive eating. If you normally avoid sugar, it is not a break of your abstinence to drink the liquid they use for a glucose tolerance test. If you are chemically dependent, you may still need some kind of analgesic (painkiller) following surgery.

As with crises, however, you may need to focus on your recovery as soon as possible, given the medical emergency.

ADDICTION PRIMARY

If there is no real crisis or primary medical condition, your recovery should have priority over all other problems in your life. This does not mean your recovery is *necessarily* more important than your family, for example, but if you don't put recovery first, you probably won't have much to offer a family member who needs your time and emotional support.

OTHER PRIMARY PROBLEM

From time to time, other problems may make demands for your undivided attention. Your job may require you to work overtime for two weeks steady. You might have a child's wedding to put on. You might be on a two-week vacation to a foreign country. These kinds of problems can be faced with the help of a Higher Power *only if your recovery has a higher priority.*

COMBINATION PROBLEM

Most problems you face are combination problems; there is a near-crisis, and your recovery is involved to some degree, and the normal things of life are going on as usual. So you have to get help from your Higher Power to order the priorities at hand, and not ignore either your recovery, the near-crisis, or daily living. Use the Serenity Prayer.

SITUATION NORMAL

For many addicts, the most dangerous time is situation normal. You may get bored with the routine, and be tempted to "stir something up."

More addicts relapse following a crisis than during it. So a return to situation normal should be a signal to give adequate focus to recovery.

You should regularly evaluate your priority system. An excellent tool for that is the daily inventory of Step Ten.

HOW

Finally, this kind of priority system helps to develop the Honesty, Openmindedness, and Willingness for recovery. Rather than a chore, prioritizing in recovery becomes another aspect of freedom. You can enjoy the knowledge that you are giving a healthy priority to things, with adequate time and effort being spent on recovery, work, and play.

Priorities, see also: Abstinence, Abuse, Aftercare, Behavior, Celebrations, Codependency, Crisis, Delusion, Dichotomous thinking, Disease concept, Family, Food addiction, Habit & structure, Halfway house, Moderation, Nicotine, Premenstrual syndrome, Pregnancy, Prevention of addiction, Relapse prevention, Sabotage of recovery, Sex, Sleep, Sponsorship, Stinking thinking, Stress & strain, Telephone, Therapy & treatment. End of path O.

Professional organizations

If you are working in the field of addictions, or if you have a counselor or other therapist who works with addictions, these professional organizations may be important to you. Contact them if you have questions about certification, about the qualifications of addictions professionals, or even if you have complaints about a person who may be certified by them.

These organizations all advocate ethical standards among their members, or those they certify. They are concerned with providing initial and ongoing training of addictions professionals. They are active in lobbying efforts to try to improve the quality of treatment for their members' clients.

EAPA

Employee Assistance Professionals Association (EAPA) supports professionals working in EAP positions. Formerly called ALMACA, this organization also offers a national certification, called Certified Employee Assistance Professional (CEAP).

EAPA
4601 N. Fairfax Dr., Suite 1001
Arlington, VA 22203
(703) 522-6272

IAEDP

The International Association of Eating Disorders Professionals (IAEDP) is the only national or international organization for professionals who work in the field of eating disorders. It is not just for people with an addiction or Twelve-Step orientation. IAEDP certifies eating disorders counselors and therapists, but certification is not necessary for membership. Anyone working exclusively or substantially with eating disorders should join.

> IAEDP, Inc.
> 123 NW 13 St., # 206
> Boca Raton, FL 33432
> (407) 388-6494

NAADAC

The National Association of Alcoholism and Drug Abuse Counselors is a membership organization that provides everything from lobbying in Washington to malpractice insurance for its members. It has a large annual conference and is affiliated with most state counselors' organizations. It offers a national certification for alcohol and drug abuse counselors, called National Certified Addiction Counselor (NCAC).

> NAADAC
> 3717 Columbia Pike, Suite 300
> Arlington, VA 22204
> (703) 920-4644
> 800-548-0497

NCCDN

The National Consortium of Chemical Dependency Nurses (NCCDN) provides training, networking, and certification for nurses who work with chemical dependency.

> NCCDN
> 975 Oak St., Suite 675
> Eugene, OR 97401
> (503) 485-4421
> 800-87-NCCDN

NCPG

The National Council on Problem Gambling, Inc., was organized to disseminate information and education on compulsive gambling as an illness and health problem. It also certifies counselors who work with compulsive gambling.

National Council on Problem Gambling
445 West 59th St.
New York, NY 10019
(212) 765-3833
800-522-4700

NCRC/AODA

The National Certification Reciprocity Consortium/Alcohol and Other Drug Abuse, Inc. is an organization of at least forty-two alcohol and drug abuse counselor certification bodies in the United States and Canada. Counselors who are certified in one state can easily obtain certification when they move to another state if both states' certifying bodies are members of the NCRC. It also offers a national credential, called Nationally Certified Alcohol and Drug Counselor.

NCRC/AODA
3725 National Drive, Suite 213
Raleigh, NC 27612
(919) 781-9734

Professional organizations, see also: Certification, Core functions, Counseling, Dual diagnosis, Employee assistance programs, Impaired professionals, Integrity & values, Therapy & treatment.

Progression

We have learned from the field of chemical dependency and alcoholism that addiction is progressive. There is certainly evidence that this is true, but to attempt to describe one model of progression into which all people will fit is a fallacy.

JELLINEK CHART

E. M. Jellinek, in his 1960 classic, *Disease Concept of Alcoholism,* described a downward progression of alcoholism. These ideas have since been spread through a U-shaped chart that has been called the Jellinek chart. People have taken this classic chart and applied it to every other addictive disease observed.

The problem is that this model does not appear to accurately describe reality for many addicts. The further you get from classic alcoholism, the less people will relate to the generalizations found on this chart. Since we use a physical, emotional, mental, and spiritual model for all addiction, we find people's experience does not always follow a downward deterioration in all these areas. Many have actually grown and made progress in many areas of their lives. So we prefer not to describe an overall model of downward progression for people to try to fit into.

PHYSICAL PROGRESSION

The one area that progression seems to fit in best is the physical aspect of the disease. This can be observed by looking at specific addiction patterns.

Rollercoaster   Many addicts' behavior resembles a rollercoaster. Drinking increases, then decreases, then increases again. The addict is confronted by family or employer, and there is a period of "good behavior" followed by a worsening condition, followed by another effort to do better. There is weight gain, weight loss, more weight gain, up and down, on and on rollercoaster-fashion.

Steady increase   Some people have simply had a steady increase of addictive behavior over the years. Drinking or using increases gradually. This pattern is most common when there is little attempt to control the addictive behavior.

Hitting bottom   The idea of "hitting bottom" is not very useful as far as we are concerned. You can be open to help depending on a variety of factors. Your awareness of the addiction, seeing that you can't control it the way you could previously, and the amount of effort needed to maintain the illusion of control are all signs that the disease is progressing. They may also be realities that make you receptive to treatment and recovery.

RECOVERY IS PROGRESSIVE

Recovery also has a pattern, but how that pattern unfolds is highly individual. Factors in the progression of recovery include:

- How seriously your addiction has affected your life
- The severity of dysfunction in your family of origin

- How much personal growth you have already done
- How addiction still affects other areas of your life
- Whether or not you have success in another Twelve-Step program

It does appear that success depends on the fact that you attempt to continue to grow spiritually, or you may easily find yourself progressing in the direction of relapse rather than recovery.

Progression, see also: Addiction, Alcoholism, Allergies, Behavior, Binge history, Bingeing, Biochemistry, Blackouts, Drugs, Employee assistance programs, Food addiction, Moodifiers, Physical aspects, Purging, Tolerance, Unmanageability, Withdrawal. End of path B. Next on path C: Emotional aspects.

Psychological problems

For years many people thought that addiction was a manifestation of moral or psychological problems. Today most addiction professionals believe it is a primary disease. Of course, addiction has emotional aspects, and these are part of the presenting problems. Many addicts seem to have no significant psychological problems except the addiction, and many psychological and psychiatric problems have nothing to do with addiction. Some addicts may have both, and they are called dual diagnosis patients. It is difficult to separate addiction and psychological problems in their ongoing behavior.

APPARENT PSYCHIATRIC BEHAVIOR
The confusion comes when you do crazy things as part of your addiction. Twelve-Step group members commonly share in meetings behavior they might have "been locked up for" when they were drinking, using, gambling, bingeing, purging, starving, or obsessed with their bodies or their addictive behavior.

While psychologists have batteries of psychological tests and clinical criteria to evaluate emotional disorders, we suggest a simple yardstick for figuring out what is going on in your Twelve-Step group meeting or with other people you meet.

First, be aware that as many as about 10 percent of the people in a recovery meeting (or almost anywhere else, for that matter) may have some kind of psychological problem that probably should receive some professional help. Of course, not all those people need to be hospitalized or present any kind of threat to themselves or others.

Then, look at how you and others respond to that person. Program members are usually fairly tolerant of eccentricities and emotional instability. But occasionally you will encounter someone who talks or behaves in a way that is enough out of the usual, even for an addict, that others have difficulty relating, and even begin to be uncomfortable or fearful because of their behavior.

We have found this to be the best test, because in a peer-group recovery program, any who cannot relate to others, or whose behavior scares people off, are simply not likely to recover without some professional help.

GENUINE PSYCHIATRIC BEHAVIOR

Psychiatric problems can exist in people with no signs of addiction. If both occur, they will aggravate each other. Some examples are depression, phobias, schizophrenia, and borderline personalities. Treatment should include intervention and treatment plans for both.

The dangers are the extremes. One is the idea that if we treat the depression, the addiction will go away. The other is that we should treat the addiction and the depression will go away.

Multiple personality   Recent research and clinical experience suggest that multiple personality disorder (MPD) is much more common than we thought. It seems to occur most often in response to severe trauma, like that of abuse, which is no stranger to many addicts' families. To avoid having to remember a horrible experience, they generate a new personality, which either does not remember or is somehow detached from the experience. Once this process begins, it becomes easier and easier to spawn new personalities when needed to protect the collective whole. Through therapy, some MPD patients have identified hundreds of personalities.

This dramatic and fascinating psychological phenomenon is usually frightening for MPD patients and their families. It is common for the personality that is usually "out" to be unaware of the other personalities, and families seldom interpret the variations in behavior as multiple personality disorder. So most MPD patients don't know they have it until it is discovered by an alert therapist. Fortunately, with proper therapy the personalities can be "integrated" so that they cooperate, and MPD families can function fairly normally.

For the rest of us, we may simply be aware that for some people, the "child within" or the extreme mood swings may be much more literal than we imagined. Addictions counselors and other professionals are learning more about MPD so they can screen for it and refer clients and their families for specialized help.

Surviving   Some people suffer from serious emotional and mental disturbances but can share honestly and fairly appropriately in meetings. If they concentrate on their problems with their addiction, and can care about others as well as themselves, they will probably fit in OK. Those who are coming primarily for recovery from their psychiatric problem and have little or no real signs of addiction should probably seek professional help instead. In some areas there may even be a group like Emotions Anonymous where they would be more comfortable.

If you are involved with someone who has significant psychiatric troubles, remember your limitations. Help if you can, but if it begins to threaten your recovery you should politely suggest that they find someone else who is better equipped to help them.

Psychological problems, see also: Addiction, Defenses, Delusion, Dichotomous thinking, Disease concept, Dual diagnosis, Emotions Anonymous, Feelings, Judgment, Magical thinking, Mental aspects, Obsession, Priorities, Sleep, Stinking thinking, Therapy & treatment, Visualizations. End of path D. Next on path E: Spiritual aspects.

Purging

Purging is usually associated with food addiction. If you think of it as an activity to offset a binge, it is easy to find parallels in other addictions. After a weekend drunk, an alcoholic may "swear off" for a few days. Gamblers may do the same thing after a huge loss. A sex addict who distributes pornography and is a child molester may get involved in an antipornography campaign. These purging activities are accompanied by fear, guilt, and attempts to control.

Purging in food addiction is an activity to try to control caloric absorption or to offset the effect of caloric consumption. All addicts should have some familiarity with this module to be in a position to help others in their Twelve-Step programs who might be experiencing these problems. We will focus on food addiction, but many of these ideas could apply to other addictions also.

LESS COMMON FORMS OF PURGING

Interestingly, the less common types of purging have gotten the most public exposure.

Vomiting food is purging, and may occur only occasionally or up to ten or more times a day. We do not call it purging if it is the occasional natural result of food poisoning or illness. Frequent involuntary vomiting when there is no desire to get rid of the food should be evaluated by a physician and possibly also by a psychiatrist.

Many people take laxatives to eliminate that full feeling, and they may think they are avoiding calories. Some bulimics take many times the recommended dosages every day. Actually less than 15 percent of the calories are avoided by laxatives, and other drastic dangers to the body are incurred. Recovery from laxative abuse can be difficult and long term.

Diuretics are taken so the scales will go down a pound or two but are of no benefit at all in lasting weight loss. Only water loss and dehydration occur.

Enemas are sometimes used to provide a feeling of purging, but are of no benefit in avoiding the consequences of food consumed.

Oral expulsion syndrome is where food is chewed and then spit out. There are records of individuals whose food addiction consisted primarily of this behavior, and others who reported using it at times. One bulimic who binged and purged reported that at times she would sit at a desk and eat candy bars, then spit them into a styrofoam cup in her desk drawer to be disposed of later.

Ruminating is vomiting up a small amount of food, chewing it, and then swallowing it again. It has been reported by some food addicts, but there is not enough information about it yet to know just where it fits—in the food addiction area, as a psychiatric problem, or as a physical/medical phenomenon.

COMMON FORMS OF PURGING

Some of the more common means of purging have not received much attention by the press.

Fasting is a common type of purging to offset the effect of excess food consumed. Eating very little or no food at one or more meals is a fasting purge, although to be considered part of bulimia it should be part of a common pattern rather than just occasionally or for religious or other purposes.

Excessive exercising to burn off calories is a common type of purge. We even see Hollywood stars advocating this type of activity "when you've been bad." It can take up many hours each day and be extremely detrimental to relationships, careers, peace of mind, and even health. It may be combined with vomiting or starving.

Extreme starvation diets are common in the obese. When you are used to several thousand calories each day, even a 1,200-calorie diet is an extreme starvation diet. Obsession about food and weight loss begins to appear similar to anorexic mentality, and over time it can be very destructive as a purging technique.

RECOVERY

Purging in any addiction perpetuates the disease. It can result in biochemical changes that become addictive themselves. The solution is Step One and the recovery program.

Purging, see also: Abstinence, Addiction, Binge history, Bingeing, Body image, Bulimia nervosa, Crisis, Edema, Exercise & activity, Moodifiers, Neurotransmitters, Progression, Stinking thinking, Unmanageability, Weight, Withdrawal. Next on path B: Constipation.

R

Recovery

Recovery is the purpose of this manual, and of the Twelve-Step programs, meetings, and fellowships.

Recovery is a threat to your addiction, and you can be sure the addiction will not surrender without a fight. But the fact that you are reading this manual is evidence that recovery has already begun, and the addiction is in trouble!

Remember that recovery is a *journey*, not a *destination*. Where do you begin? With the first, tiniest, shakiest step. "A journey of a thousand miles begins with a single step."

DETOX PERIOD

After the unpleasant effects of withdrawal, which are not always dramatic enough to be identified, many addicts, especially following treatment, get on a "pink cloud." Everything seems so wonderful, and the disease can begin to plant the seed of the idea that you are cured. Don't worry, the pink cloud won't last; enjoy it but keep working on your recovery so you'll have support when the pink cloud evaporates.

IN THE TRENCHES

The war against addiction is won in the little daily battles "in the trenches," not on the parade ground, nor even in the dramatic "breakthroughs" that signal hopes for a magic cure. Retreats and conventions may be inspirational, but the inspiration doesn't last much longer than a regular meeting.

Unfortunately, in some (non-AA) Twelve-Step Groups there is so little recovery that trying to recover is like trying to learn tennis from watching matches on TV! In these cases it is important to get a core of people very serious about recovery who will do whatever is necessary to gain abstinence from the addictive behavior, and get into recovery. Sometimes an entire community of Twelve-Step group members will improve when a few people go to a good treatment program.

YOUR "PROGRAM"

You may often hear in a meeting that somebody seems to be working a good "Program." If you are not sure what that means, we might suggest that your "Program" refers to how well you live by the principles of the Twelve Steps. When you do, others see honesty, humility, gratitude, and joy. Even if life throws you some curve balls, your Program can keep you centered. Nothing is so bad that a relapse won't make it worse.

PHASES

Around treatment programs, several phases of recovery have been identified. The first, reflecting its association with hospitals, is usually called "admission." In a more generic context, and to emphasize that it has little to do with the admission of Step One, we call it "attendance."

"Bring the body; the mind and heart will follow." Most members arrived at the doors of recovery reluctantly, skeptically, and grudgingly. In this stage of recovery, they are saying, "I'm here, I may be willing to admit that I have a problem, but I don't know if this program is right for me."

"I'll do what you say, but I'm not convinced it will work." This is the message of the compliance phase. Often there is an undercurrent of defiance, as you agree to go through the motions, or to "act as if." Probably most people leave a two- , four- , or six-week treatment program still in compliance. That's OK—many addicts comply their way right into acceptance.

The transition from compliance to acceptance is usually heralded by a growing recognition of similarities between you and other addicts.

Eventually, the realization sinks in. "I really am an addict!" You feel a sinking feeling in the pit of your stomach as you actually accept that you have a primary, progressive, chronic, and potentially fatal disease. There is a sense of identification with others in recovery, on a basic, internal level.

Finally, surrender occurs through the spiritual awakening brought about by using all Twelve Steps in your daily life. Surrender involves a level of faith seldom experienced by people in the early months of recovery. It represents abandoning the struggle and trusting in a Higher Power. It has to do with serenity.

Recovery is a process, not an event. So the phases of recovery are not static, they are dynamic. It is entirely possible to get a hint of surrender one day, be back at acceptance the next, and feel that you are essentially in attendance the next, and then back in acceptance all in the same week. The important thing is to recognize the progression of recovery, as opposed to progression of the disease. Keep moving in the overall *direction* of recovery and you *are* in recovery.

The Program offers release from the bondage of addiction and hope for a life that is good. Old-timers don't tell you to keep coming back so you will experience self-pity, resentment, fear, and misery. The promises of the Program include freedom, serenity, happiness, trust, and ultimately some real meaning for your life. Most of all it frees you to become the best you possible.

Recovery, see also: Abstinence, Acceptance, Addiction model (PEMS), Affirmations, Aftercare, Coping skills, Feelings, Freedoms, Grace, Higher Power, Humility, Humor & fun, Integrity & values, Intimacy, Love & caring, Moderation, Relapse prevention, Relationships, Steps of AA, Surrender, Tools of recovery, Unity.

Relapse prevention

Alcoholism has so influenced our thinking about addiction that most other addicts assume they have to come up with some equivalent of the first drink to identify relapse. Since alcohol is not necessary for survival, even a single drink of it indicates that relapse has progressed to the danger point. Actually, this line of thinking has limitations even for alcoholics, because an alcoholic who focuses only on not taking the first drink will not experience the joy and freedom of recovery, and is constantly in peril.

STAGES OF RELAPSE

Rather than looking at relapse as an event, we can separate relapse into three stages. This tends to shape our thinking more in the direction of a process. These stages can be called lapse, relapse, and collapse.

Lapse   If the early signs of relapse are not heeded, relapse will come along in short order. Some examples of a lapse might be (depending on your concept of sobriety or abstinence and your Program):

- Alcoholics and drug addicts: Reestablishing relationships with drinking or using buddies, or increased frequenting of drinking or drug-oriented events or environments.
- Food addicts: Eating a meal that was really too large, but not really a binge, skipping a meal, or eating a food not normally included in your food plan. If you are underweight, ignoring a significant weight loss; for others, taking no action in response to a gain of more than a few pounds, or overreacting to a weight gain.
- Compulsive gambler: You find yourself picking up the phone and dialing your bookie's number, or looking at the racing forms.
- Sex addict: Wandering into the adult section of the video store or finding yourself with an explicit magazine in your hands.
- Excitement addict: Finding yourself beginning to take risks that others might consider unusual or unnecessary. Failure to talk over a potentially exciting event or enterprise with a sponsor or others in the Program.
- Any addict: Going longer than about a week without a Twelve-Step group meeting, without having a very good reason, and perhaps not doing anything to compensate for that (like calling others or reading literature).
- Overall: Obsessive or compulsive behavior about alcohol, drugs, body image, food, weight, or other signs of the physical, emotional, mental, or spiritual aspects of the addiction.

Relapse Recovery has suffered a significant setback, and immediate action is required to get back on track. This is what we would consider breaking sobriety or abstinence. Again, the specific determination of which of these might be lapse or relapse depends on your own ideas; these are simply examples that you **might** include as relapse rather than lapse:

- Alcoholics: Taking a drink.
- Nicotine addicts: Smoking a cigarette.
- Compulsive gamblers: Placing a bet or entering a game for money.
- Drug addicts: Talking a physician into prescribing a mood-ifier (mood-altering drug) that is not clearly necessary.

- Food addicts: Eating between meals (not including a planned snack or "metabolic adjustment" if allowed on your food plan). Eating a quantity of food that clearly cannot be called a moderate meal, whether it is overeating or undereating. Eating a significant quantity of a food you know is a sensitivity for you and you have specifically excluded from your food plan, like sugary desserts. A purge, like vomiting or laxative use. This does not include legitimate illness or medical necessity.
- Compulsive spenders: Purchasing something you do not need, you have vowed not to buy, and you know is an emotional purchase.
- Sex addict: Buying a pornographic magazine.

Collapse The disease has become firmly entrenched and the whole process of recovery, from detox through early recovery must begin again as quickly as possible. This happens when lapses become relapses, and relapses do not result in immediately getting back into recovery. This may include:

- Alcoholism: Drinking continues and gets worse. Legal or medical consequences return or increase.
- Food addicts: Binges that go on for days, weeks, months, or years. Return to regular purging, starving, dieting, or excessive exercise.
- Compulsive spending: Spending binges result in severe financial problems, shoplifting, or other advanced consequences of the addiction.
- Compulsive gambling: Active involvement in gambling, borrowing, deceit, and shame and guilt.
- Sex addict: The acting-out cycle of compulsive sexual behavior that is beyond your control continues.
- All addicts: Suspension of all, or most, recovery efforts, perhaps with avoiding Twelve-Step program friends. Lying and deceitful behavior, including lying about your recovery, or not talking openly about your relapse.

REVERSE OF RECOVERY

Relapse, like recovery, is a process, not an event. Remember that usually lapse gradually turns into relapse, and that relapse over time becomes collapse. It is far more important to stop the relapse process wherever you are, rather than to split hairs over whether a given development is a lapse, relapse, or collapse.

If you have any question about whether you have broken your addiction abstinence, we recommend that you avoid making that determination until *after* you reverse the relapse trend. Often, your sponsor and friends in the Twelve-Step programs can give you valuable input, and the final determination can be between you and your Higher Power.

WARNING SIGNS

Some warning signs you should look for might include:

- Increased obsession with the substance of your addiction
- A defiant attitude about your recovery plan
- Skipping or slacking off on meetings
- Decreased contact with others in the Program, especially your sponsor
- Increased contact with those who do not support your recovery
- Placing yourself in situations dangerous to your sobriety or abstinence
- Rigid control, like dieting behavior
- Obsession with shortcomings, like weight or body shape
- Getting overextended in daily living
- Increased fear, anxiety, or hopelessness
- Reduced contact with your Higher Power
- Increasing resentments toward others
- Isolating from everyone

FOR RECOVERY

- Care about yourself at least as much as you would someone you sponsor.
- Learn from your mistakes.
- Use your Higher Power.

Relapse prevention, see also: Abstinence, Aftercare, Anger, Assertiveness, Celebrations, Chronic pain, Control, Counseling, Craving, Crisis, Dichotomous thinking, Family, Feelings, Habit & structure, Halfway house, Honesty, Intervention, Moderation, Prayer & meditation, Premenstrual syndrome, Pregnancy, Priorities, Relaxation, Resentments, Sabotage of recovery, Sanity, Sex, Sleep, Slogans, Steps of AA, Stinking thinking, Tools of recovery, Willingness. Next on path O: Sabotage of recovery.

Relationships

Addictions tend to interfere with relationships, and the inability to get and maintain healthy relationships makes recovery much harder. Fortunately, the Twelve-Step fellowships provide a way to alleviate this problem by working on recovery *through* relationships with other addicts and with a Higher Power.

When you hear the word *relationships*, you usually think about the significant people in your life—your family, friends, and coworkers. We want to broaden the idea a little to include not only other people but your relationship to yourself and to your Higher Power, and to the things that matter to you. Spirituality actually has to do with the nature or the spirit of your interactions in these areas of your life.

The first area to look at is how you relate to yourself. How do you think and feel and how do you act toward yourself? Addicts typically suffer from many negatives in this area. Addiction makes people self-centered, but that usually takes the form of fears, self-pity, resentment, and an attitude either that the world outside should conform to their wishes, or that they are inadequate, don't deserve the good things in life, and should conform to the wishes of others.

People sometimes assume the role of someone who wants to run the whole show. Rather than reflecting real grandiosity, this performance often hides deeper levels of feelings of insecurity and lack of self-worth that may be disguised in a variety of ways.

This behavior can result in looking to other people for security and satisfaction, as is typical with a people-pleaser. This could backfire when such people resist or refuse to behave or to react as you would like them to, so you become resentful.

You may even be paradoxically grandiose in believing you are the "worst whatever" that ever existed. Or maybe you feel you are the most self-sacrificing caretaker alive. There is a tendency to be all-or-nothing in addictive thinking.

BACKGROUND INFLUENCE

People come into recovery with diverse backgrounds ranging from severe abuse to mildly dysfunctional homes. It may be necessary to rethink your self-worth and build a better foundation for yourself by changing your attitudes and feelings and behaving lovingly toward yourself.

How you relate to other people is also likely to have some basis in early learning experiences. One model for looking at this is called the OK Corral in Transactional Analysis. In an oversimplification, the position taken toward others can be one of four:

- I'm not OK; you're OK—in this position, you tend to be depressed, thinking others are superior.
- I'm OK; you're not OK—here you tend to be paranoid, thinking others are out to get you.
- I'm not OK; you're not OK—you tend to be suicidal, thinking no one is worthwhile.
- I'm OK; you're OK—you feel positive about yourself and others in general and can get on with what life is all about.

Your position in the OK Corral may change when you are at work, at home, or in social situations.

THE RESCUE TRIANGLE

The rescue triangle is a model, also from Transactional Analysis, that can be used to describe how addicts who find themselves in dysfunctional relationships may relate to others.

When people grow up not learning how to get their needs met in a healthy way, nor how to get the strokes they need to develop healthy self-esteem, they learn other ways to relate to people to try to feel OK about themselves. This results in a game where each person plays a role, like that of victim, persecutor, or rescuer.

The persecutor's position is "I am better than you, you are inferior." Persecutors find victims to put down and criticize. The rescuer's position is "I know more than you, you are inadequate." The victim's position is "I am weak, I am inferior." A victim may seek either a persecutor or a rescuer (or both) to relate to. Whichever way, he reinforces his position that he is helpless, weak, or inferior.

Sometimes in the same relationship people will switch positions to keep the excitement going. This is a typical pattern for what some

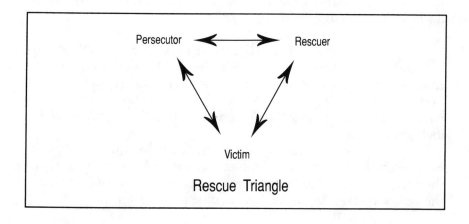

Rescue Triangle

might call relationship addiction. If one decides to recover and learn to relate in healthy, intimate ways, the game is over, and the relationship will have to change.

FRIENDSHIPS

Friendships are a very important type of relationship. You may or may not be skilled at making, keeping, or being a friend. But these skills can be learned. Remember, to be a real friend you need to feel you have something to offer, which is related to your self-esteem. YOU are the best gift you ever have to offer.

Not every friendship is balanced in terms of giving and receiving. Friendships can be horizontal or vertical, or some variation between. For example, in horizontal relationships you receive as much as you give. Your needs are met and you make a priority out of meeting your friend's needs. That feels good!

Sometimes you may just receive. For example, in early recovery you will have a sponsor from whom you mainly receive. It is supposed to be that way! Paradoxically, in giving, a sponsor does receive.

You may have some friends to whom you give a little more than you receive, or vice versa. What is important is to have a way to look at your relationships to figure out what might be working and what needs to change. You will burn out and become resentful if you are the only one who gives to the relationship.

Relationships with other people involve communication. Again, there are many people who have created models to describe how people communicate. In Transactional Analysis, they say our interactions are for exchanging strokes, which can be warm fuzzies (positive strokes) or cold pricklies (negative strokes) (Steiner, 1977).

John Powell, in *Why Am I Afraid to Tell You Who I Am?* (1969), has a model for communication that includes levels that involve cliches, facts, ideas and judgments, emotions (gut level), and peak communication, which is absolute openness and honesty. Not all communication needs to be of the peak kind, or intensely intimate, but there is real value in having the self-esteem and courage to develop a few special relationships. In these you are loved unconditionally and reveal yourself openly so you can grow into your full potential.

HIGHER POWER

A critical factor in recovery is how you can relate to and use a Higher Power that is greater than your disease. The Big Book, *Twelve Steps and Twelve Traditions,* and many other sources are available to help you understand and develop such a relationship. Your relationship with your Higher Power will set the stage for your relationship with others and with yourself.

For example, if you see your Higher Power as loving and caring, you will view other relationships in the same way. The Twelve Steps are the best tools we know for developing a recovery program that leads to satisfaction in all relationships in your life.

MODELS

There are, of course, other models available for looking at relationships. Recovery literature abounds with them. Take from each model that which fits your experience and that you find useful, rather than trying to fit yourself into any one model. There is much available to help with your journey.

Relationships, see also: Abstinence, Abuse, Adolescents, Amends, Assertiveness, Attitudes, Behavior, Children of addicts, Codependency, Control, Detachment, Emotional aspects, Enabling, Family, Family of origin, Feelings, Forgiveness, Humor & fun, Incest, Intimacy, Love & caring, Power, Recovery, Resentments, Sabotage of recovery, Self-image, Sex, Survival roles, Trust.

Relaxation

There are formal and informal techniques for relaxation that can help with sleep, with reducing obsession, and with serenity in general. These are especially valuable for most addicts, who have a history of seeking substances or addictive activities to relax.

HYPNOSIS

Hypnosis, also known as trance states, is a technique to help you focus on a specific idea or thing to the exclusion of other stimuli. It is not nearly the mysterious, dramatic event popularized in stage shows and TV dramas. Many relaxation techniques induce a trance state, where there is a change in brain wave patterns.

You have probably experienced hypnotic trance states when you were driving down a road, forgot to make a turn, and then realized you had been "out of it" for several minutes. Though not recommended in driving, trance states can help you learn to relax. Professionals can help you learn these techniques, which you can then do by yourself.

THE RELAXATION RESPONSE

In *The Relaxation Response* (1975), the relaxation and stress management classic, Herbert Benson, MD, describes the body's response to stress and an intervention technique. By mentally focusing or concentrating on one word or image, the rest of your body goes into a deep state of relaxation.

PROGRESSIVE MUSCLE RELAXATION

Another technique that can be taught by professionals and learned fairly easily is progressive muscle relaxation. Here you go through a sequence of tensing and releasing muscle groups all over your body, leaving you quite relaxed. As you learn the technique you can eventually skip the tensing step and go through it very rapidly, in less than a minute.

RELAXATION OR OTHER CLASSES

If you want something a bit more involved, look for classes in your area that relate to meditation or physical activity. You may find something that is very relaxing to you, and may be educational as well.

SIMPLE AIDS TO RELAXATION

There are also some very easy, everyday things you can do to increase your relaxation and reduce the effects of stress:

One of the simplest aids to relaxation is simply taking a deep breath. It is something you can do, without special training, at work, in the middle of a job interview, during a crisis, or anytime.

Breaks   Most employers have to allow breaks during the day. For your sanity, peace of mind, and recovery, you should take them— whether on the job or at home. You will find you can get more done after a short break than working straight through.

Meditations   There are books filled with short meditations to give your mind a thoughtful, philosophical, psychological, or spiritual message to mull over. Thinking about these messages several times throughout the day can have an effect like a break, getting you out of the rut of your daily routine.

Relaxation tapes   You can buy all sorts of cassette tapes for relaxation, from nature sounds to relaxing music, with or without a voice to guide you in a hypnotic fashion.

There is no evidence, by the way, that subliminal messages in those tapes do anything but line their producers' pockets. They may, of course, work if you *believe* they will.

Music   You may be able to listen to music while you work, and if it is conducive to relaxation, without making you sleepy, it may help calm you. And if you are trying to relax to go to sleep, the right kind of music may help.

Mind blanking   If you have some practice at meditation techniques, you may be able to just let your mind go blank for a few seconds, blocking out the tension and chaos of the moment.

A Higher Power   Whatever you use, allow the thoughts of your Higher Power, or the Program, or nature, or a combination of calming influences to help you through the day and the night.

Relaxation, see also: Acceptance, Chronic pain, Counseling, Crisis, Delusion, Dichotomous thinking, Drugs, Exercise & activity, Family, Habit & structure, Higher Power, Humor & fun, Moderation, Moodifiers, Obsession, Prayer & meditation, Premenstrual syndrome, Priorities, Relapse prevention, Sabotage of recovery, Sanity, Satiety, Serenity, Sleep, Slogans, Stress & strain, Tranquilizers. Next on path O: Sleep.

Religiosity

Religion is a specific system of belief, worship, conduct, a code of ethics, and a philosophy of living. It usually involves belief in a divine power or creator. The word comes from a Latin root that means to bind together. Religious people bind themselves to each other and to their Higher Power through their beliefs and a community of kindred spirits.

Religiosity is the quality of being extremely or excessively religious. It concerns the trappings of religion and the potential to manipulate people in the name of a certain religion or religious doctrine.

RELIGIOUS ADDICTION

Religiosity describes attitudes and beliefs that a person feels are the ultimate, only, and unquestionable truth. The extreme of these attitudes can be described as religious abuse and religious addiction. These are characterized by:

- A hunger for power
- Poor self-esteem
- Excessive guilt and shame or self-righteousness
- Dichotomous thinking
- Ideas that conflict with science
- Family dysfunction
- Authoritarianism
- Denial of reality
- Rigidity
- Idolatry
- Covert hypocritical behavior

SCANDAL

Throughout history there have been prominent religious personalities who have become involved in scandals relating to sex, money, power, and other activities, violating the trust of their followers. It is not hard to see addictive behavior involved in these transgressions. You may also remember an extreme case such as the Guyana tragedy involving Jim Jones.

CULTS

Satanic cults are perhaps the most shocking example of religiosity or religious addiction, and are more common than most of us would feel comfortable knowing. Cult leaders can work their members into such a state that they actually sacrifice children and brutally torture people, both from within and from outside the cult. Many of those who survive these activities become severely scarred emotionally. Alcohol, drugs, sex, and other addictive behaviors are integrated into the whole mess.

POWER TRIP

Religiosity is the ultimate power trip. Nothing comes close to it for its potential to control and manipulate the faithful. It is easy to see the altered states of consciousness in any of the more dramatic religious activities. Some fundamentalist revivals, the "Whirling Dervishes" of Turkey who dance themselves into a frenzy, and other emotional ceremonies and rituals involve plenty of neurochemistry.

Many religions, of course, supplement the emotional effects with drugs, from alcohol to peyote.

PEMS

Every aspect of addiction that we discuss in this manual can apply to religious addiction: physical, emotional, mental, and of course, spiritual. Recovery is difficult, because people "stung" by religiosity often take an antispiritual attitude that conflicts with Twelve-Step recovery. There is a group called Fundamentalists Anonymous, but they are not a Twelve-Step group and they do not use a Higher Power.

FR. LEO

Father Leo Booth, an Episcopal priest who is a recovering alcoholic, speaks out candidly on the subject of religious abuse and addiction in *When God Becomes a Drug: Breaking the Chains of Religious Addiction and Abuse* (1991). He says that religious abuse lies at the core of shame that fuels most addictions and codependency; it is often the cause of relapse or chronic depression. Healthy spirituality, he says, is positive, creative self-acceptance.

Religiosity, see also: Addiction, Arousal, Bingeing, Biochemistry, Celebrations, Excitement, Exercise & activity, Family, Higher Power, History of Twelve-Step groups, Moodifiers, Neurotransmitters, Power, Prevention of addiction, Purging, Sanity, Sex, Spiritual aspects, Stress & strain, Unmanageability. Next on path A: Chronic pain.

Resentments

Resentments are a combination of rehashed memories and the feelings that are elicited by those memories. Recovering addicts will find serenity elusive unless they are willing to let go of resentments. A Chinese proverb says that a leash is a rope with a noose on both ends.

"STUFFING" FEELINGS

The word *resentment* literally means "refeeling." Though some people think that chemicals from unexpressed feelings stay in the bloodstream, we have seen no evidence to support that. More likely, the anger we refeel must be brand new biochemistry produced by memories, which *are* stored in the brain. When you hear someone suggest that you are "stuffing your feelings" you may be avoiding the painful memory, and blocking the natural neurochemical responses to that memory. They might also mean that you are anesthetizing the feelings by drinking, using, bingeing, or addictive behavior.

SECRETS

Either kind of response requires energy and may block other pleasurable feelings as well. If you have not shared painful memories about your family of origin, you may be wasting emotional energy in repressing these secrets, leaving less energy for joy and spontaneity today. Ironically, you may also be blocking the happy memories from your childhood along with the painful ones.

FROZEN ANGER

One interesting image for understanding resentment is to call it frozen anger. While we do not literally believe the anger is stored, the analogy still has a useful message. Why do you put anything in your freezer? Most people will respond, "to save it," but actually you seldom freeze anything just to save it; usually it is because you want to use it later. Until you are willing to give up what benefit your addiction gets from the resentment, you are unlikely to get rid of it.

PRAYER

Many people recommend praying for the person you resent. Most people can't do this for more than a week or two without becoming willing to release the resentment. A suggestion of this method appears in the story "Freedom from Bondage" in the Big Book (p. 552).

FEEL FOOLISH

It is sometimes enough just to become aware that you are the one being hurt by the resentment, and that often the resented person doesn't even know how you feel. If this situation makes you feel foolish, you may be able to let the resentment go. You may also be able to use the tool of forgiveness to help you let go (see the modules on Amends and Forgiveness).

STEPS SIX–NINE

Steps Six through Nine are tools that should help with resentments. The Big Book even suggests that resentments are the major offender in the struggle for recovery. For many addicts other feelings play a larger part, but resentments are a major obstacle in recovery for all addicts.

RESISTANCE

There are a number of barriers that block letting resentments go:

If the resentment is still in use as a weapon, then letting it go amounts to disarmament. You may need to talk to someone about the fear you have of the person or thing you resent.

You may have grown up in an environment where it was common to hear things like, "I don't get mad—I get even." You may have to abandon the street-gang idea that honor requires you to make people pay for crossing you.

You might be afraid of letting people get close to you. You may even have developed this fear as a survival skill if your early environment was unsafe. You may now harbor resentments and blame others for your lack of intimacy.

Resentments, according to our definition, produce neurochemical imbalances that are exciting. You may need to give up this kind of self-medication.

IN RECOVERY

Share your feelings with your friends, your support system (Twelve-Step program or other group), your therapist (if applicable), and your Higher Power. If the hurt and fear are expressed directly, you will find less trouble with anger and rage. If you let go of resentments, you will open the door to serenity, love, joy, and spontaneity in your recovery.

Resentments, see also: Abuse, Acceptance, Affirmations, Anger, Assertiveness, Attitudes, Behavior, Character defects, Control, Defenses, Dichotomous thinking, Fear, Feelings, Forgiveness, Grief, Guilt & shame, Humility, Incest, Intimacy, Inventory, Love & caring, Openmindedness, Paradoxes in addiction, Perfectionism, Power, Powerlessness, Responsibility, Self-centeredness, Spirituality, Step Four, Step Six, Step Eight, Surrender, Survival roles, Trust. Next on path J: Responsibility.

Responsibility

Addiction tends to inhibit maturity. The self-centeredness that is a hallmark of addictive behavior interferes with relationships and social development. Addicts therefore are often described as irresponsible and immature. The Twelve-Step program provides the vehicle for restoring a balanced level of responsibility and maturity.

Some people see responsibility as a burden. There is a more positive way to look at it, as response-ability: the ability to respond in a way that makes you feel good about yourself. Responsibility means to be reliable and trustworthy in healthy relationships.

FAMILY OF ORIGIN

A good place to begin to understand responsibility and maturity is by looking at your family of origin. Your role models, parents and others, gave you some (possibly distorted) ideas about what responsibility and maturity were, and whether they were valuable attributes. Wherever your family fell on the spectrum between ideal and absolutely terrible played a strong part in the attitudes you developed.

Healthy families   In healthy families, children take on responsibilities appropriate for their age. This level of responsibility starts with simple things and gradually increases to the point where a teenager is taking a fair share of the duties of participating in the family. Everyone in the family, including parents, has a reasonable balance of work and play, primarily depending on their age.

Dysfunctional families   In dysfunctional families, the roles tend to be all mixed up; children are usually over- or underresponsible. You may see a ten-year-old child acting as the primary caregiver for a four-year-old sibling, because mom and dad are not available. That is too much responsibility at that age.

On the other hand, you might see a fifteen-year-old who has virtually no responsibilities toward the rest of the family. This leads to the illusion that he or she is "entitled" to a free ride from life.

Martyrdom   Some parents, many of whom are from addicted families themselves, try to give their kids what they did not have. It is easy to go overboard on this, and wind up sacrificing yourself for your children.

Think of it this way. If your children look at your life (and they do), will they see adulthood and parenthood as a desirable place to be, or as roles to be avoided as long as possible? If they see that you don't have much fun because you are sacrificing for them, what incentive do they have to grow up?

ARRESTED MATURITY

Most addicts, especially those from dysfunctional families, tend to have distorted concepts of responsibility and maturity. The most common are:

- I want what I want when I want it.
- False maturity (faking it); pseudomaturity; accepting responsibility for anyone and everything.

LEARNING

For many addicts, then, an important part of recovery is learning, or relearning, skills relating to responsibility and maturity:

Boundaries   What is appropriate behavior? If your parents and other childhood models were unable to teach you socially acceptable behavioral boundaries, you have to learn them now. Start asking people in the Program whether you're doing things right, from how close you stand to other people when talking, to how you relate to the opposite sex, and when you are isolating or being too intrusive with friends.

Balance   Balance (in most everything) is dynamic, not static or rigid. You will have times when you are more responsible, and other times when you are more carefree.

Communication   Focus on love and honesty in communication. Again, check things out with people in recovery and others in whom you sense a level of comfort or serenity with responsibility and maturity. You don't have to "reinvent the wheel."

Relationships   You will have varying levels of responsibility TO other people. Seldom if ever will you have responsibility FOR another person. Even the mother of an infant is not really responsible for her child (for every part of its well-being), although she does have lots of responsibilities for her own actions regarding it. You might be legally responsible for damages done by your teenagers, but you cannot be held morally responsible for their actions, because you cannot control them.

Spirituality   Remember that the Program runs on the energy of love and honesty. Your Higher Power and sponsors or others in the Program will be glad to help you—you have only to ask.

Responsibility, see also: Abuse, Affirmations, Amends, Assertiveness, Attitudes, Behavior, Character defects, Codependency, Defenses, Family, Feelings, Grief, Guilt & shame, Intimacy, Inventory, Judgment, Money, Paradoxes in addiction, Perfectionism, Relationships, Resentments, Self-centeredness, Service & giving, Spending, Sponsorship, Step Four, Step Six, Step Eight, Survival roles, Willingness. Next on path J: Money.

S

Sabotage of recovery

Sabotage is the intentional obstruction of or damage to some productive process, organized activity, etc. Everyone you are around will fall on some continuum between very supportive and very destructive to your recovery from your addiction(s).

Most people would help if they could, but may not know how. For example, your family may mean to help, but due to their attitudes they may make embarrassing, inappropriate, or awkward suggestions about what you should do for your recovery. Real sabotage of recovery applies to those who actively disrupt the recovering person's efforts.

Why would someone sabotage recovery? Some reasons might include:

- Protecting their own addiction(s)
- Keeping secrets, like incest
- Fear of change, if in a dysfunctional family
- Fear of abandonment; that you might outgrow them

SELF-SABOTAGE

Why do people sabotage their own recovery? For the same reasons listed above. Self-sabotage means you do not have to give up your addiction. Certainly the disease has a vested interest in that.

You may have some secrets that you fear you must own up to if you get into recovery. It is important to address these secrets directly rather than to allow the denial of them to be used as an excuse by your disease.

You may fear the changes that will take place if you recover. Fear is a natural feeling, and most people have some fear of almost any kind of change. But the pattern of responding to such fears by drinking, using, gambling, spending, smoking, bingeing, purging, or starving—this pattern is part of addiction.

COPING

If someone else seems to be trying to sabotage recovery, it may be because they are skeptical about the recovering addict's sincerity, especially if the addict has tried many methods of recovery previously. Try letting the saboteurs know exactly why it is so important that they be supportive and not sabotage recovery. Often people just don't realize how important recovery is.

If they continue to sabotage, the recovering addict will need to draw on their Higher Power for strength to either tolerate the condition, or get out of the saboteur's life, at least temporarily.

HOW TO LEAVE

How do you leave someone when it is necessary for your recovery? Often addiction and poor self-esteem conspire to make it unthinkable to change jobs or spouses, or to stop calling your parents every day.

You should begin to question how much that person loves or cares for you if they are unwilling to support your recovery when you are being honest about how important it is. At some point you might have to choose between recovery and a particular job or relationship, at least temporarily.

Sabotage of recovery, see also: Abstinence, Acceptance, Aftercare, Assertiveness, Celebrations, Chronic pain, Control, Crisis, Delusion, Dichotomous thinking, Family, Food plans, Habit & structure, Halfway house, Intervention, Prayer & meditation, Priorities, Progression, Relapse prevention, Relaxation, Sleep, Sponsorship, Steps of AA, Stinking thinking, Therapy & treatment. Next on path O: Stinking thinking.

Sanity

Addiction is a special kind of insanity. The word *insanity* is used here in a popular, not a psychiatric sense. It follows that if you are counting on a Higher Power to restore you to sanity (Step Two), then in the addiction you must have some kind of insanity.

The Big Book (*Alcoholics Anonymous*, 1976), tells about an alcoholic named Jim, who had several months of sobriety when he stopped at a roadside restaurant where they also had a bar. He ordered a sandwich and a glass of milk, and thought it couldn't possibly hurt him to drink an ounce of whiskey in the milk, since it would be on a full stomach.

"Whatever the precise definition of the word may be, we call this plain insanity. How can such a lack of proportion, of the ability to think straight, be called anything else?"

FEAR OF INSANITY

Some addicts, especially those with a history of mental illness in the family, experience fear when they think of themselves as insane. The good thing about addiction insanity is that it can easily be cured by the recovery process.

Faking sanity   Many addicts are crafty and have good persuasion skills. This actually works against you in recovery, for you can act a lot saner than you actually are. You may be able to convince family, employers, counselors, or even others in the Program that everything is going well—you might even fool yourself, unfortunately—but recovery usually comes only from honesty, and a cooperative effort between yourself, your Higher Power, and others in recovery.

Image management   Many addicts, including most women and food addicts, have some degree of distortion of body image. This kind of insanity improves only gradually, and you may simply have to accept that at times you may feel fat or ugly, and accept the word of other loving people that you are great just as you are.

RESTORING SANITY

How does the restoration of sanity come about? Gradually. At first, you may make mistakes in your recovery, taking control and charging off into poor judgment, and only realizing afterward that you could have made better choices. Later, you may be able to catch yourself before the lapse, or relapse, has fully occurred, and reach out for help then. The sooner you can recognize addictive thinking and take recovery steps, the better, of course.

SANITY IN RECOVERY

Sanity in recovery means listening for the support from your Higher Power and others in recovery, being honest, and following a course of recovery development, in physical, emotional, mental, and spiritual aspects. This is the spiritual awakening that Step Twelve talks about.

Sanity, see also: Acceptance, Crisis, Dichotomous thinking, Higher Power, Honesty, Magical thinking, Openmindedness, Power, Powerlessness, Prayer & meditation, Professional organizations, Psychological problems, Religiosity, Self-centeredness, Serenity, Step One, Step Two, Step Three, Step Seven, Step Eleven, Stinking thinking, Surrender, Trust. Next on path G: Power.

Satiety

The word *satiety* means the state of being supplied to the full extent with what is wished for. A typical addict will read that sentence and exclaim, "All RIGHT!" Satiety is one of the four major addictive states. The others are arousal, fantasy, and control.

RELIEF OF SUFFERING
Satiety involves the opiate receptors, especially in the limbic system of the brain. The limbic system is the seat of most of what we call emotions. Neuronal pathways for pain also pass through this system. Opiate neurotransmitters, like the endorphins, do not change the pain, but they mediate suffering, the *perception* of pain.

OPIATE ACTIVITIES
What do heroin, exercise, good food, and TV have in common? All increase the neurotransmitters that fill the opiate receptors in the brain, including the limbic system. They help you relax, feel good, and forget most of your worries. The main difference between heroin and the others is that it is much easier to overdose on heroin. There is no doubt that its effects are more dramatic, because it is far more concentrated. But heroin is doing the same thing in your body as exercise, good food, and TV. All that differs is the potency.

TOLERANCE
Whatever the reason you started using opiates, exercising excessively, overeating, or watching too much TV, you probably liked the effect. A lot. Remember satiety—being able to have all you want. Well, what happens when "all you want" does not satisfy as much?

You probably increased the dosage to "more than you wanted to take." This begins the tolerance, and the addiction.

MIXED STATES

Many addictions include satiety as an important addictive state. Heroin and other opiate addiction is primarily satiety, with some fantasy. Alcoholism involves satiety, but at times all the other addictive states also. Sex addiction certainly includes all four states, as the sex addict may feel extreme control, fantasy, arousal, and satiety all within a few minutes.

RECOVERY

Satiety and the other addictive states are a useful model to help understand addiction. Recovery does not mean staying out of these states. It simply means giving up the idea of taking up residence in one or more of them.

Satiety, see also: Anger, Arousal, Control, Emotional aspects, Fantasy.

Self-centeredness

Addicts using a Twelve-Step model to recover need to look at selfishness and self-centeredness. The Big Book describes the problem in the discussion of Step Three. "Selfishness—self-centeredness! That, we think, is the root of our troubles. Driven by a hundred forms of fear, self-delusion, self-seeking, and self-pity, we step on the toes of our fellows and they retaliate. Sometimes they hurt us, seemingly without provocation, but we find invariably that at some time in the past we have made decisions based on self, which placed us in a position to be hurt."

RESULTS FROM DISEASE

We believe the self-centeredness that causes addicts problems is largely a result of the disease process. Addiction requires you defer to it rather than to natural, loving, unselfish behavior.

It is not self-centeredness that makes people addicts. Rather, the addiction makes most people self-centered. Much of the shame and guilt that you experience results from behavior that violates your value system.

CONFUSING WORDS

The words *selfish* and *self-centered* confuse people. Selfishness is a problem, yet you are told this is a selfish program. Bill Wilson addresses this paradox in a letter (1967) in which he says the selfishness that is demanding and thoughtless of the welfare of others is not the AA way of life. However, without sobriety, alcoholics are of no value to others or themselves. So to be concerned with one's own recovery and spiritual growth is right and necessary.

SELF-CARING

You may be more comfortable calling your Program self-caring than selfish. This may be hard to do if you came from a dysfunctional home and were so busy learning survival skills and taking care of others that you missed learning how to get your needs met. This does not mean you think only of yourself or behave in ways that hurt or offend others. When you learn to love yourself others will benefit. People who care for you will be happy to see you free of addictive, self-destructive behavior.

Self-caring results in increased self-esteem and self-worth. Your relationships are enhanced. The greatest gift you have to offer is yourself, and you want to offer something of value to those you love.

Self-centeredness, see also: Affirmations, Assertiveness, Attitudes, Behavior, Body image, Character defects, Fear, Feelings, Guilt & shame, Inventory, Paradoxes in addiction, Perfectionism, Resentments, Responsibility, Slogans, Step Four, Step Six, Step Eight, Survival roles. Next on path J: Behavior.

Self-image

Dealing with problems of self-esteem and self-image is common for most addicts of all sorts. How you think and feel about yourself is what is involved in your self-image. It is closely tied to your self-esteem. How you feel about your looks, your talents, and your abilities is part of your self-image.

You get the foundation for your self-image from people in your family of origin, usually your parents. They should validate your worth, your feelings, your thoughts, and be models for how to deal effectively with life's problems and for how to enjoy life's pleasures. Addicts usually uncover some deficits when looking honestly at these sources for their self-image. One reason is addiction in parents or other family members.

When you are genetically predisposed to addiction, and you have these deficits, you are a sitting duck for something that initially makes you feel better, like alcohol, drugs, food, or relationships. But the alcohol or drugs soon begin to cause problems in relationships. Weight gain or other problems with bingeing, purging, or starving degrade your feelings about your body and your worth as a person. The loss of control and increasing shame and fear only call attention to your already fragile sense of worth. Dealing with your problems with self-image and self-esteem becomes an integral part of your recovery.

INVENTORY

An accurate assessment of your strengths and your areas that need improvement can be a valuable tool in recovery. Every aspect of your life, physical, emotional, mental, or spiritual, will affect your self-image.

IMPROVEMENT

Many recovery activities, like working on shame and guilt, sorting out emotional issues, dealing with abuse and incest, and codependency recovery, can help with self-image.

AFFIRMATIONS

Many addicts find the use of affirmations very helpful in improving self-image. Accepting compliments graciously, not putting yourself down, and behaving in a way that is self-loving and self-affirming—all these are important.

RELATIONSHIPS

If you are not already, you need to begin choosing to have relationships with people who will treat you with respect and love. Being around people who criticize or put you down makes it hard to feel good about yourself.

BODY IMAGE

For many addicts, especially food and sex addicts, body image improvement can help with self-image. See the module on Body image.

RECOVERY

Identifying problems in the area of self-image can be a part of your Fourth Step Inventory. Then you have the tools of Steps Six and Seven to use for improvement. A better self-image will be the natural consequence of using the Twelve Steps in your life.

Self-image, see also: Abuse, Acceptance, Adolescents, Al-Anon & Alateen, Amends, Anorexia nervosa, Assertiveness, Behavior, Body image, Children of addicts, Codependency, Dichotomous thinking, Disease concept, Emotional aspects, Enabling, Family, Family of origin, Forgiveness, Guilt & shame, Humility, Humor & fun, Incest, Intimacy, Obsession, Prayer & meditation, Recovery, Relationships, Resentments, Spiritual aspects, Survival roles.

Serenity

It is hard to appreciate the word *serenity* unless you have experienced the chaos that is its opposite. If your addiction has progressed very far, you will have plenty of experience with chaos.

CHAOS

Many addicts lived with personal chaos every day even before the development of their addictive behaviors. They had plenty of experience with it in their family of origin.

What we are describing is the kind of disruption in your life that leaves you with a sense that there is no order, no stability, no feeling that all is as it should be, and no meaningful contact with a Higher Power.

Many addicts and codependent family members respond to the chaos around them by investing psychic energy in the illusion of control. They repress their feelings and maintain a facade that everything is all right, while waging a silent war against themselves.

As you begin using Steps One, Two, and Three in your recovery, you will find that you start seeing glimpses of serenity in your life. Hope begins to return, and you can start to feel that everything is going to be OK.

SERENITY PRAYER

God grant me the serenity to accept the things I cannot change,
Courage to change the things I can, and
Wisdom to know the difference.

For many years, the Serenity Prayer was thought to be anonymous. Then several articles appeared explaining that it was part of a prayer written by Protestant theologian Reinhold Niebuhr. It may actually date back to an eighteenth-century German theologian named Friedrich Oettinger (1702–82). Whatever its origin, an early AA member handed it to Bill Wilson (cofounder of AA) in 1939. He and the AA staff liked it so much that they adopted it as AA's official prayer and worked it into AA literature.

SURRENDER

Serenity is related to surrender. While you keep struggling to change things, you are not likely to feel much serenity. For a sense of the difference, consider the following visualization:

Imagine you are swimming upstream in a large river. You are exhausted, but you feel you can't afford to rest; you will lose too much of the progress you have made. You dread seeing the places where the river narrows and gets faster, and there are sometimes rapids that take superhuman strength to get past. You have swallowed a lot of water and feel as though you are drowning. Somehow it finally occurs to you that you could be swimming downstream just as easily. As you begin to do that you find that you can make much more progress with much less effort. You can actually float at times, rest, and enjoy the beautiful scenery along your journey. You still have to swim hard at times to avoid the rapids and snags, but you now can enjoy the trip. The river is the same—but you have stopped fighting it.

Serenity, see also: Acceptance, Grace, Gratitude, Higher Power, Panic attacks, Prayer & meditation, Relapse prevention, Relaxation, Sanity, Service & giving, Spiritual aspects, Spirituality, Step Nine, Step Eleven, Step Twelve, Surrender. End of path M. Next on path N: Step Twelve.

Service & giving

CORNERSTONE OF AA

Why must you serve? Because service is vital to the continuance of Twelve-Step programs like AA, and you will need them to insure your own recovery.

You can't keep it unless you give it away. It just works that way. We might speculate on some reasons why that happens:

- Through service you feel good about yourself.
- You become grateful by seeing others where you have been.

- It helps your sense of belonging to a vital group.
- You get to hear yourself affirming your commitment to recovery.

You can give in scores of ways. You can be part of carrying the message to those who still suffer. You can locate a place to have a meeting, order literature, chair the meeting occasionally, serve as a representative to Intergroup or other service bodies, or help bring a meeting into an institution, including a treatment center.

WHEN?
The best time to start is now.

FOR HOW LONG?
Some Twelve-Step group members feel they have reached a point in their recovery where they have given enough and no longer need to be active in the fellowship. This may follow a certain length of sobriety or abstinence (or a goal weight). But real recovery results in a deep and continuing gratitude for the gift you have been given, and creates a natural need to give it back. This is true humility, and what keeps the Twelve-Step programs going.

PITFALLS OF SERVICE
There are a few dangers to avoid. The first is ego. If you are or become a big shot in the Program, your chances for long-term sobriety or abstinence, good recovery, and a spiritual awakening are less than average. There is no place for status in an anonymous program.
Don't forget balance. You will need to give enough time to your recovery, but also some to your family, your personal growth, your relationships, and your career.

Service & giving, see also: Anonymity, Enabling, Gratitude, Humility, Intervention, Love & caring, Meetings, Recovery, Responsibility, Self-centeredness, Sponsorship, Step Twelve, Tools of recovery, Traditions of AA. End of path N.

Sex

It is important to examine how addiction or disease may be using fear of sexual intimacy as an excuse to avoid continuing recovery.

Attitudes and experiences with sex need to be evaluated. If there are serious problems such as a history of sexual abuse, these certainly need to be treated. An overall negative attitude toward bodily pleasures and sensual feelings may exist. Professional help in such cases is recommended.

BULIMIA AND ANOREXIA

Studies of young women with anorexia and bulimia reveal that restricting anorexics tend to have lost any interest in sex. Bulimics are not much different from their normal counterparts in terms of sexual experience and interest. It has been theorized that the problems bulimics suffer with impulse control could be related to bingeing, which is safer than promiscuity, but this is clinical observation rather than a scientific finding at this point. Other theories could just as well explain the bingeing behavior.

ALCOHOL AND OTHER DRUGS

Many drugs, like alcohol and cocaine, seem to have a positive effect on sexuality at first. Alcohol dissolves inhibitions, so people with reservations about sexual behavior (some healthy and some unhealthy) find themselves doing things they had only dreamed about. Cocaine, because of its stimulant effect, produces an initial perception of great sexual performance. All drugs commonly abused eventually lead to impotence, however. For some it is more emotional than physical, but the expectation of drug-enhanced sex is a great myth.

Overall, addicts are likely to suffer from a variety of problems that interfere with healthy sexuality. Trust issues, negative sexual experiences, body image distortions, inability to have fun, and family of origin messages are all factors that could present problems in the ability to have satisfying sensual and sexual experiences.

Human beings have somehow devised taboos and ideas about sex that are anything but natural. Research on primates has shown that monkeys have great difficulty copulating if they have not grown up with sexually active monkeys and seen it done many times. They also become very neurotic if they are not in physical contact with other monkeys most of the time during their early lives. Mark Schwartz, ScD, a noted researcher into sexual dysfunction and sex addiction, says that he would have trouble designing a way of relating to sex that would guarantee more dysfunction than the one humanity has.

PERFORMANCE

The most common problems with sex are not medical in nature, or premature ejaculation, or anything like that. The greatest problem is fatigue. For two people who both work and have other responsibilities, to come home after a hard day, fix dinner, give "quality time" to the kids, and then, after 10 or 11 P.M., to achieve great sex including simultaneous orgasms, is expecting a bit much.

The second most common problem is overemphasis on performance. When two people accept the responsibility to satisfy the other sexually, they take on an incredible task—one that is unparalleled in nature. Most sexual therapy consists of teaching people to be responsible for their own sexuality, to slow down, take the focus off orgasm, and enjoy the experience of sex.

GAY & LESBIAN EXPERIENCE

Gay people encounter most of the sexual problems of other groups, with added stress from many sources. Society still discourages homosexuality with all sorts of subtle, obvious, and sometimes even violent discrimination. Many gays experience exile from their family of origin. The threat of AIDS may have drawn the gay community closer together, but it has added to the stress.

Studies report up to 25 percent of male bulimics and anorexics are gay. Other addictions are also common among the gay community. Outside larger metropolitan areas, there are few Twelve-Step groups that specifically encourage gays, and most of those are in AA. Many gays would feel uncomfortable discussing their problems in an ordinary meeting. Finding a meeting listed as "Gays Welcome" might help.

STARTING TO TALK

Whatever your problems regarding sex or sexuality, whether directly involving your addiction or not, the first step is to talk about it. Talk honestly with your partner, talk with others, inside the Twelve-Step programs and out. If the problem does not resolve itself through talking and your own common sense, seek competent professional help.

Many people in early recovery are especially vulnerable to others in relationships and sexuality. If you have a poor body image or poor self-esteem, you may feel starved for attention and feel trapped in a sexual or abusive relationship with the fear that you might never attract another person.

AFFAIRS

Having an affair outside a marriage or other committed relationship (including religious vows) usually creates a dangerous weakness in your integrity, and it will become more difficult to maintain rigorous honesty in your recovery and the rest of your life. It will also produce a serious barrier in that committed relationship.

Sexual affairs   Not all affairs include actual sexual activity, but most do get around to sexual behavior eventually, even if there was no intention to "go that far." When sex is involved, the guilt, the risk of pregnancy, the threat of AIDS, herpes, or other venereal disease, and other factors add to the excitement, increase the possibility of addictive behavior, and make good, solid honesty and recovery more difficult.

Prostitution   Paid sex has often been thought to be less damaging to a marriage than affairs in which there is romance or love. For most people, however, the illusion that it is harmless adds its own handicap to the recovering addict. The danger of AIDS, of arrest by legal authorities, or underworld involvement may add to the excitement and make recovery much harder.

Romantic affairs   Some affairs never reach the point of sexual activity. While this eliminates the risk of pregnancy, of AIDS, and of the guilt of inflicting these problems on the other party in the affair and the partner in the committed relationship, it also creates a few problems of its own.

People who have nonsexual romantic affairs usually live in a fantasy delusion that since sex is not involved, the relationship is "platonic," and therefore good, wholesome, and wonderful. Delusion increases as they self-righteously cast aside any hints that others suspect an affair, because "we haven't done anything wrong." This type of affair often goes on for a long time, causes severe damage to the primary committed relationship, and tends to generate lots of addictive behavior.

SEX ADDICTION

Obsession, shame and guilt, isolation, and unhealthy sexual activity are hallmarks of sexual addiction. All the usual characteristics of addiction apply to sex addiction also. Patrick Carnes (1983), a noted authority on sex addiction, has identified a four-stage cycle:

- Preoccupation—the addict is obsessed with the idea of sex and searching for sexual stimulation.
- Ritualization—this involves special routines and rituals that intensify excitement and arousal.
- Compulsive sexual behavior—acting out sexually, which the addict is powerless to stop.
- Despair—hopelessness because of the inability to stop what they don't want to do.

Carnes also identified three levels of compulsive sexual activity. Level 1 includes activities that are generally tolerated by society if they are isolated incidents. Examples are masturbation, extramarital sex, sex without considering the partner's feelings, pornography, strip shows, using prostitutes, and homosexual activities.

Level 2 acts are intrusive and may incur legal action. Voyeurism, obscene phone calls, and exhibitionism are examples.

Level 3 behavior significantly violates another's boundaries, and may involve criminal prosecution. Child molestation, rape, and incest are examples.

Biochemistry   No one can deny that the biochemistry associated with sex is extremely powerful. It satisfies survival instincts without which our species would never have lasted. Sex releases many neurotransmitters and hormones that form a physical part of the addiction.

Romance   Falling in love, romance, and relationship addiction are often intertwined with sex addiction. There is a neurochemistry here as well. Phenylethylamine (PEA) is an excitatory amine that is chemically similar to amphetamines. Its concentration increases when people are falling in love, and when it falls back to normal, the honeymoon is over. Some people get addicted to this chemistry with or without sex addiction.

Treatment   The Twelve-Step model has been very successful in treating sex addicts. Schwartz has found that a Twelve-Step approach helps sex offencers with guilt so they can get on with treatment in a positive way. Carnes also uses this approach at the Institute for Behavioral Medicine in Golden Valley, Minnesota.

Sex addiction often coexists with alcoholism, drug addiction, food addiction, or others. Recovery requires abstinence for both addictions. Alcoholics or food addicts who continue to act out sexually suffer shame and guilt to a degree that relapse with alcohol or food is almost inevitable. See the module Sex addiction groups.

Sex, see also: Addiction, Adolescents, Arousal, Assertiveness, Behavior, Binge history, Bingeing, Biochemistry, Body image, Control, Craving, Defenses, Drugs, Excitement, Exercise & activity, Guilt & shame, Incest, Intimacy, Loving & caring, Moodifiers, Neurotransmitters, Obesity, Pregnancy, Relationships, Self-image, Sex addiction groups, Sleep, Stress & strain, Therapy & treatment, Trust. Next on path A: Spending.

Sex addiction groups

The Twelve-Step groups that deal with sex addiction make an interesting study for what unites and differentiates addicts. Of these four groups for sex addicts, the main difference is how they define the problem and the resulting concept of abstinence.

SA

Sexaholics Anonymous has the most rigid definitions. Members must have "a desire to stop lusting and become sexually sober." Their First Step says they are powerless over lust. Sobriety is defined as no sex at all for single sexaholics, and sex only with the spouse for those who are married. Masturbation is excluded for all. There is also a "progressive victory over lust," whether married or single.

> Sexaholics Anonymous
> PO Box 300
> Simi Valley, CA 93062
> (818) 704-9854

SAA

Sex Addicts Anonymous members need "a desire to stop compulsive sexual behavior." In the First Step they admit they are powerless over their compulsive sexual behavior. For abstinence, members are expected to determine boundaries that exclude the behaviors that made their lives unmanageable, and that define their abstinence. Typical exclusions are anonymous, shame-producing, and victimizing sex. Within the boundaries may be intimate, committed, nurturing, and respectful sexual behaviors.

> Sex Addicts Anonymous
> PO Box 3038
> Minneapolis, MN 55403
> (612) 339-0217

SLAA

Sex and Love Addicts Anonymous, also called The Augustine Fellowship, is for people who have "the desire to stop living out a pattern of sex and love addiction." They are powerless over sex and love addiction. SLAA asks members to define their bottom-line behavior, which "leads to loss of control over rate, frequency, or duration of its recurrence, resulting in worsening self-destructive consequences." That bottom line usually excludes victimizing, secretive, and anonymous sex. SLAA has the greatest percentage of women, and romance addicts would probably feel comfortable in it.

SLAA
PO Box 119, New Town Branch
Boston, MA 02258
(617) 332-1845

SCA

Sexual Compulsives Anonymous is a much smaller group, composed mostly of gay men. Their members need "a desire to stop having compulsive sex." They admit they are powerless over their sexual compulsion, and members develop their own sexual recovery plan. This plan defines their sexual sobriety, and through it they learn to express their God-given sexuality in healthy ways.

SCA
PO Box 1585, Old Chelsea Station
New York, NY 10011
(212) 439-1123

FAMILIES

There are also several groups for family and friends of sex addicts. They are patterned after Al-Anon and are loosely affiliated with SA, SAA, and SLAA respectively:

S-Anon
PO Box 5117
Sherman Oaks, CA 91413
(818) 990-6910

COSA
PO Box 14537
Minneapolis, MN 55414
(612) 537-6904

Co-SLAA
PO Box 614
Brookline, MA 02146-9998

Sex addiction groups, see also: Adolescents, Children of addicts, Enabling, Families Anonymous, History of Twelve-Step groups, Meetings, Other support groups, Steps of AA, Therapy & treatment, Traditions of AA.

Sleep

Most addicts have some kind of difficulty with natural sleep. This is not especially surprising, since about a third of the general population has some degree of trouble sleeping.

INSOMNIA

Insomnia is a very general term meaning having trouble sleeping. Most of the time it is due to lifestyle factors, like staying up too late, drinking coffee in the evening, inadequate exercise during the day, erratic sleeping hours, or too much noise and light. Addiction to mood-altering drugs, including alcohol and possibly large amounts of sugar, is likely to disrupt the body's biochemistry enough to make sleep difficult.

SLEEP APNEA

Apnea means stopping breathing for a few seconds or longer. The sleeping disorder called sleep apnea means periods of ten seconds or more without breathing. Carbon dioxide builds up in the blood, signaling the brain to wake up enough to initiate breathing. Since this is not remembered in the morning, people with sleep apnea usually complain of sleepiness during the day rather than sleeplessness during the night.

Obstructive sleep apnea   Obstructive sleep apnea, the most severe and the most common kind, affects about 1 percent of men aged thirty to fifty, most often those who are overweight and heavy snorers, but it does affect all ages and both sexes. In this type of sleep apnea, the actual obstruction of the airway causes or contributes to the disorder.

Pickwickian syndrome   Pickwickian syndrome is named after Joe, a "fat and red-faced boy in a state of somnolence," in *The Posthumous Papers of the Pickwick Club* by Charles Dickens. This disorder, related to sleep apnea, affects very obese people. When they sit or lie in positions where the diaphragm must lift a lot of weight to breathe, the breathing becomes very shallow, and they can lose consciousness due to hypoxia. Then, after a time, their brain wakes them with a start.

OTHER SLEEP PROBLEMS

There are other sleep disturbances that may have little to do with addiction, although obesity, alcoholism, and other addictions certainly don't help them any.

Snoring   When any condition causes difficulty in breathing through the nose, you naturally breathe through the mouth. In certain positions, like lying on your back, the soft palate tends to vibrate—causing snoring.

In extreme cases snoring may be relieved by surgery, but often simply sewing an object into the pajama top near the small of the back will make it uncomfortable to sleep on your back and alleviate the symptoms.

Narcolepsy   Frequent sleep episodes and excessive sleepiness during the day may suggest this sleep disorder. It is often inherited, and treatment may include frequent naps during the day and stimulant drugs to counteract drowsiness and antidepressant drugs to suppress cataplexy (sudden loss of muscle tone without loss of consciousness).

Depression   People with certain psychiatric illnesses, including anxiety and depression, may have difficulty with sleep. Those with depression typically wake early in the morning and have trouble getting to sleep at night.

REMEDIES

While many approaches to sleep disorders are well beyond the scope of this manual, we can offer some suggestions:

Getting off all unnecessary drugs, including, of course, alcohol, nicotine, and caffeine, can help a lot. Improvement should be apparent in just a couple of weeks.

Better nutrition will insure that the body has all the raw materials to make its needed neurotransmitters and other chemicals.

Exercise during the day, especially the morning, can help with sleeping. A short walk (not vigorous exercise) just before retiring is helpful for some.

Keeping a schedule that is as regular as possible will give your body a much better chance to be regular about sleep.

The amount of sleep a person needs varies greatly, from as little as about four hours to over ten, with most being around seven to nine hours. But often there is more disturbance due to poor quality sleep than not enough of it.

Try not to use sleeping pills. For one thing, moodifiers are dangerous for addicts of any sort. Also, "sleeping pills" don't induce sleep, actually. They promote a state that is between natural sleep and a coma. The real benefits of sleep, including all four stages of sleep plus REM sleep (dreaming), don't accumulate until the drug wears off.

Certain sleep disorders, like obstructive sleep apnea, may require careful diagnosis and even surgery to correct.

DREAMS

Brain activity during sleep causes dreams. Dreams occur during REM (rapid eye movement) sleep, for some ten to twenty minutes about every ninety minutes.

Research reported in the *Lifetime Health Letter* of the University of Texas (Dec 1989) suggests that dreaming is an automatic process governed by the random firing of neurons and the release of brain chemicals during sleep. Its biological function is unidentified but believed to be important.

These firings originate in the brain stem and are transmitted to areas of the brain involved in emotion, sensory perception, and higher thought processes. Dreams appear to be a melange of events of the day, preexisting memories, and aspirations woven together in a mysterious way. In theory, when the electrical impulses reach the brain's center of higher thought, the cortex takes the information and tries to form a coherent story by relating them to stored memories.

No one knows for sure what dreams mean. The simplest explanation is that they are the by-product of the brain's filing activity and mean nothing. Others believe they reveal deep feelings, conflicts, and desires. Many therapists use dreams to help clients learn about themselves, develop intuition, or solve problems.

"Using" dreams   Many addicts report "using" dreams that involve addictive behavior. In early recovery these may be frightening. Since addiction itself is dramatic, it makes sense that memories of using and consequences would be prominent, and would be involved in dreams. Addicts years into recovery still have such dreams. Some report gratitude that it was just a dream, use it as a reminder that they are still addicts, or just dismiss them as insignificant.

Sleep, see also: Abstinence, Aftercare, Chronic pain, Drugs, Exercise & activity, Habit & structure, Prayer & meditation, Relapse prevention, Relaxation, Stress & strain, Tranquilizers. Next on path O: Pregnancy.

Slogans

The slogans of the Twelve-Step programs are simple tools that can help keep you centered. Though very useful, like any tools slogans can be misused.

EASY DOES IT

Thinking of "Easy does it" may help you break the mental set of obsession. When you feel as if you're beating your head against a wall, just stop and remind yourself that "Easy does it."

When things are busy, when you are most stressed out, these are the times when you need to stop and lighten up on yourself.

You may need the slogan when you are feeling overwhelmed, or when you are exaggerating things. Or would you rather spend your life catastrophizing and pole-vaulting over mouse droppings?

It may help to imagine that you are looking at yourself in a play, and see the responses you are making as if you were an observer not emotionally involved in the action below. See if you are being too dramatic or controlling. You might even see humor in the situation.

Another tactic is to ask yourself how significant it will be five years from now. That may give you some perspective.

Addicts can easily take anything to extreme, even a simple slogan. So people sometimes add a phrase on the end: "Easy does it . . . but do it."

LIVE AND LET LIVE

There is no common agreement about how to recover. If you listen to a variety of stories from Twelve-Step group members in recovery, you will find that some went to treatment, others did not. Some grew up in dysfunctional families, others had reasonably normal childhoods. Some alcoholics go to dance in lounges, while others avoid all such environments. Some food addicts follow a fairly rigid food plan, others have great flexibility in theirs. The longer you are around the Twelve-Step programs and the more you read of recovery literature, the more respect you will have for journeys that are different from yours.

In recovery, Dr. Bob struggled with the obsession with booze every day. Bill seemed relieved of that, but he struggled with depression for many years. Each human being is on a spiritual journey that is shared with all humankind, but also different from every other person's pilgrimage.

ONE DAY AT A TIME

The more hectic your life is, the more you need this slogan. Many addicts try to do too much too fast. This guarantees frustration, guilt, panic, and worry, which can in turn be used as an excuse to binge, purge, or starve.

Each day you can do a little planning for the future, but you can't live in the future. Make your plans one day at a time, and leave the outcome to your Higher Power.

Serenity prayer   A good way to implement *one day at a time* is to use the serenity prayer. Many addicts find it useful to mentally add the word "today" after each part:

God grant me the serenity to accept the things I cannot change *today*,
Courage to change the things I can *today*,
And wisdom to know the difference *today*.

FIRST THINGS FIRST

You should have no difficulty keeping recovery uppermost in your mind if you have suffered from addiction enough to use the First Step as a tool. This slogan is about priorities. See the module on Priorities.

Your recovery should have priority over just about everything that is not life-threatening. Prioritizing can give you freedom rather than restriction.

KEEP IT SIMPLE

Addicts often complicate things by analyzing and other mental gymnastics. Grandiose plans and ego may interfere with keeping it simple.

Dr. Bob used this slogan often. The primary purpose of most Twelve-Step fellowships is to help their members stay sober or abstinent. Sticking to the Steps and Traditions is the best way to keep it simple.

LET GO AND LET GOD

Recovery requires giving up the illusion of control. Using this slogan means you recognize that you can't control your addiction. By using Steps Two and Three you learn to "turn it over."

Many addicts apply this slogan to all the people, places, and things they want to control or change. They usually realize God, not they, has been in control all the time. What they really need to turn over is themselves, as it says in Step Three.

PROGRESS NOT PERFECTION

Recovery is about living life on a spiritual basis. The Big Book (p. 60) says, "We claim spiritual progress rather than spiritual perfection." Addicts find it helpful to apply this idea to all areas of their lives.

Giving up perfectionism will make your spiritual journey easier and more fun.

Slogans, see also: Affirmations, Attitudes, Paradoxes in addiction, Serenity. End of path J. Next on path K: Step Eight.

Spending

Many people, not just food or other addicts, have trouble with their shopping decisions. They may tend to purchase impulsively, or to be obsessive about comparing prices and products, or because of low self-esteem, feel guilty anytime they buy something for themselves, or panic if they find the same item on sale the next day. These things are not necessarily addiction, but you may need to address them.

ADDICTION

There is a point, however, when a tendency toward impulsive purchases or obsession about shopping crosses over into the realm of addiction. As with any addiction, the best tipoffs are loss of control, dishonesty, feeling guilty, or an intensive struggle required to maintain control. Compulsive spenders report issues similar to other addicts: low self-esteem, buying things to make them feel better, high expectations from parents or spouses, emotional deprivation, and lack of assertiveness.

Addictive shopping is usually a type of addiction to excitement, to the biochemical changes that take place with anticipation, fear, and a temporary relief from other problems.

Shoplifting   One direction that later-stage shopping addiction can take is shoplifting. It may begin with taking something you need or want but can't afford, but the excitement and fear are so stimulating that it can become a full-fledged addiction of its own. Drug addicts and bulimics often get into some kind of shoplifting, initially to pay for the drugs or food, or to get things they don't have money for because of spending vast amounts on their addiction. If the shoplifting becomes more than just a means to get the drugs or food, it will need specific addressing as an addictive behavior if overall recovery is a goal.

RECOVERY

Working a Twelve-Step program can help your tendency to spend compulsively. As you feel better about yourself and learn to live life on a spiritual basis, you are less likely to need things to make you feel OK.

It would be difficult to continue to spend compulsively and experience the rewards of freedom in recovery. If you buy things to try to make yourself feel better, you need to find ways to work on spirituality and self-esteem. Some people have such a problem with spending that they consider it a primary addiction and go to fellowships like Debtors Anonymous (see that module).

Spending, see also: Addiction, Adolescents, Binge history, Bingeing, Debtors Anonymous, Excitement, Gambling, Money, Moodifiers, Neurotransmitters, Unmanageability. Next on path A: Religiosity.

Spiritual aspects

Spirituality is at the core of Twelve-Step recovery from addiction. We talk about spiritual aspects, but spirituality permeates all aspects of recovery.

TWELVE STEPS

The Twelve Steps were written to explain how alcoholics used a Higher Power to quit drinking. As Dr. Bob said, the Twelve Steps tell you how to trust God, clean house, and help others. Recovering people in your Twelve-Step program can tell you how to use the Steps in your recovery, and you can read the Big Book and *Twelve Steps and Twelve Traditions* for background information.

Each person's journey in recovery is different. Look at your beliefs, your values, and the Steps. See if living life on a spiritual basis appeals to you.

DIVERSION

Sometimes Twelve-Step groups, including AA, get diverted from their primary purpose (abstinence from addictive behavior and carrying the message to others) into other issues. Dr. Bob kept reminding Bill to stick to that primary purpose. His last words to Bill were, "Remember, Bill, let's not louse this thing up. Let's keep it simple!" (*Pass It On,* p. 342.) The gift of recovery is a spiritual experience that comes from the grace of your Higher Power.

SPECIAL ADAPTATION

Each kind of addiction has its own special application of the Twelve Steps. The early alcoholics had lots of resentments and had hurt many people. Your experience may be different. The beauty of the Steps as tools is that you can use them as you need to recover from a wide variety of addictive behaviors. In your fellowship you can share how you do that with other addicts or people like yourself.

Step Twelve suggests that you practice these spiritual principles in your whole life. Refer to the modules following "see also" for more help in doing that.

Spiritual aspects, see also: Attitudes, Beliefs, Forgiveness, Higher Power, Integrity & values, Love & caring, Spirituality, Steps of AA, Surrender, Traditions of AA. Next on path E: Beliefs.

Spirituality

When you were introduced to a Twelve-Step program and heard that the Program is a spiritual one, you might have had one of two extreme reactions: a real resistance and animosity to the idea, or that you have always been a religious person and have nothing to learn. Neither attitude will be very useful in your recovery. A more productive approach would be to set aside your prejudices and see what the originators of the idea meant.

AA SPIRITUALITY

AA grew out of the experience of a Christian religious movement called the Oxford Group. Bill Wilson, AA's cofounder, had a profound religious experience while in the hospital for his alcoholism. Early AA members made no bones about the necessity of turning to God and changing their ways to stay sober. But the whole Twelve-Step movement has grown and expanded to include a variety of means by which people could find a Power greater than themselves to free them from the bonds of addiction.

By its nature, spirituality cannot be defined; it can only be described. Attempts to analyze it, to break it down into observable parts, will always lose the essence of what spirituality really is. AA gets across its message of spirituality through its members telling their stories, whether formally in a meeting or informally member-to-member. Most of the stories in the Big Book are about the spiritual concept of grace.

Spiritual awakening   To experience a spiritual awakening as talked about in Step Twelve means that you enter a state of grace with your Higher Power. This happens by living the principles of the Twelve Steps. There are specific instructions on how to do this in the Big Book of AA, specifically in chapters 5 and 6. Examples abound in the stories in the Big Book.

You are *not* God   Typically, the relationship with God or a Higher Power changes. For some, there has been no relationship at all. For others, it may change from thinking of God as an adversary, or even a supernatural servant, into a trusted guide. Many concepts or varieties of relationship with a Higher Power will work. The one that is least likely to work is the belief, however well disguised, that *you* are God.

Relationships   Spirituality is about your relationship with your-self, with others, with your Higher Power, and with the things in life that are important to you. On examination you will probably find that while you were a practicing addict, you were dishonest, unlov-ing, selfish, self-centered, resentful, self-pitying, and fearful, all to some degree. These attitudes and behaviors probably affected all your relationships.

Changes   Recovery simply means that you use your Higher Power, fellow Twelve Steppers, the Steps, and the principles of the Program in order to change.

It is true that vast emotional and spiritual changes often accom-pany the spiritual awakening referred to by Step Twelve. Fortunately, this does not have to be a dramatic event, or even happen in a certain time frame. But to be truly relieved of the bondage of addiction phys-ically, mentally, and emotionally, it does have to occur.

RELIGIOUS ADDICTION

Spirituality and healthy religion should not be confused with religious addiction, which requires specific extreme beliefs, rigid dogmas, and intolerance of others. This is really addiction to religiosity—all the excitement, power, and altered conscious states inherent in religious activity, especially of fanatical cults like the Jim Jones cult and the Guyana tragedy.

Healthy religion allows choices and focuses on the positives of human nature rather than manipulating people with shame and guilt. Do what you must to examine your experience, keep what you need, and discard what is not helpful.

RELIGION VS. SPIRITUALITY

For some people it is very important to distinguish between religion and spirituality. If you have a negative attitude toward organized religion, then you may find it comfortable to focus on the differences between them. One such difference is that religion usually includes a component of worship, which is not vital to the spirituality in AA. Most religions also have specific beliefs or dogmas that are required for membership in the particular religious group or movement.

Actually, those who have been in recovery for some time, and have a strong spirituality, have less tendency to find it important to distinguish between religion and spirituality. Perhaps this comes through the tolerance that is one hallmark of spirituality, or maybe the self-righteous condemnation of religion inhibits the development of spirituality.

Pervasive Spirituality must touch all your life, not just a portion of it. This is underscored in chapter 6 of the Big Book, "Into Action." Spirituality is the mortar that holds all the pieces of recovery in place. The majority of addiction relapses can be characterized either by not going to meetings or by not incorporating the Program into daily life. If you are living a lie in one area of your life, it will be much more difficult to be rigorously honest in the rest of your life, including your recovery from addiction.

WHAT IS REQUIRED

The spirituality that is developed by using the Twelve Steps means quite simply that you trust God, clean house, and help others. There is no specific way required to do this. You may be a person who has little difficulty fitting these principles into your life. On the other hand, you may have drastic changes to make. The Program allows for many individual differences.

Prayer and meditation are important tools for living life on a spiritual basis. Refer to the Prayer and meditation module for more information.

REWARDS OF A SPIRITUAL LIFE

The rewards of the Program are spiritual. The Promises found on pages 83 and 84 of the Big Book refer to the experiences of freedom, happiness, serenity, peace, unselfishness, faith (loss of fear), and trusting in God that come as the result of using the Steps. Note that they are found in the book after Step Nine, though many Twelve-Step group members report gaining some of these benefits even before they have actively used Steps Four through Nine.

NO MAGIC KEY

There seems to be no magic key to making the process of recovery work, though spirituality does have a touch of the mystical. Many elements are involved. Grace plays an important part, for when you do your share, God truly gives the gift, as She does when you plant the seeds and She makes the flowers grow. Recovery can provide as much joy as the beauty and fragrance of the flowers.

Spirituality, see also: Attitudes, Beliefs, Community, Forgiveness, Grace, Higher Power, Integrity & values, Religiosity, Serenity, Spiritual aspects, Steps of AA, Surrender, Traditions of AA, Unity. Next on path E: Steps of AA.

Sponsorship

At your first meeting at a Twelve-Step group, you probably heard someone talking about their sponsor, or about someone they are sponsoring, or the need to have a sponsor.

ORIGINS

Sponsorship, like much of the actual organization of AA, evolved from the Oxford Group. This was a highly successful nonsectarian Christian fellowship that flourished in the first half of the twentieth century. Its aim was to return to the spirit of first-century Christianity.

Sponsorship is not the same as counseling. A sponsor shares his or her own experience, strength, and hope with another person, primarily to work the Twelfth Step. A counselor, on the other hand, is a trained professional who uses a body of clinical knowledge, skills, and techniques to help cause a change in a client or patient.

When you ask someone to sponsor you, you are giving them an opportunity to work their own Twelfth Step. You are doing them a favor, more than the other way around. In sharing their experience, strength, and hope with you, they will build on their recovery, and they may avoid having to recycle through the revolving door of early recovery themselves.

BEING A SPONSOR

If you think of sponsorship as an activity, not an identity, it is likely to be more in line with its true purpose. In some places there is a noticeable difference in status whether you are a "qualified sponsor" or not. We believe this caste system is contrary to the spirit of the Traditions and can be avoided easily. Think of sponsorship without a capital "S"—use sponsor more as a verb than a noun.

Sponsorship, see also: Abstinence, Assertiveness, Codependency, Community, Control, Coping skills, Detachment, Higher Power, History of Twelve-Step groups, Humor & fun, Intervention, Judgment, Love & caring, Meetings, Moderation, Other support groups, Priorities, Service & giving, Slogans, Step Five, Steps of AA, Telephone, Tools of recovery, Traditions of AA, Trust, Unity.

Steps of AA

FROM AA

The Twelve Steps of all the Twelve-Step programs were adapted, usually with very minor modifications, and used by permission of Alcoholics Anonymous. In fact the only changes necessary, in most cases, are modifications for the words "powerless over alcohol" in Step One, and "carry this message to alcoholics" in Step Twelve.

THE TWELVE STEPS

1. We admitted we were powerless over alcohol, that our lives had become unmanageable.
2. Came to believe that a Power greater than ourselves could restore us to sanity.
3. Made a decision to turn our will and our lives over to the care of God *as we understood Him.*
4. Made a searching and fearless moral inventory of ourselves.
5. Admitted to God, to ourselves and to another human being the exact nature of our wrongs.

6. Were entirely ready to have God remove all these defects of character.
7. Humbly asked Him to remove our shortcomings.
8. Made a list of all persons we had harmed, and became willing to make amends to them all.
9. Made direct amends to such people wherever possible, except when to do so would injure them or others.
10. Continued to take personal inventory, and when we were wrong, promptly admitted it.
11. Sought through prayer and meditation to improve our conscious contact with God *as we understood Him,* praying only for knowledge of His will for us and the power to carry that out.
12. Having had a spiritual awakening as the result of these steps, we tried to carry this message to alcoholics and to practice these principles in all our affairs.

Steps of AA, see also: Abstinence, Alcoholics Anonymous, Attitudes, Higher Power, Honesty, Openmindedness, Spiritual aspects, Spirituality, Sponsorship, Step One, Surrender, Traditions of AA, Willingness. End of path E. Next on path F: Step One.

Step One

"We admitted we were powerless over alcohol, that our lives had become unmanageable."

Twelve Steps and Twelve Traditions presents an excellent introduction to the Steps and the Traditions of AA. The chapter on the First Step covers the following ideas and concepts:

- Why it is hard to admit defeat
- Physical allergy with a mental obsession
- Need to "raise the bottom"
- The fatal nature of addiction opens minds

Only occasionally do you see someone in Alcoholics Anonymous who tries to "work the Steps" before they stop drinking. There is a fairly universal understanding that *first* you stop drinking, and then you work the Steps so that you will stay stopped. And yet Step One says that they are powerless over alcohol, so how could they just stop?

Well, you admit you cannot do it by yourself, and the hospital, the Program, or the people in the Twelve-Step programs have a power greater than you by yourself, and that, for now, you allow that power to work for you. That is Steps One, Two, and Three, even if you have no idea what the Steps are!

HITTING BOTTOM

There is a saying in the Twelve-Step programs, that you must be "sick and tired of being sick and tired." Others call it "hitting bottom." We think it means reaching an awareness that you have exhausted your resources. It means that you have tried enough things to know that there is not likely to be another book, or spa, or gimmick that will enable you to control your addictive behavior satisfactorily, by yourself.

BOTH POWERLESSNESS AND UNMANAGEABILITY

Awareness of powerlessness and unmanageability is needed to use the First Step as a tool. If you are aware of your powerlessness over your addictive behavior, and the unmanageability that powerlessness causes in your life, then you will do whatever you need to do to recover, including using all the rest of the Steps.

If you think your life is unmanageable because of your addictive behavior, but you are still nurturing the illusion that you will be able to control it any day now, you will probably allow other priorities to supersede recovery.

Or, if you can freely admit that you can't control it, but you are maintaining a delusion that it really isn't interfering with your life very much, then you recognize powerlessness without unmanageability, and again you will not give recovery the priority it needs.

Step One, see also: Abstinence, Bingeing, Control, Crisis, Delusion, Detachment, Half-measures, Hitting bottom, Honesty, Powerlessness, Step Two, Steps of AA, Unmanageability. Next on path F: Crisis.

Step Two

"Came to believe that a Power greater than ourselves could restore us to sanity."

Twelve Steps and Twelve Traditions covers the following concepts:

- Reduction to a state of absolute helplessness
- The case of the atheist
- The hoop you have to jump through is wider than you think
- The Steps are only suggestions; AA does not demand belief
- Step Two does not have to be done all at once
- All that is needed is an open mind
- There are many roads to faith
- The case of the person who had faith but lost it
- The case of the intellectual
- Those who were disgusted with religion and hypocrisy
- The case of the devout
- Need for cleaning house, grace of God, and humility

HIGHER POWER

If you have a traditional disease, like cancer, and you admit that you cannot recover from it by yourself, then you will try to find someone who has the knowledge and skills to give you the best chance for recovery. The doctor you see is in fact a power greater than yourself. You might also have some understanding that ultimately, your life is in the care of an even greater Power.

Addiction is characterized by faulty judgment. The frustration that many professionals feel when dealing with addicts is that they seem to be doing so well and then they blow it. The addiction is not just about drinking drink number nine after you have had drink number eight. It is about buying a box of doughnuts to celebrate a fifty-pound weight loss, with the full intention of eating just one. Or stealing money to gamble after yours is gone. It is this powerlessness over the thinking process that is far more dangerous than whatever intoxication came from the nine drinks, or joints, or bets, or doughnuts.

Addicts who have a longstanding belief in a fairly traditional God often skip over Step Two, saying, "I already believe in God—that's not a problem for me." Those same people then try to work the Twelve-Step program as if God were not really involved at all. Dwell a moment on Step Two before you go on—it is critical.

The awareness of powerlessness and unmanageability from the First Step does not mean that God will give you the power to control your addiction. It means that until you surrender the "control" of your addiction to your Higher Power, you will continue to struggle with the substance or behavior, with control issues, and with the resultant confusion in your life. Step Two reinforces the idea that

God can provide the guidance and strength where your own efforts have failed.

FOR SKEPTICS

Many addicts have had trouble believing in a Higher Power. Some have such a negative reaction to even the word God that they are turned off by anything that sounds remotely spiritual. They may have plenty of experience with religious hypocrisy, perhaps in their family of origin. Or they may once have had a firm belief, but rejected it after some loss or what they might see as God's unwillingness to give them control over their addiction.

Whatever the reason for the disconnection, contact with a Higher Power is essential for success in any Twelve-Step program. Some have such fear and resistance to belief in God that they will struggle for years or decades, until finally the fear of not believing becomes greater than the fear of believing.

EASING INTO IT

Fortunately, you don't need a strong belief in God to be successful in this program. In fact, the Steps are designed to allow you to gradually become more comfortable with the idea of integrating a Higher Power into your life.

If you wish, you can start slowly, with the simple realization that there are some people in these meetings who seem to have found a way to escape from their addictions without the intense struggle that comes from trying to do it on their own. In its simplest terms, when you first ask, "How did you do it?" you are beginning to open the door to the possibility that there might be some Higher Power that can restore your sanity regarding your addiction. Sometimes that is just the power of a group of recovering people.

Later, you may find that your ideas of God, or a Higher Power, may become more traditional, or at least more encompassing. Successful recovery is usually accompanied by a growing spiritual comfort, a quiet humility, and the ability to give and receive love.

Step Two, see also: Acceptance, Higher Power, Honesty, Humility, Love & caring, Magical thinking, Openmindedness, Power, Powerlessness, Prayer & meditation, Sanity, Step One, Step Three, Step Eleven, Trust. Next on path G: Sanity.

Step Three

"Made a decision to turn our will and our lives over to the care of God *as we understood Him.*"

The chapter on Step Three includes these concepts:

- Willingness is the key to Step Three
- Requirement for action
- Just showing up at meetings is a beginning
- The paradox of becoming more independent by depending on God
- Electricity as an example
- Self-sufficiency and playing God
- The spiritual test of World War II
- Dependence on God may begin with a sponsor
- The role of willingness in Step Three
- Whole trouble was the misuse of will power

IT'S ONLY LOGICAL

Step Three assumes that you have admitted that you can't control your addictive use or behavior, that this powerlessness is ruining your life, and that you believe God or another understanding of a Higher Power can help you straighten out all this mess. If you can't do it but God can, wouldn't it be logical to let Him (or Her or It) do it? Most problems with Step Three do, in fact, result from an inadequate acceptance of Steps One and Two.

Also, for most people, Step Three is a gradual process. You make a small leap of faith, see that it works, take a bit larger jump, and so on, until one day you realize you are depending on the guidance of a Higher Power in your life.

THIRD STEP PRAYER

The "Third Step Prayer" appears on page 63 of the Big Book. Many addicts memorize it and use it as a daily affirmation of the decision to embrace the gift of recovery their Higher Power has offered.

Step Three, see also: Acceptance, Attitudes, Fear, Freedoms, Grace, Gratitude, Openmindedness, Prayer & meditation, Step Two, Step Four, Step Seven, Surrender, Trust, Willingness. Next on path H: Attitudes.

Step Four

"Made a searching and fearless moral inventory of ourselves."

Step Four includes work on these ideas:

- The use and misuse of instincts
- Examples of character defects
- Use of shortcomings as an excuse to relapse
- The delusion of self-righteousness
- A sponsor can help
- Those blinded by self-justification
- Shift from blame to humility
- The Seven Deadly Sins
- Primary instincts for sex, security, and society
- Inventory should be thorough and written

It is easier to understand the Fourth Step inventory if you look ahead to the rest of the Steps. How are you going to release the character defects in Steps Six and Seven unless you have inventoried them to know what they are? And until you have realized the kind of damage you may have caused yourself and others, you will have difficulty doing the amends of Steps Eight and Nine. The inventory is an essential step in the daily honesty of Step Ten, the spiritual contact in Step Eleven, and the spiritual awakening that Step Twelve says is THE result of working all the Steps.

Step Four, see also: Assertiveness, Behavior, Body image, Character defects, Codependency, Defenses, Dichotomous thinking, Energy levels, Family, Feelings, Honesty, Inventory, Perfectionism, Psychological problems, Self-image, Sex, Step Three, Step Five, Step Six, Step Eight, Step Ten, Survival roles. Next on path I: Step Five.

Step Five

"Admitted to God, to ourselves and to another human being the exact nature of our wrongs."

The section on the Fifth Step covers these ideas:

- All the Steps serve to deflate addicts' egos
- Fear keeps secrets still hidden, perilous for addicts
- Benefits of admitting defects, validated for centuries
- Step Five removes isolation, enhances kinship with God
- Begins forgiveness of self and others
- Humility and honesty require outside help
- Why not just you and God?
- Selecting someone to listen to Step Five
- Gaining the courage to do it

OTHER THOUGHTS

The Fifth Step is an essential part of the groundwork for the remaining steps. You have done your inventory in Step Four, but until you share it with God (or your Higher Power) and another human being, the secrets still have power, you have no idea whether someone else can accept you as you really are, and you may still have many blind spots in your inventory.

HOW TO FIND SOMEONE

You might prefer doing Step Five with a minister, priest, rabbi, or other clergy person. Religious professionals are usually suited to hearing confidences, by training and by temperament. Particularly if the cleric is a Roman Catholic priest, it is important that they understand the differences between a Fifth Step, which is a physical, emotional, mental, and spiritual inventory, and a confession, which is a sacrament for release from sin. Catholics may well need to do both.

Or you might share your inventory with a sponsor or other recovering addict in the Program. They may understand the purpose of the Step better, and you may already have developed a feeling of trust in them. It is good to know that their moral and religious views are fairly similar to yours, or else it might be difficult to share some of your darkest, most threatening secrets with them. While not likely, it is possible to be rejected by someone who, perhaps without your knowing in advance, is a lot sicker than you are.

You might even share the inventory with someone else with whom you feel very comfortable, or even with a total stranger who has been recommended by others. The only real requirement is that you be rigorously honest and as thorough as possible.

HOW TO SHARE IT

If possible, meet with this person well in advance of the Fifth Step and discuss their preferences and suggestions about how to do the inventory and how you will share it. This can reduce your anxiety about the actual sharing.

On the appointed day, be ready to share the information in some kind of organized fashion. Whether in outline or narrative form, you do not need to share everything you have written if it is extremely long. In that case, just hit the highlights, but be sure to include those things that you suspect are very important.

There are two problems with a Fifth Step that drags on longer than an hour or two. One is that most people who hear Fifth Steps are very sensitive and caring, who may not feel comfortable with telling you to speed it up as they have other things they need to do. If you are willing to listen to Fifth Steps, wouldn't you rather they average about an hour and a half instead of about four hours?

The other problem is that if you drag it out too long, you lose the ability to see general themes and tendencies because you and the person hearing the Step are smothered in detail. Remember that the purpose is to gain insight into what will need to be done for recovery, not to write a long autobiography.

WHAT TO EXPECT

You will probably feel a sense of relief as your secrets and your personality are shared and accepted by another person, who will usually give you some very encouraging and valuable feedback. They may be able to show you how you seem very hard on yourself in some areas, or some ways you have of exaggerating or minimizing certain aspects of your shortcomings, your insecurities, your talents, and your gifts.

Step Five, see also: Affirmations, Assertiveness, Character defects, Defenses, Dichotomous thinking, Energy levels, Honesty, Inventory, Perfectionism, Psychological problems, Step Three, Step Four, Step Six, Step Eight, Step Ten, Survival roles, Trust, Willingness. Next on path I: Assertiveness.

Step Six

"Were entirely ready to have God remove all these defects of character."

These ideas are found in the chapter on Step Six:

- Can God remove defects of character?
- Being "entirely ready" is a lifelong attitude
- We may enjoy our character defects

- Avoid the trap of perfectionism
- Avoid the trap of indefinite postponement
- Rebellion closes your mind against the grace of God

Why is it necessary to have a whole Step just to get ready to ask your Higher Power to remove your shortcomings? Because many people in the Twelve-Step programs have told us that their Higher Power does not come up and wrestle their character defects from them. From their collective experience it seems that it is impossible to release those shortcomings until you are thoroughly ready to let them go.

A very basic counseling skill is to recognize when someone seems to be resisting a change that would be to their benefit. A simple way to put that is to ask yourself, what mileage are you getting out of that dysfunctional or ineffective behavior. Examples:

- If you gossip about people, are you getting some superficial boost to your self-worth by putting others down? If you are not willing to let that go, you are not likely to get help with your gossiping.
- If you are often resentful of others, do you use that resentment to justify your addictive behavior, or your actions toward those people? What other side benefits are you getting from your resentment? Until you decide to get rid of that ammunition, the conflict will continue.
- If you have trouble with telling little lies, what kinds of conflicts or assertiveness or inconveniences are you avoiding? What short-term pain have the lies avoided? Realizing the long-term consequences can help you with the determination to give up the short-term benefits of lying, and open the door for your Higher Power to help you get more honest, through Step Seven.

Step Six, see also: Affirmations, Anger, Assertiveness, Attitudes, Behavior, Body image, Character defects, Fear, Feelings, Grief, Guilt & shame, Higher Power, Money, Perfectionism, Resentments, Responsibility, Self-centeredness, Spending, Step Four, Step Seven, Step Eight, Survival roles. Next on path J: Step Seven.

Step Seven

"Humbly asked Him to remove our shortcomings."

Important concepts imbedded in Step Seven include:

- What is humility?
- Material achievement vs. humility and spiritual values
- A desire to seek and do God's will
- Humiliations force learning about humility
- A wider meaning of humility
- Humility is a healer of pain
- God is not just for emergencies
- Humility is a guide to move out of yourself to others and to God

This step is relatively simple (but not necessarily easy) if you have laid the groundwork for it in Step Six. The chief obstacle to positive change is fear. You may be afraid that you or others won't like the change, or that you won't know how to cope with it, or that it will cost you in some way. In fact, it might feel more vulnerable to live honestly and to let go of those character defects, many of which are defensive in nature. But the rewards are great, including the ability to recover from your addiction.

NOT ALONE

Before you get overwhelmed with the task, remember that you don't have to do it alone. In fact, this Step clearly states that you *can't* do it alone. Humility is the key to admitting that by yourself you are inadequate for removing your shortcomings. You have the Twelve-Step program, the people in it, perhaps a counselor or therapist, other supportive people, and, of course, your Higher Power, who may work through these agents to help you remove your character defects.

Step Seven, see also: Affirmations, Assertiveness, Attitudes, Behavior, Body image, Character defects, Fear, Feelings, Grief, Guilt & shame, Higher Power, Humility, Money, Paradoxes in addiction, Perfectionism, Resentments, Responsibility, Self-centeredness, Serenity, Spending, Step Four, Step Six, Step Eight, Surrender, Survival roles. Next on path J: Character defects.

Step Eight

"Made a list of all persons we had harmed, and became willing to make amends to them all."

The chapter on Step Eight covers these ideas:

- Living with others is a great adventure for addicts
- Forgiving others and making amends are necessary to get forgiveness
- Step Eight can help discover basic flaws
- Harm causes physical, emotional, mental, or spiritual damage
- List and forgive those you have harmed in any way
- You are ending isolation from others and God

DISCUSSION

Step Eight starts a process of improving self-esteem in your relations with other people. Its objective is to get out of emotional debt. In your Fourth Step inventory, you should have found some examples of feeling guilty (for your actions that have hurt others or violated your code of conduct) or shameful (for beliefs you have incorporated into yourself, hurting yourself).

Some addictions cause more obvious damage in the family and in society. Alcohol, drugs, sex, and gambling addictions are examples. It may be easier for them to come up with a list of others that have been hurt.

More subtle   Other addicts do damage to other people, but it is often much more subtle. Most food addicts, for example, have never been arrested for eating while driving, although some have spent time in jail for shoplifting food. You may not have gotten drunk enough on food to cause an accident that severely hurt a child, but you may have given a child emotional rejection or mixed messages because of your preoccupation with food.

Has your child been embarrassed because of your appearance or your behavior? Do you have children who are suffering from your inability to provide a positive role model for their eating or other aspects of living?

Neglect   Another direction to explore about making amends is the area of neglect. Perhaps you have not done much damage to your relatives, friends, and coworkers, but have you neglected them because of your addiction? You may have avoided developing or strengthening a relationship with some people in your life because you had your hands full fighting your addiction, whatever it is. You might need to try to rectify this situation to feel good about yourself interpersonally.

Amends to yourself   We have heard some addicts say that they realized the person they had hurt the most was themselves, and that they needed to make amends to themselves as part of their recovery. We agree. What many people report as feeling ashamed has a lot to do with the damage they have done by incorporating all those ideas of being a bad or inadequate person. In this case, amends can include affirmations about your worth as an individual, and asking your Higher Power's help in treating yourself as you would like to treat someone you love.

Step Eight, see also: Abuse, Amends, Behavior, Forgiveness, Guilt & shame, Incest, Integrity & values, Relationships, Resentments, Step Nine, Step Ten, Willingness. Next on path K: Step Nine.

Step Nine

"Made direct amends to such people wherever possible, except when to do so would injure them or others."

Ideas found in the chapter on Step Nine are:

- Need for good judgment, timing, courage, and prudence
- Some amends can be made soon, others never by direct contact
- You may need to wait several weeks or even longer
- Maintain proper attitudes to avoid getting off track
- Don't talk prudence while practicing evasion
- Avoid full disclosure only when they or others would be seriously harmed
- Suggestions for whether and how to make amends

FREEDOM

Step Nine is a real freedom step. Although it is often hard to swallow your pride and apologize, it is almost always accompanied by a feeling of a burden being lifted from your shoulders. Other amends may require paying back money or some hard work to do whatever is necessary to make the amends. These, too, bring a feeling of self-confidence and self-esteem when you know that you are clearing the baggage of your past behavior.

Making arrangements   Actually, you don't have to complete the amends before realizing considerable benefit from it. A debt, for example, does not have to be paid off before Step Nine does its magic. Most of your Ninth Step happens when you own up to the debt and arrange to pay it. Even if that repayment takes years, you can go on with your recovery in the meantime.

Again, you don't have to do this step alone. You have your Higher Power and others to help. It is foolish, in fact, to think that you can or should do it by yourself.

Step Nine, see also: Amends, Delusion, Fear, Forgiveness, Guilt & shame, Incest, Relationships, Resentments, Step Eight, Step Ten. Next on path K: Amends.

Step Ten

"Continued to take personal inventory, and when we were wrong, promptly admitted it."

The section on Step Ten discusses these topics:

- Continuing look at assets and liabilities is necessary
- Eliminate emotional hangovers
- Several types of inventories; spot-check, day's end, house-cleanings, retreats
- Any disturbance should prompt a self-inventory
- Developing self-restraint
- Everyone is frequently wrong or emotionally ill to some degree
- Promptly admit failures to yourself and others
- Daily inventory includes positives and motives for wrong thoughts or acts
- One benefit is a good conscience

DAILY MAINTENANCE
Step Ten begins the daily maintenance tools of the Twelve-Step programs. Some people even call Steps Ten to Twelve maintenance

steps, although all the Steps can and should be used frequently as tools.

At least once a day, you should take a few moments to consider the day's activities, your decisions, how they worked out, your behavior, your feelings, and how you are progressing on your recovery. Many people do this at the end of the day, when they can take stock of what was productive, and what they would like to change in the future. You might also consider a few moments in the morning as you go over the day's plans and see what you can do today to enhance your recovery.

PROMPTLY ADMIT WRONGS

The other part of Step Ten says you don't have to wait until tomorrow, or even the end of the day, to correct your behavior. In fact, the skill of admitting you are wrong is one of the most powerful interpersonal skills there is, and it is a blessing of the Program.

Step Ten, see also: Anonymity, Humility, Humor & fun, Inventory, Openmindedness, Slogans, Step Eleven, Willingness. Next on path L: Humor & fun.

Step Eleven

"Sought through prayer and meditation to improve our conscious contact with God *as we understood Him,* praying only for knowledge of His will for us and the power to carry that out."

The section on Step Eleven covers:

- Resistance to prayer and meditation
- Prayer and meditation provide spiritual nourishment
- How to begin with meditation—consider a well-known prayer
- Meditation helps envision your spiritual objective
- Improves conscious contact with God, God's grace, wisdom, and love
- Practical benefit is emotional balance
- Prayer is raising the heart and mind to God
- "Knowledge of His will for us and the power to carry that out."
- Thy will, not mine, be done

- Thoughts that *seem* to come from God
- Presumption of God's will for others
- God moves in mysterious ways
- Prayer is sometimes very difficult
- Sense of belonging comes from prayer and meditation

OTHER THOUGHTS

Step Eleven calls attention to the need to nurture your contact with your Higher Power on a daily basis. This happens through prayer and meditation (see that module).

It is important to remember that whatever your situation in life, there is important work to be done. You can fulfill the purpose that God, your Higher Power, or fate has for you. Think of the spirit of a wheelchair athlete, who instead of becoming bitter and of no use to himself or anyone else, says "I can't run—but I can race!"

Step Eleven, see also: Beliefs, Control, Grace, Gratitude, Guilt & shame, Habit & structure, Higher Power, Magical thinking, Prayer & meditation, Relapse prevention, Relaxation, Serenity, Spiritual aspects, Spirituality, Step Ten, Step Twelve, Surrender. Next on path M: Prayer & meditation.

Step Twelve

"Having had a spiritual awakening as the result of these steps, we tried to carry this message to alcoholics and to practice these principles in all our affairs."

The chapter on Step Twelve contains these topics:

- Joy of living is theme; action is keyword
- Meaning of spiritual awakening
- Review of Steps One to Eleven
- Release of energy for action of AA
- Giving to another addict demands nothing in return
- Other kinds of Twelfth Step work
- Sometimes Twelfth Step work seems ineffective
- How to practice the Steps in "all our affairs"
- The danger of "two-stepping"
- Taking troubles in stride by using the AA way of life
- Attitudes about security and other people change

- Spouse and family in recovery
- Relationships in the Program
- Money and material things
- Many addicts are childish, emotionally sensitive, and grandiose
- Humble gratitude, love, and service
- Understanding builds right principles and attitudes; right action is the key to good living

SPIRITUAL AWAKENING

Note that Step Twelve does not say, "Having had a spiritual awakening as **a** result of these steps . . ." as many people read it. Instead, it says, ". . . as **the** result of these steps . . ." which implies that the spiritual awakening is the major goal of the Steps, rather than a nice by-product.

CARRYING THE MESSAGE

After you have had a spiritual awakening, through use of the Steps, you are asked to try to carry the message to those who still suffer. Carrying the message of recovery is the primary purpose of all Twelve-Step recovery groups.

Ways you carry the message include: sharing your experience, strength, and hope with others, starting new meetings, ordering literature, and sharing in meetings.

SERVICE

Dangers of overdoing Step Twelve include becoming obsessed with your own ego and encountering one or more people whose disease is stronger than your recovery. The Red Cross used to give this advice about lifesaving: "Reach, throw or row, then go."

It is also dangerous to "fake" recovery. Remember the poem:

> You can't lead where you don't go
> You can't teach what you don't know
> You can't be what you are not
> You can't give what you ain't got.

Step Twelve, see also: Control, Employee assistance programs, Enabling, Gratitude, Humility, Intervention, Love & caring, Recovery, Responsibility, Self-centeredness, Service & giving, Sponsorship, Tools of recovery, Traditions of AA. Next on path N: Intervention.

Stinking thinking

MEANS ADDICTIVE THINKING

For many years, the term *stinking thinking* has been used in AA and in other Twelve-Step organizations to mean all the thinking processes that support the disease of addiction.

Committee in the head   The committee (or the girls/boys) in the head are those voices replaying tapes from your past. Sometimes it seems so easy to get confused, with addictive thoughts and recovery thoughts going full blast and battling for dominance.

Denial   Denial is an outright rejection of what you know or suspect to be true. Alcoholics in AA have usually seen several examples of AA members who decide to have an occasional social drink, but wind up coming back after months of heavy drinking and frightening consequences. Yet through denial, they may think, "But it won't happen to me."

Rationalizing   Giving excuses for your behavior is rationalizing. "Well, everyone does it. You would too if you had a mother like mine."

Intellectualizing   With enough mental gymnastics, almost anything can sound reasonable. Addicts who get all wrapped up in theories of addiction or other intellectual subjects may have to beware of a tendency to think themselves into trouble.

Delusion   By starting with some lies, half-lies, or other misinformation, you can build a fantasy world of delusion, which gets further and further away from reality.

Histrionics   People who overdramatize are called histrionic. The addict can use this process of making mountains out of molehills as an excuse to drink, use, spend, gamble, binge, purge, starve, or make other bad decisions.

Dichotomous reasoning   The process of making things either black or white, excluding any possibility for a middle ground, carrying everything to extreme—this is called dichotomous thinking.

Diet mentality   For food addicts and other addicts concerned with weight management, diet mentality includes preoccupation with weight, weight loss, rigid food plans, ridiculous food plans, and other trappings of diets and diet clubs.

Checklist mentality   The idea that you can control your addictive behavior by "checking off" a list of prescribed actions, like attending a certain number of meetings each week, calling someone each day, doing this and doing that, is called checklist mentality. Everything we have mentioned may be useful in recovery, but checklist mentality is the subtle attitude that following the checklist will give *you* control of your addiction.

RECOGNIZING BAD THINKING

Freedom from stinking thinking occurs gradually. At first you may be doing well just to recognize after you have gotten into the stinking thinking mode, but before you have done any real damage. Later you might catch yourself just as you get into it. Eventually, through good progress on your recovery, you will be able to avoid getting into it in the first place, or will catch yourself and modify the stinking thinking.

- An alcoholic says to himself, "I could really use a drink right now." Then adds, "Like a hole in the head."
- A bulimic thinks, "I ate too much for dinner—no, I really didn't."
- A codependent says, "How long has it been since you went to a meeting?" Then adds, "Obviously *I* have been too long without one."

Stinking thinking, see also: Abstinence, Aftercare, Attitudes, Celebrations, Chronic pain, Control, Crisis, Defenses, Delusion, Dichotomous thinking, Feelings, Food plans, Habit & structure, Half-measures, Halfway house, Honesty, Judgment, Magical thinking, Moderation, Obsession, Paradoxes in addiction, Premenstrual syndrome, Priorities, Progression, Relapse prevention, Relaxation, Sabotage of recovery, Sponsorship, Visualizations. Next on path O: Celebrations.

Stress & strain

Addiction often employs stress as an excuse to use a substance or to justify other addictive behavior. You may think you cannot stop your addiction until you can somehow reduce the amount of stress in your life.

STRESS IS NATURAL

The psychological term *stress* comes from the physical disciplines, like physics and metallurgy. In recent years, stress has had a bad rap from the press and the general public. There are stress-management seminars and self-help books that are aimed at reducing stress. You can take tests in newspapers and magazines to tell you when your stress level is dangerously high.

STRAIN

Perhaps it is unfortunate that the corresponding metallurgical term *strain* was not also adopted in the model borrowed by psychology. Stress is the force that is applied to a metal from outside, to compress or bend or break it. Strain is the force within the metal that resists that compressing or bending or breaking. Metallurgists know that the strain often takes a higher toll on the metal than the stress, and the science of designing structural components has a lot to do with spreading out the strain so the part can withstand as much stress as possible.

Why is it that some people seem to flourish under a level of stress that would totally wipe out someone else? In most cases, it is strain—our *response* to the stress in our lives—that is more dangerous than the level of stress.

In fact, you function best in a certain range of stress (or, more accurately, strain). If it is too low, you get bored and perform well below your capabilities. As it increases, you perform better and better up to a point. Then you get saturated with it, and as stress continues to increase, you actually perform less, until finally you are paralyzed and unable to function at all.

For an example of stress and performance, imagine a college or pro football coach. The best coaches intuitively know just how much stress each of their players can take, and getting them "up" for the game means putting more pressure on this one, and trying to get that one to relax, depending on their ability to tolerate stress.

DECREASING STRESS

If you are suffering from too much stress, you can either lower stress, decrease the strain associated with that stress, or both.

To reduce stress, you may want to think of renegotiating contracts. Most of your contracts are not written down. You have one or more formal or informal contracts with almost everyone in your life, from your relatives to your acquaintances. It is the arrangement by which you expect what you will do for that person, and what they will do for you.

If a relationship has a contract in which you supply 90 percent of the effort and the other person supplies 10 percent, you will probably be very frustrated and experience a lot of stress. Unless that person is an infant, you ought to consider renegotiating the contract to one that is more equitable.

Another technique for reducing stress is to ask for help. Often there are others willing to help, but out of stubbornness, false pride, or low self-esteem, you may be unwilling to admit that you need help. You might not get it, but at least you should ask. Then think whether you really need this grief, and consider changing the contract.

DECREASING STRAIN

The other thing you can do is to reduce the strain—to improve your response to the stress in your life. For many addicts, part of the problem is recognizing perfectionism and realizing that your work doesn't need to be of quite that high a quality, that others might be able to help if you'd just tolerate their inability to do it as well as you can, and lower the unrealistic expectations you may have of yourself.

A valuable tool for changing your response to stress is to use Steps Six and Seven on your perfectionism and your attitudes. You can shift from self-pity to gratitude, develop assertiveness so people don't walk all over you, and get on with your life.

INCREASING STRESS AS NEEDED

Especially in early recovery, try to avoid contracting yourself for activities and obligations that will add stress to your life for a long time. Instead, if you are bored and need something to do, get involved in things you can easily pull back from if you start to get overwhelmed. If you get active in an organization, including your Twelve-Step group, volunteer for things that have a short duration, so you can assess your stress levels as you go. If someone asks you to do something, be selective and conservative, and give them fair warning you will accept it only on the condition that if it becomes too much for you, you can bail out. Then stick to *that* contract!

SERENITY PRAYER

A great tool for dealing with stress and strain is the Serenity Prayer.

Sugar

Sugar is an important test case for addiction. We know that drugs like alcohol, heroin, and cocaine are profound mood changers and mind benders. But what about other substances that are sometimes abused, like sugar. If sugar is a "moodifier," then should alcoholics and other addicts be using it regularly?

The answers to questions about sugar are vital to the treatment of food addiction, but they also help define the role of substances in all addictions.

Sugars are simple carbohydrates, consisting of a single molecule (monosaccharide) or a double molecule (disaccharide). Disaccharides must be broken down into monosaccharides before they can be used by the body.

Also called dextrose, *glucose* is the form of sugar that is used by all cells of the body as fuel. Since it is ready for use, it requires no conversion by the liver, so is metabolized very rapidly. Glucose tastes 70 percent as sweet as sucrose, and is sometimes used as a food additive.

Fructose, also called levulose, is one of the sugars commonly found in fruit. Fructose must be converted by the liver into glucose before it can be used as a fuel.

Since it tastes 1.7 times as sweet as sucrose, fructose is being used more commonly as a sweetener, often as "high fructose corn sweetener." This may be better for food addicts who are sensitive to ordinary table sugar (sucrose), but there are concerns about large amounts of fructose causing copper deficiencies.

Galactose is not very common in nature, except when combined with glucose to form lactose (see below). When it is found free in nature, it tastes 32 percent as sweet as sucrose. It takes longer to metabolize because it must be converted into glucose by the liver.

Ordinary table sugar, *sucrose*, is a combination of one fructose and one glucose. It is relatively easy for the enzymes in saliva or other digestive juices to split these two, and then there is a glucose and a fructose molecule. The glucose will be immediately available, but the fructose molecule must be converted by the liver before it can be used.

The sugar in milk is *lactose*, composed of one glucose and one galactose molecule. Since lactose tastes only 35 percent as sweet as sucrose, it could be easy to get a lot of it and not think you have had much sugar. Once it is split into glucose and galactose, the glucose is immediately available, just as with sucrose.

Maltose, or malt sugar, is two glucose units. They are split very easily, and used very rapidly. Both molecules are immediately usable by the body, and so it seems that this would be the most psychoactive sugar for food addicts. Maltose tastes only 46 percent as sweet as sucrose, so it might deceive you.

GLYCOGEN

Glycogen (animal starch) is a polysaccharide, like vegetable starch, and not a sugar. But we mention it here because it is the body's form of short-term storage for glucose. The liver, muscles, and fat cells can convert glucose into glycogen when signaled to do so by insulin, which is released by the pancreas. Another pancreatic hormone, glucagon, causes glycogen to be converted to glucose as needed.

MOOD-ALTERING?

Is sugar a mood-altering drug? While there is a scarcity of scientific evidence, people who have worked extensively with food addiction usually agree that there is some kind of mood-altering effect that has to do with sugar. Theories for this effect have to do with the blood sugar level, the insulin overshoot, the tryptophan/serotonin connection, and other effects of refined sugars.

If your blood sugar level is high, you have more energy available and feel more alert and more like doing things. If you eat refined carbohydrates, especially sugars that contain glucose, the blood sugar level can rise quickly, making you feel "better" within a few minutes.

If the blood sugar level rises very rapidly, the body will assume you have eaten a large amount of carbohydrate-containing foods, and will crank out insulin to convert the excess glucose to glycogen, preventing your body from burning yourself up with too much blood sugar.

But since these sugars are metabolized very quickly, there is then an excess of insulin and the blood sugar level may fall back below where it was when you ate the sugar. So you feel depressed—and it's back to the candy machine again.

The excess insulin also forces large neutral amino acids (LNAAs) into the muscles and other tissues of the body. One amino acid, tryptophan, is relatively unaffected by insulin, so suddenly it has less competition for the limited number of spaces on the transport molecules that cross the blood-brain barrier. Once in the brain, the tryptophan becomes serotonin, a natural tranquilizer.

Evidence of the psychoactive effect is supported by the fact that many food addicts experience blackouts, similar to those found in chemical dependency, although not usually as long-lasting or severe. These seem more common in those who have been eating a lot of sugar in their diet.

OTHER EFFECTS

Refined carbohydrates, almost by definition, have fewer amino acids, vitamins, and minerals than their unrefined counterparts. The digestion of these foods requires enzymes and other biochemical agents that the sugary foods do not replenish. This may lead to enzyme depletion or other nutritional problems, which may make good judgment more difficult, and the addiction spiral continues.

SENSITIVITY LEVELS

There is no evidence that anyone is so sensitive to sugar that a very small quantity will set off these reactions. But some factors regarding this sensitivity are:

The total quantity of sugar (especially glucose) in a meal or snack affects the speed of blood sugar rise.

It would make sense that the concentration plays a part. A tablespoon of sugar spread throughout a large meal would be metabolized more slowly than that tablespoon eaten by itself.

The more protein present in the meal or snack, the more competition the tryptophan would have for transport across the blood-brain barrier, so the less serotonin would be produced.

While not yet generally understood or documented, there seems to be a link between sugars and fats that generates cravings. For most (but not all) food addicts, sweet fats are far more powerful than sweets by themselves.

Some food addicts have been told that they should not consent to having an intravenous glucose drip while in the hospital. Unless someone has some scientific evidence or a good logical explanation, there should be no problem with an I.V. glucose drip unless it is much too rapid (and then there would be more serious problems to your health). The sensitivity is to rapid metabolism of sugar, not to the presence of glucose in your blood. If you don't have any glucose in your blood, you die.

INDUSTRIAL CONSPIRACY

Compounding the problem is the food industry, which regularly uses sugar as a food additive. Why? Because it helps products sell better. Now that the public has an increasing awareness about the nutritional problems and other concerns about sugar, the food industry has simply started to conceal sugar as an ingredient.

GLYCEMIC INDEX

Most of the literature that relates to the metabolism of sugar and other carbohydrates is intended for nutritionists who advise people with diabetes, who must be careful of foods that will increase their blood sugar too rapidly. One tool for nutritionists is a glycemic index.

This index sets glucose at a value of 100 and compares selected foods to it. The higher a food scores on the glycemic index, the faster it tends to increase the blood sugar. Maltose (which is sort of a double shot of glucose) scores 105. Fructose, which must be converted into glucose by the liver, scores 20. Sucrose (table sugar) is 59 on this scale, almost exactly between glucose and fructose, which are its two components.

High-fat and high-protein foods are low on this scale, indicating that they are metabolized more slowly. Peanuts are 13, soybeans are 15, and milk products are about 33.

There are a few surprises, however. Carrots are a speedy 92, and parsnips speed in at 97, almost as fast as glucose itself. Ice cream gets only 36.

Does this mean that people sensitive to sugar are free to eat ice cream but should leave out carrots and parsnips completely? Not a chance. It means that you need to avoid overeating any food and to be honest about how certain foods affect you.

Actually, when we do see a food addict bingeing on vegetables, carrots are usually their choice, and we know several who ate so many carrots they turned yellow from carotene poisoning.

Research has not yet determined how useful this glycemic index is for diabetics, and probably no one has even considered using it for research on food addiction. We include it only to show that there may be differences in metabolic rates, even among foods not thought to be "trigger foods." Avoiding excess of *any* food is probably the most important lesson to be learned here.

THE BOTTOM LINE

What can we conclude from all this? At the present state of the research, we can suggest that:

- Some people are much more sensitive to sugar than others.
- The combination of sugar and fat is most likely to stimulate cravings.
- There is more we don't know than we do know.
- Approach refined sugar cautiously if at all.

Sugar, see also: Alcohol, Allergies, Binge history, Bingeing, Blackouts, Craving, Drugs, Fantasy, Fats, Food addiction, Metabolism, Moodifiers, Nutrition, Sweeteners, Tolerance, Tranquilizers.

Surrender

Surrender implies turning acceptance into action. You accept your disease and surrender to the recovery process. It is an attitude you adopt when you begin a program of recovery that leads to freedom and the possibility of joy. Many addicts have a negative view of surrender that prevents this from happening.

Jacquelyn Small (*Transformers: The Therapists of the Future*, 1982) has described surrender in positive terms, and some of her ideas are the basis for this part of this module.

SURRENDER PROCESS

If you view surrender as a process where you give up and some Higher Power becomes dominant and controlling, you are likely to see yourself as weak, pitiful, and helpless. This is not what happens when you participate in the surrender process required by the first three Steps.

When you admit powerlessness over your disease, you are acknowledging that your own ego alone is inadequate to defeat the powerful forces of addiction. Next you are willing to believe that a power outside your ego can be tapped into to help you.

And Step Three is learning to use that power in your life by turning your will over to the care of your Higher Power, however you may understand Him, Her, or It.

This act of surrender is a step that allows you to let go of the illusion of control and yield yourself to the natural flow of life. When you do this you enter a transformational process in which you cooperate with the forces governing the universe rather than fighting them. It *feels* like the energy you get from "going with the flow" of a stream or a moving sidewalk.

NOT SURRENDERING

Resisting surrender results in fear, rigidity, judgmentalism, humorlessness, fatigue, and a feeling that recovery is just too hard. Sometimes even the phrase "working the Steps" indicates a struggle to do it yourself rather than surrendering to a Higher Power.

Imagine that you are a young child, and you wake up in the middle of the night. You are choking, from some acrid gas. A monster has hold of you, with a strange face and powerful arms. You scream and fight, but the monster does not let go. It carries you out of your house and into the street, with you kicking and screaming all the way. Only then do you see your parents, and they comfort you and thank the firefighter who just saved your life! Surrender may feel just like that.

FREE AND JOYOUS

Surrender, aided by acceptance, is being a full participant in life, being open, cooperating, and allowing yourself to be transformed into the person you always wanted to become. The surrender transformation allows you to become free and joyous, and have more meaning in your life.

Surrender, see also: Abuse, Acceptance, Amends, Attitudes, Fear, Freedoms, Grace, Gratitude, Openmindedness, Perfectionism, Prayer & meditation, Self-image, Step Two, Step Three, Step Seven, Trust, Willingness. End of path H. Next on path I: Step Four.

Survival roles

With the current emphasis in the field of addiction on ACOA (Adult Children of Alcoholics) issues and codependency, it is helpful to know the basis of the popularized Survival Roles of Hero, Scapegoat, Lost Child, and Mascot. Sharon Wegscheider-Cruse (1981) identified and described these roles as typical of what children do in alcoholic homes. These roles are said to surface in any seriously dysfunctional home, and people in various Twelve-Step groups describe how they adopted these roles within their family of origin.

The chaos, confusion, and pain are so severe in an alcoholic family that children must develop some way to survive. Everyone in the family feels many negative emotions, especially fear, hurt, and anger, as well as insecurity, shame, confusion, rejection, and loneliness. Because there are unspoken rules that prohibit the expression of these feelings, each family member develops defenses to survive.

DEPENDENT, CHIEF ENABLER

Typically you have one adult who is the Dependent (alcoholic father–husband, for example) and a Chief Enabler (wife–mother). All activity focuses on this duo and their unsuccessful attempts to deal with, usually by denial, an increasingly chaotic situation as alcoholism progresses.

HERO

This child is often the oldest son or daughter. Their dominant feelings are *inadequacy* and *guilt* at finding themselves in such an impossible situation. So Heroes behave in a way that makes them look very successful, giving some worth to the family. Good grades and leadership qualities are examples of ways Heroes achieve, if these characteristics are valued by the family. Sports might be an alternative route.

SCAPEGOAT

This role is fulfilled by a child who cannot possibly live up to the Hero's standards. They deal with their frustrations by acting out, causing trouble, and going outside the family to find satisfaction. The characteristic feeling they experience is *hurt,* but they appear angry, rebellious, and sullen. They might get in trouble with drugs and alcohol, and may be the first to be openly identified as having a problem.

LOST CHILD

When this child comes onto the scene, things are so chaotic that this child essentially gets lost. Their characteristic feeling is *loneliness* and they become withdrawn, shy, and overlooked. They seem to accept their lot in life, and have difficulty bonding with others and enjoying human relationships. There are Lost Children who find solace in food and become obese, which exacerbates their social problems.

MASCOT

This child is born into an already chaotic family with lots of secrets and delusions. *Fear* is the characteristic emotion of mascots; they sense something is wrong that nobody talks about. They learn early that they can obtain some relief by clowning and getting attention. Mascots' anxiety may also be manifested by hyperactivity, so the attention is not always positive.

ADULTHOOD

More often than not, these children carry these behaviors into adulthood with them. They should seek counseling for any problems involving relationships, codependency, or even for primary addictive disease, including alcoholism, drugs, food, or other addiction.

LEARNING MORE

This model is an oversimplification of a model that originally was helpful but still inadequate to explain the experience of most children of dysfunctional families. Few addiction families have only one addict. Many children changed or combined these roles, or do not fit well in any of them. We suggest you use what you can and learn more about survival roles if you find that they fit you or your family.

Survival roles, see also: Abuse, Adolescents, Behavior, Children of addicts, Codependency, Control, Defenses, Detachment, Emotional aspects, Enabling, Family, Family of origin, Forgiveness, Humor & fun, Incest, Integrity & values, Intimacy, Mental aspects, Power, Prevention of addiction, Relationships, Resentments, Sabotage of recovery, Self-image, Step Four, Surrender.

Sweeteners

Some chemical dependency treatment programs try to limit their patients' consumption of sugar and other sweeteners. Addicts of all sorts who have some concerns about weight management, including most food addicts, have some questions about sweeteners.

Sucrose is what most people mean when they say "sugar." It is the most widely known sweetener, though it now follows high fructose corn syrup as the number one sweetener in processed foods. Since sucrose is half dextrose and half fructose, the dextrose part is metabolized very quickly, while the fructose part must be converted by the liver.

High fructose corn syrup, found in everything from soft drinks to soups, contains 42 to 90 percent fructose; the rest is dextrose. Thus its rate of metabolism depends on which variety it is—the 42 percent formula would likely be metabolized much faster than the 90 percent one.

Dextrose, also known as glucose (blood sugar), is used directly by the cells of the body, so people sensitive to sugar would theoretically be more sensitive to pure dextrose than to sucrose.

Fructose (fruit sugar) must be converted to glucose by the liver before being used by the body. Therefore it takes a little longer to elevate the blood sugar level. Fruits, however, contain a mixture of sugars; oranges, peaches, and melons, for example, contain more sucrose than fructose.

Lactose (milk sugar) is a combination of glucose and galactose. The galactose part also must be changed by the liver before it can elevate the blood sugar level, but the glucose part is metabolized directly, so its general speed of metabolism should be comparable to sucrose. Since it tastes only about one-seventh as sweet as sucrose, it might be found in significant quantities in dairy products that don't taste particularly sweet.

Galactose (grape sugar) is a slower-metabolized sugar usually found as part of lactose or fruits.

Maltose, hexose, and any other -ose are probably disaccharides (other combinations of simple sugar molecules).

SUGAR ALIASES

Because of the concern that people have about eating too much sugar, the food industry is trying its best to hide it in foods. This is because food without sweeteners doesn't sell well. From a marketing standpoint, the best of both worlds is to be able to say on the package that there is "no sugar added" while loading it with "natural sweeteners" so you'll keep buying it because it tastes so good.

Corn syrup, corn syrup solids, and corn sweetener are all products of differing amounts of fructose and dextrose.

Molasses is heavy sucrose syrup that does at least have some iron remaining in it.

Brown sugar is usually ordinary table sugar to which some molasses has been added to make it brown.

Honey is a mixture of sugars, with a little more fructose than table sugar. The health food properties of honey have been overrated; it is not significantly better nutritionally than other sugars. And because of pollens and other substances included, it may actually aggravate allergies in those sensitive to airborne matter.

Natural sweetener is a euphemism for sugar.

Malted barley, also called simply malt, is germinated barley. It is used by brewers to convert starch to sugar, which is then fermented into alcohol. When malt is added to a carbohydrate, then, its function is to increase the sugar content of the food.

Maltodextrin is a starch product usually used to change the texture of foods, so it is not a sugar, but it is a processed starch. We include it here only because it sounds like a sugar.

FRUIT JUICES

These are sugars, usually with a high percentage of fructose, but sugars nevertheless. The more sensitive you are to sugars, the more careful you should be of fruit juices or dried fruit. Few people are so sensitive to sugar that they cannot tolerate eating an orange, but you can easily squeeze the juice (including the sugar) from three oranges into a glass and get about the same amount of sugar as a regular Coke.

DRIED FRUIT

When you dry fruit, you are evaporating only the water, so all the sugar stays behind in the fruit. If you eat dried fruit, like raisins, count the pieces, not the handfuls. A small box of raisins is the sugar equivalent of a pretty large bunch of grapes.

SWEET ALCOHOLS

Sorbitol, mannitol, xylitol, and similar substances are sweeteners that are classed chemically as sweet alcohols. They are only half to three-quarters as sweet as sucrose and, like sugar, contain about 4 calories per gram. They metabolize much more slowly than sugars, so they provide energy for intestinal bacteria, which attract water and produce an irritating waste that can cause diarrhea. They are marketed as "sugar free" primarily because they do not contribute to dental caries (cavities). They have other purposes, such as keeping chewing gum soft and from sticking to the paper, and because of the diarrhea, they are also laxatives if you eat very much of them. We suggest that you use them in moderation if at all.

GUMS AND MINTS

Gums, mints, etc., add up quickly, whether they contain sugar or a sweet alcohol. They should be considered as sugarless only in the sense that they don't promote tooth decay like sugar. For some food and nicotine addicts, they tend to continue the obsession by supporting the idea that you have to have something in your mouth to keep from putting food or a cigarette into it. This "substitution therapy" is a crutch at best, and a hindrance to solid recovery for many.

ARTIFICIAL SWEETENERS

Artificial sweeteners probably do not trigger the carbohydrate/insulin/serotonin reaction or directly affect blood sugar level significantly. For some food addicts, however, the very idea of eating something sweet may produce enough excitement to trigger an insulin response. This is especially true if they believe they must rigidly exclude all sugar from their diet to recover from food addiction.

Artificial sweeteners may or may not help people lose weight. People rarely cut down on fats just because they switch from sugar to artificial sweeteners. If they are used in moderation with a low-fat food plan, artificial sweeteners may help, but if they stimulate your cravings, they may hurt.

Saccharin   Saccharin is the most common purely artificial sweetener, although aspartame is catching up fast. Saccharin is up to 500 times as sweet as sucrose (table sugar). It has been implicated in cancer, but there is a controversy about how dangerous it is.

Aspartame   Aspartame goes by the trade name NutraSweet when added in bulk to processed foods, and Equal when added at the table. It has a good taste, is somewhat more expensive than saccharin, and is unstable at high temperatures, so it cannot be used in baking, for example. It is about 200 times as sweet as sucrose.

Aspartame is composed chemically of the two amino acids aspartic acid and phenylalanine, plus a methyl group. The amino acids are broken down and used as other protein fragments in the body. People with phenylketonuria (PKU) have the hereditary inability to get rid of phenylalanine when it is ingested in excess of the body's needs. Fortunately PKU is not very common, and if you have it, you would already know about it.

When aspartame's methyl group is metabolized, it briefly becomes methanol (or methyl alcohol) and then formaldehyde, and finally carbon dioxide. Moderate amounts of aspartame will not produce significant quantities of these toxic chemicals, but you might remember that the FDA gave its approval of aspartame on the assumption that no one would consume more than about 50 milligrams per kilogram of body weight. This amounts to about eighty packets of Equal per day for a 132-pound person. This sounds like a very high amount, but it could be reached with about fifteen NutraSweet soft drinks. Now that NutraSweet is in all sorts of processed foods, there is a clear danger of excess.

Others   Acesulfame-K (Sunette, Sweet One) is a newly approved artificial sweetener that tastes about as sweet and almost as good as aspartame but does not break down at high temperatures. Since it is newer, there is less information available about its safety.

SWEETENERS IN FOODS, DRUGS, VITAMINS, ETC.

If you believe you are particularly sensitive to sugars, watch the labels of all kinds of foods, drugs, vitamins, and other preparations, because sugars are often used in these products. Even packages of saccharin and aspartame have small quantities of sugar to increase the volume of the packages. Most artificial sweeteners are so concentrated that they have to add something to the packet so you won't think it is empty, and so it will pour freely. These amounts of sugar may add up if you are using much artificial sweetener.

Sweeteners, see also: Binge history, Constipation, Craving, Diet mentality, Food addiction, Food plans, Hunger & appetite, Metabolism, Moderation, Nutrition, Relapse prevention, Sabotage of recovery, Sugar.

T

Telephone

A TOOL OF RECOVERY

All Twelve-Step groups recommend the use of the telephone as a "tool" for recovery. It has value for several reasons.

As an addict, your thinking can be very erratic, spinning, and confusing. This is especially true in early recovery, when you first stop drinking, using, or behaving addictively. The telephone is a quick link to sanity. Allowing another person's serenity and words of encouragement to enter your consciousness can easily "save the day."

PHONOPHOBIA

Many people find making phone calls very difficult, particularly at first. The addiction can find all sorts of excuses for not calling, such as:

- I might be rejected.
- I don't want to bother them.
- She doesn't have time for me.
- He might not understand.
- It might not help.
- It *might* help.

None of these excuses are valid. To help with phonophobia, remember that false pride is usually the problem. It may be hard to admit to yourself or others that you need help.

All addicts in recovery know that newcomers (and many old-timers) need help. When someone talks to you on the phone, it's an opportunity for them to use their Twelfth Step—which is necessary for them and their recovery. Also, it is not unusual that the person you call might need some help, too. Almost everyone in a Twelve-Step program has had the experience of someone calling them at just the right moment, when they did not have sense enough to make a call themselves.

Occasionally the people you call may be busy or not at home, but be careful that your addiction does not use that as an excuse to give up. If you were unable to reach anyone, you will still benefit from the process; it reinforces your commitment to recovery.

Even reaching someone's answering machine can help. Just leave a message and you will feel much better.

Also, make every minute count by sharing what's going on with you without being extremely brief or extremely long-winded, then stop and listen to the feedback and sharing you receive. Usually this can be done in less than five minutes—ten minutes tops. If you are still confused or upset or lonely after ten minutes, say thanks and call someone else. That way you will increase your chances of hearing what you need at that moment.

TELEPHONITIS

Most addicts should make more use of the telephone, but there are a few who need to back off it a bit. Telephonitis (too much involvement with the phone) can be a way of avoiding the other parts of your recovery program, including meetings, reading literature, and meditation with your Higher Power.

TWELFTH STEP

The telephone, like other Twelfth-Step work, is part of the soul of the Program: one addict sharing experience, strength, and hope with another addict. As soon as you can think straight, begin reaching out to help others, not as guru or savior, but as one addict caring about another.

Telephone, see also: Assertiveness, Community, Coping skills, Crisis, Feelings, Food plans, Intervention, Love & caring, Meetings, Obsession, Other support groups, Priorities, Relapse prevention, Relationships, Service & giving, Sponsorship, Stinking thinking, Tools of recovery, Trust.

Therapy & treatment

MEDICAL TREATMENT

Obviously there are times when addiction has had physical consequences that warrant medical intervention, even hospitalization. Yet it is common for addicts to avoid going to the doctor for several reasons.

Many physicians have been judgmental, and may have preached at you, as if you didn't already have enough guilt and shame already! They may have been operating from good intentions but were ignorant or frustrated because they couldn't help you. If you have learned about your disease, and started a recovery process, try to share that with your doctor, so she or he might become more openminded, too.

If you need to be hospitalized for your addiction, be sure to choose a program with a competent medical, counseling, and nursing staff.

COUNSELING

The field of counseling is a broad area of health care that includes all kinds of knowledge and skills to help people solve their problems and improve their living skills.

You should feel free to ask about credentials, and remember that you are the employer. Many people blindly trust counselors that have far less training and experience than their automobile mechanics.

Addictions counseling is designed to help you specifically with the tools needed to recover from addiction and closely related issues. The best, most experienced counselors or therapists will have certification in your specific area of addiction (if it is available), and they will probably have advanced degrees or other educational experience.

Certification   Alcohol and drug counselors should have or at least be working toward certification at state or national level.

Eating disorders counselors should be certified or working toward certification as Certified Eating Disorders Counselors (CEDC) or as Certified Eating Disorders Therapists (CEDT) by the International Association of Eating Disorders Professionals (IAEDP).

Certification in one area of addiction counseling does not necessarily imply competence in another. For example, many certified alcoholism counselors have virtually no specific knowledge of eating disorders, and vice versa. Also, addictions counselors may be inadequately prepared to deal with issues outside the mainstream of addiction, like marriage problems, incest issues, or psychological problems.

Marriage/family therapy   If you have issues with your marriage or your family, seek a specialist in this area. An excellent credential for this area is Marriage Family Child Counselor (MFCC). Knowledge of addiction would be helpful to sort out which issues are addiction related and which may be incidental to the addiction.

Pastoral counseling   Some counselors are specially trained to deal with religious and spiritual issues, and these may be very helpful for those having problems in these areas. Often, ministers, priests, rabbis, and other pastoral counselors are also certified in marriage/family or other counseling specialties.

Psychological therapy   Mental health problems, especially those having little to do with addiction, may require the services of a psychologist or other psychotherapist. Examples are phobias, depression, anxiety, and various personality, character, or thought disorders. If physical problems or medications are involved, a psychiatrist may be helpful, having both medical and psychiatric training.

Group vs. individual   Individual therapy can be helpful to begin a concentrated look at one's own self and specific issues. It is usually more expensive than group therapy, and it can be confusing or even dangerous if you are naive and happen upon a counselor who is lacking in the experience or the integrity to know when he or she can no longer help or doesn't need to. A good counselor may refer you to someone else—nobody is universally competent.

Group therapy gives you the advantage of being able to see yourself in others, having others see your blind spots, and learning to share feelings and experiences. The power of a group has proven itself in the success of the Twelve-Step fellowships. Addicts seem to have trouble getting well in groups of two or less.

PROFESSIONAL ETHICS

Some fields of addictions counseling have established certification standards. Part of the process of establishing a profession is to adopt a statement of professional ethics. For example, the International Association of Eating Disorders Professionals requires certified counselors and therapists to pledge adherence to a six-page code of ethics relating to professional and personal conduct. The ethical principles in that code include:

Responsibility   We must be alert to pressures that might lead to misuse of our influence over the lives of others. We must provide accurate, objective, and complete information about eating disorders and related topics. We must be objective and honest in research efforts.

Competence   We can only perform those services and techniques in which we are qualified by training and experience. We maintain knowledge of current scientific and professional information related to the services we render.

We accurately represent our competence, education, training, and experience. We recognize the need for continuing education and are open to changes and new procedures.

We recognize differences in people's age, sex, economic, and cultural backgrounds. We avoid any situation in which our personal problems may harm a client, colleague, student, or others.

Moral & legal standards   We are sensitive to prevailing community standards and provide a positive role model regarding our personal patterns of eating and use/misuse of food and drugs and alcohol. We support humane treatment, civil rights, and fair laws.

Public statements   In public statements or advertising, we accurately and objectively represent our professional qualifications, affiliations, and functions, as well as those of the institutions or organizations we represent. We avoid misrepresentation through sensationalism, exaggeration, or superficiality.

Confidentiality   We reveal information about a client only with the client's permission, or when not to do so would result in a clear danger to the person or to others, or when disclosure is mandated by law.

Welfare of the consumer   We protect the welfare of our clients. If there is a conflict of interest between the client and our employing institution, we let everyone know of our commitments, and take appropriate action. We do not exploit the dependencies of clients, students, or subordinates. We avoid dual relationships, like counseling employees, students, close friends, or relatives. Sexual intimacies with clients are unethical.

We terminate a counseling relationship when it is reasonably clear that the consumer is not benefiting, offering to help locate alternative assistance.

Professional relationships   We act with respect and regard for eating disorders colleagues, other professions, and the institutions and organizations with which we or our colleagues are associated. We make full use of available professional and other resources to help our clients. We support professional training and development. We do not condone or engage in sexual harassment.

We bring minor ethical violations to the attention of the offending eating disorders counselor or therapist. Major or unresolved ethical violations are reported to the appropriate ethics committee.

Research   Any research done with human subjects must be done with respect and concern for the dignity and welfare of the participants. It must adhere to all regulations and professional standards for such research.

Therapy & treatment, see also: Abstinence, Addiction model (PEMS), Aftercare, Alcoholism, Anorexia nervosa, Certification, Codependency, Core functions, Counseling, Crisis, Disease concept, Dual diagnosis, Employee assistance programs, Family, Family of origin, Half-measures, Halfway house, Impaired professionals, Incest, Intervention, Professional organizations, Psychological problems, Sabotage of recovery, Sex, Sponsorship, Step Six, Withdrawal.

Tolerance

Applying the General Adaptation Theory (see the Allergies module) to addiction, we see that frequent toxic biological imbalances can produce a tolerance, especially in addiction-susceptible people. This forms the physical basis for addiction.

TOXICITY

Some substances are highly toxic even in small amounts. There are "designer drugs" that will produce a high from a dose of 1 microgram (1/28,000,000 ounce). Others are nontoxic in normal quantities but are toxic or psychoactive in unusually high amounts. Also, some people are far more sensitive to certain chemicals than others.

DETOX

Ingesting or producing a toxin or a toxic excess of any substance will cause the body to react swiftly to do everything in its power to rid the body of this danger, or to restore a balance. With repeated excess of the substance, the body usually learns to metabolize or excrete it more effectively, or the target cells become less sensitive to the drug. In the treatment of chemical dependency there are even programs and facilities to help an alcoholic or drug addict through this detoxification period.

If you have received a pleasurable mood change as a result of the toxin, as your body adapts you must take in or create more and more of the substance to get the same effects. You have to drink more to get the same high. That, in turn, stimulates more drinking, etc. We call this a tolerance.

Eventually, in the degenerative phase the body may lose its ability to detoxify, and a "reverse tolerance" develops where a smaller quantity of the toxic substance will produce more reaction, although not always pleasant.

TACHYPHYLAXIS

Some substances produce a very rapid tolerance, called tachyphylaxis. LSD is an example of this. After three days of regular use it loses its effect, although not using it for a few days will restore sensitivity.

KINDLING

Other substances produce an effect like starting a wood fire. They may start slowly with hardly any progress and then suddenly produce an increased effect. Cocaine, for example, may suddenly begin causing convulsions at the same dose that previously produced just a high.

For information on detoxification and withdrawal, see the Withdrawal module.

Tolerance, see also: Addiction, Alcoholism, Allergies, Bingeing, Biochemistry, Constipation, Craving, Drugs, Exercise & activity, Fantasy, Neurotransmitters, Progression, Purging, Unmanageability, Withdrawal. Next on path B: Withdrawal.

Tools of recovery

Overeaters Anonymous emphasizes a list of Tools that are important parts of the recovery process. Virtually every Twelve-Step program uses these tools, but most of them simply incorporate them into their literature and programs. We will only mention them here, because most are discussed in a module of their own in this manual.

- Abstinence
- Sponsorship
- Meetings
- Telephone
- Anonymity
- Literature
- Service
- Writing

More than 200 self-help groups have adapted the Twelve Steps of Alcoholics Anonymous to their own specific addictions or other problems. Many addicts in recovery say that successful implementation of the *Steps* as tools has given their lives peace, serenity, meaning, and freedom from addiction. Other tools are not discouraged, but long-term recovery from addiction is best assured by adopting a spiritual way of living, as found in the Steps.

Tools of recovery, see also: Abstinence, Anonymity, Coping skills, Detachment, Intervention, Love & caring, Meetings, Priorities, Service & giving, Slogans, Sponsorship, Steps of AA, Telephone, Traditions of AA, Trust.

Traditions of AA

AA's Twelve Traditions are models for practically all Twelve Steps to keep their groups healthy.

The Twelve Traditions developed in AA after more than a decade of experience with this new kind of organization and recovery process. Their purpose is to help insure that the recovery community stays healthy, while the Steps are to enable you to stay healthy.

SHORT FORM

In both the Big Book (in the appendices) and *Twelve Steps and Twelve Traditions* (in the contents and in the very back of the book) there is both a short form and a long form of the Traditions. The short form is the one most commonly heard at meetings. In the paragraphs that follow, quotations are from *Twelve Steps and Twelve Traditions* (1952) unless otherwise identified.

Tradition One   Our common welfare should come first; personal recovery depends upon AA unity.

The First Tradition tells members that they must work together if any are to survive. But that working together must be voluntary and not any abridgement of the individual's right to think, talk, and act as he or she wishes. No AA member "can compel another to do anything; nobody can be punished or expelled" (p. 129).

Tradition Two   For our group purpose there is but one ultimate authority—a loving God as He may express Himself in our group conscience. Our leaders are but trusted servants; they do not govern.

Tradition Two underscores the idea that no member holds anything like a position of authority. Any service positions that are elected should be expected to perform service conforming to the group conscience rather than their own opinions and beliefs.

Tradition Three   The only requirement for AA membership is a desire to stop drinking.

If you are in a Twelve-Step group other than AA, you simply replace "drinking" with using, gambling, eating compulsively, or whatever fits for your addiction.
Twelve Steps and Twelve Traditions says that you are an AA member "if **you** say you are. You can declare yourself in; nobody can keep you out" (p. 139).

Tradition Four   Each group should be autonomous except in matters affecting other groups or AA as a whole.

An AA group can do things just about any way they want to, provided that they don't do anything that would greatly injure AA as a whole, and they don't affiliate with anything or anybody else.

Tradition Five   Each group has but one primary purpose—to carry its message to the alcoholic who still suffers.

An addict can do one thing better than anyone else: carry the hope and message of recovery to someone still sick with the disease. Everything else in the Program is secondary to that. Also, to insure continued recovery, the addict must have someone on which to practice her or his Twelfth Step. You will hear often at meetings something to the effect that you can't keep it unless you give it away.

Tradition Six An AA group ought never endorse, finance or lend the AA name to any related facility or outside enterprise, lest problems of money, property, and prestige divert us from our primary purpose.

Watch how quickly energy gets diverted from the primary purpose of carrying the message when a Twelve-Step group gets involved in some "project." Even such things as conventions and retreats often consume far more time and energy in their social and organizational requirements than they deserve. Imagine what would happen to the singleness of purpose if Twelve-Step groups got involved in the operation of treatment centers, clubs, publishing enterprises, and other outside efforts.

Tradition Seven   Every AA group ought to be fully self-supporting, declining outside contributions.

John D. Rockefeller, Jr., is credited with keeping AA independent of outside contributions. He realized that the self-help movement was too important to risk its coming under the influence of any benefactor, no matter how supportive that might seem.

Self-support also helps members maintain some balance in responsibility, and keeps the organization out of the distractions and moral pitfalls of accepting donations.

Tradition Eight   Alcoholics Anonymous should remain forever non-professional, but our service centers may employ special workers.

Tradition Eight means that AA can hire people to perform necessary services, like secretarial and accounting work, but Twelfth-Step work should never be paid for.

A distinction can be made between paid Twelfth-Step work and working as a professional in the field of addiction. People who are recovering addicts and also counselors or other professionals are sometimes called two-hatters. When they are wearing the hat of a counselor, they should be professionals who are being paid to do a service almost unrelated to any Twelve-Step group. When they take off their professional hat and put on their anonymous group member hat, they are not paid for it, and they carry the message to help themselves stay sober or abstinent.

Tradition Nine   AA, as such, ought never be organized; but we may create service boards or committees directly responsible to those they serve.

"When Tradition Nine was first written, it said that 'Alcoholics Anonymous needs the least possible organization.' In the years since then, we have changed our minds about that. Today, we are able to say with assurance that Alcoholics Anonymous—AA as a whole—should never be organized at all" (*Twelve Steps and Twelve Traditions*, 1952 [p. 172]). This means that traditional hierarchical organization is totally absent in the structure of Twelve-Step groups. No one in AA, from the newcomer to the General Service Board Trustee, can tell any AA member she or he has to do anything! There is no authority anywhere. Service boards are responsible to those they serve, not the other way around.

Tradition Ten   Alcoholics Anonymous has no opinion on outside issues; hence the AA name ought never be drawn into public controversy.

Alcoholics Anonymous developed in the days when everyone still remembered Prohibition, and it soon became obvious that if it affiliated with any outside cause, it would become bound to the fate of that cause, and would divert needed attention away from the primary job of one addict carrying the message to another.

Tradition Eleven   Our public relations policy is based on attraction rather than promotion; we need always maintain personal anonymity at the level of press, radio, and films.

One key to understanding the difference between attraction and promotion is the focus on the principles and the work of AA, rather than on its individual members. Attraction is the opposite of promotional advertising, in which a celebrity might be enlisted to endorse a soft drink. It is better for the friends of AA to sing its praises.

Tradition Twelve   Anonymity is the spiritual foundation of all these traditions, ever reminding us to place principles before personalities.

Making Twelve-Step programs work will take a little bit of sacrifice from all its members. By setting aside the ego, strong opinions, power trips, guru identifications, personal ambitions, and other disruptive influences, the members will make the groups thrive. The miracle of the Program works, especially when members understand that all members have equal status, and each person's Higher Power works through the Steps and the Shared Story.

LONG FORM

The long form was the original form, first published in 1946. It is more explicit and gives a better idea of what the purpose of the traditions are. Also, the section on the Traditions in *Twelve Steps and Twelve Traditions* is not too long; we recommend highly that you read it along with the chapters on the Steps.

Traditions of AA, see also: Alcoholics Anonymous, Anonymity, Community, Control, History of Twelve-Step groups, Humility, Meetings, Other support groups, Responsibility, Service & giving, Spirituality, Sponsorship, Step Twelve, Unity.

Tranquilizers

The miracle prescription drugs of the 1960s were the "minor" tranquilizers, benzodiazepines (BZPs) like Valium and Librium. They were thought to be harmless. Pharmaceutical companies told physicians they were not addicting, and doctors were happy to have a safe drug to prescribe to patients who said they were struggling with anxiety. The Rolling Stones wrote a popular song that called them "Mother's Little Helper."

By 1975 Valium was the most prescribed drug in the United States. Though their addiction potential was well known among addiction treatment professionals, many doctors continued to tell patients they were safe, if taken as prescribed.

PHARMACOLOGY

BZP drugs have an affinity for certain GABA receptors. Their action decreases some norepinephrine (NE) and other neurotransmitter activity involved in anxiety. They are particularly dangerous because a tolerance develops after just a few weeks, and because they are thought to be harmless, someone can become addicted to them with little conscious awareness.

OTHER TRANQUILIZERS

There are newer tranquilizers that have different pharmacology, and it is not known how some of them work. For addicts, however, the important thought is that any attempt to "fool Mother Nature" has so far produced more varied types of addicts, and there are few legitimate psychiatric uses for these drugs, especially with people known to have addictive tendencies. For more detailed information, see the module on Drugs.

Tranquilizers, see also: Alcohol, Drugs, Energy levels, Fantasy, Fats, Marijuana, Moodifiers, Narcotics Anonymous, Nicotine, Relaxation, Serenity, Stress & strain, Sugar, Tolerance.

Trust

The issue of trust is critical for addicts, as many feel that they cannot trust other people. This can be a major obstacle to the use of a support group.

It is important to remember that trust is not an all-or-nothing situation. It is seldom either 0 percent or 100 percent. Your level of confidence in any person or thing will depend on your experience, the present situation, and the risk involved.

When you know you cannot handle your addiction by yourself, you can develop trust that there is something more powerful than your disease. The phrase "came to believe" in the Second Step indicates the need for faith. Seeing recovery in others and identifying with them is often the beginning of that trusting process.

The Twelve-Step program is pretty trustworthy. We have seen no one damaged by the Twelve Steps themselves. In fact, most clergy and many in the helping professions have called the Twelve Steps a wonderful plan for living.

It is possible for human beings to screw up a particular group or a particular implementation of the Twelve Steps. But a group of people who seem to have something in the way of recovery are more dependable than any single person.

TRUSTING PEOPLE

It is hardest to trust individual people, particularly if you have been burned before. As you develop in your recovery, you will gain an inner strength that will give you more resources, so you will be less fearful in dealing with others. You will fear people less because you will not be so vulnerable. You will feel a sense of tolerance for their shortcomings as you become more comfortable with yourself. And you will feel love and gratitude for what you have compared with what you had.

RISKING

You don't have to trust 100 percent to take a risk. All you have to do is become aware that the risk of being hurt is less than the risk of missing the opportunity for joy. That will work when you apply it to God, to the Program, or to the people in your life.

Trust, see also: Abuse, Acceptance, Amends, Attitudes, Control, Fear, Freedoms, Grace, Gratitude, Higher Power, Openmindedness, Prayer & meditation, Relationships, Self-image, Step Two, Step Three, Step Seven, Surrender, Survival roles, Willingness. Next on path H: Acceptance.

U

Unity

Unity is vital if any addicts are to recover. If you could have recovered by yourself, you would have done so long ago. This means that the early AA idea of one addict helping another is crucial to the recovery process, and so unity of the fellowship is of utmost importance.

ADDICTION AND ISOLATION

Remember that the addiction has a vested interest in your isolation. As long as you can focus on the differences between yourself and others in the Program, and while the addiction can keep Twelve-Step group members squabbling among themselves over what rules are to be followed, what food plan is correct, or who is going to run the meeting, the disease is winning.

A simple challenge for unity is what you call yourself when you begin speaking at an AA or other Twelve-Step group meeting. The traditional beginning is, "My name is _____, and I am an alcoholic." This introduction, or slight variations, reminds AA members of their primary purpose, and eases others' fears that they are in the wrong place. It also reinforces the speaker's belief that he or she is an addicted person.

RECOVERY AND UNITY

There are many threats to unity. To beat those threats one can ask these questions:

- Is there anything I can do to promote unity?

- How can I better tolerate those whose opinions differ from mine?
- Am I willing to turn this matter over to the care of my Higher Power?

The amazing thing about Twelve-Step recovery programs is that they can survive and prosper in almost any condition except rigid control. Nothing will kill the effectiveness of an anonymous fellowship quicker than trying to "make it right." Freely translated, that means to make it as *you* think it ought to be.

Unity, service, and recovery. These things are paramount in a group, and they will thrive without a shred of organization. Structure everything, and you have nothing but an institution. Leave control and ego on the doorstep, and you will find love and a Higher Power within.

Unity, see also: Alcoholics Anonymous, Anonymity, Attitudes, Community, Gratitude, History of Twelve-Step groups, Honesty, Humility, Meetings, Other support groups, Paradoxes in addiction, Service & giving, Spirituality, Step Twelve, Traditions of AA.

Unmanageability

Besides powerlessness, unmanageability is a hallmark of addiction. Few people are willing even to consider the actions necessary for recovery unless they feel a lot of unmanageability. In fact, resistance to admitting unmanageability keeps most addicts out of recovery for a long time.

ILLUSION OF CONTROL
Many addicts are reluctant to admit that they are out of control. Their addiction insists they maintain an illusion of control long after they have effectively lost it. This awareness, that you are giving up the illusion of control rather than abandoning control, may make it easier to use Step One as a tool.

SURRENDER
The point of admitting that your life is unmanageable is not to regain control of your life. It is to recognize that control is simply not your job.

To recover from addiction, you must surrender the illusion of control. The admission of powerlessness and unmanageability (Step One) prepares you for the gut-level awareness of the need for a Higher Power in your life (Step Two), and a decision to switch over to that Higher Power for guidance (Step Three).

Unmanageability, see also: Abstinence, Bingeing, Control, Crisis, Defenses, Delusion, Half-measures, Hitting bottom, Honesty, Integrity & values, Intervention, Judgment, Obsession, Powerlessness, Step One, Step Two, Step Five, Steps of AA, Stinking thinking. End of path F. Next on path G: Step Two.

V

Visualizations

Recovery from addiction involves change. Addiction convinces you that you cannot change, that anything you undertake is doomed, and that life is not worthwhile. Recovery makes hopes and dreams for a better life possible. Visualization is a tool to help shift from addictive thoughts to positive attitudes for recovery.

Meditations, guided imageries, affirmations, and relaxation techniques may use visualization. You can create visualizations to improve any area of your life—relationships, job or career, self-image, serenity, health, or spirituality.

Before you can use visualizations effectively, you must be able to relax and clear your mind. The module on Relaxation in this manual has suggestions you can use. Stress management, relaxation, or meditation techniques may help.

Shakti Gawain (1978) has a clear, practical, optimistic guide for using visualization techniques. Her philosophies and suggestions are quite compatible with working a Twelve-Step recovery program.

Gawain says the four basic steps of creating visualizations are:

- **Set your goal.** Make it something you can believe in, that is a realistic challenge. This will increase your chance of success.
- **Create a clear idea or picture.** See it as if it were already existing, with as many details as possible.
- **Focus on it often.** Take time to visualize your goal at least two or three times a day. Try to let it take shape naturally, without trying too hard.
- **Give it positive energy.** Use positive affirmations to state your belief in your goal. Let the negative thoughts gently float away.

Don't be discouraged if you have trouble seeing clear images when you try to visualize. For many, it is a learned skill. At first you may simply have thoughts, impressions, or feelings. Any use of your imagination is a good start.

Be patient. Your goals may change. Your Higher Power may have something better in store for you than you can now imagine. As long as you are working your Program, trusting in your Higher Power, and staying abstinent, clean, or sober, your use of visualization techniques can enhance your recovery.

Visualizations, see also: Assertiveness, Body image, Celebrations, Coping skills, Half-measures, Moderation, Money, Nutrition, Relapse prevention, Sabotage of recovery, Self-image, Stress & strain, Therapy & treatment, Tools of recovery.

W

Weight

Weight management is an issue for most food addicts, and many other addicts as well. We will describe the problem from the standpoint of a food addict, but we feel certain that many other addicts will also relate to weight as a problem in recovery.

One of the greatest dangers in recovery from eating disorders is that the obsession with weight is never released. This does not mean that weight is unimportant or that your weight does not matter. What it means is that the constant obsession with a few pounds, and obsession with the scales or comparing your body with others, is part of the disease you are trying to recover from.

Obsession with weight is like the tail wagging the dog. A moderate, healthy weight within a reasonable range should be one of the results of recovery. But if you focus on it, you bring up all the diet mentality that will lead to relapse.

SCALES

Many food addicts jump on the scales several times a day. They buy very accurate doctor's scales or electronic scales that keep track of their weight history. All this feeds into the obsession.

Even if you did not obsess about what the scales said, they are not helpful for recovery. Scales measure the wrong thing. All they tell you is your total body weight, which is much more sensitive to water fluctuations than to fat loss or gain. Most addicts are concerned with the amount of fat in their bodies, not the muscle or other tissue.

Each of the following factors can change your weight by several pounds on any given day, with no change in body fat at all:

- Food and liquids in the digestive tract
- Salt in the body
- Glycogen reserves
- Dehydration
- Time in the menstrual cycle
- Other health factors

Look at what the typical food addict will do with the scale reading. If you have lost a lot of weight, you can feel like celebrating (by bingeing). Even if you don't binge, you will be expecting to lose the same amount the next time you weigh.

If you have only lost a little, or weigh the same, you might get discouraged and decide your recovery is not working. You will probably get more into obsession and diet mentality in your determination to lose more next time.

If you have actually gained weight, you may panic, and you may very well use your discouragement and depression as an excuse to binge or starve (not eat, which may lead to a binge).

In short, **there is nothing the scale can tell you that will be useful for your recovery!**

The solution is to rely on a Higher Power to help you follow your abstinence and your recovery plan. Over a period of several months, if you do not seem to be getting better physically, emotionally, mentally, and spiritually, then you should discuss with your sponsor or counselor what changes you might make.

Your weight is only part of recovery. If you, your Higher Power, and your sponsor or counselor all agree that you could be gaining or losing weight more quickly, then all you need to do is allow your Higher Power to help you add or cut back **a little** on fats, and possibly adjust your activity (exercise) level.

BODY MASS INDEX

Eating disorders professionals are using another measure besides pounds. The body mass index is better than weight because it takes height into account. We like it for two reasons: it gives us a way to adjust for height, and the numbers do not have as strong an emotional attachment as pounds do. The formula is: body mass index (BMI) = Weight (in Kg) divided by Height (in meters) squared.

Because it is based on international units, it is easier to calculate if you use the following formula: BMI = Wt (lbs) divided by BMID, where BMID is a constant based on your height:

BMID values
4'4": 3.8   4'6": 4.1   4'8": 4.4   4'10": 4.8
4'5": 4.0   4'7": 4.3   4'9": 4.6   4'11": 5.0

5'0": 5.1	5'3": 5.6	5'6": 6.2	5' 9": 6.8
5'1": 5.3	5'4": 5.8	5'7": 6.4	5'10": 7.0
5'2": 5.5	5'5": 6.0	5'8": 6.6	5'11": 7.2
6'0": 7.4	6'2": 7.8	6'4": 8.2	6'6": 8.7
6'1": 7.6	6'3": 8.0	6'5": 8.4	6'7": 8.9

Suppose you are 5 feet 5 inches tall. This would mean your BMID value is 6.0. If your weight is 150 pounds, you would divide your weight by 6.0 to get a Body Mass Index of 25.0.

RANGES

As a rough idea of where you stand, remember that these ranges are **all approximate.** There are many factors, like your bone structure, your family characteristics, your age, and your own preferences that affect these generalities.

Less than 17: Much below 17 you may be emaciated, and should probably be under medical supervision.

About 17–19: This is probably underweight, and may be serious for some people, depending on bone size, age, health, etc.

About 19–21: Somewhat to slightly on the light side, but still in a normal range.

About 21–24: This is squarely in the normal range, ideal for most people.

About 24–27: Slightly to somewhat on the heavy side, but still in a normal and healthy range.

About 27–32: Slightly to fairly overweight, but not a significant health risk for most people.

About 32–48: Somewhat to fairly obese, and a health risk if gaining weight; just fine if gradually losing weight.

Over about 48: This has been called very obese or morbidly obese. Health risks increase with weight in this range but again, are more severe if gaining or cycling than if losing weight slowly.

REASONABLE GOALS

To be effective, you must avoid setting goals that have to do with losing a certain amount of weight in a set period. Your goal should be to continuue overall recovery on a daily basis and to enjoy the intermediate results as you feel better physically, emotionally, mentally, and spiritually.

Weight, see also: Binge history, Bingeing, Biochemistry, Body image, Bulimia nervosa, Diet mentality, Edema, Exercise & activity, Fats, Marijuana, Metabolism, Nicotine, Nutrition, Obesity, Physical aspects, Premenstrual syndrome, Progression, Purging, Sugar, Unmanageability. Next on path B: Progression.

Willingness

Willingness is the last part of HOW (Honesty, Openmindedness, and Willingness). If you believe that every living creature has a natural drive for health, to survive and prosper, then it makes sense that the willingness is there, somewhere.

The illusion of control and other aspects of addiction stop willingness. Recognize these characteristics, and you will become willing to surrender to recovery.

NURTURING WILLINGNESS

Willingness is an attitude that can be nurtured. Remember that the hopeless feeling may be produced by the disease itself, and is one of addiction's greatest allies. If you recognize it for what it is, you can dismiss the hopelessness as another tactic of your disease, and turn instead to willingness and gratitude.

One tiny step at a time　An ancient Oriental proverb says that a journey of a thousand miles begins with a single step. Your addiction will try to convince you it is hopeless because you have so far to go. With a Higher Power, you can, just for today, put one foot ahead of the other. The attitude that you can do that is willingness.

USING A HIGHER POWER

Willingness to recover includes daring to hope and to dream. There is a Higher Power that will give you the guidance and the power for recovery if you will only become willing to allow that Higher Power to help.

Willingness, see also: Acceptance, Amends, Attitudes, Checklist mentality, Control, Fear, Freedoms, Grace, Gratitude, Honesty, Humility, Openmindedness, Prayer & meditation, Step Two, Step Three, Step Seven, Surrender, Trust. Next on path H: Surrender.

Withdrawal

The science of withdrawal from addictive substances is critical to physicians who specialize in the treatment of addictions. For laypersons, however, it is much simpler. If an addict has developed a tolerance to the substance or activity, there will be some kind of withdrawal.

To predict how withdrawal will be, think about the effect of the drug or activity itself. How does it change the mood and the body's physical responses? The withdrawal is likely to be the negative opposite of that effect. In other words, the opposite effect, but negatively perceived.

ALCOHOL

The intoxicant effect of alcohol is depression of the inhibitions and body functions. Withdrawal produces shakes, anxiety, panic attacks, dry heaves, and in extreme cases, delirium tremens (DTs), a form of alcoholic psychosis. These are unpleasant stimulant effects. Medical treatment is strongly advised, because alcohol withdrawal can be fatal.

COCAINE

Users of cocaine experience a stimulant effect and increased perception of pleasant sensations. In withdrawal, they first experience a crash, which involves fatigue, sleep, and intense craving. They also experience anhedonia, an inability to feel pleasure or enjoyment.

MARIJUANA

Symptoms of marijuana are more vague than many drugs, and because of its fat-soluble nature, marijuana is stored in the fatty tissues of the body. This masks withdrawal symptoms, since the effects may continue for many days after the last use. During this time the marijuana addict will feel depression and agitation, loss of energy, memory loss, and apathy.

OPIOIDS

Heroin and other opioids are strong painkillers, producing a sedative hypnotic effect. Withdrawal is marked by anxiety, yawning, perspiration, running eyes and nose, and sleep disturbances. In severe cases, there can be muscular twitches, hot and cold flashes, abdominal cramps, rapid breathing and heartbeat, nausea, vomiting, diarrhea, and weight loss.

CAFFEINE

Because caffeine is a powerful stimulant drug, withdrawal from it will cause drowsiness and depression. Some food addiction treatment programs that take patients off caffeine point to the headaches and other symptoms as evidence of addiction to sugar, when those effects may be largely due to withdrawal from the caffeine. Caffeine withdrawal will add somewhat to the symptoms of withdrawal from other substances as well.

CRAVINGS

For all types of addiction withdrawal, you will probably experience some craving for the substance you are sensitive to. This is probably due to the physical and emotional deprivation from the sensitive substances, or from the activity that produces the internal chemistry of addiction.

ACTIVITIES

For any addiction that does not involve ingestion of an outside substance, withdrawals are not life-threatening. Again, look at the effects of the behavior for a clue as to what kind of neurochemistry is involved. If it is mostly a stimulant activity, like gambling or fasting, withdrawal is likely to produce depression and boredom.

For activities that produce sedative neurochemistry, like exercise or eating large quantities of food, withdrawal is more likely to cause anxiety, irritability, and sleep difficulties.

For activities that produce both kinds of neurochemistry, like sex and bulimia, withdrawal will produce most of these symptoms.

Withdrawal, see also: Addiction, Alcohol, Allergies, Behavior, Biochemistry, Constipation, Craving, Drugs, Exercise & activity, Heroin, Marijuana, Moodifiers, Nicotine, Panic attacks, Physical aspects, Progression, Purging, Sugar, Tolerance, Unmanageability. Next on path B: Biochemistry.

Bibliography

Alberti, Robert E. and Michael L. Emmons, 1982. *Your Perfect Right.* San Luis Obispo, CA: Impact Publishers. ISBN 0-915166-05-4, $6.95. A good guide to assertive living.

Alcoholics Anonymous, 3d ed., 1976. New York: Alcoholics Anonymous World Services, Inc. ISBN 0-916856-18-6. This is the basic text of AA, and of most Twelve-Step programs including Overeaters Anonymous. Highly recommended for all addicts.

Alcoholics Anonymous Comes of Age: A Brief History of A.A., 1957. New York: Alcoholics Anonymous World Services, Inc. ISBN 0-916856-02-X. This is the history of AA as written by Bill W. It is of historical interest, but probably not as accurate as *Pass It On.*

Alternative to Enabling. Van Nuys, CA: Families Anonymous. This pamphlet presents the Families Anonymous view of enabling and suggestions for families and friends.

American Diabetes Assn and American Dietetic Assn, 1987. *Family Cookbook, Volume 1.* New York: Prentice Hall Press. ISBN 0-13-003915-2, $16.95. This cookbook and volumes 2 and 3 below are easily adaptable to healthy food plans. Each recipe gives its nutritional information.

———, 1984. *Family Cookbook, Volume 2.* Englewood Cliffs, NJ: Prentice-Hall, Inc. ISBN 0-13-024910-6, $15.95.

———, 1987. *Family Cookbook, Volume 3.* New York: Prentice Hall Press. ISBN 0-13-004145-9, $16.95.

As Bill Sees It, 1967. New York: Alcoholics Anonymous World Services, Inc. ISBN 0-916856-03-8. A good collection of brief letters and other short works reflecting the thoughts of AA's cofounder.

Bass, Ellen and Laura Davis, 1988. *The Courage to Heal.* New York: Harper & Row. ISBN 0-06-096234-8. A helpful guide for identifying and healing sexual abuse.

Beattie, Melody, 1987. *Codependent No More*, Center City, MN: Hazelden. ISBN 0-89486-402-5. Comprehensive, somewhat wordy, includes just about everything people are placing under the umbrella of codependency.

———, 1990. *Codependents' Guide to the Twelve Steps.* New York: Prentice Hall Press, ISBN 0-13-140054-1, $9.95. Offers explanations of each of the Steps and suggestions for activities relating to them.

Benson, Herbert, MD, 1975. *The Relaxation Response.* New York: William Morrow and Co. ISBN 0-688-02955-8. Classic treatise on the physiological background of relaxation therapy.

Bittersweet: For Those in Other Twelve Step Programs, 1988. Baltimore, MD: Survivors of Incest Anonymous. This pamphlet describes the similarities and differences between the approach of SIA and other self-help groups.

Bloch, Douglas, 1988. *Words that Heal.* Portland, OR: Pallas Communications.

ISBN 0-929671-00-7, $9.95. Simple introduction to the use of affirmations in your own personal growth.

Blume, Sue, 1990. *Secret Survivors: Uncovering Incest and Its Aftereffects in Women.* New York: John Wiley & Sons. ISBN 0-345-36979-3, $4.95. A very professional yet compassionate book arising from the author's work with incest survivors.

Body, Mind, and Spirit, 1990. Park Ridge, IL: Parkside Publishing Corp. ISBN 0-942421-29-9. Meditation book that brings together physical, mental, and spiritual healing.

Booth, Fr. Leo, 1991. *When God Becomes a Drug: Breaking the Chains of Religious Addiction and Abuse.* Los Angeles: Jeremy P. Tarcher. ISBN 0-87477-657-0, $18.95. A good description of religious addiction including some useful suggestions for recovery.

Bradshaw, John, 1988. *Healing the Shame that Binds You.* Deerfield Beach, FL: Health Communications. ISBN 0-932194-86-9, $9.95. Says that shame is the core problem with all addictions (and everything else) and offers strategies for resolution.

Brooks, Cathleen, 1987. *The Twelve Steps: For Adult Children of Alcoholics.* Indianapolis, IN: Access. Set of two audio-cassette tapes, catalog no. A-2011, $16.95. Very good presentation outlining why the Steps are so difficult for ACOAs.

Carnes, Patrick, 1983. *Out of the Shadows: Understanding Sexual Addiction.* Minneapolis: CompCare Publishers. ISBN 0-89638-086-6, $9.95. Excellent resource for sex addiction.

————, 1991. *Don't Call It Love.* New York: Bantam. ISBN 0-553-07236-6, $19.95. First major scientific study of sexual addiction—includes study result as well as advice from addicts and coaddicts.

Cocores, James, MD, 1990. *The 800-Cocaine Book of Drug and Alcohol Recovery.* New York: Villard Books. ISBN 0-394-57404-4, $18.95. A fairly comprehensive guide to contemporary treatment for alcohol and drugs, based on the experience of the Medical Director of Fair Oaks Hospital Outpatient Recovery Centers.

Cohen, Sidney, MD, 1988. *The Chemical Brain: the Neurochemistry of Addictive Disorders.* Irvine, CA: CareInstitute. ISBN 0-917877-02-0, $8.95. Excellent source for technical information about the physical aspects of addiction.

Directory of Eating Disorders Programs, Therapists, and Services, 7th ed., June 1992. Palm Bay, FL: Center Publishing, $30.00. An update for those who have purchased previous editions is $20.00. This is the only known source for a listing of programs and professionals specializing in eating disorders. Mailing labels are also available. New editions will be produced semiannually.

Dr. Bob and the Good Oldtimers, 1980. New York: Alcoholics Anonymous World Services, Inc. ISBN 0-916856-07-0. Gives a good appreciation of Dr. Bob's contribution to the founding of AA. Along with *Pass It On,* gives the roots of the AA program.

Ebbitt, Joan, 1987a. *The Eating Illness Workbook.* Park Ridge, IL: Parkside Medical Services Corp. ISBN 0-942421-00-0. Helpful activities for physical, emotional, mental, and spiritual recovery, especially if shared with a therapist or a group of recovering people.

————, 1987b. *Spinning: Thought Patterns of Compulsive Eaters.* Park Ridge, IL: Parkside Publishing Corp. ISBN 0-942421-01-9, pamphlet. Relates to the mental aspects of food addiction.

————, 1989. *Tomorrow, Monday, or New Year's Day: Emerging Issues in Eating Disorder Recovery.* Park Ridge, IL: Parkside Publishing Corp. ISBN 0-942421-21-3. Good introductory book for eating disorders. Includes consequences, recovery, and life issues.

Emotions Anonymous, 1978. St Paul, MN: Emotions Anonymous Intl. ISBN 0-960735-60-7. The "Big Book" for EA.

Fields, Rick, et al., 1984. *Chop Wood Carry Water: A Guide to Finding Spiritual Fulfillment in Everyday Life*. Los Angeles: Jeremy P. Tarcher. ISBN 0-87477-209-5, $11.95. A great source for spiritual explorations.

Gawain, Shakti, 1978. *Creative Visualizations*. Mill Valley, CA: Whatever Publishing. ISBN 0-931432-02-2, $7.95. Description of ways to use visualization, affirmation, and mental imagery to help bring about positive changes in your life.

Hampshire, Elizabeth, 1988. *Freedom from Food*. Park Ridge, IL: Parkside Publishing Co. ISBN 0-942421-04-3. Stories of people with good recovery from compulsive overeating.

Harrison, Marvel and Catharine Stewart-Roache, 1989. *attrACTIVE Woman*. Park Ridge, IL: Parkside Publishing Corp. ISBN 0-942421-07-8, $8.95. An excellent guide to activity and exercise, with common sense suggestions for getting and staying physically active. It also integrates emotional and spiritual aspects of recovery. People who believe they are especially sensitive to certain foods, like sugar, may be uncomfortable with chapter 4, on food.

Hendricks, Gay and Kathlyn Hendricks, 1985. *Centering and the Art of Intimacy*. Englewood Cliffs, NJ: Prentice-Hall, Inc. ISBN 0-13-122250-3, $6.95. Basic book with practical ideas for improving personal relationships.

Hollis, Judi, 1985. *Fat Is a Family Affair*. Center City, MN: Hazelden. ISBN 0-89486-263-4. Classic best-selling book on food addiction and one of the few that deals with the family aspects.

"Integrated Services for the Dually-Diagnosed Client." *Addiction & Recovery* (ISSN 0899-8043), June 1990, 36–39.

Jellinek, E. M., 1960. *The Disease Concept of Alcoholism*. New Haven, CT: College and University Press. A classic in the development of the disease model for alcoholism.

Johnson, Craig and Mary E. Connors, 1987. *The Etiology and Treatment of Bulimia Nervosa: A Biopsychosocial Perspective*. New York: Basic Books, Inc. ISBN 0-465-02092-5. Good academic coverage of the treatment of bulimia.

Johnson, Vernon E., 1980. *I'll Quit Tomorrow*, revised edition. New York: Harper & Row. ISBN 0-06-250430-4. Classic book on chemical dependency and the technique of intervention.

Katahn, Martin, 1989. *The T-Factor Diet*. New York: W. W. Norton & Co. ISBN 0-393-02693-0, $18.95. Excellent explanations of the role of fats and exercise in weight management. Ignores the addiction, however.

Katherine, Anne, 1991. *Anatomy of a Food Addiction*. New York: Prentice Hall Press/Parkside. ISBN 0-13-035031-1. Order Number 6915. Explains the chemical reactions in the brain that interact with emotional conflict to make food like a drug.

———, 1991. *Boundaries*. Park Ridge, IL: Parkside Publishing Corp. ISBN 0-942421-31-0. A guide for discovering and protecting personal boundaries in relationships.

Kellermann, Joseph L., 1977. *Grief: A Basic Reaction to Alcoholism*. Center City, MN: Hazelden. ISBN 0-89486-037-2. Booklet describes losses from the disease of alcoholism. Includes good suggestions for overcoming grief.

Kolodny, Nancy J., 1987. *When Food's a Foe: How to Confront and Conquer Eating Disorders*. Boston: Little, Brown & Co. ISBN 0-316-50180-8. Written especially to help teenagers confront and conquer anorexia and bulimia. Has helpful physical and psychological suggestions.

Kurtz, Ernest, 1979. *Not-God: A History of Alcoholics Anonymous*. Center City, MN:

Hazelden. ISBN 0-89486-065-8. An excellent philosophical look at the development of AA.

_____, 1981. *Shame and Guilt: Characteristics of the Dependency Cycle.* Center City, MN: Hazelden. ISBN 0-89486-132-8. Applies the concepts of shame and guilt to addiction.

The Language of the Heart, 1988. New York: The AA Grapevine, Inc. ISBN 0-933685-16-5. A collection of odds and ends that Bill W. wrote in the *AA Grapevine*. It is excellent material, highly recommended.

Lerner, Harriet Goldhor, 1985. *The Dance of Anger: A Woman's Guide to Changing the Patterns of Intimate Relationships.* New York: Harper & Row. ISBN 0-06-091356-8, $8.95.

Living Sober, 1975. New York: Alcoholics Anonymous World Services. ISBN 0-916856-04-6.

Lovern, John D., 1988. "The Cyclic Eating Disorders: A Unified Eating Disorders Theory." Paper presented at the Eating Disorders Institute, July 1988, at Rollins College, Winter Park, Florida.

MacMahon, Alice, 1990. *Women and Hormones.* Maitland, FL: Family Publications. ISBN 0-931128-03-X. Focuses on premenstrual syndrome (PMS) with explanations and treatment options.

Madara, Edward J. and Abigail Meese, eds., 1990. *The Self-Help Sourcebook: Finding and Forming Mutual Aid Self-Help Groups, Third Edition.* Denville, NJ: Saint Clares-Riverside Medical Center. ISSN: 8756-1425. Listings of hundreds of self-help groups on all subjects, not just Twelve-Step groups. Compiled and published by the American Self-Help Clearinghouse.

Matthews, Ruth H., Pamela R. Pehrsson, and Mojgan Farhat-Sabet, 1987. *Sugar Content of Selected Foods: Individual and Total Sugars.* U.S. Department of Agriculture, Human Nutrition Information Service, Home Economics Research Report no. 48, $2.00.

May, Rollo, 1972. *Power and Innocence: A Search for the Sources of Violence.* New York: W. W. Norton & Co. ISBN 0-393-01065-1, $7.95. A deep philosophical book about violence and power. Useful model about types of power.

Mellody, Pia, 1989. *Facing Codependence: What It Is, Where It Comes from, How It Sabotages Our Lives.* San Francisco: Harper & Row. ISBN 0-06-250589-0, $10.95. Detailed model of how codependency can be traced back to childhood, resulting from a broad range of emotional, spiritual, intellectual, physical, and sexual abuses. Recovery involves reparenting oneself.

Milkman, Harvey B. and Stanley G. Sunderwirth, 1987. *Craving for Ecstasy: The Consciousness and Chemistry of Escape.* Lexington, MA: D. C. Heath and Company. ISBN 0-669-15281-1, $12.95. A very interesting mix of neurotransmitter research and theory about addictions.

Miller, Caroline Adams, 1988. *My Name Is Caroline.* New York: Doubleday. ISBN 0-385-24208-5. Bestselling story of one woman's struggle and recovery from bulimia. Good book to give bulimics and their families to understand the disease and encourage hope for recovery.

Narcotics Anonymous, 1984. Van Nuys, CA: Narcotics Anonymous World Service Office. ISBN 0-912075-02-3. This is the "Big Book" for NA.

Norwood, Robin, 1985. *Women Who Love Too Much.* New York: Pocket Books. ISBN 0-671-62049-5, $4.50. The book that brought romance addiction to popular attention.

Overeaters Anonymous, 1980. Torrance, CA: Overeaters Anonymous, Inc. This is the "Brown Book" with information and stories that resemble those in the Big Book of AA, but their spiritual message is not as powerful as those in the Big Book.

Pass It On: The Story of Bill Wilson and How the A.A. Message Reached the World, 1984.

New York: Alcoholics Anonymous World Services, Inc. ISBN 0-916856-12-7. Excellent book for AA history and for understanding how the Twelve-Step recovery program came about. Highly recommended, especially in combination with *Dr. Bob and the Good Oldtimers.*

Peck, M. Scott, MD, 1978. *The Road Less Traveled: A New Psychology of Love, Traditional Values and Spiritual Growth.* New York: Simon and Schuster, Touchstone Books. ISBN 0-671-25067-1, $5.95. A modern classic. Bestselling book that integrates psychology and spirituality. Helpful discussions about love, balance, and grace.

———, 1987. *The Different Drum: Community Making and Peace.* New York: Simon and Schuster. ISBN 0-671-60192-X, $16.95. Excellent discussion about community making. Many abstract philosophical concepts, but helpful ideas for understanding the success of an AA or OA community.

Peele, Stanton, 1989. *Diseasing of America: Addiction Treatment out of Control.* Lexington, MA: Lexington Books. ISBN 0-669-20015-8, $19.95. A general indictment of the addiction model and addiction treatment programs. Has some valid criticisms but goes overboard in the opposite direction. Not recommended for addicts in early recovery.

Pennington, Jean A. T., PhD, RD, 1989. *Food Values of Portions Commonly Used, 15th ed.* New York: Harper & Row. ISBN 0-06-096364-6, $12.95. Very useful and very complete for determining nutritional values of most foods.

Powell, John, SJ, 1969. *Why Am I Afraid to Tell You Who I Am?* Niles, IL: Argus Communications. ISBN 0-913592-02-1, $2.75. Appealing, short book on self-awareness, personal growth, and interpersonal communications. Easy to understand.

Sagan, Carl, 1977. *Dragons of Eden: Speculations on the Evolution of Human Intelligence.* New York: Ballantine Books. ISBN 0-345-32508-7. Interesting source for the model of the triune brain, which helps explain human emotions.

Schaeffer, Brenda, 1986. *Love Addiction: Help Yourself Out.* Center City, MN: Hazelden. ISBN 0-89486-383-5, $1.50. This is one of a series of booklets to help recovering addicts identify unhealthy relationships and find tools for developing healthy relationships.

Sharing Recovery through Gamblers Anonymous, 1984. Los Angeles: Gamblers Anonymous Publishing. ISBN 0-917839-00-5. The "Big Book" for GA.

Small, Jacquelyn, 1982. *Transformers: The Therapists of the Future.* Marina del Rey, CA: DeVorss & Co. ISBN 0-87516-529-X. Good for therapists interested in seeing their clients grow out of old patterns without professional interference.

Smedes, Lewis B., 1984. *Forgive & Forget: Healing the Hurts We Don't Deserve.* New York: Pocket Books. ISBN 0-671-60711-1, $3.95. Describes forgiveness as a process, not just as an event. Very useful for those snarled in resentments.

Twelve Steps and Twelve Traditions (12&12), 1952. New York: Alcoholics Anonymous World Services, Inc. ISBN 0-916856-01-1. Good description of the Steps and the Traditions. A must for any addiction recovery.

Valette, Brett, 1988. *A Parent's Guide to Eating Disorders: Prevention and Treatment of Anorexia Nervosa and Bulimia.* New York: Walker Publishing Co. ISBN 0-8027-1040-9, $18.95. A good, helpful guide for parents.

Webster's Medical Desk Dictionary, 1986. Springfield, MA: Merriam-Webster, Inc. ISBN 0-87779-025-6.

Wegscheider-Cruse, Sharon, 1985. *Choice-Making: For Co-dependents, Adult Children and Spirituality Seekers.* Pompano Beach, FL: Health Communications, Inc. ISBN 0-932194-26-5. Helpful for changing behavior and making better choices in recovery, and for getting out of old patterns.

———, 1989. *The Miracle of Recovery: Healing for Addicts, Adult Children and*

Co-Dependents. Deerfield Beach, FL: Health Communications, Inc. ISBN 1-55874-024-4. Has lots of personal history and some interesting ideas about recovery.

Williams, Margery, 1981. *The Velveteen Rabbit.* Philadelphia: Running Press. ISBN 0-89471-128-8, $3.95. Charming analogy about how love makes us become real.

Woititz, Janet Geringer, 1983. *Adult Children of Alcoholics.* Hollywood, FL: Health Communications, Inc. ISBN 0-932194-15-X. Excellent descriptions and prescriptions for overcoming the deficits resulting from growing up in an addictive family.

Wurtman, Judith J., 1986. *Managing Your Mind & Mood through Food.* New York: Harper & Row. ISBN 0-06-097138-X, $7.95. Good information about the moodifier effect of carbohydrates and protein, but sometimes reminds us of Timothy Leary talking about LSD.

Yoder, Barbara, 1990. *The Recovery Resource Book.* New York: Fireside. ISBN 0-671-66873-0, $12.95. An excellent resource for organizations and information relating to recovery from all addictions.

Appendix—Addresses

Adult Children of Alcoholics
PO Box 3216
Torrance, CA 90510
(213) 534-1815

Al-Anon Family Groups
PO Box 862, Midtown Station
New York, NY 10018-0862
(212) 302-7240
800-356-9996

Alcoholics Anonymous (AA)
PO Box 459, Grand Central Station
New York, NY 10163
(212) 870-3400

American Self-Help Clearinghouse
Saint Clares-Riverside Medical
   Center
Denville, NJ 07834
(201) 625-7101

American Society of Addiction
   Medicine (ASAM) (formerly
   AMSAODD)
12 West 21st St.
New York, NY 10010
(212) 206-6770

Cocaine Anonymous
6125 Washington Blvd., Suite 202
Los Angeles, CA 90230
(213) 559-5833

Co-Dependents Anonymous
PO Box 33577
Phoenix, AZ 85067-3577
(602) 277-7991

Compulsive Stutterers Anonymous
Box 1406
Park Ridge, IL 60068
(815) 895-9848

COSA
   (families/friends of sex addicts)
PO Box 14537
Minneapolis, MN 55414
(612) 537-6904

Co-SLAA
   (families/friends of sex & love
   addicts)
PO Box 614
Brookline, MA 02146-9998

Cult Awareness Network
2421 W. Platt Blvd., Suite 1173
Chicago, IL 60645
(312) 267-7777

Daytop Village
54 West 40th St.
New York, NY 10018
(212) 354-6000

Debtors Anonymous
PO Box 20322
New York, NY 10025-9992
(212) 642-8222

Delancey Street
2563 Divisadero St.
San Francisco, CA 94115
(415) 882-5427

Drugs Anonymous
   (formerly Pills Anonymous)
PO Box 473, Ansonia Station
New York, NY 10023
(212) 874-0700

Emotional Health Anonymous
PO Box 429
Glendale, CA 91209
(818) 240-3215

Emotions Anonymous
PO Box 4245
St. Paul, MN 55104
(612) 647-9712

Employee Assistance Professionals
  Assoc (EAPA) (formerly
  ALMACA)
4601 N. Fairfax Dr., Suite 1001
Arlington, VA 22203
(703) 522-6272

Families Anonymous
PO Box 528
Van Nuys, CA 91408
800-736-9805

Fundamentalists Anonymous
PO Box 20324, Greeley Square
  Station
New York, NY 10001
(212) 696-0420

Gam-Anon Family Groups
PO Box 157
Whitestone, NY 11357
(718) 352-1671

Gamblers Anonymous (GA)
PO Box 17173
Los Angeles, CA 90017
(213) 386-8789

HIVIES (HIV positives)
610 Greenwood
Glenview, IL 60025
(708) 724-3832

Incest Survivors Anonymous
Box 5613
Long Beach, CA 90805-0613
(213) 428-5599

International Association of Eating
  Disorders Professionals, Inc.
  (IAEDP)
123 NW 13 St., #206
Boca Raton, FL 33432
(407) 388-6494

Messies Anonymous
5025 SW 114th Ave.
Miami, FL 33165
(305) 271-8404

Nar-Anon Family Groups
PO Box 2562
Palos Verdes, CA 90274-0119
(213) 547-5800

Narcotics Anonymous (NA)
PO Box 9999
Van Nuys, CA 91409
(818) 780-3951

National AIDS Hotline
800-342-AIDS
(for deaf access: 800-AIDS-TTY)

National Alliance for the Mentally Ill
2101 Wilson Blvd., #302
Arlington, VA 22201-3008
(703) 524-7600

National Anorexic Aid Society
  (NAAS)
c/o C.T.E.D.
1925 E. Dublin Granville Rd.
Columbus, OH 43229-3517
(614) 846-2833

National Association of Alcohol and
  Drug Abuse Counselors
  (NAADAC)
3717 Columbia Pike, Suite 300
Arlington, VA 22204
(703) 920-4644
800-548-0497

National Association of Anorexia
  Nervosa and Related Disorders
  (ANAD)
Box 7
Highland Park, IL 60035
(312) 831-3438

National Certification Reciprocity
  Consortium/Alcohol and Other
  Drug Abuse (CRC/AODA)
3725 National Drive, Suite 213
Raleigh, NC 27612
(919) 781-9734

National Chronic Pain Outreach
7979 Old Georgetown Rd., Suite 100
Bethesda, MD 20814
(301) 652-4948

National Consortium of Chemical
  Dependency Nurses (NCCDN)
975 Oak St., Suite 675
Eugene, OR 97401
(503) 485-4421
800-87-NCCDN

National Council on Problem
  Gambling
445 West 59th St.
New York, NY 10019
(212) 765-3833
800-522-4700

National Self-Help Clearinghouse
CUNY Graduate Center
25 West 43rd St., Room 620
New York, NY 10036
(212) 642-2944

National Sexually Transmitted
  Diseases Hotline
800-227-8922

Nicotine Anonymous
  (formerly Smokers Anonymous)
2118 Greenwich St.
San Francisco, CA 94123
(415) 922-8575

O-Anon Family Groups
  (family/friends of compulsive
  overeaters)
PO Box 4305
San Pedro, CA 90731

Obsessive-Compulsive Anonymous
PO Box 215
New Hyde Park, NY 11040
(516) 741-4901

Overcomers Outreach
  (Christian orientation)
2290 W. Whittier Blvd., Suite A/D
La Habra, CA 90631
(213) 697-3994

Overeaters Anonymous
Box 92870
Los Angeles, CA 90009
800-743-8703

Parents Anonymous
6733 S. Sepulveda Blvd., #270
Los Angeles, CA 90045
800-421-0353

Pill Addicts Anonymous
PO Box 278
Reading, PA 19603
(215) 372-1128

Prostitutes Anonymous
11225 Magnolia Blvd. #181
North Hollywood, CA 91601
(818) 905-2188

Rational Recovery Systems
Lois E. Trimpey, Manager
PO Box 800
Lotus, CA 95651
(916) 621-4374

Recovery, Inc.
  (mental health self-help)
802 N. Dearborn St.
Chicago, IL 60610
(312) 337-5661

S-Anon
  (families/friends of sexaholics)
PO Box 5117
Sherman Oaks, CA 91413
(818) 990-6910

Secular Organizations for Sobriety
James Christopher
PO Box 5
Buffalo, NY 14215
(716) 834-2922

Sexaholics Anonymous
PO Box 300
Simi Valley, CA 93062
(818) 704-9854

Sex Addicts Anonymous
PO Box 3038
Minneapolis, MN 55403
(612) 339-0217

Sex and Love Addicts Anonymous
  (SLAA)
PO Box 119, New Town Branch
Boston, MA 02258
(617) 332-1845

Sexual Compulsives Anonymous
  (SCA) (gays/lesbians welcome)
PO Box 1585, Old Chelsea Station
New York, NY 10011
(212) 439-1123

Survivors of Incest Anonymous
PO Box 21817
Baltimore, MD 21222-6817
(301) 282-3400

Workaholics Anonymous
PO Box 661501
Los Angeles, CA 90066
(310) 859-5804

Index

397